Global Perspectives on Human Capital-Intensive Firms

Cécile Cézanne
Université Côte d'Azur, France

Laurence Saglietto
Université Côte d'Azur, France

A volume in the Advances in Logistics, Operations, and Management Science (ALOMS) Book Series

IGI Global
DISSEMINATOR OF KNOWLEDGE

Published in the United States of America by
IGI Global
Business Science Reference (an imprint of IGI Global)
701 E. Chocolate Avenue
Hershey PA, USA 17033
Tel: 717-533-8845
Fax: 717-533-8661
E-mail: cust@igi-global.com
Web site: http://www.igi-global.com

Library of Congress Cataloging-in-Publication Data

Names: Cezanne, Cecile, 1981- editor. | Saglietto, Laurence, editor.
Title: Global perspectives on human capital-intensive firms / Cecile Cezanne and Laurence Saglietto, editors.
Description: Hershey : Business Science Reference, [2019]
Identifiers: LCCN 2018028036| ISBN 9781522574262 (hardcover) | ISBN 9781522574279 (ebook)
Subjects: LCSH: Human capital. | Industrial management. | International business enterprises--Management. | Labor supply.
Classification: LCC HD4904.7 .G565 2019 | DDC 658.3/01--dc23 LC record available at https://lccn.loc.gov/2018028036

This book is published in the IGI Global book series Advances in Logistics, Operations, and Management Science (ALOMS) (ISSN: 2327-350X; eISSN: 2327-3518)

British Cataloguing in Publication Data
A Cataloguing in Publication record for this book is available from the British Library.

Advances in Logistics, Operations, and Management Science (ALOMS) Book Series

ISSN:2327-350X
EISSN:2327-3518

Editor-in-Chief: John Wang, Montclair State University, USA

MISSION

Operations research and management science continue to influence business processes, administration, and management information systems, particularly in covering the application methods for decision-making processes. New case studies and applications on management science, operations management, social sciences, and other behavioral sciences have been incorporated into business and organizations real-world objectives.

The **Advances in Logistics, Operations, and Management Science** (ALOMS) Book Series provides a collection of reference publications on the current trends, applications, theories, and practices in the management science field. Providing relevant and current research, this series and its individual publications would be useful for academics, researchers, scholars, and practitioners interested in improving decision making models and business functions.

COVERAGE

- Political Science
- Decision analysis and decision support
- Information Management
- Services management
- Computing and information technologies
- Networks
- Operations management
- Marketing engineering
- Production management
- Finance

IGI Global is currently accepting manuscripts for publication within this series. To submit a proposal for a volume in this series, please contact our Acquisition Editors at Acquisitions@igi-global.com or visit: http://www.igi-global.com/publish/.

The Advances in Logistics, Operations, and Management Science (ALOMS) Book Series (ISSN 2327-350X) is published by IGI Global, 701 E. Chocolate Avenue, Hershey, PA 17033-1240, USA, www.igi-global.com. This series is composed of titles available for purchase individually; each title is edited to be contextually exclusive from any other title within the series. For pricing and ordering information please visit http://www.igi-global.com/book-series/advances-logistics-operations-management-science/37170. Postmaster: Send all address changes to above address.

Titles in this Series

For a list of additional titles in this series, please visit:
https://www.igi-global.com/book-series/advances-logistics-operations-management-science/37170

Technological Developments in Industry 4.0 for Business Applications
Luis Ferreira (Polytechnic Institute of Cávado and Ave, Portugal) Nuno Lopes (Polytechnic Institute of Cávado and Ave, Portugal) Joaquim Silva (Polytechnic Institute of Cávado and Ave, Portugal) Goran D. Putnik (University of Minho, Portugal) Maria Manuela Cruz-Cunha (Polytechnic Institute of Cávado and Ave, Portugal) and Paulo Silva Ávila (Polytechnic of Porto, ortugal)
Business Science Reference • ©2019 • 451pp • H/C (ISBN: 9781522549369) • US $225.00

Advanced Methodologies and Technologies in Business Operations and Management
Mehdi Khosrow-Pour, D.B.A. (Information Resources Management Association, USA)
Business Science Reference • ©2019 • 1482pp • H/C (ISBN: 9781522573623) • US $495.00

Emerging Applications in Supply Chains for Sustainable Business Development
M. Vijaya Kumar (National Institute of Technology Warangal, India) Goran D. Putnik (University of Minho, Portugal) K. Jayakrishna (Vellore Institute of Technology University, India) V. Madhusudanan Pillai (National Institute of Technology Calicut, India) and Leonilde Varela (University of Minho, Portugal)
Business Science Reference • ©2019 • 345pp • H/C (ISBN: 9781522554240) • US $225.00

Crowdsourcing and Knowledge Management in Contemporary Business Environments
Regina Lenart-Gansiniec (Jagiellonian University, Poland)
Business Science Reference • ©2019 • 304pp • H/C (ISBN: 9781522542001) • US $195.00

Burstiness Management for Smart, Sustainable and Inclusive Growth Emerging Research and...
Andreas Ahrens (Hochschule Wismar, Germany) Ojaras Purvinis (Kaunas University of Technology, Lithuania) Jeļena Zaščerinska (Centre for Education and Innovation Research, Latvia) Diana Micevičienė (Kaunas University of Technology, Lithuania) and Arūnas Tautkus (Kaunas University of Technology, Lithuania)
Business Science Reference • ©2019 • 194pp • H/C (ISBN: 9781522554424) • US $185.00

For an entire list of titles in this series, please visit:
https://www.igi-global.com/book-series/advances-logistics-operations-management-science/37170

IGI Global
DISSEMINATOR OF KNOWLEDGE

701 East Chocolate Avenue, Hershey, PA 17033, USA
Tel: 717-533-8845 x100 • Fax: 717-533-8661
E-Mail: cust@igi-global.com • www.igi-global.com

Editorial Advisory Board

Table of Contents

Preface xiii

Acknowledgment xviii

Section 1
Organization, Management Practices, and Human Capital

Chapter 1
A Survey of the Literature on Human Capital-Intensive Firms: A Bibliometric Analysis 1
Cécile Cézanne, Université Côte d'Azur, France
Laurence Saglietto, Université Côte d'Azur, France

Chapter 2
HRM Practices in Human Capital-Intensive Firms: An Empirical Study of IBM Corporation......... 30
Sabrina Loufrani-Fedida, Université Côte d'Azur, France

Chapter 3
Collaborating Without (Formal) Organization: How Do Freelancers Question the Definition and the Role of Organizations?......... 53
Anthony Hussenot, Université Côte d'Azur, France
Viviane Sergi, Université du Québec à Montréal, Canada

Section 2
Corporate Governance: New Developments

Chapter 4
The Governance of Human Capital-Intensive Firms: A Motivational Issue 73
Cécile Cézanne, Université Côte d'Azur, France

Chapter 5
The Role of Human Resource Accounting in the Business Environment 99
Ahmet Özcan, Adana Science and Technology University, Turkey

Chapter 6
How Are Innovation, Growth, and HCIF Affected by Natural Resources? 121
Seyed Mohammad Amir Mousavi, National Iranian Oil Refining and Distribution Company, Iran & Université Côte d'Azur, France

Section 3
Capabilities, Innovation, and Performance

Chapter 7
Knowledge Inflows and Knowledge Creation Capabilities Among MNC Subsidiaries in Malaysia: Human Capital in Host Country as a Moderator 156
Vijayalakchimi Subramaniam, University Science Malaysia, Malaysia
Shankar Chelliah, University Science Malaysia, Malaysia

Chapter 8
Organizational Learning and Collective Human Capital Relationship With Firm Performance Among MNEs in the Northern Region of Malaysia 176
Phynthamilkumaran Siea Dass, Universiti Sains Malaysia, Malaysia
Shankar Chelliah, Universiti Sains Malaysia, Malaysia

Chapter 9
A Supply Chain Management View of Human Capital-Intensive Firms 198
Laurence Saglietto, Université Côte d'Azur, France
Dominique Bonet Fernandez, IPAG Business School, France
Alban Quillaud, Independent Researcher, France
Gilles Paché, Aix-Marseille University, France

Compilation of References 220

About the Contributors 262

Index 265

Detailed Table of Contents

Preface xiii

Acknowledgment xviii

Section 1
Organization, Management Practices, and Human Capital

Chapter 1
A Survey of the Literature on Human Capital-Intensive Firms: A Bibliometric Analysis 1
Cécile Cézanne, Université Côte d'Azur, France
Laurence Saglietto, Université Côte d'Azur, France

The aim of this chapter is to provide a survey of the academic research dedicated to human capital-intensive firms (HCIF) both at a theoretical and empirical level. The authors conduct a thematic inventory of the published works in this area to assess the dynamism of the field research and provide an exploratory analysis. They develop a bibliometric analysis based on the three widely used databases (Econlit, Science Direct, and Wiley) over the time period 1992-2018. From a cluster analysis, the chapter draws a portrait of HCIF based on the highlighted distinctive features. It also gets more information on the scope of existing research and the issues, limits, and prospects involved.

Chapter 2
HRM Practices in Human Capital-Intensive Firms: An Empirical Study of IBM Corporation 30
Sabrina Loufrani-Fedida, Université Côte d'Azur, France

This chapter focuses on examining the human resource management (HRM) practices that are used in human capital-intensive firms (HCIFs). In the specialized literature on HCIFs, human resources (HR) are recognized as constituting an infinite value potential. Nevertheless, we know little in the literature about "how to manage" these

HR in the specific context of HCIFs. First of all, in this chapter, a literature review provides a clarification of the HR's key concepts (human capital, competence, and talent) on the one hand and introduces the relevance to study HRM practices underlying human capital management on the other hand. Then, based on the case study of IBM Corporation, a synthesis of the wide variety of HRM practices is proposed into three processes: identifying, assessing and developing, and finally, motivating and retaining human capital. The IBM case is representative of the HCIFs insofar as the company puts its human capital at the heart of its overall strategy and, in order to do this, provides a sophisticated HRM policy and, in addition, has implemented formalized HRM practices. For IBM, the aim is to improve resource assets of its employees necessary to generate innovation, value, and performance.

Chapter 3
Collaborating Without (Formal) Organization: How Do Freelancers Question the Definition and the Role of Organizations?..53
Anthony Hussenot, Université Côte d'Azur, France
Viviane Sergi, Université du Québec à Montréal, Canada

This chapter focuses on independent workers and on the organizational specificities of the independent workers' phenomenon. The authors treat independent workers as an emergent and continually shifting organizational phenomenon questioning some of our assumptions about what organizations are and revealing trends that are currently reshaping work. They suggest viewing the independent workers' phenomenon as an open organizational phenomenon in which activities are project-oriented, temporality-oriented, and inclusive. This chapter contributes to an understanding of the independent workers' phenomenon as an organizational one that constantly (re) defines rules, roles, and statuses making the activities possible. It also contributes to a broader reflection on the matter of organization. Considered as an open organizational phenomenon, the independent workers' phenomenon calls the organization-society dualism into question. Finally, revealing the organizational aspects of independent workers' activities allows us to better understand some of the transformations that are nowadays affecting more traditional forms of work.

Section 2
Corporate Governance: New Developments

Chapter 4
The Governance of Human Capital-Intensive Firms: A Motivational Issue 73
Cécile Cézanne, Université Côte d'Azur, France

For the past 30 years, the organization and functioning of firms have considerably changed, especially with the growing importance of human capital. In parallel, the primacy of the shareholder governance model has maintained. The aim of this chapter is to review the main theoretical and empirical elements of this paradox and to propose a renewed model of firm governance that takes into account the intrinsic nature of critical human capital incorporated by key employees. The chapter shows that the inalienable residual rights of control inherent to specific human capital are inconsistent with traditional disciplinary models of corporate governance. They rather call for a model of regulation of economic power exercising based on work motivation. This original model that the author calls the "multi-resource model" aims to encourage, retain, and collectively enrich critical resources by using an original operational device based on complementary instruments of incentive and coordination.

Chapter 5
The Role of Human Resource Accounting in the Business Environment 99
Ahmet Özcan, Adana Science and Technology University, Turkey

In this chapter, human resources accounting is comprehensively analyzed. Human capital has been often neglected or inaccurately reported in the financial statements due to its nature. In the new economy, financial market participants such as investors, creditors, and shareholders would like to get information about the firm's investment in human capital. Over the last decades, some accounting methods have been developed for human capital. In this chapter, the methods used in the accounting treatment of human capital are analyzed, and a total of 288 operating reports of banks listed on Borsa Istanbul for the period between 2010 and 2017 are examined through content analysis. The results of content analysis indicate that there is a growing trend in human capital disclosure by banks listed on Borsa Istanbul between the period of 2010 and 2017, implying that banks listed on Borsa Istanbul have become more aware of the importance of human capital.

Chapter 6
How Are Innovation, Growth, and HCIF Affected by Natural Resources? 121
Seyed Mohammad Amir Mousavi, National Iranian Oil Refining and Distribution Company, Iran & Université Côte d'Azur, France

This chapter demystifies in detail the transmission mechanisms of how the natural resource industry (NRI) harms the growth and innovation in human capital-intensive firms (HCIF). Two important phenomena were studied qualitatively: rent seeking (RS) and Dutch disease (DD) which result from the abundance of natural resources (NR). RS pushes down the return of production and DD results in uncompetitive production. The empirical results for a cross-section of 81 countries show a significant evidence that with recent data, oil rent hinders human capital as a proxy for innovation. Meanwhile, the indicators of resource governance show a significant and positive impact on human capital accumulation. A growing amount of literature focuses on growth and human capital, while this chapter emphasizes HCIF and innovation, elaborating the transmission mechanisms of underperforming economic growth through the hindrance of innovation in the firms and awkwardness of HC.

Section 3
Capabilities, Innovation, and Performance

Chapter 7
Knowledge Inflows and Knowledge Creation Capabilities Among MNC Subsidiaries in Malaysia: Human Capital in Host Country as a Moderator......156
Vijayalakchimi Subramaniam, University Science Malaysia, Malaysia
Shankar Chelliah, University Science Malaysia, Malaysia

In a volatile business environment and a global landscape, knowledge creation capability plays an important role in ensuring that MNC subsidiaries stay competitive. In this respect, knowledge inflows from different parts of the MNC knowledge network are vital to a subsidiary's capability to create new knowledge. Briefly, knowledge creation capability refers to the successful implementation of creative ideas within an organization. However, innovation-based competitiveness always starts with creativity that is rooted in individual workers in an organization. The human capital of the organization, therefore, is considered to be one of the main sources of knowledge-based competitive advantage. Therefore, besides knowledge inflows from the MNC network, subsidiaries also need human capital to allow for knowledge flows to be utilized creatively in order to remain competitive.

Chapter 8
Organizational Learning and Collective Human Capital Relationship With Firm Performance Among MNEs in the Northern Region of Malaysia............176
Phynthamilkumaran Siea Dass, Universiti Sains Malaysia, Malaysia
Shankar Chelliah, Universiti Sains Malaysia, Malaysia

The main objective in this chapter is to understand the organizational learning challenges of multinational enterprises and their performance in Malaysia. At the same time, it also explores how organizational learning and collective human capital with competitive advantage as a mediating factor affect MNEs' performance in Malaysia through employee movement. This research concluded knowledge acquisition, knowledge distribution, and organizational memory is positively significant towards competitive advantage. Only knowledge acquisition and organizational memory are positively significant when competitive advantage mediates organizational learning towards firm performance. Collective human capital is positively significant towards competitive advantage as well as towards firm performance when competitive advantage mediates. Through this research it was found that MNEs in Malaysia are weak in knowledge interpretation and knowledge distribution due to employee movement in the northern region of Malaysia.

Chapter 9
A Supply Chain Management View of Human Capital-Intensive Firms 198
Laurence Saglietto, Université Côte d'Azur, France
Dominique Bonet Fernandez, IPAG Business School, France
Alban Quillaud, Independent Researcher, France
Gilles Paché, Aix-Marseille University, France

Logistics and supply chain management (SCM) is benefiting from today's disruptive information technologies. Disruptive technologies based on massive data capabilities offer new opportunities for growth in international trade, through supply networks and real-time management. The authors aim to shed light on the impact of digitization and digitalization and disruptive technologies on human-capital-intensive firms (HCIFs), particularly in the logistics sector. Three case studies of control towers, business spheres, and supply chain cockpits seem to indicate that a new generation of high value-added human capital is entering the logistics sector in the context of massive data.

Compilation of References 220

About the Contributors 262

Index 265

Preface

Since the mid-1990s, firms' productive activity is mainly based on human capital resources. It is widely recognised that the capacity of most modern firms to generate innovation, value and performance depends on the knowledge and skills of their founders, managers and employees and on the ability of organisations to combine them efficiently. They are the bedrock of firms' competitive advantage. In this context, Human Capital-Intensive Firms (HCIF) are an interesting object of study as they capture the transformation and complexity of productive organisations in today's globalised economies, relying more and more on human assets and resources. In this sense, it is crucial to grasp the scope and breadth of HCIF and its impact in relation to value creation.

Although it is difficult to establish a precise definition of human capital-intensive firms (HCIF), the investigation of the past and recent literature on the subject allows to characterize them as enterprises whose productive activity is largely dependent on the specialised and complementary human assets embodied by their critical partners, who may be firm employees or external partners.

In this context, HCIF include a wide variety of organisations, ranging from law firms whose prosperity depends essentially on the expertise of the lawyers they employ, advertising agencies whose reputation is based on the talent of the artists and designers in their creative departments, IT companies whose activity is essentially built around skilled computer specialists and programmers, and pharmaceutical laboratories whose success and performance depends largely on their researchers and especially 'star scientists'. In other words, HCIF operate in entirely different branches from knowledge-intensive business services (commonly known as KIBS) to high-tech manufacturing industries, readily identifiable in the diverse classifications of economic activities.

In the end, HCIF encompass the large majority of productive organizations whose activity requires not only traditional production factors such as fixed capital and labor but also and especially the intangible assets of skills, structures and organisational procedures, and a corporate culture along with specific human assets. Consequently, although HCIF might appear to be an extreme case of a productive organisation, they in reality are widespread in business and are essential sources of technological and organizational innovation. Thus, HCIF are an ideal focus for the study of modern firms, both at an analytical and empirical level.

Many current issues and future challenges must be explored: how can the HCIF's boundaries and governance can be analysed? How do HCIF manage their network of critical and complementary intangibles assets on which they are built? To what extent skills assessment and intellectual management is decisive for HCIF? What about funding innovation for these types of firms? etc.

The objective of this book is to provide an advanced analysis of a widespread and valuable organizations of the modern capitalism which is yet difficult to precisely define and underexplored in the theoretical and empirical literature. In this perspective, a transdisciplinary approach (economics of the firm, corporate finance, accounting, human resource management, sociology, psychology, organization theory…) is required to examine HCIF.

This book offers a broad overview of the major works on the field and advances innovative research directions, building on different methods of research (theoretical models, case studies, empirical evidence and testimonials, historical analysis…).

Studying HCIF will impact the economics and management of the firm because the book will:

- highlight an under-studied concept;
- show the role of HCIF in different fields of research;
- explore the evolution of HCIF in different sectors, their internal and external organizations, their performance, and their key strenghts that could be easily transferred;
- propose a pluridisplinary approach on a transversal topic.

This book is considered to be of aid to the following prospective audiences:

- First of all, students (both at undergraduate and postgraduate level) who study Operations Management, Logistics, supply chain management, intermediation and business administration.
- Moreover, researchers in the above fields.
- Managers, consultants, practitioners who are experts in economics, management or in other social and applied sciences to build decision support systems.
- The target audience for this book is very large. It includes academic researchers, teachers, advanced students and PhD students in various disciplines like economics, business and management, organization, sociology… It could be an essential support for fellowship programs in operational research,

organizational research and/or historical theses. This book is also intended for managers, consultants, practitioners who are experts in economics, management or in other social sciences to build human resource decision.

The editor's intention was to help the above groups by giving them an easy to read and understand book with the right depth and the right volume.

ORGANIZATION OF THE BOOK

The book is organized into nine chapters. A brief description of each of the chapters follows:

- **Chapter 1: A Survey of the Literature on Human Capital-Intensive Firms – A Bibliometric Analysis**. This chapter provides a survey of the theoretical and empirical literature on HCIF based on a bibliometric analysis. In particular, this chapter identify and map research on HCIF by highlighting three dominant themes that can be used to discuss the implications of this concept: 'human resources and performance' (theme 1), 'specific intangible assets and strategies of the firm' (theme 2), and 'firm boundaries, innovation and competitive advantage' (theme 3). It also sheds light on the limitations and prospects involved.
- **Chapter 2: HRM Practices in Human Capital-Intensive Firms – An Empirical Study of IBM Corporation.** This chapter identifies and examine the different mechanisms to develop human resources internally in order to optimize human capital (skills, knowledge, and ability) of the employees within HCIF. Based on a qualitative approach centered on a single case study: IBM Corporation, this chapter shows tht IBM Corporation proposes a sophisticated HRM policy and has implemented formalized HRM practices to generate innovation, value and performance.
- **Chapter 3: Collaborating Without (Formal) Organization – How Do Freelancers Question the Definition and the Role of Organization?** This chapter analyses the specificities of the freelancing movement as an activity of identities' construction and relation in which all the elements that define the collaboration are re/defined through practices and only exist through these situated and relational practices. In such, this chapter contributes in the understanding of freelancing as an organizational phenomenon consisting in constantly re/defining the actors, their tools and their governance.

- **Chapter 4: The Governance of Human Capital-Intensive Firms – A Motivational Issue.** This chapter proposes a detailed analytical reading of the governance of HCIF and suggests an original operational system supporting a renewed model of firm governance. In particular, the chapter advances that the governance of HCIF is based on a global issue of motivation of long-term specific relationships. In this perspective, the chapter provides an operational model built on a combination of vertical incentive practices, horizontal work methods and decentralized decision-making.
- **Chapter 5: The Role of Human Resource Accounting in the Business Environment.** This chapter analyzes various aspects of human resource accounting. It discusses advantages and disadvantages of the dominant measurement methods of human resource accounting. Based on a content analysis of operating reports of banks listed on Borsa Istanbul between 2010 and 2017, the chapter notably shows that the most reported category in human capital disclosure is firm's philosophy about human capital followed by directors' year of experience whereas the least reported category is employee compensation plan.
- **Chapter 6: How Are Innovation, Growth, and HCIF Affected by Natural Resources?** This chapter sheds some light on the impact of the abundance of natural resources on HCIF and the mechanism of creation of innovation by human capital. It discusses the Rent Seeking and Dutch Disease theories and demystifies their effects on human capital, innovation, and economic growth. Based on multiple linear regression models applied for a cross-section of 81 resource governance index ranked countries, the chapter reveals that oil rent is inversely related to human capital accumulation. This implies that the higher the share of oil rent in national income, the more is the likelihood for the government to concentrate on its natural resource windfall, by this means neglecting other capitals like human capital.
- **Chapter 7: Knowledge Inflows and Knowledge Creation Capabilities Among MNC Subsidiaries in Malaysia – Human Capital in Host Country as a Moderator**. This chapter shows that knowledge creation capability at the organizational level, based on human capital incorporated by individual workers are decisive for the competitiveness of multinational companies' subsidiaries. Based on Malaysian case, the authors argue that beyond knowledge inflows from the MNC network, subsidiaries need human capital to allow for knowledge flows to be utilized creatively in order to remain competitive.

- **Chapter 8: Organizational Learning and Collective Human Capital Relationship With Firm Performance Among MNEs in the Northern Region of Malaysia.** This chapter provides an analysis of Multinational Enterprises (MNEs) performance in Malaysia. In particular, it explores how does organizational learning, collective human capital with competitive advantage as mediating factor which affects MNEs performances in Malaysia itself. This chapter intends to be a guide and reference for MNEs in Malaysia to pursue and retain their operation by expending their knowledge acquisition and organizational memory practices while retaining and developing their performance.
- **Chapter 9: A Supply Chain Management View of Human Capital-Intensive Firms.** This chapter sheds light on the impact of digitization and digitalization and disruptive technologies on human capital-intensive firms (HCIFs), particularly in the logistics sector. The three case studies of control towers, business spheres and supply chain cockpits suggest that a new generation of high value-added human capital will be required to manage the massive data in logistics. The chapter identifies the human factor i.e. the skills and knowledge of employees, is essential for efficient implementation of disruptive technologies in HCIFs along the supply chain.

Acknowledgment

The editors would like to acknowledge the help of all the people involved in this project and, more specifically, to the authors and reviewers that took part in the review process. Without their support, this book would not have become a reality.

First, the editors would like to thank each one of the authors for their contributions. Our sincere gratitude goes to the chapter's authors who contributed their time and expertise to this book.

Second, the editors wish to acknowledge the valuable contributions of the reviewers regarding the improvement of quality, coherence, and content presentation of chapters.

Third, the editors would like to thank all the members of the Editorial Advisory Board for their helpful advice and guidance.

Cécile Cézanne
Université Côte d'Azur, France

Laurence Saglietto
Université Côte d'Azur, France

Section 1

Organization, Management Practices, and Human Capital

Chapter 1
A Survey of the Literature on Human Capital-Intensive Firms:
A Bibliometric Analysis

Cécile Cézanne
Université Côte d'Azur, France

Laurence Saglietto
Université Côte d'Azur, France

ABSTRACT

The aim of this chapter is to provide a survey of the academic research dedicated to human capital-intensive firms (HCIF) both at a theoretical and empirical level. The authors conduct a thematic inventory of the published works in this area to assess the dynamism of the field research and provide an exploratory analysis. They develop a bibliometric analysis based on the three widely used databases (Econlit, Science Direct, and Wiley) over the time period 1992-2018. From a cluster analysis, the chapter draws a portrait of HCIF based on the highlighted distinctive features. It also gets more information on the scope of existing research and the issues, limits, and prospects involved.

DOI: 10.4018/978-1-5225-7426-2.ch001

INTRODUCTION

Since the mid-1990s, human capital has been identified indisputably as the single most important resource for the productive activity of firms (Myers, 1999; Roberts and Van den Steen, 2000; Rajan and Zingales, 2001; Qian, 2003; Burton-Jones and Spender, 2011). It is widely recognised that the capacity of most modern firms to generate wealth depends on the knowledge and skills of their employees and on the ability of organisations to combine them efficiently (Blair, 1995). Employees add value to firms' innovation strategies based on their skills and talents and, according to Moavenzadeh et al. (2012), human capital is one of the essential factors that will shape the future of competition among firms, and among countries. In this respect, human capital is the bedrock of firms' competitive advantage and their functioning and activities (Coff, 1997, 1999; Lepak and Snell, 1999; Kraaijenbrink, 2011). How is human capital defined? What are its particularities and what organisational effects can it generate? Why do some firms use it so intensively in the context of their productive activities?

Human Capital-Intensive Firms (HCIF) are an interesting object for study because they demonstrate the extension to the firm's boundaries and also the transformations to and complexity of productive organisations in today's globalised economies which are inducing an evolution in economic and managerial theories. Nevertheless, HCIF also reflect both a reality and a concept that are yet ill-defined, since the recent literature would suggest that they appear to refer to several different aspects. The aim of this chapter, therefore, is to identify as clearly as possible the research on HCIF, to evaluate its theoretical structure and, thus, to determine its rhetorical and prospective significance. The authors conduct a thematic inventory of the work in this area in order to assess the dynamism of this research and provide an exploratory bibliometric analysis. This is challenging empirically, and according to the authors, is the first research to focus precisely on the genesis of the concept of HCIF. So far, study of HCIF has given rise to heterogeneous works around a number of different themes. The analysis in this chapter allows the authors to portray HCIF based on their different aspects, as well as the different theoretical perspectives exploited and depth of their analysis. This examination of HCIF dataset should shed light on three main research themes, the scope of existing research, and the issues, limits and prospects involved. The chapter concludes by discussing the significance and limitations of the present study.

BACKGROUND

In pioneering work in economics on human capital theory (Mincer, 1958; Schultz, 1961; Becker, 1964), the concept of capital' refers to the idea of immaterial stock (which can accumulate and depreciate), resulting from an investment that can be evaluated as the difference between the initial outlay (spending on education and training, opportunity costs) and the discounted future income. Human capital includes the concept of 'human assets' applied mainly in contractual theories of the firm (Alchian and Demsetz, 1972; Jensen and Meckling, 1976; Williamson, 1975, 1985; Grossman and Hart, 1986; Hart and Moore, 1990; Hart, 1995; Gibbons, 2005) to define a factor essential to a productive activity in progress. In particular, it represents the 'labour' factor in the context of the firm's production activity and transactions with partners. It is particular in being non-appropriable (in the legal understanding) by the firm or its partners. According to the contractualist approach understanding, an individual cannot promise residual rights of control over his/her human capital to another party based on an incomplete contract for any period. It is impossible to separate human capital from its holder; 'the human capital of [these] workers belongs to them both before and after the acquisition' (Hart, 1995, p. 29), while Blair (2011, p. 52) emphasises that: 'Human capital is, obviously, a trait of the worker and cannot be separated or conveyed or traded to another party'. In other words, human assets are incorporated in individuals who cannot legally be owned. However, they can be observed at a given moment in time from the perspective of static analysis of the firm and of the market competitive structure. Finally, human capital is increasingly considered to include the concept of 'human resources' which, according to the Resource-Based View, (RBV) comprises 'the training, experience, judgment, intelligence, relationships, and insight of individual managers and workers in a firm' (Barney, 1991, p. 101). So, in addition to the firm's physical and organisational capital, its human capital resources allow reductions in costs and increased value. The RBV introduces a dynamic perspective because human resources imply long-term investment (Prahalad and Hamel, 1990; Mahoney and Pandian, 1992), which enhances long-term competitive advantage based especially on innovation (Coff, 1999, 2011; Lepak and Snell, 1999; Wang et al., 2009). In this chapter, the authors use the terms 'capital', 'asset' and 'resource' interchangeably to indicate the breadth of the concept of resource. This allows to examine human capital according to its general or specific nature, and its impact in relation to value creation. Human capital theory distinguishes between general and specific human capital. It considers human capital is intangible stock attributable to the individual if it is general, and to the organisation if it is specific (Becker, 1964). General human capital can be transferred throughout the whole labour market whereas specific human capital is productive within the firm, but barely if at all productive outside it. Thus, the specificity of human capital can be captured by incentive payment practices which reveal the firm's fear of losing capital as a result of failure to recover, through higher productivity, the specific investment made (e.g. through departure of specialised workers). From this perspective, the wage hierarchy is explained by differences in the productivity of employees, which, in turn, stem from differences in specific investments in quantities of human capital (Mincer, 1970). The neo-institutional approach, which extends human capital theory, defines specific (or idiosyncratic) human assets as employees' knowledge and skills that have limited application outside of the firm relationship in which they have been developed (Williamson et al., 1975; Klein et al., 1978). These assets become specific from the moment that an employment relationship with the firm proves to be more efficient than a temporary work contract with an external individual. Economics approaches to the firm based on asset specificity can be likened to managerial views based on skills and resources (Prahalad and Hamel, 1990; Mahoney and Pandian, 1992). This similarity lies in the convergence between the definitions of non-transferability or inalienability of human capital that generates surplus value. Since the seminal work of Penrose (1959), it has been generally accepted that it is only firm-specific resources that provide the firm with lasting competitive advantage. To do so, they must satisfy certain criteria related to value (they must be critical or decisive for the firm), rarity, inimitability and non-substitutability. Firm specific resources require specific long-term investment and are the only resources capable of producing a value greater than their individual value (Barney, 1991). Also, the specific human capital of workers tends to appreciate over time, and life-long training, 'learning by doing', team working, and the variety of the tasks assigned to workers, enriches their human capital. It appreciates through the different production activities and collaborations in which they engage allowing the acquisition of new knowledge and diverse skills which may be more efficient and, therefore, more value-creating in the future. In these circumstances, it is clear that long-term employment relationships are necessary for the firm to be profitable (Blair, 2011). Specific human capital is also used to create new knowledge, to generate innovations (improvements to organisational procedures, industrial patenting activity, etc.). Although the authors concur with these definitions, the concept is broader because the specificity of human assets cannot be reduced only to the conditions of the employment relationship. The complexity of firms' tasks obliges firms also to establish long-term relationships with specialised external partners that possess knowledge and know-how indispensable to their productive activities. The human capital of these partners becomes specific to the firm that needs it. Ultimately, despite fundamental methodological and analytical differences between the economics and managerial approaches to the firm, there would appear to be some consensus around the definition of human capital and its specificity: generally speaking, specific human capital corresponds to all the knowledge, skills, talents and other attributes that an individual controls and exploits in a particular economic situation. However, it is less straightforward to identify the firms concerned, that is, the organisations endowed with high levels of specific human capital.

The link between productive organisations and their specific human capital is core to the depiction of HCIF. HCIF were first characterized in William H. Starbuck's seminal managerial contribution 'Learning by knowledge-intensive firms' published in 1992. This paper focuses on the activities inside knowledge-intensive firms. It reviews work expertise and describes organisational learning. Built on managing training, personnel turnover, organisational culture or even social capital, these firms develop long-term strategic development, including multinational expansion. Starbuck (1992) notably insists on the importance of intra and inter-organisational networks between experts decisive to firms' productive activities and identifies that social networks make the boundaries of the knowledge-intensive firm porous. In our view, in the economics, these 'new firms' (Rajan and Zingales, 2000; Zingales, 2000) can be considered a legacy of Rajan and Zingales's (1998) seminal piece 'Power in a Theory of the Firm', which gave rise to Critical Resource Theory (CRT) (Rajan and Zingales, 2001; Zingales, 2000). Similar to the RBV (Penrose, 1959; Wernerfelt, 1984; Barney, 1991; Amit and Schoemaker, 1993), CRT considers production and competition dynamics as fundamental to its analysis. In addition, in order to move beyond the incomplete contracts approach from which this theory developed (Grossman and Hart, 1986; Hart and Moore, 1990; Hart, 1995), CRT proposes a definition of the firm in which competitive advantage depends on the specificity of human capital and the specialisation of individuals. However, no homogeneous theoretical approach has been developed for HCIF. Isolated studies addressing diverse themes and using diverse terminologies in very different disciplinary fields, have multiplied making it difficult to identify HCIF in the literature.

From an analytical point of view, various more or less precise designations refer to HCIF: 'knowledge-based firms', 'innovative firms', 'high-tech firms', 'new firms', 'knowledge-intensive firms', etc. However, the authors persist with the term 'HCIF', which they consider to be both more inclusive and more explicit because of its direct reference to the specific human capital on which these firms depend. Some authors define HCIF as productive organisations whose value depends primarily on the ability of their employees to generate innovations (Fulghieri and Sevilir, 2009); others see them as sets of human assets possessed by individuals with complete access to them (Subramanian, 2007); yet others consider HCIF as depending mainly on their human capital and, therefore, on the efforts and creativity of a group of key workers (Qian, 2003). What is common to these definitions is that they refer to firms whose productive activity is largely dependent on the specialised and complementary human assets embodied by their critical partners, who may be firm employees and/or external partners (Cézanne and Rubinstein, 2012).

From an empirical perspective, HCIF include a wide variety of organisations, ranging from law firms whose prosperity depends essentially on the expertise of the lawyers they employ, to advertising agencies whose reputation is based on the talent of the artists in their creative departments, to including IT companies whose activity is essentially built around skilled computer specialists and programmers, or pharmaceutical laboratories whose success and performance depends largely on their researchers and especially 'star scientists'. In other words, HCIF encompass the large majority of productive organisations in the 'new economy'. Their productive activity requires not only traditional production factors such as fixed capital and labour but also and especially the intangible assets of skills, structures and organisational procedures, and a corporate culture (Brynjolfsson et al., 2002) along with specific human assets (Fulghieri and Sevilir, 2009). Consequently, although HCIF might appear to be an extreme case of a productive organisation, they in reality are widespread in business and are essential sources of technological and organisational innovation and added value. Thus, HCIF are an ideal focus for the study of modern firms, and notably include – with their own specific characteristics, the entrepreneurial firm (Alchian and Demsetz, 1972), and the Japanese firm (Aoki, 1988; 1990). As applies to the study of other types of firms, the domains of study related to HCIF are the modern theories of the firm and its related fields, with new developments that reflect the emergence of these 'new firms'.

MAIN FOCUS OF THE CHAPTER

Research Protocol

To explore the concept of HCIF, the authors construct a sample of 100 academic papers in Economics and Management derived from three recognized databases: ScienceDirect, Ebscot and Wiley. They consider this sample as the most significant articles to study HCIF. The authors construct a research protocol drawn from the works of Newbert (2007) and of David and Han (2004) who conduct bibliometric research respectively on the RBV and transaction cost economics firm theories. They develop similar research protocols and adopt their method for this study. In addition, the authors draw on classic measures in bibliometric analysis to better describe and appraise the concept of HCIF. The bibliometric approach is recognised in several disciplines as a means to evaluate, describe and map science.

Following Newbert's (2007) and David and Han's (2004) recommendations, the authors select items from the criteria shown in Table 1.

Table 1. The different steps of the research protocol

Steps	Explanations
1. *Type of publication*	The review is restricted to published peer-reviewed, academic articles in international journals.
2. *Database*	The review is restricted to published articles contained in the following three databases: EconLit, ScienceDirect and Wiley. These databases are suitable for our purposes because of their multidisciplinary nature in economics and business topics. Science Direct covers over 2,500 peer-reviewed journals from around the world, and Wiley 1400. Econlit indexes over 500 journals and over 600 collected volume articles per year.
3. *Topic choice*	The authors ensure substantive relevance by requiring firstly that selected articles contain at least 'Firm*' and 'Human capital' keywords in their titles or abstracts.
4. *Complementary topic choice*	Based on the discussion of HCIF presented above, the ensure substantive relevance by requiring also that selected articles contain at least one of the six following keywords in their titles or abstracts: 'Knowledge', 'intangible*', 'asset', 'innov*', 'R&D', 'skill*'. Note that these keywords were chosen in order to identify articles that were substantively relevant to describing HCIF.
5. *Nature of the content of the publication*	The author ensure empirical content by requiring that selected articles also contain at least one of the following seven 'methodological' keywords in their title or abstract: 'data', 'empirical', 'test*', 'statistical, finding*', 'result' or 'evidence' (Newbert, 2007; David and Han, 2004).
6. *Consolidation*	To ensure substantive context and empirical relevance, the author read all remaining articles in their entirety.
7. *Coherence*	The authors eliminate duplicate articles.
To this set of criteria, the authors add the following complementary criteria:	
8. *Year of publication*	For each item selected, the authors take into account date of publication.
9. *Period chosen*	The authors choose the 100 most significant articles to analyze HCIF between 1992 (Starbuck's seminal contribution) and 2018.
10. *Language*	English. For consistence, the authors retain only one language.
11. *Names of the authors*	The authors include all article authors because they contribute equally to the development of the science. This test also identifies research communities with the same publication practices.

In addition, the authors use classic bibliometric analysis measures.

- **Bradford's Law:** Aims to identify the core journals that best address a given subject. Scientific journals are ranked in decreasing order of productivity on the subject.
- **Lotka's Law:** Aims to count the number of publications by each author, which indicates, first, each author's contribution to scientific progress, and second, the structure of a disciplinary field.

- **Zipf's Law:** Aims to analyse the appearance of words by counting the number of occurrences and ranking them in decreasing order of frequency.

The authors also use univariate indicators. These are purely quantitative measures based on a simple count of different bibliographical elements: date of publication, publication by journal, author, keywords, etc.

Lastly, the authors use relational indicators. These are based on an analysis of the co-occurrence of associated words (repeated segments) and analysis of co-authors. Associated words are a valuable source of information because the concept being analysed, HCIF, is itself an association of words. Multiple authorship indicates different collaborations (within or between different schools of thought, research teams, universities and/or countries. Out of the possible procedures for counting authors (normal count, fractional authorship, straight count, modified straight count), the authors chose normal count, which gives the same weight to all the authors of an article because it allows us to count all the articles to which an author puts his or her name.

A Systematic Review of the Evidence on HCIF

The portrait of HCIF is based on the criteria chosen for the research protocol. The study involves three stages with increasingly high degrees of precision in the study of titles, keywords and abstracts. Finally, to discuss the results and take the analysis further, the authors read all of the articles selected.

In relation to date of publication, 2011 was the most prolific year with 10 articles published in diverse journals (see Table 2).

Using Zipf's law and counting occurrences and co-occurrences, the authors evaluate the articles, then the keywords and, last, the abstracts. The abstracts of the 100 articles were analysed using bibliometric measures to identify themes (and the authors read the complete articles to obtain complete information). The authors derive an overview of the empirical research in relation to geographical location, method, sector, theory and scope. The results are ranked in decreasing order of frequency.

- **Geographical Location:** United States, Europe, Asia, India and Africa;
- **Research Methods Employed:** The authors observe a wide variety of methods, with a predominance of statistical and econometric analyses (favouring various types of regression, logit or probit models, OLS, structural equations. Case studies with sample sizes ranging from 1 to 15,319 cases, are relatively infrequent. There is an interesting proportion of articles based on very substantial literature reviews;

Table 2. Publication dates and journal names

Date	Number of Articles	Journals
2018	4	*Academy of Management Perspectives, Small Business Economics, The International Journal of Human Resource Management, Human Resource Management Journal*
2017	5	*Journal of Business Research, Strategic Management Journal, The Journal of Technology Transfer, The International Journal of Human Resource Management*
2016	2	*Journal of Business Research*
2015	6	*Strategic Management Journal, Technovation, Managerial and Decision Economics, Management Science, Annual Review of Economics*
2014	3	*Thunderbird International Business Review, Journal of Management, Research Policy*
2013	2	*Journal of Finance, Structural Change and Economic Dynamics*
2012	4	*British Journal of Management, Research Policy, Technovation, Journal of Management Studies*
2011	10	*Industrial and Corporate Change, Small Business Economics, Education Economics, Expert Systems with Applications, Production and Operations Management, Economic Papers, Entrepreneurship Theory and Practice, Strategic Entrepreneurship Journal, Papers in Regional Science,*
2010	9	*Journal of Economic Surveys, Journal of World Business, Problems and Perspectives in Management, Review of Regional Research, The Leadership Quarterly, Economics of Innovation and New Technology, Papers in Regional Science, Technological Forecasting and Social Change*
2009	6	*Entrepreneurship Theory and Practice, Singapore Economic Review, Research Policy, British Journal of Management, Journal of Banking and Finance, Strategic Management Journal*
2008	5	*Public Policy Review, Taiwan Economic Review, Labour Economics, Journal of Urban Economics, Strategic Management Journal*
2007	5	*RAND Journal of Economics, Economic Record, Journal of Law and Economics, Research Policy, Journal of Rural Studies*
2006	3	*Economic Journal, Journal of Accounting and Public Policy, Review of Pacific Basin Financial Markets and Policies*
2005	6	*Journal of Economic Behavior and Organization, R&D Management, Strategic Management Journal, International Journal of Industrial Organization, Journal of Labor Economics*
2004	8	*Small Business Economics, Management, International Journal of Industrial Organization, Human Resource Management Journal, Strategic Management Journal, Industry and Innovation, Journal of Business Logistics, Research Policy*
2003	3	*Journal of Economics and Management Strategy, Small Business Economics, Human Resource Management Journal*
2002	7	*Journal of Management, Human Resource Management Journal, International Journal of Management Reviews, International Journal of Production Economics, Journal of Evolutionary Economics, Economic Development Quarterly*
2001	3	*Labour Economics, Economic Inquiry, Asian Economic Journal*
2000	3	*Environment and Planning, International Journal of Management Reviews, Journal of High Technology Management Research*
1999	1	*Journal of Development Economics*
1998	1	*Sociological Quarterly*
1997	1	*Academy of Management Review*
1996	1	*Resarch Policy*
1993	1	*Resarch Policy*
1992	1	*Journal of Management Studies*

Note: There may be several articles in the same journal and the same year.

- **Sectors:** The authors observe an appreciable bias towards general technology sectors (high-tech, biotech, software, electronics, semiconductors) and manufacturing industries, followed by cross-cutting sectors, law, and very diverse, isolated sectors (such as education or sport). Unsurprisingly, the sectors with a stronger presence require advanced technologies;
- **Theoretical Approaches:** The RBV is the most frequent approach used to appraise HCIF, followed by human capital theory, innovation theories, human resource management theory, growth theories, social capital theory, agency theory, and other isolated theories.

To deepen the analysis, the authors next distinguish between the dependent and independent variables. For the dependent variables, after 'human capital' (cited more than 120 times) and 'firm specific', the ranking (in decreasing order) is 'knowledge', 'innovation', 'R&D', 'labour productivity', 'employment', and experienced human resources ('education', 'intangible assets', 'specific skill', 'intellectual capital'). The notion of performance emerges strongly. HCIF are closely tied to the concept of performance (the abstracts included 80 occurrences of the term performance) and profit. The impact, influence or effects of performance on HCIF are a recurrent theme (cited 84 times) and impact is mainly positive (cited 36 times). The results for each independent variable are presented in decreasing order in Table 3.

Table 3. The independent variables

Categories	Independent Variables
Human capital	Specific, intensive, leveraging, evolution, organisational
Other capital	Intellectual, social, intangible, organisation*, intensive, knowledge, stock, technological, performance, productivity,
Size and type of firms	Small, young venture, new venture, large, start up, medium
Type of Industry	Specific, intensive
Concept of cooperation	Relationship, cooperation, apprenticeship training, business network, cluster, inter-firm, interactions
Economics	Economic, competitive advantage, international*, productivity*, region, investments, labour market, environment, business, entrepreneurship, economic growth, export*
Employees and Organisation	Experience, worker, entrepreneur*, organisational, manager*, marketing capabilities, organisational innovation, team, specific training, cognitive ability, expert human capital leveraging, human resource, leadership
Dynamics	Transfer*, interaction, dynamic capabilities, intensi*, capabilities innovative, boundaries
Firm specific	Skills, human capital, intensive
Type of innovation	Organisational

The 100 articles in the database are published in 65 different journals (see table 2). Following Bradford's law, there are four core journals which publish the most articles on HCIF: *Strategic Management Journal* (cited 9 times), *Research Policy* (7), *Human Resource Management Journal* (4), and *Small Business Economics* (4). These journals give a good representation of the scope of the domain of HCIF studies, while making an important contribution to the communication of research results. They have a high h-index[1]: *Strategic Management Journal*: 506, *Research Policy*: 359, *Human Resource Management Journal*: 107, and *Small Business Economics*: 206. The h-index quantifies the journal's scientific production, and its impact measured by number of citations to the articles it publishes. Publication is essential both for communicating results and as a vector of scientific recognition of researchers. Publishing in a journal with a high h-index guarantees wide circulation of the results and signals the interest in the subject.

207 authors write the 100 articles. 22 are single-authored and 78 are multiple-authored (43 have 2 authors, 26 have 3 authors and 9 have 4 authors). Grouping authors according to frequency of publication provides the following results. Very few authors published a large number of articles. This grouping of authors follows Lotka's law, that is, a distribution with a centre-periphery curve. Consequently, it is possible to evaluate both the contribution of each author to scientific progress, and the structure of a disciplinary field. These results for normal count can be refined in several ways: for example, the contribution of an author is often weighted by the number of co-authors of the article. Likewise, the results can be treated by taking account of the rate of citation (through the h-index), in other words the impact of articles in the core of the distribution.

Among the sample, the authors chose to retain the 17 articles with citation rates of 100 or above calculated by the bibliometric software 'Publish or Perish' using Google Scholar Metrics[2]. These 17 articles bring to light 3 main themes which the authors use to categorise the 100 articles in the sample. These 3 themes constitute the main research areas on HCIF in the period 1992-2018.

Table 4. Synthesis: The three main themes

Themes	References (The 17 Articles Most Often Cited)
Theme 1: human resources and performance	Boxall and Purcell (2000); Hatch and Dyer (2004); Lepak and Snell (2002); Nyberg et al. (2014).
Theme 2: specific intangible assets and strategies of the firm	Audretsch et al. (2009); Bosma (2004); Eisfeldt and Papanikolaou (2013); Kor and Leblebici (2005); Leiponen (2005); Moen (2005).
Theme 3: boundaries of the firm, innovation and competitive advantage	Ballot et al. (2001); Colombo et al. (2004); Hayton (2005); Loof and Heshmati (2002); Macpherson and Holt (2007); Negassi (2004); Ranft and Lord (2000).

SOLUTIONS AND RECOMMENDATIONS

The aim of this chapter was to identify and map research on HCIF. The analysis identifies three dominant themes (see table 4) that can be used to discuss the implications of this concept: 'human resources and performance' (theme 1), 'specific intangible assets and strategies of the firm' (theme 2), and 'firm boundaries, innovation and competitive advantage' (theme 3). Analysis of the 100 articles reveals a consensus over the development of specific human capital and its consequences within firms.

Firstly, organisations build and/or enrich the specific human capital embodied in their key employees. In the process, they encounter obstacles, because ensuring a core of specialised human capital dedicated to the firm's activities and functioning requires more than simply winning their loyalty. In addition to traditional incentive systems, firms need human resource management practices that will attract, retain and improve complementary skills and talents whose quality and specificity is not measurable by the number of hours spent in the workplace. Theme 1 explores these issues and their limits by assigning central importance to human capital in the employment relationship, and to the new forms of motivation within a collective value creation perspective that includes both employees, and the firm as their employer. The authors identify three subgroups of contributions on this theme 1.

The first subgroup includes articles that analyse the role of the employment relationship in the formation of specific human capital – which comprises all the knowledge, skills and know-how developed by and embodied in the employees within the organisation and which have little or no value outside that organisation. In this respect, training that is specific to the firm is one of the functions in the employment relationship that shape specific human capital (Antonelli et al., 2010). Specific human capital is difficult to transfer (Thomas and Ong, 2002), and especially in relation to family businesses, which are characterised by knowledge structures and combinations of skills, talents and qualities that differ from those of other companies (Patel and Fiet, 2011). However, some studies suggest that employees with high levels of potential and skill, constitute a labour force that can be redeployed quite easily (Huang, 2001). This diverging opinion is supported further by the complexity and diversity of the systems used to evaluate human capital (Elias and Scarbrough, 2004).

The second subgroup of articles focuses on how firms, first, can attract, retain and motivate employees with critical and scarce abilities, and second, develop efficient knowledge based work organisation processes to form a source of competitive advantage (Boxall and Purcell, 2000; Ballot et al., 2001). Despite the inalienable nature of human capital, employees with specific skills have a certain power over the firm which can affect their investment behaviour. This applies, for example, in the case of managers of logistics service providers (Myers et al., 2004) or partners in law firms (Chatain and Meyer-Doyle, 2017). It can even lead to the exercise of the legal right to leave the organisation, to take one's human capital elsewhere – perhaps by setting up a spin-off or a start-up firm (Appold, 2000). Firms can limit this hold-up risk by adopting human resource (HR) management practices appropriate to different types of human capital and job roles (Lepak and Snell, 2002), firm's sector of activity (Hunter et al., 2002), or accord to the centrality of client relationships (Swart and Kinnie, 2003). These practices may involve adapting wages and other forms of employee remuneration according to the types of human capital embodies (Huang et al., 2012) and according to their experience, level of education (Serneels, 2008), and gender (Amoroso et al., 2018; Huang, 2001). Knowledge workers can also be motivated by allowing them to benefit from non-financial gains, for example from greater autonomy (Gambardella et al., 2015)

The third subgroup of articles considers specific human capital, training and the formation of HR as the sources of HCIF performance. These articles are in broad agreement about the positive impact of these aspects on the firm while increasing knowledge about human capital within organizations (Nyberg et al., 2014; Boon et al., 2018). For example, Cater (2004) shows that firms' competitive advantage depends on the singularity of the knowledge they possess and the way it is coordinated. In particular, specific investment in human capital has a positive influence on firm performance (Hatch and Dyer, 2004; Lepak and Snell, 2002), whether measured by innovation (Bornay-Barrachina et al., 2012; Simonen and McCann, 2008, 2010), survival, profit and job creation (Bosma, 2004), or market valuation (Lajili and Zéghal, 2006). Refinements can be made according to the nature of the human capital (general or specific) and the sector involved (goods or services) (Wynn and Mueller, 1998). Also, the dominant frameworks on 'best practice' in HR show that the strategies adopted by firms are highly influenced by contextual contingencies, including national, sectoral and organisational factors. In addition, intellectual capital and processes of learning and adaptation in the organisation are largely studied (Kianto et al., 2017; Vomberg et al., 2015). In this perspective, since the knowledge and skills inherent in human capital are increasingly being recognised as vital for competitive advantage, firms are turning to diversified training programmes in order to develop and benefit from these resources (Schneider et al., 2010; Linnehan and De Carolis, 2005). Level of education, professional status and experience all influence HCIF performance (Schneider et al., 2010) and play a crucial role in access to international markets (Padmasiri, 2011).

Secondly, firms develop strategies that are based not only on the specific human capital they employ but also and more widely on the intangible assets that complement it (such as culture, patents and licences). Theme 2 examines the issues and limits related to this approach by focusing on the roles played by innovation and employee expertise in the competitive strategies of firms. Both factors contribute to the organisation's value creation through the endowment of strategic capabilities and key talents (Eisfeldt and Papanikolaou, 2013). This is particularly convincing in industrial sectors with high technological potential (Glenn et al., 2001; De and Dutta, 2007; De, 2009; Lynskey, 2004) and notably for firms whose R&D activities are conducted by star researchers, which procures for them strong real and symbolic value (Luo et al., 2009). These strategic capacities vary across different institutional environments (Griffith et al., 2010), but always contribute to long-term performance. They also influence the localisation of firms (Surinach and Moreno, 2011). The authors identify two subgroups of contributions on this theme 2.

The first subgroup analyses intangible assets as decisive factors in the competitive strategies of firms. Attention focuses, in turn, on the specific roles of the knowledge, abilities, experience, intellectual capital and talent of employees for enabling the firm to maintain its performance and to achieve long-term competitive advantage (Bosma, 2004; Ramirez and Hachiya, 2006; Wang and Lim, 2008). Generally, the alignment of intangible assets (human, informational and organisational) has a positive impact on the innovation process and the innovative capacity of firms (Huang et al., 2011). Certain investments in general human capital that complement specific human capital, also can contribute to this (Kessler and Lulfesmann, 2006). This essentially is due to the non-transferable nature of the resources embodied in employees (Wang and Lim, 2008), which then become entry barriers for many firms (Wang et al., 2009). The high level of expertise of certain employees can be seen as leveraging the implementation of diversification strategies. The recruitment of experts helps firms to build new knowledge bases and to exploit opportunities for growth (Kor and Leblebici, 2005). The high level of expertise of certain employees is also often considered to be a key element of corporate acquisition strategies (Coff, 2002).

The second subgroup of articles focuses on a form of intangible assets, intellectual capital, and the particular position it occupies in the innovative strategies of firms. R&D activity develops knowledge that is specific to the firm and, also, a form of intellectual capital that can be applied in other organisations. For example, inventors might be tempted to exploit their research results by joining a rival firm (Møen, 2005). This raises the question of propensity to innovate; in the context of young innovative firms, if innovators have high levels of specific abilities and are experienced in patent registration, they will be more likely to develop patents from the outset through their new firms (Audretsch et al., 2009; Balconi and Fontana, 2011). In other words, the specific professional skills and the managerial and entrepreneurial experience of founders play a central role in the production of patents (Audretsch et al., 2011), the success of projects (Colombo et al., 2004) and the technological development that contributes to the firm's economic growth (Hayton, 2005; Leiponen, 2005). More generally, intellectual capital (and, therefore, patents) influences the technical performance of innovation projects via the expertise of employees, the quality of information exchange, and the psychological security (Lee et al., 2011). Intellectual capital is decisive in the functioning and activity of HCIF, although it can include various realities. Some authors consider it to include human capital, intellectual property and reputational capital (Hayton, 2005); others see it as comprising human capital, organisational capital and customer capital (Kaya et al., 2010). Because it influences the present and future success of firms, intellectual capital attracts a good deal of attention and prompts some organisations to invest in staff training with the sole aim of increasing their intellectual capital (Kaya et al., 2010).

Thirdly, as just discussed, in the race for innovation and competitive advantage, specific human capital is the focus of corporate concern. It obliges firms to rethink their boundaries and their governance (Cézanne, 2008). This is the area explored by theme 3. When a firm develops its productive activity around the skills, knowledge, talents, etc. that are inseparable from the partners who control them, it faces the problem of regulating the power granted by specific human capital both within the legal perimeters of the firm and in the context of its key cooperation relationships. Theme 3 focuses on this last stage and the theoretical and empirical problem of the economic boundaries of HCIF. In this category, the authors groupe the articles that examine the origins and consequences of changes to the boundaries of the firm and identified two subgroups of articles.

The first of these subgroups studies the factors determining modifications to the boundaries of the firm. To ensure their growth or even just survival, HCIF need a number of specialised intangible assets that are both complementary and specific (Macpherson and Holt, 2007; Peneder, 2002). Their exploitable stock of knowledge depends on a strong link between investments in R&D and investments in human capital (Gómez and Vargas, 2012). This stock of knowledge comes either directly from the firm's hierarchical organisation or from disintegrated external relationships (Garicano and Hubbard, 2005, 2007). The specific training offered by the firm (Geel et al., 2011) or the creative leadership of CEOs (Makri and Scandura, 2010) on the one hand, and partnerships with other firms, for example spin-offs (Taheri and Van Geenhuizen, 2011) on the other, exemplify the underlying debates related to expansion of the firm's boundaries. In other words, the growing importance of specific human capital that is largely inimitable and non-transferable, in the productive activity and transactional relations of HCIF, has revolutionized the understanding of firm boundaries (Chou, 2007). In the context of the race for competitive advantage based on innovation, this is a central theoretical challenge in industrial economics. HCIF are increasingly adopting an innovation strategy centring on associations with other firms, in the form of cooperation, partnerships, acquisitions, new ventures, etc. (Ranft and Lord, 2000).

The second subgroup of articles explores the possible organisational consequences of changes to the firm's boundaries. The accumulation of specific human capital is a major source of economic growth (Peretto, 1999; Fukuda and Owen, 2008; Desmarchelier et al., 2013). The valuable resources embodied in the HCIF's key partners complement those embodied in the HCIF's key employees and both contribute to the HCIF's innovation process (Gersbach and Schmutzler, 2003; Al-Laham et al., 2011; Leiponen, 2005; Huang et al., 2011) and to their performance improvement (Lööf and Heshmati, 2002; Huang et al., 2012; Svendsen and Sørensen, 2007). This phenomenon is based on cooperation for R&D: these inter-firm relationships, which enable the transfer of key knowledge and skills, favour minimisation of decreasing returns from technology creation and, therefore, promote innovation (Negassi, 2004; Domenech et al, 2016). The geographical dimension, which includes the importance of different forms of proximities that are emblematic of local networks of organisations (e.g., clusters), is highlighted by several works (Kramer et al., 2010; Simonen and McCann, 2008; Steinfield et al., 2010). Ultimately, the alliances between HCIF and dense networks of partners introduce questions related to the scope and expansion of firms' boundaries, and even of their governance (Audretsch et al., 2009; Huang, 2003; Perdreau et al., 2015). They complicate the market valuation of firms (Johnson et al., 2002; Pantzalis and Park, 2009).

FUTURE RESEARCH DIRECTIONS

Although it is difficult to establish a precise definition of HCIF, this investigation of the past and recent literature on the subject allows us to delimit the field of study. The authors identified four elements that are fundamental to understand the HCIF: the existence of resources critical for the firm, the expansion of the firm's boundaries, the changing balance of power between employer and key partners (employees and external suppliers), and the transformations to human resource management practices. These four elements describe the productive entities that can be considered HCIF.

Firstly, HCIF are characterised by critical resources which can take the form of skills, talents and know-how that are essential for or indispensable to the long term productive activity of the firm. They are very important and/or irreplaceable sources of value. More precisely, 'critical' human assets allow the firm to exploit existing growth opportunities and explore new opportunities, following the principle of duality proposed by March (1991). In addition, these assets are at the heart of the dynamic process of firms' creation of economic, financial and symbolic value. These types of resources, held by both the firm and its key productive partners, necessarily modify the firm's scope of action in its coordination of these specific assets.

Consequently, secondly, HCIF are characterised by the expansion of their boundaries. Unlike tangible resources (factories, machinery) and certain transferable intangible resources (patents, brands), human capital, because it is immaterial, non-transferable and inimitable, cannot be appropriated by others. Therefore, human capital endows its providers with inalienable residual rights of control. Key employees and decisive external productive partners can exercise these inalienable residual rights of control; rent-seeking occurs not only within the firm but also between firms. Therefore, legal property cannot be considered an efficient method for coordinating the exercise of power. The boundaries of the firm must be studied in economic terms and no longer simply in legal terms. Along the same lines, the number and diversity of providers of critical human assets, both inside and outside the legal perimeters of the firm, calls for a complete rethinking of power struggles.

In this perspective, thirdly, HCIF are characterised by a change in the balance of power between the firm-employer and key productive partners. This represents a multilateral economic dependency relationship in which each party needs the other. On the one side, key employees and decisive suppliers need the assets of the firm to accomplish or extract value from their productive activity, and, therefore to activate their specific and complementary human assets. On the other side, the firm needs the co-specific assets of all these partners to develop its productive activity and to remain competitive. Under these circumstances, firm governance needs to be re-formulated. Since it has been recognised that corporate governance and ownership structure influence human resource management, the fragmentation of power into the hands of a large number of critical partners requires the firm to transform its human resource management.

Thus, fourthly, HCIF are characterised by innovative human resource management practices. Because of the growing importance of holders of specific human assets, the firm can no longer rely only on disciplinary management. It must address the broader problem of motivating its productive partners which requires a composite operational system. It may take the form of what are known as high-performance work practices which combine different vertical incentive mechanisms and horizontal work and coordination methods.

These four elements should become the basis for reflection and discussion related to future research aimed at improving the definition of HCIF and could contribute to the construction of an inclusive theoretical framework. The study of HCIF needs a coherent theoretical framework which at the same time is holistic and encompasses the diversity of possible approaches as well as more transversal methods of heuristic analysis. Many recent and forthcoming works on HCIF embrace this priority and make relevant propositions.

CONCLUSION

The aim of this chapter was to paint a picture of HCIF that shows its increasing importance place in the economy and need for theoretical legitimacy. The interdisciplinary scientific community that recognises HCIF is limited, but their portrayal in this study includes the contributions of each discipline and each theoretical approach to our understanding of this phenomenon. The sample of articles allowed the authors to analyse the characteristics of HCIF through numerous empirical studies conducted throughout the world, and to shed light on their commonalities, and the questions that remain open. This was enabled by a meticulous data gathering methodology and analysis to ensure the relevance and representativeness of the sample of articles.

However, this chapter has some limitations which should be highlighted. Firstly, the sample is not exhaustive. As Newert (2007) and David and Han (2004) observe, the used databases – Econlit, Science Direct and Wiley – do not contain all the published studies of HCIF, and other databases could be included, such as Emerald Publishing, for example. Nevertheless, because of the complete nature of the chosen databases, the sample can be considered representative of the whole population of articles on HCIF, and the results presented in this chapter are generalizable. Furthermore, since the criteria used to select articles are very strict to achieve a degree of objectivity, some purely conceptual articles, with no empirical content, were discarded. It would be possible to consider less restrictive criteria to expand the scope of the articles studied. Despite these limitations, the results of this chapter make a real contribution to the understanding of HCIF.

REFERENCES

Abramo, G., D'angelo, A. C., & Viel, F. (2013). Assessing the accuracy of the h- and g-indexes for measuring researchers' productivity. *Journal of the American Society for Information Science and Technology*, *64*(6), 1224–1234. doi:10.1002/asi.22828

Al-Laham, A., Tzabbar, D., & Amburgey, T. L. (2011). The dynamics of knowledge stocks and knowledge flows: Innovation consequences of recruitment and collaboration in Biotech. *Industrial and Corporate Change*, *20*(2), 555–583. doi:10.1093/icc/dtr001

Alchian, A. A., & Demsetz, H. (1972). Production, information xcosts, and economic organization. *The American Economic Review*, *62*(5), 777–795.

Amit, R., & Schoemaker, P. J. H. (1993). Strategic assets and organizational rent. *Strategic Management Journal, 14*(1), 33–46. doi:10.1002mj.4250140105

Amoroso, S., & Link, A. (2018). Under the AEGIS of knowledge intensive entrepreneurship: Employment growth and gender of founders among European firms. *Small Business Economics, 50*(4), 899–915. doi:10.100711187-017-9920-4

Antonelli, G., Antonietti, R., & Guidetti, G. (2010). Organizational change, skill formation, human capital measurement: Evidence from Italian manufacturing firms. *Journal of Economic Surveys, 24*(2), 206–247. doi:10.1111/j.1467-6419.2009.00615.x

Aoki, M. (1988). *Information, Incentives and Bargaining in the Japanese Economy*. Cambridge, UK: Cambridge University Press. doi:10.1017/CBO9780511571701

Aoki, M. (1990). Towards an economic model of the Japanese firm. *Journal of Economic Literature, 28*(1), 1–27.

Appold, S. J. (2000). The control of high-skill labor and entrepreneurship in the early US semiconductor industry. *Environment & Planning A, 32*(12), 2133–2160. doi:10.1068/a3372

Audretsch, D. B., Lehmann, E. E., & Plummer, L. A. (2009). Agency and governance in strategic entrepreneurship. *Entrepreneurship Theory and Practice, 33*(1), 149–166. doi:10.1111/j.1540-6520.2008.00284.x

Balconi, M., & Fontana, R. (2011). Entry and innovation: An analysis of the fabless semiconductor business. *Small Business Economics, 37*(1), 87–106. doi:10.100711187-009-9231-5

Ballot, G., Fakhfakh, F., & Taymaz, E. (2001). Firms' human capital, R&D and performance: A study on French and Swedish firms. *Labour Economics, 8*(4), 443–462. doi:10.1016/S0927-5371(01)00038-0

Barney, J. B. (1991). Firm resources and sustained competitive advantage. *Journal of Management, 17*(1), 99–120. doi:10.1177/014920639101700108

Becker, G. S. (1964). Human Capital: A Theoretical and Empirical Analysis, with Special Reference to Education (3rd ed.). University of Chicago Press.

Blair, M. M. (1995). *Ownership and Control: Rethinking Corporate Governance for the Twenty-First Century*. Washington, DC: Brookings Institution Press.

Blair, M. M. (2011). An economic perspective on the notion of 'human capital. In The Oxford Handbook of Human Capital, Part 1: The nature of human capital. Oxford.

Boon, C., Eckardt, R., Lepak, D. P., & Boselie, P. (2018). Integrating strategic human capital and strategic human resource management. *International Journal of Human Resource Management, 29*(1), 34–67. doi:10.1080/09585192.2017.1380063

Bornay-Barrachina, M., De la Rosa-Navarro, D., López-Cabrales, A., & Valle-Cabrera, R. (2012). Employment relationships and firm innovation: The double role of human capital. *British Journal of Management, 23*(2), 223–240. doi:10.1111/j.1467-8551.2010.00735.x

Bosma, N., van Praag, M., Thurik, R., & de Wit, G. (2004). The value of human and social capital investments for the business performance of start-ups. *Small Business Economics, 23*(3), 227–236. doi:10.1023/B:SBEJ.0000032032.21192.72

Boxall, P., & Purcell, J. (2000). Strategic human resource management: Where have we come from and where should we be going? *International Journal of Management Reviews, 2*(2), 183–203. doi:10.1111/1468-2370.00037

Brynjolfsson, E., Hitt, L. M., & Yang, S. (2002). Intangible Assets: Computers and Organizational Capital. *Brookings Papers on Economic Activity, 1*(1), 137–198. doi:10.1353/eca.2002.0003

Burton-Jones, A., & Spender, J. (2011). *The Oxford handbook of human capital*. Oxford, UK: Oxford University Press. doi:10.1093/oxfordhb/9780199532162.001.0001

Cater, T. (2004). The relevance of the knowledge-based school of thought on the sources of a firm's competitive advantage. *Management, 9*(1), 1–26.

Cézanne, C. (2008). Modern corporate changes: Reinstating the link between the nature, boundaries and governance of the Firm. *International Review of Applied Economics, 22*(4), 447–461. doi:10.1080/02692170802137596

Cézanne, C., & Rubinstein, M. (2012). The role of CSR in the governance of the 'new firm': An empirical study of the French telecommunications industry. *The IUP Journal of Corporate Governance, 11*(4), 17–38.

Chatain, O., & Meyer-Doyle, P. (2017). Alleviating managerial dilemmas in human-capital-intensive firms through incentives: Evidence from M&A legal advisors. *Strategic Management Journal, 38*(2), 232–254. doi:10.1002mj.2473

Chou, E. S. (2007). The boundaries of firms as information barriers. *The Rand Journal of Economics, 38*(3), 733–746. doi:10.1111/j.0741-6261.2007.00109.x

Coff, R. W. (1997). Human assets and management dilemmas: Coping with hazards on the road to resource-based theory. *Academy of Management Review, 22*(2), 374–402. doi:10.5465/amr.1997.9707154063

Coff, R. W. (1999). When competitive advantage doesn't lead to performance: The resource-based view and stakeholder bargaining power. *Organization Science, 10*(2), 119–133. doi:10.1287/orsc.10.2.119

Coff, R. W. (2002). Human capital, shared expertise, and the likelihood of impasse in corporate acquisitions. *Journal of Management, 28*(1), 107–128. doi:10.1177/014920630202800107

Coff, R. W. (2011). Maximizing value from human capital. In *The Oxford Handbook of Human Capital* (pp. 359–381). Oxford, UK: Oxford University Press.

Colombo, M. G., Delmastro, M., & Grilli, L. (2004). Entrepreneurs' human capital and the start-up size of new technology-based firms. *International Journal of Industrial Organization, 22*(8–9), 1183–1211. doi:10.1016/j.ijindorg.2004.06.006

David, R. J., & Han, S.-K. (2004). A systematic assessment of the empirical support for transaction cost economics. *Strategic Management Journal, 25*(1), 39–58. doi:10.1002mj.359

De, S. (2009). Intangible determinants of market value in the new economy: A dynamic panel data analysis of the Indian software industry. *The Singapore Economic Review, 54*(3), 379–398. doi:10.1142/S0217590809003392

De, S., & Dutta, D. (2007). Impact of intangible capital on productivity and growth: Lessons from the Indian information technology software industry. *The Economic Record, 83*(s1), S73–S86. doi:10.1111/j.1475-4932.2007.00406.x

Desmarchelier, B., Djellal, F., & Gallouj, F. (2013). Knowledge intensive business services and long term growth. *Structural Change and Economic Dynamics, 25*(0), 188–205. doi:10.1016/j.strueco.2012.07.003

Domenech, J., Escamilla, R., & Roig-Tierno, N. (2016). Explaining knowledge-intensive activities from a regional perspective. *Journal of Business Research, 69*(4), 1301–1306. doi:10.1016/j.jbusres.2015.10.096

Eisfeldt, A., & Papanikolaou, D. (2013). Organization capital and the cross-section of expected returns. *The Journal of Finance, 68*(4), 1365–1406. doi:10.1111/jofi.12034

Elias, J., & Scarbrough, H. (2004). Evaluating human capital: An exploratory study of management practice. *Human Resource Management Journal, 14*(4), 21–40. doi:10.1111/j.1748-8583.2004.tb00131.x

Fukuda, S., & Owen, R. F. (2008). Human capital and economic growth: Dynamic implications of insider-outsider problem for macroeconomics. *Public Policy Review, 4*(1), 133–158.

Fulghieri, P., & Sevilir, M. (2009). *Size and scope of human capital intensive firms*. Working paper, CEPR and ECGI University of North Carolina.

Gambardella, A., Panico, C., & Valentini, G. (2015). Strategic incentives to human capital. *Strategic Management Journal*, *36*(1), 37–52. doi:10.1002mj.2200

Garicano, L., & Hubbard, T. N. (2005). Hierarchical sorting and learning costs: Theory and evidence from the law. *Journal of Economic Behavior & Organization*, *58*(2), 349–369. doi:10.1016/j.jebo.2004.03.021

Garicano, L., & Hubbard, T. N. (2007). Managerial leverage is limited by the extent of the market: Hierarchies, specialization, and the utilization of lawyers' human capital. *The Journal of Law & Economics*, *50*(1), 1–43. doi:10.1086/508313

Geel, R., Mure, J., & Backes-Gellner, U. (2011). Specificity of occupational training and occupational mobility: An empirical study based on Lazear's skill-weights approach. *Education Economics*, *19*(5), 519–535. doi:10.1080/09645291003726483

Gersbach, H., & Schmutzler, A. (2003). Endogenous technological spillovers: Causes and consequences. *Journal of Economics & Management Strategy*, *12*(2), 179–205. doi:10.1162/105864003766754198

Gibbons, R. (2005). Four formal(izable) theories of the firm? *Journal of Economic Behavior & Organization*, *58*(2), 200–245. doi:10.1016/j.jebo.2004.09.010

Glenn, A., McGarrity, J. P., & Weller, J. (2001). Firm-specific human capital, job matching, and turnover: Evidence from major league baseball, 1900–1992. *Economic Inquiry*, *39*(1), 86–93. doi:10.1093/ei/39.1.86

Gómez, J., & Vargas, P. (2012). Intangible resources and technology adoption in manufacturing firms. *Research Policy*, *41*(9), 1607–1618. doi:10.1016/j.respol.2012.04.016

Griffith, D. A., Yalcinkaya, G., & Calantone, R. J. (2010). Do marketing capabilities consistently mediate effects of firm intangible capital on performance across institutional environments? *Journal of World Business*, *45*(3), 217–227. doi:10.1016/j.jwb.2009.09.008

Grossman, S. J., & Hart, O. D. (1986). The costs and benefits of ownership: A theory of vertical and lateral integration. *Journal of Political Economy*, *94*(4), 691–719. doi:10.1086/261404

Hart, O. D. (1995). *Firms, Contracts, and Financial Structure*. Oxford, UK: Oxford University Press – Clarendon Press. doi:10.1093/0198288816.001.0001

Hart, O. D., & Moore, J. (1990). Property rights and the nature of the firm. *Journal of Political Economy*, *98*(6), 1119–1158. doi:10.1086/261729

Hatch, N. W., & Dyer, J. H. (2004). Human capital and learning as a source of sustainable competitive advantage. *Strategic Management Journal*, *25*(12), 1155–1178. doi:10.1002mj.421

Hayton, J. C. (2005). Competing in the new economy: The effect of intellectual capital on corporate entrepreneurship in high-technology new ventures. *R & D Management*, *35*(2), 137–155. doi:10.1111/j.1467-9310.2005.00379.x

Hirsch, J. E. (2005). An index to quantify an individual's scientific research output. *Proceedings of the National Academy of Sciences of the United States of America*, *102*(46), 16569–16572. doi:10.1073/pnas.0507655102 PMID:16275915

Huang, H.-C., Lai, M.-C., & Lin, T.-H. (2011). Aligning intangible assets to innovation in biopharmaceutical industry. *Expert Systems with Applications*, *38*(4), 3827–3834. doi:10.1016/j.eswa.2010.09.043

Huang, H.-C., Lai, M.-C., & Lo, K.-W. (2012). Do founders' own resources matter? The influence of business networks on start-up innovation and performance. *Technovation*, *32*(5), 316–327. doi:10.1016/j.technovation.2011.12.004

Huang, L.-H. (2001). Industry-specific human capital and wage determination in Taiwan. *Asian Economic Journal*, *15*(1), 19–37. doi:10.1111/1467-8381.00121

Huang, L.-H. (2003). Industry-specific human capital, occupation and firm size: Evidence from Taiwan. *Small Business Economics*, *20*(3), 205–218. doi:10.1023/A:1022845929500

Hunter, L., Beaumont, P., & Lee, M. (2002). Knowledge management practice in Scottish law firms. *Human Resource Management Journal*, *12*(2), 4–21. doi:10.1111/j.1748-8583.2002.tb00061.x

Jensen, M. C., & Meckling, W. H. (1976). Theory of the firm: Managerial behavior, agency costs and ownership structure. *Journal of Financial Economics*, *3*(4), 305–360. doi:10.1016/0304-405X(76)90026-X

Johnson, L. D., Neave, E. H., & Pazderka, B. (2002). Knowledge, innovation and share value. *International Journal of Management Reviews*, *4*(2), 101–134. doi:10.1111/1468-2370.00080

Kaya, F. B., Sahin, G. G., & Gurson, P. (2010). Intellectual capital in organizations. *Problems and Perspectives in Management*, *8*(1), 153–160.

Kessler, A. S., & Lulfesmann, C. (2006). The theory of human capital revisited: On the interaction of general and specific investments. *Economic Journal (London), 116*(514), 903–923. doi:10.1111/j.1468-0297.2006.01116.x

Kianto, A., Sáenz, J., & Aramburu, N. (2017). Knowledge-based human resource management practices, intellectual capital and innovation. *Journal of Business Research, 81*, 11–20. doi:10.1016/j.jbusres.2017.07.018

Klein, B., Crawford, R., & Alchian, A. (1978). Vertical integration, appropriable rents, and the competitive contracting process. *The Journal of Law & Economics, 21*(2), 297–326. doi:10.1086/466922

Kor, Y. Y., & Leblebici, H. (2005). How do interdependencies among human-capital deployment, development, and diversification strategies affect firms' financial performance? *Strategic Management Journal, 26*(10), 967–985. doi:10.1002mj.485

Kraaijenbrink, J. (2011). Human capital in the Resource-Based View. In A. Burton-Jones & J.-C. Spender (Eds.), *The Oxford Handbook of Human Capital, Part 2: The nature of human capital and the firm* (pp. 218–237). Oxford.

Kramer, J.-P., Revilla Diez, J., Marinelli, E., & Iammarino, S. (2010). Intangible assets and MNEs' locational strategies for innovation-or: Why the regional matters: Empirical insights from Germany and the UK. *Review of Regional Research, 30*(2), 129–157. doi:10.100710037-010-0046-2

Lajili, K., & Zéghal, D. (2006). Market performance impacts of human capital disclosures. *Journal of Accounting and Public Policy, 25*(2), 171–194. doi:10.1016/j.jaccpubpol.2006.01.006

Lee, J. Y., Swink, M., & Pandejpong, T. (2011). The roles of worker expertise, information sharing quality, and psychological safety in manufacturing process innovation: An intellectual capital perspective. *Production and Operations Management, 20*(4), 556–570. doi:10.1111/j.1937-5956.2010.01172.x

Leiponen, A. (2005). Skills and innovation. *International Journal of Industrial Organization, 23*(5–6), 303–323. doi:10.1016/j.ijindorg.2005.03.005

Lepak, D. P., & Snell, S. A. (1999). The human resource architecture: Toward a theory of human capital allocation and development. *Academy of Management Review, 24*(1), 31–48. doi:10.5465/amr.1999.1580439

Lepak, D. P., & Snell, S. A. (2002). Examining the human resource architecture: The relationships among human capital, employment, and human resource configurations. *Journal of Management, 28*(4), 517–543. doi:10.1177/014920630202800403

Linnehan, F., & De Carolis, D. (2005). Strategic frameworks for understanding employer participation in school-to-work programs. *Strategic Management Journal, 26*(6), 523–539. doi:10.1002mj.467

Lööf, H., & Heshmati, A. (2002). Knowledge capital and performance heterogeneity: A firm-level innovation study. *International Journal of Production Economics, 76*(1), 61–85. doi:10.1016/S0925-5273(01)00147-5

Luo, X., Koput, K., & Powell, W. (2009). Intellectual capital or signal? The effects of scientists on alliance formation in knowledge-intensive industries. *Research Policy, 38*(8), 1313–1325. doi:10.1016/j.respol.2009.06.001

Lynskey, M. (2004). Knowledge, finance and human capital: The role of social institutional variables on entrepreneurship in Japan. *Industry and Innovation, 11*(4), 373–405. doi:10.1080/1366271042000289379

Macpherson, A., & Holt, R. (2007). Knowledge, learning and small firm growth: A systematic review of the evidence. *Research Policy, 36*(2), 172–192. doi:10.1016/j.respol.2006.10.001

Mahoney, J., & Pandian, J. (1992). The resource-based view within the conversation of strategic management. *Strategic Management Journal, 15*(5), 363–380. doi:10.1002mj.4250130505

Makri, M., & Scandura, T. A. (2010). Exploring the effects of creative CEO leadership on innovation in high-technology firms. *The Leadership Quarterly, 21*(1), 75–88. doi:10.1016/j.leaqua.2009.10.006

March, J. G. (1991). Exploration and exploitation in organizational learning. *Organization Science, 2*(1), 71–87. doi:10.1287/orsc.2.1.71

Mincer, J. (1958). Investment in human capital and personal income distribution. *Journal of Political Economy, 66*(4), 281–302. doi:10.1086/258055

Mincer, J. (1970). The distribution of labor incomes: A survey with special reference to the human capital approach. *Journal of Economic Literature, 8*(1), 1–26.

Moavenzadeh, J., Bernard, M., Giffi, C. A., & Powers, D. (2012). *Manufacturing for growth strategies for driving growth and employment.* A World Economic Forum Report, April.

Moen, J. (2005). Is mobility of technical personnel a source of R&D spillovers? *Journal of Labor Economics, 23*(1), 81–114. doi:10.1086/425434

Myers, M. B., Griffith, D. A., Daugherty, P. J., & Lusch, R. F. (2004). Maximizing the human capital equation in logistics: Education, experience and skills. *Journal of Business Logistics*, *25*(1), 211–232. doi:10.1002/j.2158-1592.2004.tb00175.x

Myers, S. C. (1999). Financial architecture. *European Financial Management*, *5*(2), 133–141. doi:10.1111/1468-036X.00086

Negassi, S. (2004). R&D co-operation and innovation a microeconometric study on French firms. *Research Policy*, *33*(3), 365–384. doi:10.1016/j.respol.2003.09.010

Newbert, S. L. (2007). Empirical research on the resource-based view of the firm: An assessment and suggestions for future research. *Strategic Management Journal*, *28*(2), 121–146. doi:10.1002mj.573

Nyberg, A., Moniterno, T., Hale, D., & Lepak, D. (2014). Resource-based perspective on unit-level human capital: A review and integration. *Journal of Management*, *40*(1), 316–346. doi:10.1177/0149206312458703

Padmasiri, H. M. N. (2011). The role of human capital in the development process of industrial clusters: Evidence from metalworking clusters in Sri Lanka. *Economic Papers*, *30*(1), 109–117. doi:10.1111/j.1759-3441.2010.00092.x

Pantzalis, C., & Park, J. C. (2009). Equity market valuation of human capital and stock returns. *Journal of Banking & Finance*, *33*(9), 1610–1623. doi:10.1016/j.jbankfin.2009.03.008

Patel, P. C., & Fiet, J. O. (2011). Knowledge combination and the potential advantages of family firms in searching for opportunities. *Entrepreneurship Theory and Practice*, *35*(6), 1179–1197. doi:10.1111/j.1540-6520.2011.00497.x

Peneder, M. (2002). Intangible investment and human resources. *Journal of Evolutionary Economics*, *12*(1-2), 107–134. doi:10.100700191-002-0103-2

Penrose, E. T. (1959). The Theory of the Growth of the Firm. Oxford University Press.

Perdreau, F., Nadant, L., & Cliquet, G. (2015). Human capital intangibles and performance of franchise networks: A complementary view between agency and critical resource perspectives. *Managerial and Decision Economics*, *36*(2), 121–138. doi:10.1002/mde.2656

Peretto, P. F. (1999). Industrial development, technological change, and long-run growth. *Journal of Development Economics*, *59*(2), 389–417. doi:10.1016/S0304-3878(99)00018-8

Prahalad, C. K., & Hamel, G. (1990). The core competence of the corporation. *Harvard Business Review, 68*(3), 79–91.

Qian, Y. (2003). *Human capital-Intensive firms: Incentives and capital structure.* Working Paper Series, University of Iowa – Department of Finance.

Rajan, R. G., & Zingales, L. G. (1998). Power in a theory of the firm. *The Quarterly Journal of Economics, 113*(2), 387–432. doi:10.1162/003355398555630

Rajan, R. G., & Zingales, L. G. (2000). The Governance of the New Enterprise. In X. Vives (Ed.), *Corporate Governance: Theoretical and Empirical Perspectives* (pp. 201–227). Cambridge, UK: Cambridge University Press. doi:10.1017/CBO9781139175333.007

Rajan, R. G., & Zingales, L. G. (2001). The influence of the financial revolution on the nature of firms. *The American Economic Review, 91*(2), 206–211. doi:10.1257/aer.91.2.206

Ramirez, P. G., & Hachiya, T. (2006). Measuring firm-specific organizational capital and its impact on value and productivity: Evidence from Japan. *Review of Pacific Basin Financial Markets and Policies, 9*(4), 549–574. doi:10.1142/S0219091506000860

Ranft, A. L., & Lord, M. D. (2000). Acquiring new knowledge: The role of retaining human capital in acquisitions of high-tech firms. *The Journal of High Technology Management Research, 11*(2), 295–319. doi:10.1016/S1047-8310(00)00034-1

Roberts, J., & Van den Steen, E. (2000). *Stakeholder interests, human capital investment and corporate governance.* Stanford GSB Working Paper Series, n°1631.

Schneider, L., Gunther, J., & Brandenburg, B. (2010). Innovation and skills from a sectoral perspective: A linked employer-employee analysis. *Economics of Innovation and New Technology, 19*(1-2), 185–202. doi:10.1080/10438590902872887

Schultz, T. W. (1961). Investment in human capital. *The American Economic Review, 51*(1), 1–17.

Serneels, P. (2008). Human capital revisited: The role of experience and education when controlling for performance and cognitive skills. *Labour Economics, 15*(6), 1143–1161. doi:10.1016/j.labeco.2007.10.003

Simonen, J., & McCann, P. (2008). Firm innovation: The influence of R&D cooperation and the geography of human capital inputs. *Journal of Urban Economics, 64*(1), 146–154. doi:10.1016/j.jue.2007.10.002

Simonen, J., & McCann, P. (2010). Knowledge transfers and innovation: The role of labour markets and R&D co-operation between agents and institutions. *Papers in Regional Science, 89*(2), 295–309. doi:10.1111/j.1435-5957.2010.00299.x

Starbuck, W. (1992). Learning by knowledge-intensive firms. *Journal of Management Studies, 29*(6), 713–740. doi:10.1111/j.1467-6486.1992.tb00686.x

Steinfield, C., Scupola, A., & López-Nicolás, C. (2010). Social capital, ICT use and company performance: Findings from the Medicon Valley Biotech Cluster. *Technological Forecasting and Social Change, 77*(7), 1156–1166. doi:10.1016/j.techfore.2010.03.004

Subramanian, K. (2007). *Firm boundaries in the new economy: Theory and evidence.* 2007 Annual Meeting Allied Social Science Associations, AEA Conference, Chicago, IL.

Surinach, J., & Moreno, R. (2011). The role of intangible assets in the regional economic growth. *Investigaciones Regionales,* (20), 165-93.

Svendsen, G., & Sørensen, J. F. (2007). There's more to the picture than meets the eye: Measuring tangible and intangible capital in two marginal communities in rural Denmark. *Journal of Rural Studies, 23*(4), 453–471. doi:10.1016/j.jrurstud.2007.01.008

Swart, J., & Kinnie, N. (2003). Knowledge-intensive firms: The influence of the client on HR systems. *Human Resource Management Journal, 13*(3), 37–55. doi:10.1111/j.1748-8583.2003.tb00097.x

Taheri, M., & van Geenhuizen, M. (2011). How human capital and social networks may influence the patterns of international learning among academic spin-off firms. *Papers in Regional Science, 90*(2), 287–311. doi:10.1111/j.1435-5957.2011.00363.x

Thomas, W. F., & Ong, P. (2002). Barriers to rehiring of displaced workers: A study of Aerospace engineers in California. *Economic Development Quarterly, 16*(2), 167–178. doi:10.1177/0891242402016002006

Vomberg, A., Homburg, C., & Bornemann, T. (2015). Talented people and strong brands: The contribution of human capital and brand equity to firm value. *Strategic Management Journal, 36*(13), 2122–2131. doi:10.1002mj.2328

Wang, H., & Lim, S. (2008). Real options and real value: The role of employee incentives to make specific knowledge investments. *Strategic Management Journal, 29*(7), 701–721. doi:10.1002mj.681

Wang, H. C., He, J., & Mahoney, J. T. (2009). Firm-specific knowledge resources and competitive advantage: The roles of economic- and relationship-based employee governance mechanisms. *Strategic Management Journal*, *30*(12), 1265–1285. doi:10.1002mj.787

Wernerfelt, B. (1984). A resource-based view of the firm. *Strategic Management Journal*, *5*(2), 171–180. doi:10.1002mj.4250050207

Williamson, O. E. (1975). *Markets and Hierarchy: Analysis and Antitrust Implications*. New York: Free Press.

Williamson, O. E. (1985). *The Economic Institutions of Capitalism: Firms, Markets, Relational Contracting*. New York: Free Press.

Williamson, O. E., Wachter, M. L., & Harris, J. E. (1975). Understanding the employment relation: The analysis of idiosyncratic exchange. *The Bell Journal of Economics*, *6*(1), 250–278. doi:10.2307/3003224

Wynn, T., & Mueller, C. W. (1998). Product characteristics, human capital and labor market segments. *The Sociological Quarterly*, *39*(4), 597–622. doi:10.1111/j.1533-8525.1998.tb00520.x

Zingales, L. (2000). In search of new foundations. *The Journal of Finance*, *55*(4), 1623–1653. doi:10.1111/0022-1082.00262

ENDNOTES

1 In 2005, the physicist J.E. Hirsch achieved an intuitive breakthrough with the proposal of the index that is now named after him (Hirsch, 2005). The 'h-index' represents the maximum number h of works by a scientist that have at least h citations each (Abramo et al., 2013).

2 As of 31/05/2018.

Chapter 2
HRM Practices in Human Capital-Intensive Firms:
An Empirical Study of IBM Corporation

Sabrina Loufrani-Fedida
Université Côte d'Azur, France

ABSTRACT

This chapter focuses on examining the human resource management (HRM) practices that are used in human capital-intensive firms (HCIFs). In the specialized literature on HCIFs, human resources (HR) are recognized as constituting an infinite value potential. Nevertheless, we know little in the literature about "how to manage" these HR in the specific context of HCIFs. First of all, in this chapter, a literature review provides a clarification of the HR's key concepts (human capital, competence, and talent) on the one hand and introduces the relevance to study HRM practices underlying human capital management on the other hand. Then, based on the case study of IBM Corporation, a synthesis of the wide variety of HRM practices is proposed into three processes: identifying, assessing and developing, and finally, motivating and retaining human capital. The IBM case is representative of the HCIFs insofar as the company puts its human capital at the heart of its overall strategy and, in order to do this, provides a sophisticated HRM policy and, in addition, has implemented formalized HRM practices. For IBM, the aim is to improve resource assets of its employees necessary to generate innovation, value, and performance.

DOI: 10.4018/978-1-5225-7426-2.ch002

INTRODUCTION

In the current competitive environment where intensive and repeated innovation plays a fundamental role (Brown & Eisenhardt, 1997; Lew & Sinkovics, 2013), many firms are part of a development process based on knowledge-intensive products and/or services (Starbuck, 1992; Makani & Marche, 2010). According to Cézanne and Saglietto (2016, p. 62), Human Capital-Intensive Firms (HCIFs) are identified as "small and large innovative modern firms operating in both knowledge-intensive service sectors and high-tech manufacturing industries whose results in terms of the growth of production and/or turnover are better than those of other types of firms". HCIFs are built on "resources that are, by nature, intangible, inalienable and difficult to reproduce instantaneously" (ibid., p. 63). In other words, they are built on specific human capital which is defined as the skills, knowledge and competencies that produce value only within the firm in which it has been accumulated (Becker, 1964).

According to Armstrong and Taylor (2014), Human Resource Management (HRM) includes activities covering strategic HRM (SHRM), human capital and knowledge management, corporate social responsibility (CSR), organization development, resourcing (including HR planning, recruitment, selection, and retention), learning and development, performance and reward management, employee relations and well-being, as well as international HRM (IHRM). HRM consists of a set of HRM practices, which, according to Ngo et al. (2008), are defined as mechanisms to develop HR internally in order to optimize the skills, knowledge, and ability of the employees and to increase their motivation. These practices are notably aimed at employee selection, recruitment, development, and retention (Marchington et al., 2016).

In a context of strengthening HCIFs, the question of HRM practices has become a rising issue both for companies and management research. Companies are interested in jointly managing human resource development and developing innovative products and services. In the specialized literature on HCIFs, human resources are recognized as constituting an infinite value potential (Becker et al., 1997; Cézanne and Saglietto, 2014). Human capital can be regarded as the prime asset of an organization and businesses need to invest in that asset to ensure their survival and growth. As explained by Armstrong and Taylor (2014), HRM aims to ensure that the organization obtains and retains the skilled, committed and well-motivated workforce it needs. Studies of HRM practices in HCIFs environments have emphasized the difficulties of operationalizing human capital management (Fulmer & Ployhart, 2014; Nyberg et al., 2014). As stated by Fulmer and Ployhart (2014), we consider that contributions are limited in the specification of HRM practices that are used to manage human capital. In other words, we know little in the literature about 'how to manage' human resources in the specific context of

HCIFs. The purpose of our study is precisely to highlight and examine the different mechanisms to develop HR internally in order to optimize human capital (skills, knowledge, and ability) of the employees. Accordingly, we seek to provide answers to the following question: *What are the HRM practices underpinning human capital management in HCIFs, and how are they used?*

To address this question, our research is based on a qualitative approach centred on a single case study: IBM Corporation. The IBM case is worthwhile and interesting as a research subject in so far as the company puts its human capital at the heart of its overall strategy, and in order to do this, provides a sophisticated HRM policy and has implemented formalized HRM practices. For IBM, the aim is to improve resource assets of its employees, necessary to generate innovation, value and performance.

The chapter is organized as follows. In the first part, we carry out a literature review on the different concepts in order to characterize HR (human capital, competence, talent) and introduce the relevance of studying HRM practices underpinning human capital management in HCIFs. Then, in the second part, we briefly describe our research methodology. In the third part, based on the case study of IBM Corporation, acknowledged as a HCIF, we propose summarizing of the wide variety of HRM practices into three processes: identifying, assessing & developing, and motivating & retaining human capital. Finally, in the fourth part, we discuss and conclude the chapter by providing implications for research and practice, and identifying limitations and suggestions for future research directions.

LITERATURE REVIEW

Human Capital, Competence, Talent

The concepts of human capital, competence and talent are part of a series of key concepts that have led to HRM becoming operationalized over more than 50 years. Indeed, one of the major concerns of HR practitioners is to find key terms to measure human activity and be able to predict the future career path of the individual. Nowadays, individuals at work are sometimes characterized by their human capital, sometimes by their competencies, sometimes by their talent, and sometimes by all the three. We therefore need to distinguish these concepts by introducing them successively and by comparing them in the same time.

The term 'human capital' was coined by Schultz (1961) who developed his concept in 1982 as follows: "Consider all human abilities to be either innate or acquired. Attributes… which are valuable and can be augmented by appropriate investment will be human capital". A more detailed definition was put forward by Bontis et al. (1999) as follows: Human capital represents the human factor in the organization; the combined intelligence, skills and expertise that gives the organization its distinctive character. Since the founding works initiated by economists such as Schultz (1961, 1982) and Becker (1964), the notion of human capital has gradually become the subject of controversy due to the disputes between disciplines, the levels of analysis used, the terminology and typologies used (specific and general human capital) and the difficulties associated with measuring and valuing it (Ployhart & Moliterno, 2011; Fulmer & Ployhart, 2014; Nyberg et al., 2014). In particular, for these authors, human capital can be understood as a multi-level concept. From the individual point of view, Ployhart and Moliterno (2011) propose defining it as a set of KSAOs (knowledge, skills, abilities and other characteristics) held by an individual. From an organizational point of view, the company's human capital can be a strategic resource based on its value and rarity (Lepak & Snell 1999; Hatch & Dyer, 2004). Fulmer and Ployhart (2014) retain the term of collective human capital (i.e., at the firm or unit level). For Armstrong and Taylor (2014), the human capital of an organization consists of the people who work there and on whom the success of the business depends. For these HRM researchers, the human capital individuals of the organization are those that are capable of learning, changing, innovating, and providing the creative thrust, which if properly motivated, can ensure the long-term survival of the organization.

The term 'competence' emerged in the 1980s. Many contradictions in the current literature stem from two alternative ways of considering competence: 'worker' and 'work' viewpoints (Håland & Tjora, 2006). The 'worker' view considers competence as a set of resources, namely 'knowledge, skills and attitudes' (KSA) (Delamare Le Deist & Winterton, 2005). It is therefore possible to consider that individual competence is built on knowledge and practical experience (know-how), while relying on a behavioural foundation (know-how or faculty of adaptability). McClelland (1973) was one of the founders of this approach. This 'worker' view is a deterministic, universal or even ideal view of competencies required by individuals: we seek to identify 'good' competencies (Boyatsis, 1982; Spencer & Spencer, 2008). Accordingly, the 'worker' perspective of competence is very close to that of human capital because they both consider human resources as 'human assets'. The 'work' view of individual competence proposes a perspective based more on the work that the person actually does (Singleton, 1978; Capaldo et al., 2006). Here, individual competence is highly contingent on a given professional situation and therefore corresponds to a context. Individuals are not competent themselves but in relation to something. Therefore, appreciating whether an individual possesses a competence can only be revealed by a specific work situation. Competence is an unstable and flexible construct, interacting between the individual and its context (Sandberg, 2000; Häland & Tjora, 2006; Sandberg & Pinnington, 2009; Lindberg & Rantatalo, 2015). As a combination of work and worker views, a hybrid view considers individual competence as a combination of resources (knowledge, skills and attitudes) that makes a person at work capable of doing something in a professional situation, "in a specific context" (Defelix et al., 2006).

Finally, since the early 2000s, the term 'talent' has 'invaded' HRM. Based on the 'Parable of the Talents' in the New Testament (Gospel of Matthew, 25: 14-30), Tansley (2011) suggests that talent is used as a synonym for human capital because of the translation of the Greek word talent into the new English word capital. Research literature, articles, and books are falling short of providing a clear and universal definition of what talent is and who talents are. Nevertheless, our analysis of the literature on this 'new' concept qualifying and measuring human resources shows that there cannot be talent without competence, even if the talent is more than the competence (Farndale et al., 2010). Dejoux and Thévenet (2012) define talent "as a rare combination of rare competencies", and emphasize that talent (as a person) will be distinguished from others through unique and original competencies. For their part, Ulrich and Smallwood (2012, p. 60) consider that a person must possess and use three characteristics to be recognized as talented, according to the following formula: "*Talent = competence x commitment x contribution*". The interest of this conception of talent is to consider what a person contributes to achieving organizational objectives. Moreover, three major debates on the nature and design of talent cross the literature. (1) The first stresses two views of the concept of talent in the workplace (Gallardo-Gallardo et al., 2013): subject and object. Whereas in the 'subject' view, talent corresponds to the specific person (to be a talent); in the 'object' view, talent corresponds to a characteristic of a person (to have a talent). (2) The second debate concerns the origin and provenance of talent, with two streams of complementary definitions (Meyers et al., 2013). In the first stream, talent is mainly innate: it can be likened to a 'gift', as something that people are either born with, conferred on exceptional people. The second stream favours abilities acquired over time: talent is then a combination of different competencies that the subject (the person) has accumulated over his/her experiences. Accordingly, talent can be developed and managed (Collings & Mellahi, 2009). (3) Finally, according to Gallardo-Gallardo et al. (2013) and Al Ariss et al. (2014), an important question for defining talent in the workplace is whether everybody can be considered as a talent (inclusive view) or whether talent is unique and applies only to a rather small elite group of individuals (exclusive view). Very often in this exclusive view, top performers, high potentials and experts are cited as examples (Chabault et al., 2012). A High Potential is someone who is considered by his/her organization to have the ability to hold a leadership position. The expert is considered to be a professional with a particularly high degree of ability in a specific field of competence.

To conclude this section, we observe that theoretical foundations appear to be the same between human capital, competence (in a 'worker' perspective) and talent. Whether individuals are recognized as human capital, competent or talented, these 'workers' are independent from their work, or in other words from their context. A combination of different resources (knowledge, skills, abilities and other characteristics) allow them to succeed in their jobs.

HRM Practices Underlying Human Capital Management

There is an emerging literature on Human Capital Management (HCM), emphasizing it as the key point that a firm's human resources and subsequently its HRM system can be more than just a cost to be reduced (Becker et al., 1997; Baron, 2007; Ketchen Jr, 2017). This means taking steps to assess and satisfy future staff needs and enhance and develop people's inherent capacities– their contributions, potential and employability – by providing learning and continuous development opportunities. According to Armstrong and Taylor (2014), this involves obtaining, analysing and reporting on data that informs top management on value-adding people management and strategic investment & operational decisions at the corporate level as well as at the level of front-line management. The defining characteristic of HCM is this use of metrics to offer guidance in managing people by regarding them as assets and emphasizing that competitive advantage is achieved by strategic investments in those assets through employee engagement & retention, talent management & learning and development programmes. HCM points the way to achieving a human capital advantage by highlighting where and how investments in people generate the highest returns. It ensures that HRM policies and practices are developed to achieve this end. These policies include knowledge management, resourcing, talent management, performance management, learning and development programmes, as well as reward and recognition processes (Armstrong & Taylor, 2014).

Although the concept of HRM is not consistently defined, there is a significant amount of academic literature focusing on HRM perspectives and practices including but not limited to employee selection, recruitment, development, and retention (Marchington et al., 2016). Armstrong and Taylor (2014, p. 1) refer to HRM as "a philosophy about how people should be managed, which is underpinned by a number of theories relating to the behaviour of people and organizations," and which contributes to improving organizational effectiveness. Despite the numerous research studies on HRM practices, there is no clear consensus on how HRM practices are understood, and no consistency as to the type or number of practices used and included under the HR function. According to Delaney and Huselid (1996, p. 967), "no two studies measure HRM practices in the same way." In our research, we understand HRM practices as mechanisms to develop HR internally in order to optimize employee skills, knowledge and ability, and to increase their motivation levels (Ngo et al., 2008). This approach is based on the AMO (ability, motivation, opportunity) framework (Appelbaum et al., 2000; Purcell & Hutchinson, 2007), maintaining that HRM practices can positively affect the skills, competencies, and abilities as well as the motivation and commitment of employees, while offering career and development opportunities can have a positive influence on organizational outcomes.

Over the past decades, research in the field of HRM experienced a shift from the micro-analytic level to the macro level that considers the strategic perspective of HRM (Delery & Roumpi, 2017). This development redefined classical HRM as SHRM, linking HRM to company strategy by analysing the impact of HRM practices on performance. Armstrong and Taylor (2014, p. 16) suggest that SHRM is "a strategic, integrated and coherent process (...) that involves adopting a broad and long-term view of where the business is going". Schuler and Jackson (2007) conclude that the main purpose of SHRM is to systematically link people with the organization. Ever since HRM research began, academics have aimed to demonstrate the strategic importance and impact of HRM practices on company performance (e.g., Wright & Snell, 1991; Ferris et al., 2004; Wright et al., 2005; Lengnick-Hall et al., 2009). In the same vein, while research in economics and psychology has focused on human capital at the individual level (Becker, 1964; Schmidt & Hunter, 1998; Schultz, 1961, 1982), strategic management research has focused on firm-level human capital resources through the resource-based view (Barney, 1991). More recent research has begun to recognize that human capital is inherently a multi-level phenomenon (e.g., Coff & Kryscynski, 2011; Molloy et al., 2011; Ployhart & Moliterno, 2011; Barney & Felin, 2013). Work on talent and human capital indeed provides a promising way to study micro-foundations in organization theory, management, and strategy (Barney & Felin, 2013). Due to the similar interest of both the HRM and HCM literature for strategic management which are strong on multi-level theory and conceptualization about human capital resources, current research is interested in further integrating strategic human capital and strategic HRM (Delery & Roumpi, 2017; Boon et al., 2018).

Nevertheless, the recent literature on strategic human capital/strategic HRM is largely silent on the actual operationalization of HRM practices. In particular, Fulmer and Ployhart (2014) call for more research on practice in HCM. We still know little about how to concretely manage human resources in the specific context of HCIFs. Studies of HRM practices in HCIFs environments have emphasized the difficulties of operationalizing human capital management (Fulmer & Ployhart, 2014; Nyberg et al., 2014). As stated by Fulmer and Ployhart (2014), we consider that contributions are limited in the specification of HRM practices that are used to manage human capital. The aim of our study is precisely to highlight and examine the different mechanisms for developing HR internally in order to optimize the human capital (skills, knowledge, and ability) of employees. Accordingly, we seek to provide answers to the following question: *What are the HRM practices underpinning human capital management in HCIFs, and how are they used?*

METHODOLOGY

Research Design and Setting

To address this question, our empirical research relies on a qualitative approach focused on a unique case study: IBM Corporation. In line with the common recommendations for qualitative research focused on case studies (Eisenhardt, 1989; Eisenhardt & Graebner, 2007; Siggelkow, 2007; Yin, 2008), we selected the IBM case study because it is representative of HCIFs: the company puts its human capital at the heart of its overall strategy, and in order to do this, provides a sophisticated HRM policy and has implemented formalized HRM practices. For IBM, the aim is to improve the resource assets of its employees, needed to foster innovation, value and performance. Indeed, anticipating, reacting quickly and adapting in order to remain competitive requires first of all, positioning human capital at the heart of the company's overall strategy. For IBM, which is facing an increasingly competitive environment, optimizing HRM is therefore a key development factor, which directly contributes to customer satisfaction. Table 1 presents the main characteristics of our case study.

Table 1. Characteristics of the IBM case study

Characteristics	IBM Corporation
Business sector	Computer technologies and services
Unit/Department studied	IBM Global Services
Total staff in the group at the time of the study	325 000
Nationality	American
Strategic and organizational context	Strategic reorientation towards computer services and solutions, resulting in a reorganization by projects and jobs
Number of interviews	15
People interviewed	CEO (1), HR partners (3), line managers (3), projects managers (6), engineers (2)

Data Collection and Analysis

The data was mainly sourced from individual interviews. In total and in order to obtain an overall view of the phenomenon studied, 15 semi-structured interviews lasting on average 1.5 hours were carried out in France with employees in various positions and functions on the issue of managing human capital: one Chief Executive Officer (CEO), 3 Human Resources partners, 3 line-managers, 6 projects managers, and 2 engineers. Individual interviews were carried out using interview guides specific to the case and employees under study. These interview guides were created after the literature review and the first interviews. The interviews dealt with three common themes: (1) strategic human capital in links with competence and talent; (2) HRM practices; (3) support facilities (staff, entities, tools, resources, etc.). In total, about 25 hours of interviews were recorded and 80 single-spaced pages were transcribed.

These interviews were supplemented by relevant documents (competency frameworks, archives and interviewee's personal notes, press articles, etc.), non-participant observation (carried out while we were present onsite for the interviews), and informal dialogues (including conversations with interviewees via email, telephone, or conversations without any prior arrangement). We transcribed our observations into a research journal. These four sources of data (interviews, documents, observations, and informal discussions) add richness to the findings and also help with triangulation (Yin, 2008).

For data analysis, we used multiple tools, most of which were recommended by Miles and Huberman (1994): interview summary sheets, data coding, and reports. Based on an abductive approach, the analytic strategy (Yin, 2008) consisted of the technique of 'open coding' (Strauss & Corbin, 1990) and 'thematic coding' (Miles & Huberman, 1994). Open coding was used to identify HRM practices for managing human capital. Thematic coding was used to highlight the process associated with HRM practices: identifying, assessing & developing, and motivating & retaining human capital. All data were coded: interviews, documents, daily journal, and emails. Finally, a report of approximately fifty pages was written about the phenomenon studied in the company and submitted to key people identified at IBM, to obtain their agreement, validate our interpretations and thus increase the validity of both the construct and the internal research (Yin, 2008).

CASE STUDY

The Company and Its Context

As presented by Ahamed et al. (2013), International Business Machine (IBM) is the world leading computer and technology firm, established in 1911, which offers a variety of products and services in information and communication technology (ICT) industry. IBM operates across five business segments, and is present in markets in the United States, Europe, Asia, Africa, Oceania, etc. Until the mid-1990s, IBM specialized in selling and developing computer hardware and software, but an ultra-competitive market, changes in customers' needs and ongoing business demand led the company to redirect its strategy towards computer services and solutions. To support this strategic change, IBM had to thoroughly review its organization and operations to put the client at the centre of its priorities. This transformation resulted in a project-based organization which organized IBM competencies by jobs. Competencies were then considered as independent from the company's business segments: "*There was no other way for us to position ourselves fundamentally in relation to the demand of our customers and in order to develop competencies in services*" (IBM France CEO).

This company reorganization resulted in prioritizing individual competence management. "*IBM's future depends on the competencies of the individuals who make up the company, because company success depends on its employees (...). At IBM, competencies are considered to be what really differentiates us from our competitors and one of the main reasons why our clients trust us*" (Head of jobs and qualifications). This is why IBM is now considered to be the pioneer in human capital management through its implementation of formalized HRM practices which encourage the development of individual competencies and aim at improving staff employability (above all internally, but also externally). Moreover, it is important to note that at IBM, the HR function is delegated to management: the HR department provides managers with support and advice on how to manage the competencies in their unit.

The purpose of this part is to highlight the main HRM practices implemented by the company to encourage human capital management. Personal skills updates, talent detection, personal business commitments, internal job certification, training and mentoring, career management and job rotation are the main mechanisms of this global challenge. We propose structuring the presentation of these HRM practices according to the three major processes: (1) identifying (2) evaluating & developing (3) motivating & retaining human capital.

Identifying Human Capital

Personal Skills Update (PSU)

The PSU is a personalized skills framework, developed at IBM in the form of a database. Specifically, it is a system of managing each employee's key technical skills in real time. According to the company's own method, employees identify and self-evaluate their skills (from levels 0-5). This self-evaluation is usually validated by the line manager. The skills recorded in the PSU are systematically and strictly updated by the different people concerned. Once or twice a year, all employees are asked to update their profile of technical skills in the database. These updates are checked by their line managers. Through the PSU tool, all employees are given a specific skill capital. This specific capital of owned skills is built up gradually over their careers. "*Thanks to the PSU database, we know, at every moment, who is competent in Linux, Java, and so on. We have databases that show the technical skills of individuals. We have databases that show the degree of potentiality of people for a particular skill-set*" (Director of the IBM Nice-La Gaude and the e-business solutions centre). "*With this repository, we know exactly who are the experts and top talents in the company*" (HR Director). "*We all have to populate a database by describing our skills. This makes assessment possible, but we are also able to find the person best suited for a specific project*" (Project Manager).

Talent Detection

Next, with the objective of profiling, IBM has invested in an HR policy to detect and manage talents and high potentials. The company distinguishes 'technical resources' from 'managerial resources'. 10% of technical resources are 'technical *gurus*', or individuals acknowledged as having high levels of technical competence. Within this classification, competencies are graded and each grade has a corresponding title, a competence scope, personal responsibilities, and a salary scale. Appointments to these grades are similar to appointments to higher positions. They are made and reviewed every year by managers who are asked to spot young engineers with high potential in their teams. As for individuals acknowledged as having 'managerial resources', these are the company's future executive managers. To be appointed, they have to take a three-day course in an assessment centre in order to confirm their managerial competencies objectively, notably using role-playing exercises. These assessments are carried out by top-level executive managers.

Evaluating and Developing Human Capital

Personal Business Commitments (PBC)

To encourage everyone to develop within the company and validate an employee's suitability to its objectives, an individual performance appraisal system, called "Personal Business Commitments" (PBC), is set up. At the beginning of the year, in agreement with their line managers, employees determine their personal objectives, as well as how they will contribute to achieving the objectives of their unit. This type of moral contract constitutes the basis of the interviews with the managerial staff leading to an individual performance appraisal. The purpose of this interview is mainly to fix salary raises, as well as promotions. At the end of the performance appraisal, employees receive a score between 1 to 5 from their managers. The best, rated 1, receive substantial bonuses. The worst, rated 5, are denied any raise or promotion.

Internal Job Certification

Internal job certification is a key assessment practice of individual competence management at IBM. In line with this, IBM has developed internal job certifications in order to manage jobs and careers. In this large American international company, individual competence management is based on internal qualifications that attest to a certain level of individual competencies in a particular job. The company thus widely encourages employees to become certified in all domains, including technical areas, in order to improve their employability (both inside and outside the company). Certification is also often a prerequisite for promotion.

From a study on its development projects for innovative products and services, the company has defined four main job functions requiring qualification certificates: consultants, architects, specialists, and project managers. The main characteristic of these certifiable jobs is that they span all the company's business units. For example, an architect for computer solutions can work just as well in the company's hardware division as in software or services. An individual competence certification for a job is valid for three years: to qualify for recertification, employees have to continue practicing their job, increase their individual competencies & contributions and accumulate 40 hours of training over 3 years. "*Recertification is a way of questioning oneself and forcing people to progress and keep themselves up to date*" (Project Manager).

The Internal Job Certification Process at IBM

The certification process consists of three main steps:

1. Candidates prepare their application. The application has four components: professional experience, individual skills (this part is taken from employees' individual skills sheet, recorded in the Personal Skills Update - PSU database); their contribution to IBM's business (here, candidates choose three commitments to business projects - for each commitment, candidates must prove to what extent they have contributed to the success of a sale, a product or a service); and finally, their contribution to sharing their experiences (here, candidates must testify to their influence inside and outside the company, for example by giving courses, talking at conferences, or writing documents in order to share them). The certification application must be extremely detailed, so that the assessors can evaluate the applicants' individual skills. When creating their application and undergoing certification, candidates can ask for the help from one or more mentors who have already gone through the certification process.
2. The application is reviewed by three peers. Once the certification application has been created, it is presented and reviewed by peers, who are people with the same job function as the certification applicant, but not necessarily in the same field. As a general rule, three randomly named peers (excepting the mentor who cannot be an assessor) are appointed for each candidate; making a total of three reviews.
3. The certification board. During this meeting, candidates present and explain their application in front of the panel of peers. After interviewing each applicant, the council deliberates by sharing the peer reviews, and decides generally by consensus.

Job competence certification serves to acknowledge and promote the value of individuals' competencies both inside and outside the company. HR can thus be transferred among divisions and the process provides an evaluation of individuals' competencies that is independent of and complementary to that carried out by the unit manager: "*Someone who has a problem with their line manager can even ask to get their competencies recognized and become qualified outside of the company. And this situation happens fairly often*" (Head of jobs and qualifications). Finally, job certification also guarantees that people are employable outside of the company. For example, if IBM closes a business unit, the architect who belonged to that unit may very well work for another business unit, since individual competencies developed by an architect are not bound to a product or technology but to a job: "*True mobility is the possibility to go from one organization to another while remaining in the same job*" (Head of jobs and qualifications).

Training and Mentoring

Furthermore, job certification is supported by training and mentoring programmes that reinforce the required competencies. Firstly, employees consider training (to which IBM devotes around 7% of its payroll costs) as key to developing their knowledge and skills. The company offers many specialized training programmes in various formats (courses, lectures, e-learning, etc.) to maintain staff employability in a constantly changing technological environment. "*In the company, there is always the desire to get education and training at a relatively high level*" (E-business solutions specialist). "*Access to knowledge and skills development is one of the core business areas, especially in companies that sell intellectual property, such as IBM*" (Technical Director). Every year in an interview with their line managers, employees draw up an 'Individual development plan' aimed at increasing their in-job competencies or acquiring new competencies that will enable them to take on another job within the company. During the training interview, employees set out what type of training they would like to take. Managers approve the requests and/or suggest other training possibilities depending on the company's/department's needs. This individual training plan enables employees and managers, to think about their future both inside and outside the company. This is the whole point of supported employability: "*The annual training interview is a time for discussion and exchange where employees can state their needs and assess their employability*" (HR Manager).

Secondly, in IBM, mentoring is recognized as an important practice for developing competencies. It relies on two individuals coming together: the 'mentor' who possesses significant experience and a 'mentee' whose role is to acquire competencies. At IBM, mentoring is offered to four employee categories: new recruits, certification applicants, people with acknowledged technical potential and candidates for management and leadership functions. The role of the seniors is not to train the juniors themselves, but rather to support them as they gradually acquire professional knowledge, making themselves available to them, making a point of going to see them, making sure that the difficulties raised by a project are identified and assisting them in researching or developing answers to questions they might have. "*Mentoring is as beneficial to the 'mentee', who improves their competencies, as to the 'tutor' who improves their coaching, management and personal qualities*" (Project Manager).

Motivating and Retaining Human Capital

Career Management and Job Rotation

At IBM, there are many jobs in areas as diverse as services, sales, marketing, manufacturing, research and development, project management, finance, purchasing and human resources. Mobility is an essential part of IBM's HR policy, especially because for the company, career management can no longer be based on fixed or only vertical paths. In fact, encouraging cross-functional mobility allows individuals to vary their tasks and also to enrich the organization by constantly shuffling competencies.

Because of its size, diversity and culture, IBM has the advantage of offering multiple careers and career development opportunities. One employee in three changes jobs every year internally. This flexibility is highly valued at IBM, so that individuals improve their competencies by not staying in their role for eternity. "*IBM is a company that is large enough to allow you to try out all the roles, and thus pick up all the desired experiences and competencies*" (Technical Director). "*Anyone can move from one job to another. A typical case is to transition from being a specialist to an architect (...). There are also specialists who become project managers, project managers who become architects, architects who become consultants (...). Employees do not stay in the same job for life*" (Business Manager and Qualification of Technical Professionals).

By way of illustration, IBM has reviewed how its career paths and job transitions are organized internally, reflecting on the career development between jobs (see Figure 1).

Figure 1. Career development between jobs at IBM

Consultant	Consultant	Consultant	Senior Consultant	Managing Consultant	Associate Partner, Executive Cons, Principal
Education	Education Specialist	Advisory Education Specialist	Senior Education Specialist	Consulting Education Specialist	Senior Consulting Education Specialist
IT Architect			IT Architect	Consulting IT Architect	Senior Consulting IT Architect
IT Specialist	IT Specialist	Advisory IT Specialist	Senior IT Specialist	Consulting IT Specialist	Senior Consulting IT Specialist
Project Mgmt.		Associate Project Manager	Advisory Project Manager, Advisory Program Mgr	Senior Project Manager, Senior Program Manager	Executive Project Manager, Executive Program Mgr

DISCUSSION AND CONCLUSION

Our IBM case study highlights eight HRM practices underpinning human capital management: personal skills update, talent detection, personal business commitments, internal job certification, training and mentoring, career management and job rotation. Accordingly, we can affirm that IBM is a HCIF that gives individuals the means to increase and continuously improve their human capital. To do this, the company continues to develop HRM practices to help manage and develop employee competencies. Each employee must learn faster, find better ways to anticipate new situations and adapt to new markets with more ease. "*The company must arouse the curiosity of its employees and inculcate in them a willingness to manage their own career. It must also give them the means to achieve this*" (HR Director). By offering its employees dynamic organizational support in developing their individual competencies, IBM Corporation is determined to continue to be competitive in its markets. However, even if IBM provides this organizational support, the company encourages employees to be active in developing their own competencies, in order to future-proof their employability. This encouragement is only performed to remind employees of their own responsibility for their careers: "*IBM's career principle is that nobody develops your career for you – you do it yourself*" (Project Manager).

From a theoretical point of view, our research widens the findings of the existing literature by identifying HRM practices that are used to concretely manage human resources in the specific context of HCIFs. In a nutshell, by investigating mechanisms to optimize human capital (skills, knowledge, and ability) of employees we can improve our understanding of HRM in HCIFs. Thanks to the IBM case study, we are able to provide some answers to the call of researchers (Fulmer and Ployhart, 2014; Nyberg et al., 2014) for more research on practice in HCM. Moreover, the focus of our research on HRM practices highlights an operational level of observation for the main HRM components of a conceptual dimension of HCM. This operational level of observation provides a more detailed analysis of how people operate in HCIFs. Therefore, HRM practices help to link conceptual analysis and practical action of HCM.

From a managerial point of view, this chapter offers managers an illustration of HRM practices used by an acknowledged world leader in computer and technology that is highly competitive in its industrial sector. This chapter could therefore be of use to them as a source of information and support for future changes. In particular, the findings of this research show that companies permanently invent or adapt HRM practices, enabling them to obtain the best possible balance between human capital and business strategy.

Despite the theoretical and managerial contributions of our work, there are some ontological and methodological limitations. From an ontological point of view, in this chapter, we have positioned our work in an instrumental and positive vision as here, we have considered human capital as human assets, and HRM practices as macro mechanisms to develop and optimize employee skills, knowledge, and abilities. From a methodological point of view, the principal limitation concerns the external validity of the stated results, due to limited sampling. At this stage of our research, we cannot claim that our findings are broadly applicable. However, the initial aim of our work was not to make statistical generalizations, but rather analytical generalizations (Yin, 2008), with the aim of enriching the most recent work on HRM practices in HCIFs.

To conclude, this work reveals four interesting avenues for future research. One perspective would aim at a better understanding of how the different identified corporate HRM practices are combined and complemented. Indeed, the link between HRM practices and HCM will be powerful and sustainable for companies that succeed in attaining a high degree of coherence and complementarity between the different practices identified. A second promising research perspective would be to adopt a process and practice-based approach in order to go beyond the description of official corporate discourse (HRM practices) by analysing the individuals' practices placed in the concrete and daily dynamics of the organization (Gherardi, 2000). In the IBM case study, this new perspective would make it possible to better consider the complexity of the company, the heterogeneity of the work practices implemented by employees, as well as governance in different departments and business units. A third interesting avenue would extend the procedure to new investigative fields in other branches of industry. The aim would be to test and enrich the results obtained by including new contexts, new case studies to improve the external validity and reliability of the results. It is also pertinent to ask whether a manager should favour one HRM practice more than another. A fourth relevant research perspective would lie in studying emerging HRM practices and individuals' practices in line with the different levels of (macro and micro) analysis, according to a multi-level perspective (e.g., Coff & Kryscynski, 2011; Molloy et al., 2011; Ployhart & Moliterno, 2011; Barney & Felin, 2013). This perspective would give a deeper understanding of how corporate HRM practices are really applied, appropriated and interpreted by employees in work situations.

Ultimately, we hope to have provided a deeper understanding of HRM practices for managing human capital in HCIFs. More generally, this chapter is a step forward, among others, in understanding HRM in HCIFs.

REFERENCES

Ahamed, Z., Inohara, T., & Kamoshida, A. (2013). The servitization of manufacturing: An empirical case study of IBM Corporation. *International Journal of Business Administration*, *4*(2), 18. doi:10.5430/ijba.v4n2p18

Al Ariss, A., Cascio, W. F., & Paauwe, J. (2014). Talent management: Current theories and future research directions. *Journal of World Business*, *49*(2), 173–179. doi:10.1016/j.jwb.2013.11.001

Appelbaum, E., Bailey, T., Berg, P. B., Kalleberg, A. L., & Bailey, T. A. (2000). *Manufacturing advantage: Why high-performance work systems pay off*. Cornell University Press.

Armstrong, M., & Taylor, S. (2014). *Armstrong's handbook of human resource management practice*. Kogan Page Publishers.

Barney, J. (1991). Firm resources and sustained competitive advantage. *Journal of Management*, *17*(1), 99–120. doi:10.1177/014920639101700108

Barney, J., & Felin, T. (2013). What are microfoundations? *The Academy of Management Perspectives*, *27*(2), 138–155. doi:10.5465/amp.2012.0107

Barney, J. B., & Wright, P. M. (1998). On becoming a strategic partner: The role of human resources in gaining competitive advantage. *Human Resource Management (1986-1998)*, *37*(1), 31.

Baron, A. (2007). *Human capital management: Achieving added value through people*. Kogan Page Publishers.

Becker, B. E., Huselid, M. A., Pickus, P. S., & Spratt, M. F. (1997). HR as a source of shareholder value: Research and recommendations. *Human Resource Management*, *36*(1), 39–47. doi:10.1002/(SICI)1099-050X(199721)36:1<39::AID-HRM8>3.0.CO;2-X

Becker, G. S. (1964). *Human capital: A theoretical and empirical analysis, with special reference to education*. New York: University of Chicago Press and NBER.

Bontis, N., Dragonetti, N. C., Jacobsen, K., & Roos, G. (1999). The knowledge toolbox: A review of the tools available to measure and manage intangible resources. *European Management Journal*, *17*(4), 391–402. doi:10.1016/S0263-2373(99)00019-5

Boon, C., Eckardt, R., Lepak, D. P., & Boselie, P. (2018). Integrating strategic human capital and strategic human resource management. *International Journal of Human Resource Management*, *29*(1), 34–67. doi:10.1080/09585192.2017.1380063

Boxall, P. (1998). Achieving competitive advantage through human resource strategy: Towards a theory of industry dynamics. *Human Resource Management Review*, *8*(3), 265–288. doi:10.1016/S1053-4822(98)90005-5

Boyatsis, R. E. (1982). *The competent manager: A model for effective performance*. New York: Wiley.

Brown, S. L., & Eisenhardt, K. M. (1997). The art of continuous change: Linking complexity theory and time-paced evolution in relentlessly shifting organizations. *Administrative Science Quarterly*, *42*(1), 1–34. doi:10.2307/2393807

Capaldo, G., Iandoli, L., & Zollo, G. (2006). A situationalist perspective to competency management. *Human Resource Management*, *45*(3), 429–448. doi:10.1002/hrm.20121

Cézanne, C., & Saglietto, L. (2014). Human Capital-Intensive Firms and symbolic value creation. *Timisoara. Journal of Economics and Business*, *7*(1), 70–88.

Cézanne, C., & Saglietto, L. (2016). Human Capital-Intensive Firms and 4PLs: A Specific Partnership. *Journal of Economics and Management*, *12*(1), 61–83.

Chabault, D., Hulin, A., & Soparnot, R. (2012). Talent management in clusters. *Organizational Dynamics*, *41*(4), 327–335. doi:10.1016/j.orgdyn.2012.08.008

Coff, R., & Kryscynski, D. (2011). Drilling for micro-foundations of human capital-based competitive advantages. *Journal of Management*, *37*(5), 1429–1443. doi:10.1177/0149206310397772

Collings, D. G., & Mellahi, K. (2009). Strategic talent management: A review and research agenda. *Human Resource Management Review*, *19*(4), 304–313. doi:10.1016/j.hrmr.2009.04.001

Defélix, C., Klarsfeld, A., & Oiry, E. (2006). *Introduction de l'ouvrage – Nouveaux regards sur la gestion des compétences* (pp. 1–9). Paris: Vuibert.

Dejoux, C., & Thévenet, M. (2012). *Talent management*. Paris: Dunod.

Delaney, J. T., & Huselid, M. A. (1996). The impact of human resource management practices on perceptions of organizational performance. *Academy of Management Journal*, *39*(4), 949–969.

Delery, J. E., & Roumpi, D. (2017). Strategic human resource management, human capital and competitive advantage: Is the field going in circles? *Human Resource Management Journal*, *27*(1), 1–21. doi:10.1111/1748-8583.12137

Eisenhardt, K. M. (1989). Building theories from case study research. *Academy of Management Review*, *14*(4), 532–550. doi:10.5465/amr.1989.4308385

Eisenhardt, K. M., & Graebner, M. E. (2007). Theory building from cases: Opportunities and challenges. *Academy of Management Journal, 50*(1), 25–32. doi:10.5465/amj.2007.24160888

Farndale, E., Scullion, H., & Sparrow, P. (2010). The role of the corporate HR function in global talent management. *Journal of World Business, 45*(2), 161–168. doi:10.1016/j.jwb.2009.09.012

Ferris, G. R., Hall, A. T., Royle, M. T., & Martocchio, J. J. (2004). Theoretical development in the field of human resources management: Issues and challenges for the future. *Organizational Analysis, 12*(3), 231–254.

Fulmer, I. S., & Ployhart, R. E. (2014). "Our most important asset": A multidisciplinary/multilevel review of human capital valuation for research and practice. *Journal of Management, 40*(1), 161–192. doi:10.1177/0149206313511271

Gallardo-Gallardo, E., Dries, N., & González-Cruz, T. F. (2013). What is the meaning of 'talent' in the world of work? *Human Resource Management Review, 23*(4), 290–300. doi:10.1016/j.hrmr.2013.05.002

Gherardi, S. (2000). Practice-based theorizing on learning and knowing in organizations. *Organization, 7*(2), 211–223. doi:10.1177/135050840072001

Håland, E., & Tjora, A. (2006). Between asset and process: Developing competence by implementing a learning management system. *Human Relations, 59*(7), 993–1016. doi:10.1177/0018726706067599

Hatch, N. W., & Dyer, J. H. (2004). Human capital and learning as a source of sustainable competitive advantage. *Strategic Management Journal, 25*(12), 1155–1178. doi:10.1002mj.421

Ketchen, D. J. Jr, Crook, T. R., Todd, S. Y., Combs, J. G., & Woehr, D. J. (2017). *Managing human capital.* The Oxford Handbook of Strategy Implementation.

Le Deist, F. D., & Winterton, J. (2005). What is competence? *Human Resource Development International, 8*(1), 27–46. doi:10.1080/1367886042000338227

Lengnick-Hall, M. L., Lengnick-Hall, C. A., Andrade, L. S., & Drake, B. (2009). Strategic human resource management: The evolution of the field. *Human Resource Management Review, 19*(2), 64–85. doi:10.1016/j.hrmr.2009.01.002

Lepak, D. P., & Snell, S. A. (1999). The human resource architecture: Toward a theory of human capital allocation and development. *Academy of Management Review, 24*(1), 31–48. doi:10.5465/amr.1999.1580439

Lew, Y. K., & Sinkovics, R. R. (2013). Crossing borders and industry sectors: Behavioral governance in strategic alliances and product innovation for competitive advantage. *Long Range Planning*, *46*(1-2), 13–38. doi:10.1016/j.lrp.2012.09.006

Lindberg, O., & Rantatalo, O. (2015). Competence in professional practice: A practice theory analysis of police and doctors. *Human Relations*, *68*(4), 561–582. doi:10.1177/0018726714532666

Makani, J., & Marche, S. (2010). Towards a typology of knowledge-intensive organizations: Determinant factors. *Knowledge Management Research and Practice*, *8*(3), 265–277. doi:10.1057/kmrp.2010.13

Marchington, M., Wilkinson, A., Donnelly, R., & Kynighou, A. (2016). *Human resource management at work*. Kogan Page Publishers.

McClelland, D. C. (1973). Testing for competence rather than for "intelligence". *The American Psychologist*, *28*(1), 1–14. doi:10.1037/h0034092 PMID:4684069

Meyers, M. C., Van Woerkom, M., & Dries, N. (2013). Talent – Innate or acquired? Theoretical considerations and their implications for. *Human Resource Management Review*, *23*(4), 305–321. doi:10.1016/j.hrmr.2013.05.003

Miles, M. B., & Huberman, A. M. (1994). *Qualitative data analysis: An expanded sourcebook*. Sage Publications, Incorporated.

Molloy, J. C., Ployhart, R. E., & Wright, P. M. (2011). The myth of "the" micro-macro divide: Bridging system-level and disciplinary divides. *Journal of Management*, *37*(2), 581–609. doi:10.1177/0149206310365000

Ngo, H. Y., Lau, C. M., & Foley, S. (2008). Strategic human resource management, firm performance, and employee relations climate in China. *Human Resource Management*, *47*(1), 73–90. doi:10.1002/hrm.20198

Nyberg, A. J., Moliterno, T. P., Hale, D. Jr, & Lepak, D. P. (2014). Resource-based perspectives on unit-level human capital: A review and integration. *Journal of Management*, *40*(1), 316–346. doi:10.1177/0149206312458703

Ployhart, R. E., & Moliterno, T. P. (2011). Emergence of the human capital resource: A multilevel model. *Academy of Management Review*, *36*(1), 127–150. doi:10.5465/amr.2009.0318

Purcell, J., & Hutchinson, S. (2007). Front-line managers as agents in the HRM-performance causal chain: Theory, analysis and evidence. *Human Resource Management Journal*, *17*(1), 3–20. doi:10.1111/j.1748-8583.2007.00022.x

Sandberg, J. (2000). Understanding human competence at work: An interpretative approach. *Academy of Management Journal, 43*(1), 9–25.

Sandberg, J., & Pinnington, A. H. (2009). Professional competence as ways of being: An existential ontological perspective. *Journal of Management Studies, 46*(7), 1138–1170. doi:10.1111/j.1467-6486.2009.00845.x

Schmidt, F. L., & Hunter, J. E. (1998). The validity and utility of selection methods in personnel psychology: Practical and theoretical implications of 85 years of research findings. *Psychological Bulletin, 124*(2), 262–274. doi:10.1037/0033-2909.124.2.262

Schuler, R. S., & Jackson, S. E. (2007). *Strategic human resource management* (2nd ed.). Oxford, UK: Blackwell.

Schultz, T. W. (1961). Investment in human capital. *The American Economic Review, 51*(1), 1–17.

Schultz, T. W. (1982). *Investing in people: The economics of population quality.* University of California Press.

Siggelkow, N. (2007). Persuasion with case studies. *Academy of Management Journal, 50*(1), 20–24. doi:10.5465/amj.2007.24160882

Singleton, W. T. (1978). *Study of real skills: Vol. 1. The analysis of practical skills.* Academic Press.

Skaggs, B. C., & Youndt, M. (2004). Strategic positioning, human capital, and performance in service organizations: A customer interaction approach. *Strategic Management Journal, 25*(1), 85–99. doi:10.1002mj.365

Spencer, L. M., & Spencer, P. S. M. (2008). *Competence at Work models for superior performance.* John Wiley & Sons.

Starbuck, W. H. (1992). Learning by knowledge-intensive firms. *Journal of Management Studies, 29*(6), 713–740. doi:10.1111/j.1467-6486.1992.tb00686.x

Strauss, A., & Corbin, J. (1990). *Basics of qualitative research: Grounded theory procedures and techniques.* London: Sage Publications.

Tansley, C. (2011). What do we mean by the term "talent" in talent management? *Industrial and Commercial Training, 43*(5), 266–274. doi:10.1108/00197851111145853

Ulrich, D., & Smallwood, N. (2012). What is talent? *Leader to Leader, 2012*(63), 55–61. doi:10.1002/ltl.20011

Wright, P. M., Gardner, T. M., Moynihan, L. M., & Allen, M. R. (2005). The relationship between HR practices and firm performance: Examining causal order. *Personnel Psychology*, *58*(2), 409–446. doi:10.1111/j.1744-6570.2005.00487.x

Wright, P. M., & Snell, S. A. (1991). Toward an integrative view of strategic human resource management. *Human Resource Management Review*, *1*(3), 203–225. doi:10.1016/1053-4822(91)90015-5

Yin, R. K. (2008). *Case study research: Design and methods* (4th ed.). London: Sage Publication.

Chapter 3
Collaborating Without (Formal) Organization:
How Do Freelancers Question the Definition and the Role of Organizations?

Anthony Hussenot
Université Côte d'Azur, France

Viviane Sergi
Université du Québec à Montréal, Canada

ABSTRACT

This chapter focuses on independent workers and on the organizational specificities of the independent workers' phenomenon. The authors treat independent workers as an emergent and continually shifting organizational phenomenon questioning some of our assumptions about what organizations are and revealing trends that are currently reshaping work. They suggest viewing the independent workers' phenomenon as an open organizational phenomenon in which activities are project-oriented, temporality-oriented, and inclusive. This chapter contributes to an understanding of the independent workers' phenomenon as an organizational one that constantly (re)defines rules, roles, and statuses making the activities possible. It also contributes to a broader reflection on the matter of organization. Considered as an open organizational phenomenon, the independent workers' phenomenon calls the organization-society dualism into question. Finally, revealing the organizational aspects of independent workers' activities allows us to better understand some of the transformations that are nowadays affecting more traditional forms of work.

DOI: 10.4018/978-1-5225-7426-2.ch003

INTRODUCTION

Makers (Anderson, 2012; Dougherty, 2012; Hatch, 2013), creative freelancers (Debra, 2010), coworkers (Spinuzzi, 2012), and digital nomads (Makimoto & Manners, 1997; Nash, Jarrahi, Sutherland, & Phillips, 2018) have been under the media spotlight for a while as they redefine the way people work, collaborate, and are involved in society. All of them can be called "independent workers" (or "self-employees"), as they are not attached to any company or government, but rather are their own bosses (Bögenhold & Klinglmair, 2016; Leighton, 2016). "Independent" means there is no subordinate relation between them and their collaborators or clients, but only temporary contracts with the aim of achieving a specific goal (Burke, 2015; Cappelli & Keller, 2013).

This does not mean that independent workers work alone. In addition to examining the specific situation of each of these independent workers, we can also look at them as an ensemble, and see in their collective activities an organizational form that emerges and may persist for a while. In this sense, the independent workers' phenomenon is an intensive human capital phenomenon (Ployhart, Nyberg, Reilly, & Maltarich, 2014; Schultz, 1961; Wright & McMahan, 2011), as each worker is involved in numerous projects, with various clients, companies, and other independent workers. Seeing this as an organizational phenomenon can seem a bit unusual, but it is also an interesting way to understand how people collaborate in an expanding world of self-employed work.

Although an exact appreciation of the size of this movement is difficult to establish, some studies indicate that the independent workers' movement already represents about 35% of the US workforce and that the majority of workers could be freelancers by 2027.[1] In Europe, the rate is not as high, but independent workers represent 16% of the workforce, with an important increase shown since 2004.[2] While it was the common way to work and collaborate during the 19th century – at least in countries such as France - (Marchand, 1998), independent working has reappeared as a key trend after a century of decline. Of course, the jobs, skills, and tools have evolved since, but the core principles of independent work remain the same: the workers are free (they are not attached to an organization in a stable way), but their work entails the need to collaborate intensively with each other and with various organizations.

As wage employment has been the dominant model in Western society during the 20th century, organization scholars have mainly conceptualized the organization as a social structure based on working contracts. In this, organization has been defined as a rational-action system (Selznick, 1948), with a specific behavior (Cyert & March, 1963; March & Simon, 1958), and evolving in a given environment (Burns & Stalker, 1961; Lawrence & Lorsch, 1967). Mainly inspired by the sociology of bureaucracy (Merton, 1968; Weber, 1922) and the economic view of organizations

(Coase, 1937; Jensen & Meckling, 1976), this approach was also influenced by the empirical sites that inspired them, mainly large industrial companies (Augier, March, & Sullivan, 2005; March, 2007), and has been anchored in an economic and social context dominated by mass production and standardized goods and services. It thus provided a functionalist and restricted view of organization, in which the organization's borders are clearly defined and its structure of governance is imposed on the workers. Studies have consequently focused on the generative mechanisms inside the organizations or the relations between them, taking for granted the existence of the organizations themselves. Although these conceptions of the organization have been challenged, criticized, and complemented with other perspectives, they have laid the foundations on which organization theories have developed (Chia, 1997; Parker, 1992). In other words, organization theories have been dominated by a view that understands organization as a social or economic entity separate from the rest of society (Chia, 2003). Recent empirical phenomena such as the rise of the independent workers have contributed to questioning assumptions about what constitutes an organization.

A traditional view of organizations would probably not recognize the presence of an "organization" in the independent workers' phenomenon, given its distinctly open and individualized nature. Consequently, mainstream organization studies generally struggle to understand these open phenomena. This is why an alternative perspective that offers a way to see organization as an open phenomenon, always evolving, is needed. We suggest turning toward process ontology (Chia, 1999; Helin, Hernes, Hjorth, & Holt, 2014; Langley and Tsoukas, 2010, 2017) and a perspective called the "communicative constitution of organizations" (hereafter, "CCO"; see Brummans, Cooren, Robichaud, & Taylor, 2014 or Cooren, Kuhn, Cornelissen, & Clark, 2011 for overviews) to extend our understanding of organization. These perspectives are mainly anchored in the assumption that organizations are continuously moving and changing, and that they need to be constantly constituted and reconstituted to endure, albeit not necessarily in the exact same shape, over time. These perspectives place becoming, rather than stability (Rescher, 1996), at the heart of all matters, including organizations. In such a view, organization has no predefined limitations and is intertwined with the rest of society. Based on these tenets about organization, we claim that this view is especially relevant to understanding the independent workers' activities and, more precisely, how the characteristics of their modes of working and collaborating call into question the matter of organization.

This chapter makes two contributions. First, we contribute to the understanding of the independent workers' phenomenon as an open organizational phenomenon. More precisely, we suggest understanding this organizational phenomenon based on three characteristics of the collaborations that independent workers pursue, which is that they are project-oriented, temporality-oriented, and inclusive. Second, working from the idea that the independent workers represent an open organizational phenomenon, this chapter challenges the classic view of organization and offers some insights into understanding the matter of organization in a general context of evolving collaboration practices and transformation of work.

Based on these two contributions, we discuss two implications of this phenomenon. First, we discuss how the independent workers' movement calls the organization–society dualism into question. Then we discuss the impact of such an understanding on traditional organizations, such as established companies. In a context in which some traditional organizations are experimenting with new work arrangements (Cappelli & Keller, 2013), this inquiry into independent workers is not only about workers opting for this way of working, but also about organizations whose boundaries are becoming blurrier.

This chapter is structured as follows. The first section will introduce the independent workers by highlighting the difference between those working for companies as temporary collaborators (freelancers) and those running their own companies (solopreneurs). The second section will deal with the specificities of the organizational phenomenon emerging from the independent workers' collaborations. The last section will introduce the implications of such an organizational conception of independent workers.

BACKGROUND: FREELANCING AND SOLOPRENEURSHIP

Freelancers, solopreneurs, sole proprietors, mompreneurs, fempreneurs, self-entrepreneurs, digital nomads, coworkers, makers, etc.: given the existence of a variety of labels designating independent workers, it is not easy to define these workers. These notions are often used in the media without any distinction, and are mobilized to refer to self-employed people having a "cool" job, such as photographers or community managers, and working in trendy places such as coworking spaces, coffee shops, libraries, or fablabs. These workers are presented as the trendiest workers of the moment, hipsters spending their day in a shabby-chic coffee shop, drinking lattes, and being creative on their laptops. Print and social media play an important role in spreading this idealized image, but it is also partly built up by the workers themselves. Actually, there is much more to independent work than what is seen in this idealistic, even caricatured, image.

In order to move beyond this image of independent workers, we suggest categorizing them based on the nature of their activities and relation to others.[3] More specifically, we will make a distinction between *freelancers* (people who work for a company as temporary collaborators) and *solopreneurs* (those who deliver products and services to clients). The next section presents these two main ways of being independent workers and the nature of their activities.

Freelancer: A Short-Term Collaborator in a Company With a Specific Objective

Visiting freelancers' social media accounts—such as Instagram—is an interesting exercise, as one can see the way freelancers portray themselves. For example, hashtags[4] such as #freelancing (62,777 posts), #freelancelife (261,584 posts), #freelancers (87,582 posts), #freelance (2,295,800 posts), and others like these offer plenty of pictures from thousands of accounts showing how freelancers have a creative job and lead an exciting lifestyle. These snapshots summarize the promises of freelancing: freedom, creativity, and a "chill" lifestyle. In reality, these workers' daily lives are often far more complex and less glamorous than they appear, yet it seems important for them to craft this image, since independent workers sell their skills and expertise rather than ready-to-use products or services. They are their own brand and product.

However, this "cool and relaxed" image has not always been associated with the word "freelance," as this word initially referred to a medieval mercenary, a "free-lance," selling his services to any lord ready to pay. "Free-lance" thus meant that the mercenary was not permanently sworn to any lord's service as the contract between the lord and the free-lance was temporary. The Scottish novelist and historian Walter Scott (1771–1832) apparently coined the word in his famous novel *Ivanhoe* (1820). "Freelance" then gained a figurative meaning around the 1860s.[5] This brief historical and etymological overview of the word "freelance" helps us define what freelancing is. As the medieval mercenary (*free-lance*) was hired by a lord to fight in a specific battle or campaign, the contemporary freelancer is usually hired by a company to complete a specific task.

In a restrictive sense, freelancers are short-term collaborators with a specific objective. Consequently, they are not supposed to sign a full-time employment contract, and always remain independent. However, the freelancer's independence can vary considerably from one project to another. While freelancers do not normally need to work in a company's offices, some companies employing them will demand that they do work there with the regular employees for the duration of their contract. In that case, freelancers have no choice but to apply the company's rules to their own work. Companies thus sometimes impose work conditions and hours on freelancers. The working life of freelancers can sometimes resemble that of any employee of the company, as they are temporarily in a hierarchical relationship with the client for whom they are providing a specific service. Typically, companies hire freelancers to join and help a project team in the completion of certain tasks, such as the development of software, or social media communications. However, freelancers do not always work in their clients' offices, as many of them work remotely. This remoteness can even be appreciated by some clients, as they do not have to provide desks, computers, and other materials to the freelancer. Freelancing is often perceived as a way for companies to make their business more flexible and adaptable to change. Finally, freelancers can have several clients at the same time. In this case, they manage many projects simultaneously, working for different companies. Generally speaking, freelancers have to constantly find the right organization for their work and make sure all the tasks requested from their different clients are completed on time.

Solopreneur: An Entrepreneur Without Employees

In opposition to a freelancer, a solopreneur sells products and services, which can be customized or not. A solopreneur thus has a proper company and can create a brand, logo, website, and social media accounts to promote his or her business. So, what is the difference with other companies? We usually speak of "solopreneur" when the company is run only by the owner, without a cofounder or other employees. The solopreneur often manages everything alone and has to complete very different tasks and master different skills in various fields such as communications, sales, product development, finances, or networking.

Solopreneurship is quite a trend nowadays, as much as freelancing, and one can easily see this by searching Instagram for hashtags such as #solopreneur (556,940 posts), #solopreneurs (40,930 posts), or #solopreneurship (3,670 posts). The iconography is rather the same as for freelancing. The pictures are a mix of people showing off their lifestyle with inspirational quotes encouraging independent workers to work harder to achieve their goals. Among the new management gurus promoting this activity, Timothy Ferriss, with his globally successful book *The 4-Hour Workweek: Escape 9-5, Live Anywhere, and Join the New Rich*, is a good example of that. In this book, the author explains how he became rich and successful by being a solopreneur and working only a few hours a week. Given the popularity of this book (more than two million copies sold in North America[6]), it is not difficult to imagine that it has inspired millions of independent workers in the way they have managed their work and life.

Differentiating Between Freelancers and Solopreneurs

Based on this distinction, we can now easily differentiate between independent workers hired by companies (freelancers) and those having their own companies who sell products and services (solopreneurs)... at least, the distinction is clear on paper. Indeed, these two categories of workers are often confused with one another and the definition of each mainly depends on the type of projects people are working on. A freelancer can also be a solopreneur, as much as a solopreneur can sometimes work as a freelancer. This is the case, for example, when freelancers do not only work with companies, but develop their own projects with other freelancers as well. More specifically, the restrictive sense of "freelancing" means that the workers will be "renting out" their expertise to a company to complete a specific task, such as proofreading a document, shooting photos for events, or writing a press release before the launch of a new product. However, freelancers often collaborate with other independent workers to develop their own products or services. This can be a part-time or full-time job. In other words, freelancers can also be solopreneurs.

Beyond the distinction between freelancers and solopreneurs, and as mentioned previously, there are plenty of other labels, such as *sole proprietor*, *mompreneur*, *fempreneur*, *self-entrepreneur*, *digital nomad*, *coworker*, and *maker*, that can refer to work situations akin to either freelancing or solopreneurship. If we look at these labels, we quickly realize that some of them are closer to identity claims (e.g., *mompreneur*), while others refer more to the form work takes or to its location (e.g., *digital nomad*). On the one hand, a sole proprietor can be defined as a company owned by one person. *Mompreneur* and *fempreneur* refer to female entrepreneurs. These notions are a way to empower and encourage women to create their own businesses in spite of social pressures or home duties. These labels highlight who the worker is. On the other hand, *digital nomad* refers to independent workers who travel the world while running a business. *Coworker* refers to being a member of a coworking space (Gandini, 2015). *Makers* are independent workers who develop products (Anderson, 2012). They may or may not be members of a "makerspace," i.e., a workspace that provides the resources they need to develop their innovative products.

Ultimately, our main argument is not about the need to have clear-cut categories to label these independent workers, as their meanings can overlap and evolve over time. Rather, the blurriness of these categories should attest to the constant evolution of the working world today.

Numerous Projects and Intensive Collaborations

Whatever the label, one of the main features of the independent workers' phenomenon is the heterogeneous and intensive collaborations that these people develop constantly. The sustainability of their business is based on their ability to collaborate and generate new opportunities. Of course, some of them can only work on their own, or prefer to do so. Traditional artisans are a good example of people able to work alone without needing to develop new collaborations, but many have to constantly develop new projects or accept new tasks with new companies. This is particularly the case with creative independent workers who have to produce original and unique deliverables for clients, which often requires numerous skills. These workers cannot work alone, and their activity is often divided into several projects, while the actors, rules, purpose, etc. can be very different from one project to another.

As a consequence, the organizational forms that emerge from these projects are not defined by an imposed hierarchical structure. Each project has its own specific organizational form, which can evolve over time in order to follow the possible evolution of the project (aim, budget, deliverables, etc.). As much as it is difficult to define what independent workers are, it is even more difficult to conceptualize in an unequivocal way how they collaborate. In this context, the traditional understanding of organizations makes it almost impossible to see how independent workers temporarily collaborating together contribute in some way or another to an organized phenomenon. For all of these reasons, independent work is particularly tricky to understand from an organization studies point of view.

To date, scholars have mainly focused on formal organization (Chia, 2003; March, 2007). Classic organization studies have been relevant for studying formal organizations such as companies, but the field has not been developed to deal with independent workers involved in various projects with numerous actors, especially since the activities of these workers might be diversified in terms of purpose, location, etc. As a consequence, this kind of informal or barely formalized organizational form requires a specific theoretical development that would embrace the openness and the constant evolution of such a phenomenon. This is the basis of our proposition, which builds on process ontology. The next section introduces the theoretical development needed to understand the features of the independent workers' phenomenon.

THE INDEPENDENT WORKERS' ACTIVITIES AS AN OPEN ORGANIZATIONAL PHENOMENON

To embrace the particularity of the organizational form emerging from the collaborations between independent workers, one needs to establish some tenets about what an organization is. We start from the idea that an organization is something more informal than it is usually thought and constantly evolving. More specifically, we suggest considering activities first in our understanding of organization, because rules, statuses, and roles are defined through activities, and are not imposed on actors. It follows that everything that defines and makes the activity possible only exists in activities.[7] It means that the organizational features are not given but rather always re/produced through activities. The collaboration rules, the roles of the independent workers in their project, their projects' temporality are defined and maintained for the very purpose of the activity. This is an important shift in comparison to the bureaucratic organization, in which rules are set first, forcing organizational actors to act in precise ways, whatever their activity.

These ideas also echo those at the heart of some recent approaches in organization studies, such as process studies (Helin et al., 2014; Langley & Tsoukas, 2010, 2017) and the CCO perspective (Brummans et al., 2014; Cooren et al., 2011), that have emerged in order to bypass the limits of classic organization theories. These views suggest seeing reality as a movement, or a flow, in which things only exist as hubs of activities and through their relations. Here, organization is not a predefined entity, but rather "*an ongoing aggregative world-making activity*" (Chia, 2003) in which, first, humans, technologies, and rules are constantly (re)defined through activities, and second, the organization is not an element apart from society, but the very movement of the constitution of it. In relation to the notion of organization, and working with the ideas of CCO, Dobusch and Schoeneborn (2015) have introduced the idea of *organizationality* to transform the notion of what is (or is not) an organization. Their view consists in enlarging the category of "organization," allowing it to include social collectives that are more open and fluid than traditional organizations. This opening up of the notion of organization toward informal and more social phenomena—such as social movements and artistic performances, among others—is particularly welcomed as the independent workers belongs to this new range of organizational phenomena,[8] far from the formal ones.

These approaches might be useful to understand the organizational phenomenon related to the independent workers, as it is mainly defined through all of the independent workers' activities. This phenomenon should not be seen as a kind of formal organization, like an association to which independent workers would choose to belong or not. Based on the theoretical perspectives we have introduced, this phenomenon must be understood as an emergent effect stemming from all the activities of independent workers. It is constantly evolving and its contours are not fixed. It does not occur in a delimited time, space, and structure of governance, but rather emerges through independent workers' activities. However, it does not mean that there is not a sense of continuity in such organizational phenomena, but rather this continuity is always fragile and uncertain. As stated by the philosopher Alfred North Whitehead (1929/1978), the continuity is always in a state of becoming, and it is constantly reproduced and maintained through the independent workers' activities; but it is not imposed by means of a corporate structure of governance.

Although going into the details of the contributions of these perspectives to the reconceptualization of organizations is beyond the scope of this chapter, our brief introduction to these perspectives already provides us with enough theoretical elements to lay the basis for seeing an organizational phenomenon in all independent workers' activities. Based on these theoretical assumptions, we suggest going deeper into our understanding of the organizational phenomenon related to the independent workers by focusing on three core aspects of their activities: the fact that these activities are project-based, temporality-based, and inclusive. We suggest that we can understand the organizational phenomenon related to the independent workers as a collection of – more or less interrelated – temporary collaborations between actors. Moreover, as we will discuss in the last section, these properties of independent workers' activities not only extend to the organizational phenomenon that they constitute, but also reflect broader trends with which more traditional organizations should be concerned.

Project-Based Activities

As their activities are always temporary and oriented toward a specific goal, independent workers are organized around projects. Projects become the independent workers' unit of activity and are also a way to evaluate their work. Independent workers are a good example of what Jensen, Thuesen, and Geraldi (2016) called the "project society," i.e., a society 1) organized around professional and personal projects, 2) oriented toward the future and novelty, 3) in which people define themselves and evolve through their projects, 4) with the aim of living multiple personal and professional lives and achieving as much as possible. In such a project-based society, the organizational phenomenon is multiple and constantly evolving as independent workers work on many projects at the same time, with different actors (companies, other independent workers, etc.), while the tasks can be performed in different spaces (as is the case with coworking or café-working), online (with collaborative apps such as Trello and Slack), or on the move. Each project adds a layer of relations, emergence, and complexity. However, projects are not clearly separate but are interrelated, as the actors involved can be partly the same, the tasks can be complementary, or synergies can be created between projects. This is particularly the case when several independent workers group together to offer more or less the same services to many different clients. As a consequence, each project is not defined based on a spatio-temporal structure, but rather different temporalities and work places emerge and are entangled.

As such, the organization can no longer be represented as a static structure, like the traditional pyramidal or functional model, but has to be understood as evolving, multiple, and open. With independent workers, the organization is a tangle of interrelated projects in which each project can be both new and a continuation of the previous ones. In such an organizational form, independent workers can partly rely on previous experiences, results, teams, etc., but they also have to innovate by creating new tools, as well as defining new roles and new governance, mainly for the sake of the development of new products or services. The common phenomenon stemming from these projects is a flow of new organizational forms emerging, interrelating, and resembling one another. Every project has its own definition and identity, while it can also partly integrate previous projects through its members, history, results, tools, etc.

In this flow of organizational forms resulting from the involvement of actors in various projects, past forms are enacted to appreciate the present shape of the organizational forms, while these present forms are a potential for future forms (Hernes, 2014). Previous projects are kept present by their shaping of the current ones, and the continuity of independent workers' business comes from the potential new projects, missions, and collaborations that stem from their past and present projects. This is how the organization is a continuation of what has come before and is also constantly renewed. In this view, novelty and stability are concomitant—and not separate—stages, as opposed to what is conceptualized in mainstream organization studies (Langley, Smallman, Tsoukas, & Van de Ven, 2013).

Temporality-Based Activities

As the activities are not repeated simply based on past routines but take the form of projects, their time and space have to be (re)defined as well. In any new project—especially when the independent workers have to develop something new, like a product or service—the time to accomplish this project is always difficult to estimate, while the scheduling of tasks and steps has to often be redefined, and the deadline renegotiated as the project progresses. Independent workers have to define temporalities for their projects, which are both unique to each project and interrelated, when other projects are taken into consideration. A temporality means that the projects are organized based on past, present, and future events related to these projects. These events are constantly redefined, retained, forgotten, and configured in a specific order to make sense of the project and allow the action to take place (Hussenot & Missonier, 2016). A good example of this is the use of the Gantt tool when managing a project from a classic approach, or the Kanban tool when managing a project from an agile approach. By using these tools, actors define and configure events (called "tasks" or "milestones") in a way that makes the collaboration possible. These events form a continuum that enables members to make sense of what they have done, what they are doing, and what they will do.

Temporality is not only a way to re/define the past, present and future tasks. It really defines what the organization is (Hernes, 2014). As independent workers can work from anywhere and still always be connected—thanks to mobile technologies—localization and space are not what defines the area of collaboration. Rather, temporality defines the organizational phenomenon, as it defines the very potential to make the activities possible. When independent workers have to collaborate while they live or travel in different countries, the rules of collaboration emerge from the combination of various events. The list of tasks done and to be done, the scheduling of meetings, and the deadlines for deliverables participate in defining a structure of governance from which the independent workers are able to make decisions and define responsibilities among the project's members. According to this view, the organization is primarily defined by and as a temporality, which implies that continuity and ordering of activities do not come primarily from the sharing of a work space (building, office, etc.). Rather, such continuity and ordering come from the actors who define the past, present, and future steps of the projects.

Inclusive Activities

By not being defined by a pre-existing governance structure, the organizational form of the independent workers' activities is open. "Open" means that it does not exist as a circumscribed entity evolving in an environment with a defined membership. Consequently, the organizational phenomenon that emerges from the independent workers' activities is inclusive, as it does not exclude anything on the basis of an imposed delimitation. To date, organizations have been mainly conceptualized as delimited spaces, with a specific economic purpose and predefined structure of governance. This view positions a wide variety of actors as being "outside" the organization, thus excluding many stakeholders, and not considering societal stakes as part of the organization's purpose. This separation between organizations (especially companies) and society has even been enshrined in law in most countries, such as in the French Civil Code (articles 1832 and 1833). Conversely, the independent workers' phenomenon offers another conceptualization of the organization: one that is more inclusive and does not distinguish between what would be inside and outside the organization—because everything is defined through activities, whoever the actors involved and whatever the field or purpose.

Consequently, with the independent workers' phenomenon, the organization cannot be reduced to a space or even to a stable nexus of contracts (which would be mainly made up of employees), as any project can bring together various people from different sectors, professionals or not. This is particularly obvious in the maker movement, where projects can be managed by specialists (designers, artisans, etc.), students, or enthusiasts like hackers or DIYers. Even if the maker movement has an economic purpose (Anderson, 2012), it also includes a political purpose aimed at changing capitalism and society (Lallement, 2015). As such, the maker movement combines economic and political purposes, and unites professionals and enthusiasts, while the makers can have different backgrounds and work on various projects. The organizational phenomenon of the makers is not outside of society, but participates in its transformation and redefinition. For example, the maker movement is playing an important role in the evolution of the education and industry sectors (Dougherty &

Conrad, 2016). This openness can be observed among other independent workers as well, when workers explain their decision to shift from a full-time job as employees to a much more precarious status by their eagerness to reshape their work–life balance. Becoming independent allows them to redefine their family life, hobbies, and even sometimes their role in society. A good example of this is digital nomadism, since one of the main reasons people become independent workers is to travel and seek adventure (Nash et al., 2018). By being digital nomads—i.e., independent workers traveling, working, and living in different countries while running a business—people can both embrace a professional career and have a fulfilling personal life. Contrary to traditional views of organizations, open organizational forms like the ones we discuss here limit neither who is a member of the organization nor what should or should not be part of its mission.

CONCLUSION

In this final section, we bring together the ideas we have put forward in the previous sections, and draw a few preliminary conclusions about the organizational phenomena behind all independent workers' activities. We touch upon two main implications: considering independent workers' activities allows us to rethink organizations, especially traditional companies, and move beyond the organization–society dualism.

First, we note that the rise in independent work is concomitant with transformations in more traditional organizations. Companies and public organizations are becoming more "projectified" (Midler, 1995), as organizations have been steadily adopting project-based organizing over the last two decades. In a similar way to independent workers, to have employees involved in several projects at the same time is not unusual today. As shown by several recent studies,[9] workers and employees have been asking for more autonomy in their daily work life, and organizations have started (albeit timidly) to grant them more freedom, be it in the form of more possibilities to work remotely, of renewed workspaces designed to be more open and activity-based, or of more participatory management practices. In terms of the spatial transformations of organizations, some companies are even opening their doors to workers who do not belong to the organization. This trend is called "corporate coworking" or "corpoworking," and it consists of welcoming other companies or independent workers into the company's building in order to create opportunities to collaborate and innovate together. All of these practices tend to make stable employees slightly more independent from their organization, compared to their situation a few decades ago.

Moreover, these transformations also indicate that organizational boundaries, which used to be more closed (at least, from a traditional viewpoint), now tend to become blurrier. Not only are regular employees working more and more outside the organization, but independent workers are now entering the organization. In fact, big companies hire more and more independent workers to collaborate on their projects (Corporaal & Lehdonvirta, 2017). These workers can work online or have a desk in the company's building. In the latter case, it is not always easy to distinguish the freelancers from the employees as they can work together on similar projects.

A second implication is that this more open and fluid organizational form allows us to think differently about the strict divisions between organizations and society, or between business and society. As highlighted in the previous sections, traditional understandings of organizations have led to conceptualize the existence of a separation between organizations and society. Yet, when one moves from this perspective to a more processual one, as suggested in these pages, such separations appear artificial. Indeed, no organization—be it a traditional company or an open movement—is separate from the rest of society. Organizations are not seen as by-products of society, but as the very definition of it (Chia, 1999). As noted above, the independent workers' phenomenon is not only an economic challenge, it is also a social one, as it changes not only the way we work, but the way we live, the way we differentiate between life and work, etc. Modifying how we think about organizations is stimulating in theoretical terms, but is also relevant, given the social and environmental challenges we face nowadays.

What we see in these two broad implications is in fact larger trends that are at the heart of current organizational transformations, and are challenging widespread management practices: the "projectification" of work, the rise of mobility and autonomy, and the growing importance of reconnecting the organization to society. The independent workers' phenomenon is therefore a good opportunity for both scholars and practitioners to question implicit hypotheses about work, management, and organization, especially in a context in which independent work is on the rise.

ACKNOWLEDGMENT

This research was supported by the Fonds de recherche du Québec Société et culture (FRQSC) [grant number 2016-NP-193126].

REFERENCES

Anderson, C. (2012). *Makers: The New Industrial Revolution*. Crown Business.

Augier, M., March, J. G., & Sullivan, B. N. (2005). Notes on the evolution of a research community: Organization studies in Anglophone North America, 1945–2000. *Organization Science, 16*(1), 85–95. doi:10.1287/orsc.1040.0108

Bögenhold, D., & Klinglmair, A. (2016). Independent work, modern organizations and entrepreneurial labor: Diversity and hybridity of freelancers and self-employment. *Journal of Management & Organization, 22*(6), 843–858. doi:10.1017/jmo.2016.29

Brummans, B., Cooren, F., Robichaud, D., & Taylor, J. R. (2014). Approaches in research on the communicative constitution of organizations. In L. L. Putnam & D. Mumby (Eds.), *The SAGE Handbook of Organizational Communication* (3rd ed.; pp. 173–194). London, UK: Sage.

Burke, A. (Ed.). (2015). *The Handbook of Research on Freelancing and Self-Employment*. Dublin, Ireland: Senate Hall Academic Publishing.

Burns, T., & Stalker, G. M. (1961). *The Management of Innovation*. London, UK: Tavistock.

Cappelli, P., & Keller, J. R. (2013). Classifying work in the new economy. *Academy of Management Review, 38*(4), 575–596. doi:10.5465/amr.2011.0302

Chia, R. (1995). From Modern to Postmodern Organizational Analysis. *Organization Studies, 16*(4), 579–604. doi:10.1177/017084069501600406

Chia, R. (1997). Essai: Thirty years on: From organizational structures to the organization of thought. *Organization Studies, 18*(4), 684–707. doi:10.1177/017084069701800406

Chia, R. (1999). A "rhizomic" model of organizational change and transformation: Perspective from a metaphysics of change. *British Journal of Management, 10*(3), 209–227. doi:10.1111/1467-8551.00128

Chia, R. (2003). Organization theory as postmodern science. In H. Tsoukas & C. Knudsen (Eds.), *The Oxford Handbook of Organization Theory*. Oxford University Press.

Coase, R. H. (1937). The nature of the firm. *Economica, 4*(16), 386–405. doi:10.1111/j.1468-0335.1937.tb00002.x

Cooren, F., Kuhn, T. R., Cornelissen, J. P., & Clark, T. (2011). Communication, organizing and organization: An overview and introduction to the special issue. *Organization Studies*, *32*(9), 1149–1170. doi:10.1177/0170840611410836

Corporaal, G. F., & Lehdonvirta, V. (2017). *Platform Sourcing: How Fortune 500 Firms Are Adopting Online Freelancing Platforms*. Oxford, UK: Oxford Internet Institute - University of Oxford.

Cyert, R. M., & March, J. G. (1963). *A Behavioral Theory of the Firm*. Englewood Cliffs, NJ: Prentice-Hall.

Dobusch, L., & Schoeneborn, D. (2015). Fluidity, identity, and organizationality: The communicative constitution of Anonymous. *Journal of Management Studies*, *52*(8), 1005–1035. doi:10.1111/joms.12139

Dougherty, D. (2012). The maker movement. *Innovations*, *7*(3), 11–14. doi:10.1162/INOV_a_00135

Dougherty, D., & Conrad, A. (2016). *Free to Make: How the Maker Movement is Changing our Schools, our Jobs, and our Minds*. Berkeley, CA: North Atlantic Books.

Gandini, A. (2015). The rise of coworking spaces: A literature review. *Ephemera*, *15*(1), 193–215.

Hatch, M. (2013). *The Maker Movement Manifesto: Rules for Innovation in the New World of Crafters, Hackers, and Tinkerers*. McGraw-Hill Professional.

Helin, J., Hernes, T., Hjorth, D., & Holt, R. (Eds.). (2014). *Process Philosophy and Organization Studies*. Oxford, UK: Oxford Press University. doi:10.1093/oxfordhb/9780199669356.001.0001

Hernes, T. (2014). *A Process Theory of Organization*. Oxford, UK: Oxford University Press. doi:10.1093/acprof:oso/9780199695072.001.0001

Hussenot, A., De Vaujany, F. X., & Chanlat, J. F. (2016). Changements socio-économiques et théories des organisations. In *Théories des organisations: nouveaux tournants* (pp. 11–24). Paris, France: Economica.

Osnowitz, D. (2010). *Freelancing Expertise: Contract Professionals in the New Economy*. Cornell University Press.

Hussenot, A., & Missonier, S. (2016). Encompassing stability and novelty in organization studies: An events-based approach. *Organization Studies*, *37*(4), 523–546.

Jensen, A., Thuesen, C., & Geraldi, J. (2016). The projectification of everything: Projects as a human condition. *Project Management Journal, 47*(3), 21–34.

Jensen, M. C., & Meckling, W. H. (1976). Theory of the firm: Managerial behavior, agency costs and ownership structure. *Journal of Financial Economics, 3*(4), 305–360. doi:10.1016/0304-405X(76)90026-X

Lallement, M. (2015). *L'âge du faire. Hacking, travail, anarchie*. Paris, France: Seuil.

Langley, A., Smallman, C., Tsoukas, H., & Van de Ven, A. H. (2013). Process studies of change in organization and management: Unveiling temporality, activity, and flow. *Academy of Management Journal, 56*(1), 1–13. doi:10.5465/amj.2013.4001

Langley, A., & Tsoukas, H. (2010). Introducing "Perspectives on process organization studies.". In T. Hernes & S. Maitlis (Eds.), *Process, Sensemaking and Organizing* (pp. 1–26). Oxford, UK: Oxford University Press. doi:10.1093/acprof:oso/9780199594566.003.0001

Langley, A., & Tsoukas, H. (2017). Introduction: Process thinking, process theorizing and process researching. In A. Langley & H. Tsoukas (Eds.), *The SAGE Handbook of Process Organization Studies* (pp. 1–26). London, UK: Sage. doi:10.7765/MG/9781526125491.01

Lawrence, P. R., & Lorsch, J. W. (1967). Differentiation and integration in complex organizations. *Administrative Science Quarterly, 12*(1), 1–47. doi:10.2307/2391211

Leibniz, G. W. (2011). *«La monadologie». Les classiques des sciences sociales.* Retrieved from http://classiques.uqac.ca/classiques/Leibniz/La_Monadologie/La_Monadologie.html

Leighton, P. (2016). Professional self-employment, new power and the sharing economy: Some cautionary tales from Uber. *Journal of Management & Organization, 22*(6), 859–874. doi:10.1017/jmo.2016.30

Makimoto, T., & Manners, D. (1997). *Digital Nomad*. Chichester, UK: Wiley.

March, J. G. (2007). The study of organizations and organizing since 1945. *Organization Studies, 28*(1), 9–19. doi:10.1177/0170840607075277

March, J. G., & Simon, H. A. (1958). *Organizations*. New York, NY: Wiley.

Marchand, O. (1998). Salariat et non-salariat dans une perspective historique. *Economie & Statistique, 319-320*(1), 3–11. doi:10.3406/estat.1998.2666

Merton, R. K. (1968). *Social Theory and Social Structure*. New York, NY: The Free Press.

Midler, C. (1995). Projectification of the firm: The Renault case. *Scandinavian Journal of Management, 11*(4), 363–375. doi:10.1016/0956-5221(95)00035-T

Nash, C., Jarrahi, M. H., Sutherland, W., & Phillips, G. (2018). Digital nomads beyond the buzzword: Defining digital nomadic work and use of digital technologies. In G. Chowdhury, J. McLeod, V. Gillet, & P. Willett (Eds.), Lecture Notes in Computer Science: Vol. 10766. *Transforming Digital Worlds. iConference 2018*. Cham, Switzerland: Springer. doi:10.1007/978-3-319-78105-1_25

Osnowitz, D. (2010). *Freelancing Expertise: Contract Professionals in the New Economy*. Ithaca, NY: Cornell University Press.

Parker, M. (1992). Post-modern organizations or postmodern organization theories. *Organization Studies, 13*(1), 1–17. doi:10.1177/017084069201300103

Ployhart, R. E., Nyberg, A. J., Reilly, G., & Maltarich, M. A. (2014). Human capital is dead; Long live human capital resources! *Journal of Management, 40*(2), 371–398. doi:10.1177/0149206313512152

Rescher, N. (1996). *Process Metaphysics: An Introduction to Process Philosophy*. New York: State University of New York Press.

Rescher, N. (2012, Summer). Process philosophy. *The Stanford Encyclopedia of Philosophy*. Retrieved from https://plato.stanford.edu/archives/sum2012/entries/process-philosophy/

Schultz, T. W. (1961). Investment in human capital. *The American Economic Review, 51*, 1–17.

Scott, S. W. (2000). Ivanhoe. London, UK: Wordsworth Classics. (Original work published 1820)

Selznick, P. (1948). Foundations of the theory of organization. *American Sociological Review, 13*(1), 25–35. doi:10.2307/2086752

Spinuzzi, C. (2012). Working alone together: Coworking as emergent collaborative activity. *Journal of Business and Technical Communication, 26*(4), 399–441. doi:10.1177/1050651912444070

Weber, M. (1922). *Economy and Society*. Routledge.

Whitehead, A. N. (1978). *Process and Reality*. New York, NY: The Free Press. (Original work published 1929)

Wright, P. M., & McMahan, G. C. (2011). Exploring human capital: Putting "human" back into strategic human resource management. *Human Resource Management Journal, 21*(2), 93–104. doi:10.1111/j.1748-8583.2010.00165.x

ENDNOTES

1 According to a survey commissioned by Upwork and Freelance Union in 2017 (https://www.upwork.com/i/freelancing-in-america/2017/). This higher rate of independent workers in the United States may also be explained by the variety of workers included under this label.

2 According to the Organisation for Economic Co-operation and Development (https://www.oecd-ilibrary.org/employment/oecd-employment-outlook_19991266). These percentages should only be seen as indications of the increase in independent work, as each country or economic zone defines "independent workers" in different terms.

3 This categorization should be seen as an analytical way to make the phenomenon understandable.

4 Instagram hashtags consulted on February 20, 2018.

5 Merriam-Webster. (n.d.). *The surprising history of freelance.* Retrieved from https://www.merriam-webster.com/words-at-play/freelance-origin-meaning.

6 According to Publishers Marketplace: https://www.publishersmarketplace.com/members/swhanselma/.

7 This tenet is anchored in process philosophy (Rescher, 1996, 2002) and, even more precisely, in the philosophy of Leibniz (1840/2011).

8 By "new," we mean that the interest for these phenomena are relatively recent in organization studies (Hussenot, DeVaujany, & Chanlat, 2016).

9 Many surveys made by consulting companies have led to the same conclusion about the evolution of work practices in companies. For example, see the 2018 McKinsey study *Skill shift: Automation and the future of the workforce* (https://www.mckinsey.com/featured-insights/future-of-organizations-and-work/skill-shift-automation-and-the-future-of-the-workforce) or the 2018 Fuze study *Workforce futures* (https://www.fuze.com/workforce-futures).

Section 2

Corporate Governance:
New Developments

Chapter 4
The Governance of Human Capital-Intensive Firms:
A Motivational Issue

Cécile Cézanne
Université Côte d'Azur, France

ABSTRACT

For the past 30 years, the organization and functioning of firms have considerably changed, especially with the growing importance of human capital. In parallel, the primacy of the shareholder governance model has maintained. The aim of this chapter is to review the main theoretical and empirical elements of this paradox and to propose a renewed model of firm governance that takes into account the intrinsic nature of critical human capital incorporated by key employees. The chapter shows that the inalienable residual rights of control inherent to specific human capital are inconsistent with traditional disciplinary models of corporate governance. They rather call for a model of regulation of economic power exercising based on work motivation. This original model that the author calls the "multi-resource model" aims to encourage, retain, and collectively enrich critical resources by using an original operational device based on complementary instruments of incentive and coordination.

DOI: 10.4018/978-1-5225-7426-2.ch004

INTRODUCTION

Competition based on innovation races has heightened since the early 1990s. Yet, in globalized economies, innovation gives rise to two contradictory phenomena. On the one hand, companies' propensity to innovate depends on increasing needs for financing. This situation has led to financial deregulation and to the development of new instruments to control and share risk in a context of accelerated financialization (Aglietta and Rebérioux, 2012; Lazonick, 2010; Lippert et al., 2014). It has also attracted external investors and given more control to shareholders while stock market use has extended. In this context, the shareholder model of corporate governance, emblematic of joint-stock companies, became established: during the three last decades, corporate strategies in favor of shareholder value creation have been intensified. Corporations have adopted a "downsize and distribute" principle based on cutting the size of their labor force (*downsize*), in an attempt to increase the return on equity to increase dividends (*distribute*) (Lazonick and O'Sullivan, 2000, p. 18; Cordonnier and Van de Velde, 2014)[1]. On the other hand, companies' propensity to innovate depends on increasing needs for specific intangible resources. In particular, the demand for innovative process and quality improvement can only be satisfied by specialized and mobile employees and external experts. Innovation comes from specific human capital at every stage of the production process. Therefore, human capital tends to be more important than physical assets and employees tend to get involved in participative forms of work organization (Arundel et al., 2007; Boxall and Macky, 2009). Specialized employees with a unique skill or a particular know-how represent valuable resources which are immaterial, inalienable and non-imitable instantaneously (Kochan and Rubinstein, 2000; Wang et al., 2009). Specialized employees control assets able to minimize many transactional and productive costs so that the firm can improve its competitive position. As the importance of human capital has grown, power has moved away from the top management; power is much more widely dispersed through the firm, in particular in the hands of key employees because they represent and control decisive functional resources for the firm. Finally, the separation between ownership and control, recognized as the source of corporate governance issues (Berle and Means, 1932), becomes blurred in the present firm but does not challenge the shareholder primacy view of corporate governance. This paradoxical situation has largely been responsible for the harmful drift of financial capitalism of the beginning of the 21th century (Dore, 2008; Lazonick, 2011).

The author suggests that maximizing shareholder value is inconsistent with a value creation process achieved by a group of employees. While this idea is not new (Marx, 1867), the negative effects of these growing contradictory trends have not been taken into account. The author advances that equating all assets to a financial asset, at least at a conceptual level, amounts to considering that human assets are generic, transferable, and separable from the individual that invests them. Actually, innovation resulting from partnerships strategies is not incompatible with the deep development of funds and information exchanges; however, human assets that support innovation cannot be coordinated and controlled solely by pure financial mechanisms. Consequently, if the paradox of shareholder primacy is maintained, the long-term viability of firms may be called into question. Furthermore, since specific human capital is a key element of economic power in the firm, traditional disciplinary methods of solving conflicts of interests and risk-sharing are obsolete. Other solutions are needed to deal with the intangible, inalienable and irreproducible nature of valuable human assets (Blair and Roe, 2010; Chassagnon, 2011; Klein et al., 2012; Rajan and Zingales, 2000). In view of these observations, the author suggests that firm governance has to be reconsidered to take into account the changing nature of firms since the 1990s which are precisely built on specific human capital. This chapter considers firm governance as the general system by which the exercise of power on specific non-human and human assets is regulated.

This chapter has a dual purpose: (1) to propose a detailed analytical reading of the governance of human capital-intensive firms; (2) to suggest an original operational system supporting a renewed model of firm governance. Given the multidisciplinary nature of firm governance and moving beyond the legal-financial approach to corporate governance, this chapter seeks to found an integrative theory of firm governance. It aims to propose new predictions and/or explain phenomena that cannot be explained by theories considered separately (Foss, 2000; Ravix, 2008).

The chapter is organized as follows. The Background section shows that the role of specific human capital, frequently neglected by economists writing about the firm, calls for a renewed model of firm governance. The section focusing on the Main Focus of the Chapter conceptually describes the main purposes of this model, which the author calls the 'multi-resource model'. It has to maintain and strengthen the links of economic dependency between the key members of the firm viewed as critical co-specific[2] resources. Thus, firms built on specific human capital have to maximize their collective value potential; they have to optimize their multi-resource value. The Solutions and Recommendations section reformulates the central issue of the multi-resource model and tries to infer underlying operational modes of human capital-intensive firm governance. It presents the multi-resource governance as a composite model of internal regulation able to effectively mobilize specific human resources by motivating key employees. Such a model of firm governance is achieved by the simultaneous use of vertical mechanisms of incentive, horizontal modes of work and decentralized decision-making processes. The Future Research Directions will be presented before ending the chapter by a Conclusion section providing discussion of the overall coverage of the chapter and concluding remarks on the governance of human capital-intensive firms.

BACKGROUND

At a conceptual level, human capital-intensive firm (HCIF) can be defined as a firm whose value mainly depends on the human assets of the members (in particular the employees) it works with. This conception inevitably implies that human capital is specific by nature; the field of application of specific human capital is limited outside the relationship in which it has been developed (Williamson et al., 1975; Klein et al., 1978). At an empirical level, HCIFs include a wide variety of organizations: law firms whose prosperity depends essentially on the expertise of the lawyers they employ; advertising agencies whose reputation is based on the talent of the artists and designers in their creative departments; IT companies whose activity is essentially built around skilled computer specialists and programmers; or even pharmaceutical laboratories whose success and performance depends largely on their researchers and especially 'star scientists'. In other words, HCIFs operate in entirely different branches from knowledge-intensive business services (commonly known as KIBS) (Hipp and Grupp, 2005; Doloreux et al., 2008; Lau and Lo, 2015) to high-tech manufacturing industries (O'Regan and Sims, 2008; Harbi et al., 2009; Yam et al., 2011). They are readily identifiable in the diverse classifications of economic activities (notably in Statistical Classification of Economic Activities in the European Community). In the end, HCIFs encompass the large majority of productive organisations whose activity requires not only traditional production factors such as fixed capital and labour but also and especially the intangible assets of skills, structures and organisational procedures, and a corporate culture (Brynjolfsson et al., 2002) along with specific human assets (Fulghieri and Sevilir, 2009). Consequently, although HCIFs might appear to be an extreme case of a productive organisation, they in reality are widespread in business and are essential sources of technological and organisational innovation. In this context, this chapter aim to study the majority of current firms.

The critical resource theory (Rajan and Zingales, 1998; Zingales, 2000) can be taken as the preferred framework to analyze HCIFs. According to this contractual approach, the firm is viewed as a nexus of specific investments in human capital. Since human capital cannot be legally appropriated, the firm has an enlarged role of coordination: by giving access to a heterogeneous group of productive partners who participate in the division of labor, the firm manages *ex ante* the co-specialization of critical resources within its economic boundaries (Rajan and Zingales, 1998; Cézanne and Saglietto, 2015). In parallel, the multiple key partners controlling inalienable resources that are fundamental for the firm, in particular specialized employees have strong economic power; the firm does need their resources to develop its activity, to grow or even to survive. Following this representation of the firm, the problem of governance is to limit the exercise of power by strategic employees, on the one hand, and by the firm, on the other. The regulation of power relationships is central to protecting productive synergies within the firm and thus to creating a total value superior to the market value of the sum of individual contributions. Since power is fragmented, firm governance does not aim to protect the surplus of only one group of agents; economic dependency links between the firm and strategic employees call for a reconsideration of the internal power structure. Some economists have highlighted this rethinking of firm governance (Rajan and Zingales, 2000; Keenan and Aggestam, 2001, Klein Mahoney, McGahan, and Pitelis, 2012; Chassagnon and Hollandts, 2014) but, as far as the author knows, no specific studies have been made of it.

Employment contracts are more incomplete than any other forms of contract because they concern human capital which is by nature intangible and non-transferable. Firstly, employees' human capital is difficult to measure. Secondly, the value created by human capital is difficult to distinguish from the value created by other assets. Finally, the employment relationship is affected by a dual expropriation risk resulting from the economic interdependency between the employer and key employees. Each party would like to capture *ex post* a bigger share of the joint value they can create together (Tirole, 1988, Schmitz, 2001). On the one hand, since specific human capital is inalienable (Hart and Moore, 1994), and since contracts are not complete, the firm can expropriate a share of the quasi-rent superior to the value that its specific investments could pay. Such behavior is a major obstacle to productive cooperation and to an efficient distribution of costs and surplus. On the other hand, critical employees know that their human capital is crucial for the productive activity and the competitiveness of the firm. They have inalienable residual rights of control over their critical resources, and thus over the firm (Gibbons, 2005; Grandori, 2013). As soon as production process starts, strategic employees hold strong economic power, and consequently substantial negotiating power. These employees could expropriate a large fraction of the value of the firm by developing outside opportunities. When they accumulate enough power, central employees can underinvest or even exercise their legal right to leave the firm (Baron and Kreps, 1999). In particular, they can threaten to break the employment contract. Since contract breakdown cannot occur without loss for at least one of the contractual parties (Klein et al., 1978), such a situation is very detrimental even if, most of the time, the firm is the party that breaks the contract[3]. When a decisive employee leaves the firm, he reduces organizational and reputational values of the firm (Teece, 2003). By taking a part of the production team's human capital, the employee deprives the firm of a critical link in the chain of specific investments. He can also cause the chain departure of specialized team members, that is to say workers who depend on him. In sum, a key employee can undermine the integrity of the firm.

Finally, to survive, the firm must maintain specific relationships with key employees. HCIFs must use governance mechanisms to incite *ex post* employees to invest in human capital within valuable firm activities (Wang and Barney, 2006). This is a *sine qua non* for the long-term viability of firms, especially for innovative ones. Firms that operate on complex high-tech markets characterized by high levels of R&D investments and specialized patented applications need their key employees to invest continuously and specifically in human capital (Guilhon, 2004). Thus, firm governance has to go beyond the traditional issues with which it has concerned itself. As power and rents depend mainly on critical inalienable resources, firm governance must not deal with efficient modes of conflict-solving, to maximize shareholder or stakeholder value, but encourage key employees not to quit the firm, and to continuously make firm-specific human capital investments. In other words, strategic employees have to be encouraged to pursue their relationship with the firm so that the latter can retain the wealth indispensable to its productive activity. The governance of HCIFs, described in this chapter as the 'multi-resource model' recognizes specialized employees as valuable complementary resources that enhance the collective value of the firm and ensure its long-term viability. The final objective of the multi-resource model is to maximize the value of the various critical inalienable assets owned by key employees in the nexus of specific investments, *i.e.* to maximize multi-resource value. To reach this objective, the firm has to promote the superiority of collective interests over personal ones. This incentive issue may be considered traditional, but it is essential to prevent conflicts between productive partners and to avoid the decline or even the death of the firm.

Even now, contractual theories of the firm agree that the question of interest alignment is an importance aspect of firm governance (Nyberg, Fulmer, Gerhart and Carpenter, 2010). But this issue is treated differently according to the definition of the firm. On the one hand, agency theory advocates that behavior has to be aligned to a superior individual interest, that of the principal, who is described as the unique residual claimant in the firm (Alchian and Demsetz, 1972; Jensen and Meckling, 1976). On the other hand, transaction cost approaches suggest that interest alignment is ensured when everybody acts to satisfy the owner(s) of the property rights (Grossman and Hart, 1986; Hart and Moore, 1990; Hart, 1995). Despite analytical differences, contractual theories of the firm develop a legal vision of the firm in which the centralization of residual rights of control coordinates *ex ante* and *ex post* incentives. Therefore, they support a disciplinary vision of firm governance. Instead, the conception of the firm as a nexus of specific investments in human capital, proposed by the critical resource theory, suggests that interest alignment should be reexamined in the light of the fragmentation of power resulting from the dispersion of inalienable residual rights of control (Rajan and Zingales, 2000; Zingales, 1998; Zingales, 2000; Chassagnon, 2011). Hold-up threats inherent to specific human capital incorporated by critical employees should be prevented to reach a superior collective goal. In what follows, the author suggests, through the proposition of the multi-resource model, some avenues to rethink firm governance issues and instruments.

MAIN FOCUS OF THE CHAPTER

Contrary to dominant approaches, this chapter advances that firm governance should aim to satisfy neither shareholder value nor stakeholder value. Since the firm is built on specific human capital (as represented by the critical resource theory), economic power is fragmented in the hand of the multiple and complementary decisive members of the firm so that they must already adhere to the same purpose. In other words, shareholder primacy and stakeholder legitimacy based on the satisfaction of particular residual claimant interests are challenged. The author provides the framework for an original model of firm governance ensuring the alignment of collective interests.

Each key partner has to be encouraged to give up his own ambitions to commit himself collectively in favor of the organizational welfare. From this perspective, firms can be considered as systems of cooperation of human activity (Barnard, 1938). Now, cooperation can be reached if the efforts of all critical resource-holders are focused on a common preferable goal. In particular, the maximization of multi-resource value depends on the complementarity links between all the critical resources, and requires incentives to organizational interest alignment. According to Gottschalg and Zollo (2007, p. 420), "*organizational interest alignment can be defined as the degree to which the members of the organization are motivated to behave in line with organizational goals*".

The author proposes to analyze how different critical firm members can coordinate their actions to reach a collective goal without requiring an authoritarian or non-authoritarian external intervention by focusing on key employees who incorporate specific human capital within the employment relationship. Key employees have inalienable rights of control and need to be encouraged to behave in line with organizational goals, which are the employer's goals. Like shareholders and managers, they are viewed as partners of the firm: they own generic resources and automatically behave in line with organizational goals. In this sense, what matters is the degree to which collective goals and key employees' individual goals are aligned. Contrary to traditional approaches, the author advances that understanding how objectives have been set and who has prioritized them is of little use. The author suggests that critical resource-holders in HCIFs should embrace a common purpose from the beginning of the relationship with the firm. To serve this purpose, the multi-resource model of firm governance should perpetuate the organizational interest alignment, and can thus maximize the creation of collective value and distribution of the surplus.

Lasting commitment from key employees within the firm depends both on contract evolution and on outside options. More precisely, it depends on their negotiating power and on a fundamental right linked to their organizational membership. To prevent underinvestment risks resulting from key employees' exercise of power, the multi-resource model of firm governance has to convince them that investing specifically is of benefit to them as much as it is to the firm. One solution could be to build a system that minimizes in all the stages of the employment relationship the distance between the diverse individual preferences, thereby reducing the tension in power relationships (Grandori and Soda, 2004). In this context, employment relationship models and incentive systems need to be integrated, as McGregor (1960) suggests in the Y Theory. Lessons have been drawn from this seminal theory, and it has recently been reconsidered in incentive theory focused on the human dimension (Ellingsen and Johannesson, 2008). The main idea is to create conditions so that firm members can reach their own goals by turning their efforts towards the success of the firm. Preventing hold-up threats is not the only problem of the multi-resource model of firm governance. Since the firm is economically dependent on strategic employees, the maximization of its value potential requires to co-specialize *ex post* key resource holders.

The collection of specific human resources within the production team (*i.e.* the firm) is a decisive factor of organizational quasi-rent creation. Because of productive synergies, the value of the firm is higher than the sum of the individual critical resource-holders' values (Engelen and Vanderberghe, 2005). This chapter argues that the co-specialization of key employees is a central issue to optimize the multi-resource value: in this way, the firm should meet two challenges, retaining and enriching the critical resources these employees represent.

Retaining critical resources within the firm implies to guarantee decisive employee loyalty, which means consolidating the employment relationship by empowering them. On the one hand, maintaining critical resources within the firm prevents reduction of the multi-resource value. Indeed, the firm can maximize multi-resource value if decisive employees are not incited to seize their outside opportunities. So, the firm should ensure key employees' commitment over the long term by setting up obstacles to the exploitation of their human capital in another productive entity (Coff, 1997; Rajan and Zingales, 2000). However, the power of the firm should not be weakened too far, for fear that a disproportionate counter-power might jeopardize the joint value they can create together. On the other hand, the purpose of ensuring key employee loyalty is to obtain and protect the best possible combination of workers. Yet, contrary to what some authors argue (Grandori and Soda, 2004), it is no use securing the team of workers that maximize, at any given moment in time, investments in critical resources. In other words, a controlled turnover of labor-force within a bounded external market is not a solution. Employees who extend their knowledge portfolio energize the internal labor market but strengthen at the same time their employability, their outside opportunities, and thus their *ex post* negotiating power. A less wasteful solution would consist in retaining within the firm the same employees whose human capital would be maintained at the level of the market demand and needs by using accumulation and enrichment methods. In this way, specific human capital is enriched within the firm itself.

Enriching critical resources hold by firm-specific employees implies to improve the stock of specific human capital. Consequently, specific human capital is endogenous within the context of the creative function of the firm. Moreover, even if the value creation process requires the use of co-specific resources that increase workers' productivity only within the firm that employs them, it should not change these co-specific resources in core rigidities by maintaining too narrow a base of core skills (Leonard-Barton, 1992). Rather, the firm and key employees should act in synergy to enrich specific resources. An appropriate internal market, characterized by a limited number of outside options during careers, can create such a favorable situation at the collective level. Indeed, employees who hold down a stable job foresee that it is in their interest to promote the firm's prosperity and to behave cooperatively. As for the employer, he improves the efficiency of human resources allocation. The necessity to invest specifically in human capital consists in preventing its depreciation and its transferability.

This chapter advances that a governance model adapted to HCIFs should optimize the combination of specific human assets in the most wealth-creative activities. In this way, the author proposes that the multi-resource model aims to (1) incite key workers to invest specifically and durably in human capital and (2) protect the firm's investments themselves, to develop and exploit growth opportunities. This renewed model of firm governance is endogenous to the intangible, inalienable and difficult-to-reproduce nature of specific human assets (Rajan and Zingales, 1998; Wang et al., 2009). It is based on the reinforcement of inalienable residual rights of control held individually by decisive employees. In this perspective, the author shows that the multi-resource governance model consists in collectively encouraging, retaining and enriching key employees. Employees who hold specific competences should be empowered to create value for all the critical resources that make up the firm, which is to say for themselves and for the firm (Rajan and Zingales, 2000). The multi-resource value approach is not reduced to a strict incentive issue; it aims to meet the global challenge of motivating key employees, which could be based on a multidimensional operational system.

SOLUTIONS AND RECOMMANDATIONS

Work motivation points out that the firm's success depends on collective performances which themselves depend on individual results (Pinder, 2014). Thus, a strong work motivation results in more employees' commitment, more innovation and more flexibility. In line with self-determination theory (SDT) (Deci and Ryan, 1975; 1985; 2002), the author suggests that a "motivational continuum" can depict the degree to which key employees, viewed as critical resource-holders, commit themselves to work (Gagné and Deci, 2005; Gagné, 2014). This motivational continuum defines the level of self-determined motivation reached by an employee according to the degree of satisfaction of his need for autonomy. When the effects of the activity are external to him, a decisive employee finds reasons for commitment in the environment, for example because of controls, constraints, promises or rewards. After amotivation, which defines the absence of self-determined motivation, external regulation is the weakest level of self-determined motivation that is called "extrinsic motivation". On the contrary, when the effects of the activity are internal to the key employee, motivation is self-determined or self-regulated: the activity is enjoyed for itself and not for somebody or for reasons included in his environment. Thus, the individual need for autonomy is completely satisfied. Finally, if the effects of the activity are internal to the employee and external to the task accomplished, internalized extrinsic motivation is described. Internalized extrinsic motivation is a hybrid form of motivation that depends on the degree of internalization of the external regulation by the individual (*idem*)[4]. Based on the SDT framework, this chapter supports that the firm can decide either to extrinsically motivate employees through an incentive system or to influence self-determined motivations to "naturally" shape their behavior. The author also provides some operational instruments that support the multi-resource governance model.

Firstly, purely extrinsic motivation means that an agent acts only in order to obtain an outcome which is external to himself and to the task performed. In the domain of work, the employee is extrinsically motivated by getting results distinct from the work itself (Baron and Kreps, 1999; Deci and Ryan, 2000). He is also extrinsically motivated by certain actions and decisions of others, since they influence the consequences of his activities. Purely extrinsic motivation encourages the employee's involvement in an activity for its monetary consequences (obtaining a higher remuneration through performance bonuses or a professional advancement), material consequences (improvement of work conveniences) and social consequences (search for reputation, for gratitude). Purely extrinsic motivation largely depends on contractual hierarchical mechanisms oriented by incentives and control: the disciplinary effect partly determines the balance between the increase of individual employees' productivity and the regulation of opportunistic behavior. Several studies on financial remuneration modes and performance evaluation highlight the positive correlation between the use of such incentive mechanisms and employees' purely extrinsic motivation (Lazear, 2000; Nagin et al., 2002), in line with the recommendations of contractual theories of the firm. As explained above, the multi-resource governance model has to meet the challenge of encouraging critical resource-holders to behave according to the collective interest. This incentive issue can be solved by developing individual systems of external regulation. For example, financial and institutional participation systems or different forms of compensation extrinsically motivate key employees. Indeed, key employees are satisfied because they obtain an important financial return on their investments, or because they are identified as central members in the firm that allocates them formal residual rights of control (French and Rosenstein, 1984). Consequently, the author emphasizes that the role of the hierarchy in fixing remunerations is a major determinant in the multi-resource model of firm governance.

Secondly, intrinsic motivation comes from rewards inherent to an activity itself: it stems from the enjoyment of performing a task and from a need for immediate satisfaction (Deci and Ryan, 2000). Intrinsic motivation is the perfect incarnation of self-determination. The activity itself is the reason why an intrinsically-motivated individual commits himself. No direct or indirect valuable consequences through incentives, constraints or sanctions are necessary for the individual to invest himself. Thus, an individual is intrinsically motivated when he voluntarily performs activities; he acts out of interest for the activity without expecting rewards and without hoping to avoid feeling guilty. Within the employment relationship, key employees are intrinsically motivated if they can directly satisfy their needs by working. Among others, cooperative relationships and willingly accepted organizational practices and work conditions support intrinsic motivation. In the context of the multi-resource model, granting autonomy and giving employees a sense of responsibility relieves them of the feeling of hierarchical control. In addition, it encourages self-subordination to the collective organizational interest. Freedom of action, liberty granted to employees, "*raises the perceived self-determination of employees and therewith strengthens intrinsic motivation*" (Osterloh and Frey, 2000, pp. 543). In turn, this may lead to an increase of their creativity in the pursuit of organizational goals (Foss et al., 2006). Moreover, a positive correlation may link employee participation, on the one hand, with trust levels, intrinsic compensation, involvement in organization, work satisfaction and the stress level, on the other hand. From this perspective, labor organization and labor division underpin interest alignment and the co-specialization of specific human capital when social capital is favorable. The durability of employment relationships is ensured by organizational practices that are innovative, attractive and useful in themselves. Intrinsic motivation creates a common will to increase the value of the team production's collective specificity.

In addition, Baard et al. (2004) empirically highlight a positive correlation between a work organization favorable to autonomy and competences and, on the one hand, a high degree of intrinsic motivation, adaptability and changes and on the other, high levels of performance.

Thirdly, like intrinsic motivation, internalized extrinsic motivation depends on self-determination, since individuals undertake an activity because they want to. Deci and Ryan (2000) argue that self-determination can be analyzed beyond the principle of satisfying the vital need for autonomy. According to these authors, internalization takes place when individuals perform an activity not because this activity is interesting and satisfies a need in itself, but because it is fundamental and has a value for them. In other words, internalized extrinsic motivation corresponds to individuals' commitment to the importance that they give to values, norms and other significations represented by the activity undertaken and the resulting satisfaction (Ouchi, 1980). From this perspective, notably, a key employee accepts voluntarily to undertake pro-social actions, which are actions aiming to help or benefit others (Eisenberg, 1982; Bénabou and Tirole, 2006; Grant and Berry, 2011). More generally, a decisive employee deliberately adopts an observable behavior aimed at supporting the collective benefit or sharing costs and benefits with the group. As far as the multi-resource model of firm governance is concerned, the author advances that the representation of the most essential employees on the board of directors, for example, does not affect intrinsic motivation because of long and tiresome assemblies or even hard debates concerning strategies of the firm. Rather, it affects internalized extrinsic motivation by asserting the employees' point of view and aiming to safeguard co-specific resources within the firm. The motivating factor does not come from the task itself, which can be uninteresting; it comes from the meaning of the motivation, moral values and social norms that employees' representation promotes or allows to reach through its effects, and from the resulting collective utility. A key employee internalizes these externalities and does not need to be extrinsically motivated by disciplinary incentives.

The author believes that self-regulated motivations self-strengthen the power of the employer and of strategic employees in HCIFs. On the one hand, key employees are aware that they control critical resources, and need to be intrinsically motivated because they hold inalienable residual rights of decision on them. Thus, they want to enjoy their specific relationship with the firm. On the other hand, key employees should acknowledge that respecting collective interests and guaranteeing co-specialization are two vital issues for the durability and the growth of the firm. Under these conditions, they internalize extrinsic sources of motivation. The HCIF should set up mechanisms allowing its crucial employees to internalize the constraint of the long-term employment relationship; these latter do not need strong autonomy to behave according to organizational goals and to enrich the specific human capital that they control. Finally, balanced powers between the employer and critical employees entails offsetting the different forms of motivation. Thus, the author proposes that the multi-resource value approach aims to tackle the global issue of motivating key employees from the perspective of "motivational self-reinforcement". If the economic literature has focused on the effects of extrinsic regulations on intrinsic motivation (*crowding theory of motivation*: Frey, 1997; Osterloh and Frey, 2000; Frey and Jegen, 2001), no consensus has emerged about the nature of those effects. By suggesting that there is a reciprocal (not a one-way) dynamic relationship between the purely extrinsic motivation and the intrinsic motivation of individuals, the author is taking position in favor of motivational complementarity. According to the theory of supermodularity (Milgrom and Roberts, 1995), the marginal efficiency of a factor – in this case the purely extrinsic motivation – increases with the level of another factor – in this case the intrinsic motivation, and *vice versa*. When contracts are incomplete, the key advantage of intrinsic motivation is that it can remedy the inefficiency of incentives. Intrinsic motivation is indispensable when extrinsic motivation cannot resolve certain extracontractual problems, because employees' behavior cannot be observed or because the results cannot be attributed to individuals (Osterloh and Frey, 2004). The intrinsic dimension protects the specific relationship between specialized employees and the employer by strengthening the attraction of employees to their work and favoring their attachment to the firm. It also contributes to the creation and pooling of knowledge by ensuring the involvement and collaboration of employees in production teams. Ultimately, intrinsic motivation offsets the harmful effects of tangible forms of external regulation. For example, an employee may be handsomely paid for the work he does, but if he derives no satisfaction from accomplishing his task, he may eventually decide to leave the firm, taking with him a share of the organizational rent. But if the firm succeeds in coupling the extrinsic motivation of financial incentive with a system that favors intrinsic motivation, by giving employees more responsibility or initiative, for example, then it can maintain the specificity of the employment relationship over the long term.

The self-reinforcement of motivations is taken to an extreme when internalized extrinsic motivation is considered, hitherto neglected by many authors who have classified it too hastily in the domain of the extrinsic, or confusedly in the domain of the intrinsic (Amabile, 1993; Frey, 1997; Kreps, 1997; Osterloh and Frey, 2000; Bénabou and Tirole, 2003). Internalized extrinsic motivation is an intermediate form of self-determination with an intrinsic component and an extrinsic component. Yet, an appropriate degree of assimilation and acceptance of the external constraint by a key employee achieves a balance between the need to transmit the rules to him and the satisfaction of his need for autonomy. Moreover, introducing a measure of control based on individual self-regulation (not only based on external regulation) can be effective because it generates a feedback effect on the individual's need for skill and social relations without negating the need for autonomy. In turn, the internalization of incentives has a positive influence on the employee's behavior at work. Therefore, it is important to recognize the role of internalized extrinsic motivation in developing the loyalty and commitment of employees, especially managerial staff.

Ultimately, purely extrinsic motivation and self-regulated motivation should be combined. The overall motivation of key employees is a fundamental condition of the regulation of powers in the employment relationship. The multi-resource governance model supports this point of view in terms of both the issues and the methods involved. The authors argue that this HCIF governance model can achieve the self-reinforcement of motivations with the help of different instruments that are themselves complementary.

To operationalize the multi-resource model of firm governance, the author suggests that three decisive elements in the new vision of the firm should be considered: (*i*) the importance of human capital and its inappropriable and inimitable nature, (*ii*) the complementarity and inseparability of assets, and (*iii*) the incompleteness of contracts. Since it is not possible to contractualize the income to be expected from investments in specific human capital and because the value-added of each individual's contributions is hard to measure, other methods should be developed than the simple use of incentives or purely extrinsic motivation. Instruments of collective interest protection and critical human capital retention and enrichment are endogenous to the firm and therefore take into account the specificity of its critical resources. The multi-resource firm governance should be built on extrinsic motivation and self-regulated motivation mechanisms. In other words, the complementarity of motivations suggests a complementarity in the governance practices that seek to promote them. The multi-resource value approach requires a balanced combination of financial and non-financial controlling mechanisms (purely extrinsic motivation) and a new set of practices of organization and coordination (self-regulated motivations). This combination allows to take into account the double location of sources of motivation and to evaluate the effects of the composite operational system on the regulation of power within the organization (Deci and Ryan, 2000). The combination of extrinsic and intrinsic dimensions generates an effect of virtuous synergy for the firm: it guarantees control over the multilateral risks of *ex post* expropriation and valorization of the co-specific resources. Consequently, the multi-resource model can be operationalized to protect specific employment relationships. In line with March and Simon (1958), this chapter advances that individuals' decisions to cooperate and effectively participate in the firm are organizational incentive and coordination issues.

The conditions of use of the labor force in the productive activity, viewed from the microeconomic perspective of the motivation to work rather than the increase in production capacities, can serve as the basis for a characterization of the operational instruments of the multi-resource model of firm governance. The trend towards more individualized wage practices and the shift in productive coordination towards a more collective approach supply tangible elements of the redistribution of powers within the modern firm. In other words, vertical incentives and horizontal work organization account for innovative high-performance work practices (Macky and Boxall, 2007) or high road of work organization (Lippert et al., 2014); they aim at guaranteeing jobs that will be durably qualified and specialized in favorable working conditions. Most of the literature views these new forms of remuneration and coordination as an expression of a degradation of the employment relationship in favor of the employer (Ramsey et al., 2000). Indeed, it is often argued that the aim of current human resources management policies is to improve labor productivity and flexibility to the detriment of employees' welfare (Green, 2004; Tregaskis et al., 2013). But this point of view has been hotly challenged based on documented studies (Berg, 1999; Appelbaum and Berg, 2000). Whereas the new forms of labor force organization may possibly constitute a toughening of work conditions for employees with generic human capital, the same is not true in the case of employees with specific human capital. For the latter, they represent a way of making voluntary the application and enrichment of the knowledge and skills underlying the improvement of the relationships specific to the organization. Consequently, vertical incentives and horizontal work practices can be considered as key instruments of work motivation and not as the manifestation of an intensive use of the labor force. In addition to these two modern practices for strengthening key employees' commitment, the third fundamental dimension is the decentralization of operational and strategic decision-making, in other words the delegation of residual rights of control in the domains of production and management. In broad outline, the author suggests that the combination of these three types of strategic practices create a work environment favorable to the intrinsic motivation of employees (horizontal work organization) and the internalization of external regulation (decentralized decision-making) while at the same time rewarding the development of specific skills (vertical incentives). Without appropriate economic incentives, interesting work content and shared norms and values, strategic employees may be discouraged from investing in non-transferable specific human capital, preferring to invest in more general skills that can be exploited outside the firm.

FUTURE RESEARCH DIRECTIONS

Specific human assets motivation practices are not strictly part of the mechanisms of governance; they lie outside the field of what is traditionally covered by the term corporate governance or firm governance. Nevertheless, their objectives undoubtedly involve the value creation and preservation. There is a point, therefore, where the forms of human resources management (HRM) and the mechanisms of governance interpenetrate (Lippert et al., 2014) while it is acknowledged that firm governance and the ownership structure of firms influence HRM (Deakin et al., 2006; Deakin and Rebérioux, 2009). In this perspective, the most recent theories of the firm maintain, like Blair (1999), that the regulation of power relationships between strategic employees and the firm should no longer be treated separately from firm governance. Even if executive officers mainly determine the general policy of the firm and are in charge of value maximization, the centrality of human capital prohibits from neglecting the role assigned to HRM in firm governance. Therefore, the operational model of HCIF governance can be considered in a broader perspective than the traditional models that are strictly limited to the legal conditions of the allocation of alienable control rights among stakeholders. The multi-resource model should be considered as the whole set of mechanisms motivating key employees to work together to maximize in the long-term the rents of co-specific human capital and make them completely available.

The research agenda about the multi-resource model of firm governance is not exhausted. If it is adapted to the valorization of co-specific human assets, the multi-resource model of firm governance will help to create competitive advantages and so generate gains for the firm that implements it. These gains find expression in the maintenance and exploration of growth opportunities contained in inimitable assets and in the extension and exploitation of growth opportunities by the implementation of multi-resource governance. In other words, future research would have to show that key resources and the complementary tools of governance that mobilize them are a joint source of performance for HCIFs. Such an avenue for research could question the field of corporate social responsibility (Jamali et al., 2008; Sacconi et al., 2010).

CONCLUSION

This chapter showed that the mobilization of specific human assets in the division of labor calls for a rethinking of the regulation of power exercise within a context of preservation of economic dependence relationships. It proposed a revised model of governance adapted to HCIFs that the author calls the multi-resource model of firm governance. Unlike traditional disciplinary models, which seek to satisfy residual claimants' particular interests, this new model of governance is collective by nature: it aims to ensure that the co-specific investments in key resources are lasting and prosperous. This chapter advanced that the maximization of multi-resource value requires to encourage, retain and enhance employees' specific human capital within a logic of productive complementarities; ultimately, it is based on a global issue of motivation of long-term specific relationships. The multi-resource value can only be maximized by and for individuals who are rewarded and self-determined. In addition, the author advanced that the multi-resource model should ensure that in the future the key employees of the firm would receive appropriate rent and satisfaction; to achieve the self-reinforcement of motivations, it should make a synergic use of operational mechanisms. Thus, to encourage its key employees to adhere to a common organizational purpose and to guarantee continuously the co-specialization of valuable knowledge, skills and expertise, HCIFs should set up a combination of vertical incentive practices, horizontal work methods and decentralized decision-making. In other words, a balanced power relationship within HCIFs requires a mutual strengthening of more horizontal working practices where the decision-making is decentralized, decisive employees are more autonomous and where overarching dynamics are preferred and evaluation and remuneration modes are vertical and individualized.

REFERENCES

Aglietta, M., & Rebérioux, A. (2012). 23 Financialization and the firm. *Handbook on the Economics and Theory of the Firm*, 308.

Alchian, A., & Demsetz, H. (1972). Production, Information Costs, and Economic Organization. *The American Economic Review*, *62*(5), 777–795.

Amabile, T. (1988). A Model of Creativity and Innovation in Organizations. In B. Staw & L. Cummings (Eds.), *Research in Organizational Behavior* (pp. 123–167). Greenwich, CT: J.A.I. Press.

Amabile, T. (1993). Motivational Synergy: Toward New Conceptualizations of Intrinsic and Extrinsic Motivation in the Workplace. *Human Resource Management Review*, *3*(3), 185–201. doi:10.1016/1053-4822(93)90012-S

Appelbaum, E., & Berg, P. (2000). High-Performance Work Systems: Giving Workers a Stake. In M. Blair & T. Kochan (Eds.), *The New Relationship: Human Capital in the American Corporation* (pp. 102–138). Washington, DC: Brookings Institution Press.

Arundel, A., Lorenz, E., Lundvall, B. Å., & Valeyre, A. (2007). How Europe's economies learn: A comparison of work organization and innovation mode for the EU-15. *Industrial and Corporate Change*, *16*(6), 1175–1210. doi:10.1093/icc/dtm035

Baard, P., Deci, E., & Ryan, R. (2004). Intrinsic Need Satisfaction: A Motivational Basis of Performance and Well-Being in Two Work Settings. *Journal of Applied Social Psychology*, *34*(10), 2045–2068. doi:10.1111/j.1559-1816.2004.tb02690.x

Baker, G., Gibbons, R., & Murphy, K. (2002). Relational Contracts and the Theory of the Firm. *The Quarterly Journal of Economics*, *117*(1), 39–84. doi:10.1162/003355302753399445

Baker, G., Jensen, M., & Murphy, K. (1988). Compensation and Incentives: Practice vs. Theory. *The Journal of Finance*, *43*(3), 593–616. doi:10.1111/j.1540-6261.1988.tb04593.x

Baldwin, C., & Clark, K. (2000). *Design Rules: The Power of Modularity* (Vol. 1). Cambridge, MA: The MIT Press.

Barnard, C. (1938). *The Functions of the Executive*. Cambridge, MA: Harvard University Press.

Baron, J., & Kreps, D. (1999). *Strategic Human Resources: Frameworks for General Managers*. New York: Wiley and Sons.

Bénabou, R., & Tirole, J. (2003). Intrinsic and Extrinsic Motivation. *The Review of Economic Studies*, *70*(3), 489–520. doi:10.1111/1467-937X.00253

Bénabou, R., & Tirole, J. (2006). Incentives and Prosocial Behavior. *The American Economic Review*, *96*(5), 1652–1678. doi:10.1257/aer.96.5.1652

Berg, P. (1999). The Effects of High Performance Work Pratices on Job Satisfaction in the United States Steel Industry. *Relations Industrielles. Industrial Relations*, *54*(1), 111–134. doi:10.7202/051222ar

Berle, A., & Means, G. (1932). *The Modern Corporation and Private Property*. New York: Harcourt, Brace and World.

Biondi, Y., & Rebérioux, A. (2012, December). The governance of intangibles: Rethinking financial reporting and the board of directors. *Accounting Forum*, *36*(4), 279–293. doi:10.1016/j.accfor.2012.03.003

Blair, M. (1999). Firm-Specific Human Capital and Theories of the Firm. In M. Blair & M. Roe (Eds.), *Employees and Corporate Governance* (pp. 58–90). Washington, DC: Brookings Institution Press.

Blair, M. M. (2010). *Wealth creation and wealth sharing: A colloquium on corporate governance and investments in human capital.* Brookings Institution Press.

Blair, M. M. (2012). In the best interest of the corporation: Directors' duties in the wake of the global crisis. In The SAGE Handbook of Corporate Governance (pp. 62-80). Sage. doi:10.4135/9781446200995.n3

Blair, M. M., & Roe, M. J. (Eds.). (2010). *Employees and corporate governance.* Brookings Institution Press.

Boxall, P., & Macky, K. (2009). Research and theory on high-performance work systems: Progressing the high-involvement stream. *Human Resource Management Journal, 19*(1), 3–23. doi:10.1111/j.1748-8583.2008.00082.x

Brynjolfsson, E., Hitt, L., & Yang, S. (2002). Intangible Assets: Computers and Organizational Capital. *Brookings Papers on Economic Activity, 1*(1), 137–198. doi:10.1353/eca.2002.0003

Calder, B., & Staw, B. (1975). Self-Perceptions of Intrinsic and Extrinsic Motivation. *Journal of Personality and Social Psychology, 31*(4), 599–605. doi:10.1037/h0077100 PMID:1159610

Chassagnon, V. (2011). The law and economics of the modern firm: A new governance structure of power relationships. *Revue d'Economie Industrielle*, (2): 25–50. doi:10.4000/rei.4983

Chassagnon, V., & Hollandts, X. (2014). Who are the owners of the firm: Shareholders, employees or no one? *Journal of Institutional Economics, 10*(1), 47–69. doi:10.1017/S1744137413000301

Clarke, T. (2014). Dangerous frontiers in corporate governance. *Journal of Management & Organization, 20*(3), 268–286. doi:10.1017/jmo.2014.37

Clarke, T. (2015). Changing paradigms in corporate governance: New cycles and new responsibilities. *Society and Business Review, 10*(3), 306–326. doi:10.1108/SBR-07-2015-0027

Coff, R. (1997). Human Assets and Management Dilemmas: Coping With Hazards on the Road to Resource-Based Theory. *Academy of Management Review, 22*(2), 374–402. doi:10.5465/amr.1997.9707154063

Cordonnier, L., & Van de Velde, F. (2014). The demands of finance and the glass ceiling of profit without investment. *Cambridge Journal of Economics, 39*(3), 871–885. doi:10.1093/cje/beu064

Cornell, B., & Shapiro, A. (1987). Corporate Shareholders and Corporate Finance. *Financial Management*, *16*(1), 5–14. doi:10.2307/3665543

Deakin, S., Hobbs, R., Konzelmann, S., & Wilkinson, F. (2002). Partnership, ownership and control: The impact of corporate governance on employment relations. *Employee Relations*, *24*(3), 335–352. doi:10.1108/01425450210428480

Deakin, S., Hobbs, R., Konzelmann, S., & Wilkinson, F. (2006). Anglo-American Corporate Governance and the Employment Relationship: A Case to Answer? *Socio-economic Review*, *4*(1), 155–174. doi:10.1093/SER/mwj037

Deakin, S., & Rebérioux, A. (2009). Corporate Governance, Labour Relations and Human Resource Management in Britain and France: Convergence or Divergence? In J.-P. Touffut (Ed.), *Does Company Ownership Matter?* Cheltenham, UK: Edward Elgar. doi:10.4337/9781781953297.00014

Deci, E., & Ryan, R. (1985). *Intrinsic Motivation and Self-Determination in Human Behavior*. New York: Plenum Press. doi:10.1007/978-1-4899-2271-7

Deci, E., & Ryan, R. (2000). Self-Determination Theory and the Facilitation of Intrinsic Motivation, Social Development, and Well-Being. *The American Psychologist*, *55*(1), 68–78. doi:10.1037/0003-066X.55.1.68 PMID:11392867

Deci, E. L., & Ryan, R. M. (Eds.). (2002). *Handbook of self-determination research*. University Rochester Press.

Dore, R. (2008). Financialization of the global economy. *Industrial and Corporate Change*, *17*(6), 1097–1112. doi:10.1093/icc/dtn041

Eisenberg, N. (1982). *The Development of Prosocial Behavior*. London: Academic Press.

Ellingsen, T., & Johannesson, M. (2008). Pride and Prejudice: The Human Side of Incentive Theory. *The American Economic Review*, *98*(3), 990–1008. doi:10.1257/aer.98.3.990

Engelen, P.-J., & Vanderberghe, A.-S. (2005). Boundary Defense in Human Capital Intensive Firms: Coping With the Problem of Collective Departure of Employees. *22nd Annual Conference of the European Association for Law and Economics*, 15-17.

Foss, K., Foss, N., & Vazquez, X. (2006). 'Tying the Manager's Hands': Constraining Opportunistic Managerial Intervention. *Cambridge Journal of Economics*, *30*(5), 797–818. doi:10.1093/cje/bei107

Foss, N. (2000). The Dangers and Attractions of Theoretical Eclectism. *Journal of Macromarketing, 20*(1), 65–67. doi:10.1177/0276146700201007

French, J., & Rosenstein, J. (1984). Employee Ownership Work Attitudes and Power Relationships. *Academy of Management Journal, 27*(4), 861–869.

Frey, B. (1997). *Not Just for the Money - An Economic Theory of Personal Motivation*. Cheltenham, UK: Edward Elgar.

Frey, B., & Jegen, R. (2001). Motivation Crowding Theory. *Journal of Economic Surveys, 15*(5), 589–611. doi:10.1111/1467-6419.00150

Gagné, M. (Ed.). (2014). *The Oxford handbook of work engagement, motivation, and self-determination theory*. Oxford Library of Psychology. doi:10.1093/oxfordhb/9780199794911.001.0001

Gagné, M., & Deci, E. (2005). Self-Determination Theory and Work Motivation. *Journal of Organizational Behavior, 26*(4), 331–362. doi:10.1002/job.322

Gibbons, R. (2005). Four Formal(izable) Theories of the Firm? *Journal of Economic Behavior & Organization, 58*(2), 200–245. doi:10.1016/j.jebo.2004.09.010

Gottschalg, O., & Zollo, M. (2007). Interest Alignment and Competitive Advantage. *Academy of Management Review, 32*(2), 418–437. doi:10.5465/amr.2007.24351356

Grandori, A. (2013). Human capital and property rights. Handbook of Economic Organization: Integrating Economic and Organization Theory, 273.

Grandori, A., & Soda, G. (2004). Governing with Multiple Principals: An Empirically-Based Analysis of Capital Providers' Preferences and Superior Governance Structures. In A. Grandori (Ed.), *Corporate Governance and Firm Organization: Microfoundations and Structural Forms* (pp. 67–88). New York: Oxford University Press. doi:10.1093/acprof:oso/9780199269761.003.0004

Grant, A. M., & Berry, J. W. (2011). The necessity of others is the mother of invention: Intrinsic and prosocial motivations, perspective taking, and creativity. *Academy of Management Journal, 54*(1), 73–96. doi:10.5465/amj.2011.59215085

Green, F. (2004). Whay Has Work Effort Become More Intense? *Relations Industrielles. Industrial Relations, 43*(4), 709–741. doi:10.1111/j.0019-8676.2004.00359.x

Grossman, S., & Hart, O. (1986). The Costs and Benefits of Ownership: A Theory of Vertical and Lateral Integration. *Journal of Political Economy, 94*(4), 691–719. doi:10.1086/261404

Guilhon, B. (2004). Markets for Knowledge: Problems, Scope and Economic Implications. *Economics of Innovation and New Technology*, *13*(2), 165–181. doi: 10.1080/10438590410001628134

Hall, P., & Soskice, D. (2001). Introduction. In P. Hall & D. Soskice (Eds.), *Varieties of Capitalism* (pp. 1–68). Oxford, UK: Oxford University Press. doi:10.1093/0199247757.003.0001

Hart, O. (1995). Corporate Governance: Some Theory and Implications. *Economic Journal (London)*, *105*(430), 678–689. doi:10.2307/2235027

Hart, O., & Moore, J. (1990). Property Rights and the Nature of the Firm. *Journal of Political Economy*, *98*(6), 1119–1158. doi:10.1086/261729

Hart, O., & Moore, J. (1994). A theory of debt based on the inalienability of human capital. *The Quarterly Journal of Economics*, *109*(4), 841–879. doi:10.2307/2118350

Jamali, D., Safieddine, A. M., & Rabbath, M. (2008). Corporate governance and corporate social responsibility synergies and interrelationships. *Corporate Governance*, *16*(5), 443–459. doi:10.1111/j.1467-8683.2008.00702.x

Jensen, M., & Meckling, W. (1976). Theory of the Firm: Managerial Behavior, Agency Costs and Ownership Structure. *Journal of Financial Economics*, *3*(4), 305–360. doi:10.1016/0304-405X(76)90026-X

Keenan, J., & Aggestam, M. (2001). Corporate Governance and Intellectual Capital: Some Conceptualizations. *Empirical Research-Based and Theory-Building Papers*, *9*(4), 259–275.

Klein, B., Crawford, R., & Alchian, A. (1978). Vertical Integration, Appropriable Rents, and the Competitive Contracting Process. *The Journal of Law & Economics*, *21*(2), 297–326. doi:10.1086/466922

Klein, P. G., Mahoney, J. T., McGahan, A. M., & Pitelis, C. N. (2012). Who is in charge? A property rights perspective on stakeholder governance. *Strategic Organization*, *10*(3), 304–315. doi:10.1177/1476127012453108

Kleinknecht, R. H. (2015). Employee participation in corporate governance: Implications for company resilience. *European Journal of Industrial Relations*, *21*(1), 57–72. doi:10.1177/0959680114523820

Kochan, T., & Rubinstein, S. (2000). Toward a Stakeholder Theory of the Firm: The Saturn Partnership. *Organization Science*, *11*(4), 367–386. doi:10.1287/orsc.11.4.367.14601

Kreps, D. (1997). Intrinsic Motivation and Extrinsic Incentives. *The American Economic Review*, *87*(2), 359–364.

Lazear, E. (2000). The Power of Incentives. *The American Economic Review*, *90*(2), 410–414. doi:10.1257/aer.90.2.410

Lazonick, W. (2010). Innovative business models and varieties of capitalism: Financialization of the US corporation. *Business History Review*, *84*(4), 675–702. doi:10.1017/S0007680500001987

Lazonick, W. (2011). From innovation to financialization: how shareholder value ideology is destroying the US Economy. The handbook of the political economy of financial crises, 491-511.

Lazonick, W., & O'Sullivan, M. (2000). Maximizing Shareholder Value: A New Ideology for Corporate Governance. *Economy and Society*, *29*(1), 13–35. doi:10.1080/030851400360541

Leonard-Barton, D. (1992). Core Capabilities and Core Rigidities: A Paradox in Managing New Product Development. *Strategic Management Journal*, *13*(special issue), 111–125. doi:10.1002mj.4250131009

Lippert, I., Huzzard, T., Jürgens, U., & Lazonick, W. (2014). *Corporate governance, employee voice, and work organization: sustaining high-road jobs in the automotive supply industry*. Oxford University Press. doi:10.1093/acprof:oso/9780199681075.001.0001

Macky, K., & Boxall, P. (2007). The relationship between 'high-performance work practices' and employee attitudes: An investigation of additive and interaction effects. *International Journal of Human Resource Management*, *18*(4), 537–567. doi:10.1080/09585190601178745

March, J., & Simon, H. (1958). *Organizations*. New York: John Wiley and Sons.

Marx, K. (1867). *Le Capital*. Presses Universitaires de France, Coll. Quadridge.

McGregor, D. (1960). *The Human Side of Enterprise*. New York: McGraw-Hill.

Milgrom, P., & Roberts, D. (1995). Complementarities and Fit: Strategy, Sructure, and Organizational Change in Manufacturing. *Journal of Accounting and Economics*, *19*(2-3), 179–208. doi:10.1016/0165-4101(94)00382-F

Nagin, D., Rebitzer, J., Sanders, S., & Taylor, L. (2002). Monitoring, Motivation and Management: The Determinants of Opportunistic Behavior in a Field Experiment. *The American Economic Review*, *92*(4), 850–873. doi:10.1257/00028280260344498

Osterloh, M., & Frey, B. (2000). Motivation, Knowledge Transfer, and Organizational Forms. *Organization Science, 11*(5), 538–550. doi:10.1287/orsc.11.5.538.15204

Osterloh, M., & Frey, B. (2004). Corporate Governance for Crooks? The Case for Corporate Virtue. In A. Grandori (Ed.), *Corporate Governance and Firm Organization: Microfoundations and Structural Forms* (pp. 191–211). New York: Oxford University Press. doi:10.1093/acprof:oso/9780199269761.003.0009

Ouchi, W. (1980). Markets, Bureaucracies and Clans. *Administrative Science Quarterly, 25*(1), 129–141. doi:10.2307/2392231

Perraudin, C., Petit, H., & Rebérioux, A. (2008). The stock market and human resource management: Evidence from a survey of French establishments. *Recherches Economiques de Louvain, 74*(4), 541–581. doi:10.3917/rel.744.0541

Pinder, C. C. (2014). *Work motivation in organizational behavior*. Psychology Press.

Rajan, R., & Zingales, L. (1998). Power in a Theory of the Firm. *The Quarterly Journal of Economics, 113*(2), 387–432. doi:10.1162/003355398555630

Rajan, R., & Zingales, L. (2000). The Governance of the New Enterprise. In X. Vives (Ed.), *Corporate Governance: Theoretical and Empirical Perspectives* (pp. 201–227). Cambridge, UK: Cambridge University Press. doi:10.1017/CBO9781139175333.007

Rajan, R., & Zingales, L. (2001). The Influence of the Financial Revolution on the Nature of Firms. *The American Economic Review, 91*(2), 206–211. doi:10.1257/aer.91.2.206

Ramsey, H., Scholarios, D., & Harley, B. (2000). Employees and High-Performance Work Systems: Testing Inside the Black Box. *British Journal of Industrial Relations, 38*(4), 501–531. doi:10.1111/1467-8543.00178

Ravix, J. L. (2008). Nature and governance of the firm: In search of an integrated perspective. *International Review of Applied Economics, 22*(4), 463–478. doi:10.1080/02692170802137620

Sacconi, L., Blair, M., & Freeman, R. E. (2010). *Corporate social responsibility and corporate governance: The contribution of economic theory and related disciplines*. Springer.

Schmitz, P. W. (2001). The Hold-Up Problem and Incomplete Contracts: A Survey of Recent Topics in Contract Theory. *Bulletin of Economic Research, 53*(1), 1–17. doi:10.1111/1467-8586.00114

Teece, D. (2003). Expert Talent and the Design of (Professional Services) Firms. *Industrial and Corporate Change*, *12*(4), 895–916. doi:10.1093/icc/12.4.895

Tirole, J. (1988). *The theory of industrial organization*. MIT Press.

Tregaskis, O., Daniels, K., Glover, L., Butler, P., & Meyer, M. (2013). High performance work practices and firm performance: A longitudinal case study. *British Journal of Management*, *24*(2), 225–244. doi:10.1111/j.1467-8551.2011.00800.x

Wang, H., & Barney, J. (2006). Employee Incentives to Make Firm-Specific Investments: Implications for Resource-Based Theories of Corporate Diversification. *Academy of Management Review*, *31*(2), 466–476. doi:10.5465/amr.2006.20208691

Wang, H., He, J., & Mahoney, J. (2009). Firm-Specific Knowledge Resources and Competitive Advantage: The Roles of Economic- and Relationship-Based Employee Governance Mechanisms. *Strategic Management Journal*, *30*(12), 1265–1285. doi:10.1002mj.787

Wang, H. C., He, J., & Mahoney, J. T. (2009). Firm-specific knowledge resources and competitive advantage: The roles of economic-and relationship-based employee governance mechanisms. *Strategic Management Journal*, *30*(12), 1265–1285. doi:10.1002mj.787

Williamson, O., Wachter, M., & Harris, J. (1975). Understanding the Employment Relation: The Analysis of Idiosyncratic Exchange. *The Bell Journal of Economics*, *6*(1), 250–278. doi:10.2307/3003224

Zingales, L. (1998). Corporate Governance. In D. Newman (Ed.), *The New Palgrave Dictionary of Economics and the Law* (pp. 497–502). London: Stockton Press.

Zingales, L. (2000). In Search of New Foundations. *The Journal of Finance*, *55*(4), 1623–1653. doi:10.1111/0022-1082.00262

ENDNOTES

1 The "downsize and redistribute" regime follows a corporate governance principle already based on the maximization of shareholder value. The latter is called "retain and reinvest" (Lazonick and O'Sullivan, 2000, p. 14). In this previous regime, corporations tended to *retain* both the money that they earned and the people whom they employed, and to *reinvest* in physical capital and complementary human resources.

2 According to Hall and Soskice (2001), co-specific assets are assets whose returns depend heavily on the active cooperation of other specific assets, which cannot readily be turned to another purpose.

3 Generally, the firm has to adapt its strategy to a competitive environment; thus the firm can decide to fire employees because their human capital is getting obsolete i.e. unsuited to market demand. In this case, employees' power is noticeably reduced (Cornell and Shapiro, 1987).

4 According to SDT, internalization is an overarching term that refers to three different processes: introjection, identification, and integration. For more details, see Gagné & Deci (2005, pp. 334-336).

Chapter 5
The Role of Human Resource Accounting in the Business Environment

Ahmet Özcan
Adana Science and Technology University, Turkey

ABSTRACT

In this chapter, human resources accounting is comprehensively analyzed. Human capital has been often neglected or inaccurately reported in the financial statements due to its nature. In the new economy, financial market participants such as investors, creditors, and shareholders would like to get information about the firm's investment in human capital. Over the last decades, some accounting methods have been developed for human capital. In this chapter, the methods used in the accounting treatment of human capital are analyzed, and a total of 288 operating reports of banks listed on Borsa Istanbul for the period between 2010 and 2017 are examined through content analysis. The results of content analysis indicate that there is a growing trend in human capital disclosure by banks listed on Borsa Istanbul between the period of 2010 and 2017, implying that banks listed on Borsa Istanbul have become more aware of the importance of human capital.

DOI: 10.4018/978-1-5225-7426-2.ch005

INTRODUCTION

Firms' financial statements are used by financial market participants to assess firms' financial position and performance. Financial market participants heavily need financial statements when making investment decisions. The financial statements that truly reflect financial performance and position are one of the key components of well-functioning financial markets. According to full disclosure principle, firms should report all types of information that can influence the decisions of financial market participants.

As the world economy is becoming much more globalized than before, economic competitiveness among firms significantly increases. Over the last two decades, firms have developed new management and production process to gain advantages over competitors. Firms should effectively utilize their capital to maximize the shareholders' wealth. Due to economic globalization, firms should effectively use all types of capital to increase their operational efficiency. In the new economy, knowledge has become one of the important factors that shape firms' operational efficiency. The efficiently use of knowledge can prominently contribute to the firms' value added of products.

The rapid globalization of world economy makes knowledge one of key resources in the current business climate. Knowledge-based firms play more active role in the economy. The production process of knowledge-based firms is not dominated by capital and labor. Knowledge is the major input of knowledge-based firms' production process (Asimakou, 2009). Strategic and organizational features of the firm influence the role of knowledge in the firm (Carlucci et al., 2004). Therefore, the same knowledge can affect different firms differently. Malhotra (1998) and Tapp (1997) claim that firms increasingly adopt organizational learning mechanisms. This is because firms are aware of the fact that best performing firms value knowledge and know how to effectively manage it in the new economy. A well- established knowledge management system enables firms to acquire and use human capital and create new business opportunities. In some cases knowledge can be a valuable asset for the firms' operations and only available for firms that can afford it (Carel, 2010).

There is a significant interaction between human capital and innovation. Human capital is one of the key contributors to innovation. Minai et al. (2016) stated that innovation is one of the results of explorative activities managed by individual or a team over a period of time. Innovation processes are influenced by firm-specific factors such as human capital, organizational structure and firm policies. The higher education level of workforce is a driving force of innovativeness of firms. Moreover education enables firms to facilitate effective use of human capital. More educated employee can easily adopt and introduce new technology. Educated employees are important keys to importing and managing innovations. Human capital investments increase the productivity of knowledge-intensive activities (Dakhli and Clercq, 2004). Innovation can be considered a knowledge-intensive activities. Teixeira and Shu (2012), D'amoria and Iorio (2017), Scott and Bruce (1994) and Amabile (1988) state that firms heavily depend on human capital for the creation and application of new ideas. The involvement in research and development activities implies the continuous improvement in innovation activities. High-quality human capital can play prominent role in fostering individual innovation within firms.

Human capital-intensive firms are inevitable part of the global economic environment. Past research studies indicate that human-capital intensive firms tend to play more active role in economic activities. Human capital- intensive firms are very special since the most important asset of these firms is human capital. These firms are expected to provide remarkable incentives to suppliers of human capital. The operations of human capital-intensive firms are based on human capital. In the human capital- intensive firms, employees have high educational levels and professionalism in the workplace. Problem solving ability of human capital-intensive firms' employees in a volatile industry is a critically important ability to sustain growth and operational efficiency. Human capital is considered a key engine of well-functioning economy (Ahmed et al., 2011; Grossman and Helpman, 1991; Romer, 1986). Governments around the world spend huge amount of money to create high-quality human capital with the expectation of enhancing innovation capacity (Gelübcke, 2013). Human capital-intensive firms heavily rely on the loyalty of key employees. When key employees leave the firm, this human capital-intensive firm may face serious operational risks.

The accurate measurement of human capital increases the quality of financial statements. It is worth mentioning that the structure of capital has huge impacts on the firms' financial performance. Financial market participants such as creditors, investors and stockholders meticulously analyze firms' human capital structure when making investment decisions. Although the significance of human capital is constantly increasing, many firms still face problems in the measurement of human capital (Andrikopoulos, 2005; Nazari and Herremans, 2007).

In the global business climate, not all assets can be considered strategic assets. For instance, an equipment may be classified as an asset, yet it is not a strategic asset for the firm, since other firms can easily acquire or duplicate it. A strategic asset should enable firms to have sustainable competitive advantage in the economic environment (Flamholtz and Randle, 2012). Human capital is a strategic asset since it is difficult to imitate by other firms and provides sustainable competitive advantage over other firms in the same sector.

Human capital is one of the most debated issues in the knowledge-based economy. Human capital is viewed as a driving force for the competition. To remain competitive, more and more firms are investing in human capital. In the new economy, wealth is the outcome of the human capital. Human capital is heavily needed by firms to create sustainable wealth. Undoubtedly if the firm management manages knowledge efficiently, the quality of firm's human capital will soar up. Human capital is considered the most significant capital a firm can have in the current business climate in which innovation technology and knowledge play prominent roles in the business success. García et al. (2005) defined intellectual capital as knowledge, human property or experience that can increase shareholders' wealth. Intellectual capital is divided into three parts as follows.

- Structural capital
- Relational capital
- Human capital

Structural capital is one of the critical elements of intellectual capital. Structural capital can be considered an asset or capital, it depends on how financial market participants evaluate the performance of firm's structural capital. The list of clients, any useful knowledge created by employees, organizational principles adopted by the firm and know-how research are among the examples of structural capital.

Dyer and Singh (1998) defines relational capital as a resource created by the firm's social network processes. In other words, relational capital refers to relationships established among firms and it is considered the extension of human capital. An effective relational capital is one of the important keys to long-term business success.

Although human capital significantly contributes to the business success, interestingly little attention has been paid to the reporting of human capital. Flamholtz et al. (2012) stated that human resources are vital component of firms' intangible assets. There have been massive efforts to value human capital financially.

With the advent of rapid globalization, multiple measures have been introduced to value human capital. Lev and Schwartz (1971) state that the total amount of human capital can be calculated as the present value of an employee's future earnings. This book chapter also discusses the different measures for human capital. Bullen and Eyler (2010) stated that human resource accounting may provide important information for firms' management in making long-run strategic decisions.

The accounting for human capital is very new field in the accounting science. This book chapter seeks to discuss the nature and objectives of human capital, the evolution of human capital accounting and current accounting challenges toward human capital. Past experiences prove that human capital is significantly related with knowledge, experience and innovation. The accounting for human capital is highly complex issue. All factors that contribute to the development of human capital should be meticulously considered by firms' management. The results of the book chapter may invigorate the research in the area of human resource accounting.

The list of the most valuable firms in the global economic environment enables us to understand the significance of knowledge. These firms share a common trait, human capital can significantly increase the effectiveness of these firms' production process. In these firms, human beings play a vital role in the accumulation of capital, thus the operations of these firms are human capital intensive. The financial statements of these firms indicate that these firms have higher amounts of intangible assets such as patent, software, trademark, research and development than other firms.

THE NATURE OF HUMAN RESOURCE ACCOUNTING

Stakeholder theory states that all stakeholders of the firms have an indisputable right to have information regarding how the firm activities influence their decision-making process even if these firm activities have no impact on the firm survival (Deegan, 2000). Effective investment decisions strongly depend on the availability of high quality information. Human resource accounting has emerged to meet demands of firms that have difficulty in measuring and reporting human capital. Accounting standard setting bodies such as International Accounting Standards Board (IASB) and Financial Accounting Standards Board (FASB) have significant efforts for accounting treatment of human capital. Generally speaking, human capital issues were only considered in internal control mechanisms. As a result, financial market participants cannot clearly comprehend firms' human capital structures. A systematic and well-established academic activity for human capital began in the early 1960s.

According to the traditional bookkeeping, intangible assets primarily created by human capital are reported in the firm's financial statements yet human capital cannot be reported in the firm's financial statements. For the last few decades, firms have been encouraged to disclose human capital information in their annual operating reports. With the advent of globalization and technological development, the measurement and reporting of human capital grab the attention of financial market participants. In a highly competitive economic environment, investors are more willing to invest in the stocks of firms with better human capital. Chen et al. (2005) analyze the relationship between human capital and financial performance. They concluded that firms that have better human capital efficiency show higher profitability and earnings growth.

Firms may face various challenges during the implementation of human resource accounting. The disclosure of human resource accounting information may provide vital insights into the firms' competitors or even could cause negative image in the eyes of stakeholders. Bureaucratic factors may deter the development of human resource accounting. Jasrotia (2004) claim that low level of acceptance and awareness of human resource accounting significantly deter the progress in this field. It is worth mentioning that free mobility of firms' employees is one of the risks that threat the efficiency of human resource accounting. Even though human capital has great importance in the business world, human beings are not recognized as assets by tax laws around the world. In addition to these challenges, a well-established and globally accepted method for the accurately measuring human capital has not yet been established.

Stewart (1999), Edvinsson and Malone (1997) claim that intangible asset is the most important asset of successful firms operating in a highly competitive economic environment. All human capital theories claim that firms, country economies and individuals can enhance financial and non-financial performance by investing in education. Solow (1956) and Mankiw et al. (1992) support the assertion that competitive capability and sustainable economic growth largely depend on technological progress created by human capital.

Möller et al. (2011) state that human capital cannot solely create financial value, firstly human capital should interact with the firm's financial and physical assets. The nature of human capital has been carefully investigated in prior research studies. Schultz (1961) and Becker (1975) state that just like physical capital, human capital is one of the primary production factors and provides important benefits to firms and society. Bartel (1991) investigated the impacts of human capital investment on productivity growth. He found that human capital investment positively influences productivity growth in firms. Bontis (1999) claimed that human capital is critically important for firms since it is a primary source of innovation and entrepreneurship.

Hansson (2004) analyzed the impacts of human capital on market value and stock returns using financial statement data of firms listed on Stockholm stock exchange. The results of empirical analysis indicate that human capital positively influences stock returns and market value in the long-run and firms that rely more on human capital than physical assets generate larger amounts of positive cash flow.

Flamholtz (1976) analyzed the impacts of human resource accounting information on firms' management decisions. He concluded that the management of firms and external parties such as creditors, investors and government agencies need information provided by human resource accounting. Additionally, he claimed that information provided by human resource accounting significantly increases the quality of investment decisions. Falmholtz et al. (2002) stated that academic research studies on human resource accounting began in 1960s. He explained the evolutionary process of human resource accounting as follows.

1960-1967: Primary concepts of human resources accounting were derived from other business sciences such as management, organizational behavior and theory.

1967-1971: During this era, there was a huge need for human resource accounting. A number of methods and models were developed to assess and manage human capital of firms.

1971-1976: In this period, there was a growing interest in human resource accounting. Firms faced serious problems in the application of human resource accounting.

1976-1980: The methods and models used in human resource accounting were heavily criticized. Academic interest on human resource accounting was decreased.

1980-Until Now: After 1980, intellectual capital has played a more critical role in the operations of firms and earning power of firms has been more dependent on human capital than other assets. Thus, firms have paid close attention to human resource accounting.

Oweyo (2013) conducted a content analysis of financial statements of twelve firms operating in Nigeria. He found that human resource accounting disclosure index of financial firms is significantly higher than that of manufacturing firms. He also note that firms should consider the valuation models for human resources to enhance financial statements disclosures. Firm size measured by total assets and total sales revenue are important factors affecting voluntary reporting (Gray et al., 1995).

Human resource manager should pay enough attention to human resource accounting concepts.

Uden et al. (2014) investigate the impacts of human capital investments on the innovation at the firm. The empirical data is collected from the firms operating in Uganda, Tanzania and Kenya. They found that firms that invest in human capital are more likely to adopt innovative production process compared to firms that do not invest in human capital.

Vomberg et al. (2015) investigated the joint effects of human capital and brand equity in enhancing firm value. By using a sample that includes 211 firms between 2002 and 2009, they conclude that brand equity has strong positive impacts on firm value, however human capital has no direct effect on firm value. They also claimed that human capital positively influences operational performance when employees use their knowledge and skills for the firm's objectives.

Teixeira and Lehmann (2014) analyzed the effects of foreign direct investment on human capital. By using the data collected via questionnaire sent to 703 firms operating in Portugal, they found that foreign direct investment significantly fosters a firm's human capital in terms of education and skills. Additionally, they state that the relationship between human capital and foreign ownership is highly complex. Slaughter (2002) put the forward that foreign multinational corporations increase the demand and supply of human capital. On one side, the operations of foreign multinational corporations are based on advanced technology (Slaughter, 2002), hence foreign multinational corporations demand high-skilled and educated employees to work along their technological assets.

The global business climate has tremendously changed over the last decades. The twenty-first century economy has been dominated by knowledge assets. Human capital has positive impacts on the creation of intangible assets such as patent, software, trademark, license, research and development. Financial capital has no feelings and emotions, whereas human capital have feelings and emotions.

The primary objectives of human resource accounting are as follows;

1. Identification of human capital aspects
2. Accurately measurement of cost and benefits of human capital to firms
3. Facilitation human capital planning
4. Analyzing of the impacts of human capital on return on investment
5. Effective utilization of human capital
6. Dissemination of reliable and relevant qualitative and quantitative information about human capital
7. Effectively analyzing the investment in human capital
8. Monitoring the use of human capital by the firm management
9. Helping firms' employees in enhancing their performance. Each employee can understand his contribution to the firm in relation to expenditure for him through human resource accounting.

American Association of Accountants (AAA) stated that h*uman resource* accounting is "a *process* of *identifying* and *measuring* data regarding *human capital* and *communicating* this accounting information to *financial market participants*". Human resource accounting enables firms to correctly measure recruiting, selection, hiring, placing, orientation and training costs.

There are two main costs in human resource accounting; acquisition costs and learning costs. Direct and indirect costs of recruitment, selection, hiring and placement are considered acquisition costs. Direct and indirect costs of orientation and on-the-job training are components of learning costs. Using human resource accounting, firms can identify high-performers, high-potentials and poor performers and take corrective actions to enhance the performance of poor performers. The main cost items used in human resource accounting are presented in Table 1 and 2 in more detail.

According to the accounting theory, firms' assets are divided into three categories, financial assets, tangible assets and intangible assets. Assets are held by firms in order to generate future economic benefits. Each type of assets serves different economic purposes. Workforce education, experience, research and development activities can be used as a proxy for firm' human capital.

Table 1. Acquisition costs

Type of Costs	Definitions
Recruitment	Emerges with the search for human capital. Recruiting costs include the cost of job boards such as Linkedin and Indeed, the salary of internal recruiters' salaries, recruitment agency fees and interviewing technology.
Selection	It includes the cost of reference checking, the organization of detailed tests and interviews.
Hiring	Emerges when the needed employee is selected. Hiring costs include travel, accommodation and similar costs.
Placing	After orientation program, placing process begins. It is associated with situating the newly hired employee in his or her job and includes various administrative costs incurred in the placement process.

Table 2. Learning costs

Type of Costs	Definitions
Orientation	It includes costs incurred in familiarizing the newly hired employee with firm policies, procedures, products and services offered by the firm.
Training	It includes costs of training programs such documents and equipments. The greatest cost in training activity is department director's lost time while training newly hired employee to do job accurately and effectively.

International Accounting Standards Board issues international accounting standards (IAS) and international financial reporting standards (IFRS). International financial reporting standards are used by more than 150 countries. Firms are expected to prepare their financial statements in accordance with International Financial Reporting Standards. International Accounting Standards Board published IAS 38 that outlines the financial reporting for intangible assets such as patent, trademark, copyright and license. It is worth mentioning that IAS 38 can be a useful guideline in the accounting treatment for human capital. There are two primary financial statements that disseminate information regarding intangibles; balance sheet and profit and loss statement.

Items reported in balance sheet

- Capitalized research and development costs
- Internally generated intangible assets
- Intangible assets from other business parties

Items reported in profit and loss statements

- Sale, general and administrative expenses
- Research and development expenses
- Wage and salary expenses

Items reported in notes to financial statements

- Accounting treatment method for research and development costs
- Detailed explanation of the nature of intangible assets

Intangible assets are reported as long-term assets. IAS 38 defines intangible assets as ‘‘an identifiable non-monetary asset without physical substance’’. Unfortunately tax laws around the business world treat all expenditures related with human resources as expenses rather than assets. IAS 30 Disclosures in the Financial Statements of Banks and Similar Financial Institutions encourages firms operating in the financial industry to adopt human resource accounting in order to provide fair and reliable disclosure of firms' financial position and performance. The adoption IFRS increases the transparency of firms' financial statements and decreases the uncertainties and accounting irregularities. The quality of financial information can be increased by well–established mechanisms that can mitigate information asymmetry and accounting irregularities.

Lack of a reliable and accurate valuation model in human resources discourages accounting standard setting bodies to develop a specific standard that effectively outlines the human resource accounting. The following information disclosed by human resource accounting can be used by the firm management in the evaluation of human capital efficiency.

- The amount of shareholders' wealth generated per employee
- The average salary and wage for each employee
- Employee turnover rate
- Absenteeism rates among employee
- The ratio of salary and wage paid to employee to the corporate earnings

There are some limitations in financial statements without human capital. In traditional accounting, the investments in human capital are recorded as expenses rather than assets. This results in distorted profit and loss statement. Moreover, the balance sheet of the firm is distorted since total assets do not contain human assets. Traditional accounting treats money spent by a firm's management to create human capital as an expense, despite these expenses are incurred with the aim of generating future economic benefits. Under traditional accounting practices, a firm that invests into human capital to improve the earning power reports lower net income. Therefore, the firm investing in human capital may appear to have financial problems when in fact the firm has stable financial performance and position.

Table 3 and 4 illustrate how income statement and balance sheet of Mediterranean appear under traditional and human resource accounting. Mediterranean Corporation operates in the steel industry. Historical financial statements indicate that Mediterranean Corporation has a stable earnings growth rate. Mediterranean Corporation expected tremendous business growth in the next years and therefore it has substantially invested in human capital. Mediterranean Corporation has incurred the following costs.

- **Recruitment Costs:** $30,000
- **Selection Costs:** $30,000
- **Orientation Costs:** $ 10,000
- **Training Costs:** $90,000

Mediterranean Corporation estimated that recruitment costs, selection costs, orientation costs and training costs have a useful life of ten years. Mediterranean Corporation uses straight-line method for the amortization of human assets. The amortization expense for human resources is $16,000 during the useful life. Under traditional accounting, all of these investments in human capital are reported as expenses for the current year. On the other hand, all of these investments in human capital are capitalized and will be amortized over their useful life under human resource accounting. Therefore, if Mediterranean Corporation uses human resource accounting, it would report a higher net profit. Table 4 illustrates how Mediterranean Corporation's balance sheet would appear under traditional and human resource accounting. Balance sheet shows investment in human resource is $144,000. According to table 4, Mediterranean Corporation's total amount of assets increases when human resource accounting is used. In the traditional accounting, Mediterranean Corporation expenses employee costs immediately, thus total assets of Mediterranean Corporation are understated.

MEASUREMENT METHODS IN HUMAN RESOURCE ACCOUNTING

Using human resource accounting, firms can calculate the economic value of human capital. Objectivity principle plays a key role in the calculation of present value of human capital. Firms are motivated by financial reporting standard setting bodies to measure their human capital and provide structured information related with human capital to the financial markets that can improve the perceptions of

Table 3. Income statement of mediterranean corporation for the year ending December 31, 201X

Accounts	Traditional Accounting	Human Resource Accounting
Gross Sales Reveneu	$2,250,000	$2,250,000
Sales Discounts	150,000	150,000
Sales Returns and Allowances	100,000	100,000
Net Sales Reveneu	2,000,000	2,000,000
Total Expenses (Excluding depreciation and amortization)	1,660,000	1,500,000
Depreciation andAmortization Expenses	N/A	16,000
Earnings before Taxes	340,000	484,000
Corporate Tax (20%)	68,000	96,800
Net Income After Corporate Tax	**272,000**	**387,200**

Table 4. Balance sheet of Mediterranean corporation for the year ending December 31, 201X

Accounts	Traditional Accounting	Human Resource Accounting
Current Assets	2,000,000	2,000,000
Cash	1,500,000	1,500,000
Notes Receivable	260,000	260,000
Inventories	200,000	200,000
Supplies	40,000	40,000
Long-Term Assets	150,000	294,000
Land	100,000	100,000
Patent	50,000	50,000
Human Resource Investments, net*	N/A	144,000
Total Assets	2,150,000	2,294,000

the firm. An asset is an economic resource that should be fully controlled by the business entity and the cost of an asset at the time of acquisition should be accurately measurable. According to this definition, human capital should satisfy four criteria to be recognized as an asset (Miller, 1996).

Criteria 1: Human capital should be an economic resource that will provide future economic benefits to the firm.

Criteria 2: It is essential that human capital should be fully controlled and tracked by the firm when acquired.
Criteria 3: The acquisition cost of human capital should be fairly determined.
Criteria 4: Financial market participants should recognize the output of human capital.

Many firms are facing serious problems in the management of human capital due to difficulties in measuring human capital in the current business climate. There are three primary methods used in the human resource accounting. Each method has its own advantages and limitations. The correctly use of these methods is expected to boost the quality of firms' financial statements. These methods are as follows;

- Historical Cost Method
- Replacement Cost Method
- Opportunity Cost Method
- Standard Cost Method

According to historical cost method, the cost of recruiting, selection, hiring, placement, orientation and training are capitalized and amortized over employees' useful life. Historical cost method is easy to use for the accounting treatment of human resources. The main criticism on historical cost method is that it fails to reflect current costs of recruiting, selection, hiring, placement, orientation and training on the firms' financial statements.

Replacement costs are dynamic and can change according to the market conditions. Replacement cost method considers all type of costs such as recruiting, selection, hiring, placement, orientation and training incurred in replacing human assets. Policymakers and economists claim that replacement cost method yields more relevant results than historical cost method does. Replacement cost method enables firms to accurately reflect the current market value of firms' human assets.

Opportunity cost model, also called as competitive bidding model, is introduced to overcome the limitations of historical cost method and replacement cost method. Opportunity cost model is used to determine the value of human resources based on the best alternative use. Using opportunity cost model, firms can quantitatively plan, assess and improve their human resources.

Standard cost method is much easier than other measurements. According to standard cost, recruiting, selection, hiring, placement, orientation and training costs are determined annually. In this method, the firm management compares the standard costs with actual costs and conducts variances analysis. If there exists variance between standard cost and actual cost, firm management is expected to take corrective measures. Total standard costs are used to determine the value of human resources.

CONTENT ANALYSIS OF HUMAN RESOURCE ACCOUNTING DISCLOSURES BY TURKISH BANKS

The content of information disclosures by firms in their operating reports grabs the attention of academicians and financial market participants. Past research studies (Bontis, 2003; Brennan, 2001; Bozzolan et al., 2003) employ content analysis to derive and analyze information disclosed by firms in their annual operating reports and financial statements. Content analysis enables researchers to effectively, systematically and accurately analyze the information disclosed by firms (Guthrie and Parker, 1990). Guthrie et al. (2004) investigate the usefulness of content analysis in understanding intellectual capital reporting. They posit that content analysis is tremendously effective in investigating the trends in reporting of intellectual capital.

Content analysis is one of the most widely used research methods in the accounting science (Beattie, 2005). The objective of this section is to analyze human capital disclosures by banks operating in Turkey by using content analysis. Content analysis is employed to capture information associated with human capital in operating reports and financial statements of sampled banks between 2010 and 2017.

The sample includes twelve banks listed on Borsa Istanbul. Operating reports and financial statements of sampled banks are available at the website of public disclosure platform and Borsa Istanbul. Operating reports can provide important opportunity for human capital reporting. Firms are not required to follow financial reporting standards in the preparation of operating reports. A total of 288 operating reports for the period between 2010 and 2017 are used in the content analysis. The list of sample banks is listed as shown in Table 5.

Eleven categories of human capital disclosures are used in the content analysis. These measures are taken from previous studies (Ridhuan and Ahmed, 2016; Abeysekera, 2007; Abeysekera and Guthrie, 2004). In the content analysis, key words related with human capital disclosures are searched in the operating reports of sample banks. Table 6 presents the frequency distribution of human capital disclosure categories between 2010 and 2017.

According to Table 6, firm's philosophy about human capital is the most popular disclosed information with a frequency of 240, followed by directors' year of experience (227) and directors' skills (216). Moreover, directors' expertise, career development and recruitment policy also attained significance with a frequency of 200, 194 and 186 respectively. The least reported information about human capital

Table 5. Sample banks

Name	Origin
Akbank T.A.Ş.	Domestic
Albaraka Turk Katılım Bankası A.Ş.	Foreign
Denizbank A.Ş.	Foreign
ICBC Turkey A.Ş.	Foreign
Finansbank A.Ş.	Foreign
Şekerbank A.Ş.	Foreign
Türkiye Garanti Bankası A.Ş.	Foreign
Türkiye Halkbank A.Ş.	Domestic
Türkiye İş Bankası A.Ş.	Domestic
Türkiye Vakıflar Bank A.Ş.	Domestic
Türkiye Yapı Kredi Bank A.Ş.	Domestic
Türkiye Sınai Kalkınma Bankası A.Ş.	Domestic

Table 6. The distribution of human capital disclosures between 2010 and 2017

The Categories of Human Capital Disclosures	Frequency	Percentages
Firm's philosophy about human capital	240	14.1%
Directors' year of experience	227	13.3%
Directors' skills	216	12.7%
Directors' expertise	200	11.7%
Career development	194	11.4%
Recruitment policy	186	10.9%
Training programs	140	8.2%
Orientation programs	110	6.4%
Educational background of human capital	78	4.5%
Employment health insurance benefits	64	3.7%
Employee compensation plan	43	2.5%
Total	1698	100

in the operating reports of banks are educational background of human capital (78), employment health insurance benefits (64) and employee compensation plan (43).

Table 7 presents the number of disclosures per bank between 2010 and 2017. Garanti Bank is the top discloser with 218 disclosures followed by İş Bankası (212). ICBC Turkey provided the least disclosure in human resource. Generally speaking, firms with higher asset volume report a higher number of human resource disclosures. Additionally, Table 7 indicates that the domestic banks are top disclosers in the sample.

Figure 1 shows the frequency of human capital disclosures for years since 2010. Graph shows that in 2010 the frequency of human capital disclosures by sample banks is 84 and in 2011 the frequency of human capital disclosures by sample banks rose to 113. After 2013, the frequency of human capital disclosures by sample banks slightly increased and in 2017 the frequency of human capital disclosures by sample banks reached to 267. The graph reveals that the increases in the number of human capital disclosures confirm the increasing awareness of sample banks to value their human capital.

CONCLUSION

In this book chapter, it is aimed to analyze various aspects of human resource accounting. Human resources enable firms to have sustainable competitive advantages in the economic environment. As the world economy is becoming much more globalized than before, financial market participants want to analyze firms from different perspectives.

Table 7. The number of human resource disclosure by banks

No	Name of Bank	Frequency
1	Türkiye Garanti Bankası A.Ş.	218
2	Türkiye İş Bankası A.Ş.	212
3	Türkiye Yapı Kredi Bank A.Ş.	201
4	Akbank T.A.Ş.	194
5	Türkiye Halkbank A.Ş.	178
6	Türkiye Vakıflar Bank A.Ş.	167
7	Denizbank A.Ş.	116
8	Şekerbank A.Ş.	113
9	Finansbank A.Ş.	102
10	Albaraka Turk Katılım Bankası A.Ş.	87
11	Türkiye Sınai Kalkınma Bankası A.Ş.	84
12	ICBC Turkey A.Ş.	26
	Total	1698

Figure 1. Human capital disclosure frequency, 2010-2018

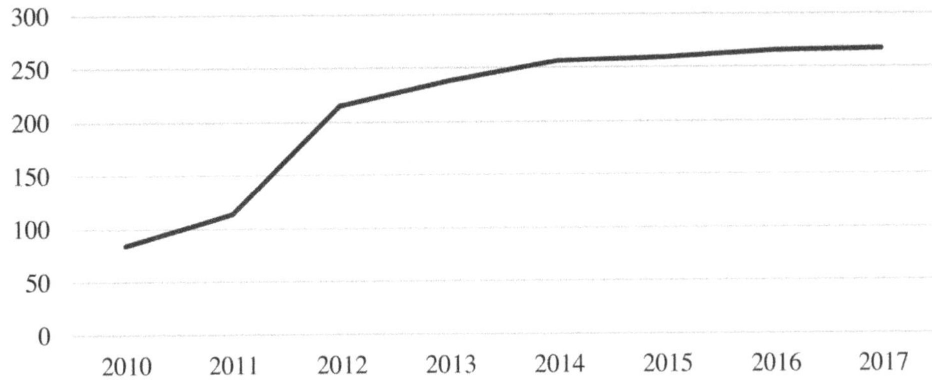

In the current business climate, human capital plays a prominent role in the business success. The importance of human capital has tremendously increased over recent decades. Past research studies demonstrate that human capital investment is a key to development of strategic assets and innovation. Organizational systems, culture, strategies, policies and skills developed to meet the expectations of stakeholders are elements of internal capital. Human capital is one of the internal capital owned by firms. Human resource accounting is one of the newest fields in the accounting science. Accounting standard setting bodies are expected to establish standards that outline the accounting treatment for human resources.

Human capital disclosures enable financial market participants to assess the efficiency of human capital in firms operations. In the current business environment, there are few methods that can correctly measure the total value of human capital. Measurements of human resource accounting are discussed in the study. It should be emphasized that each measurement method has its own advantages and disadvantages. Thus, firms should select the appropriate measurement method according to their organizational structure and industry. Current accounting practices treat all employee costs, including recruiting, selection, hiring, placing, orientation and training as expenses.

Content analysis that enables us to investigate the frequency and type of human capital disclosures is used as a research method in this study. A total of 288 operating reports of banks listed on Borsa Istanbul for the period between 2010 and 2017 are used in the content analysis. The results of content analysis indicate that the most reported category in human capital disclosure is firm's philosophy about human capital followed by directors' year of experience. The least reported category is employee compensation plan. The results of content analysis reveal that there is an increasing trend in human capital disclosure between the period of 2010 and 2017.

However, the firms operating in Turkey should take more actions that enhances human capital disclosures.

Future research studies are strongly required to validate the results of the content analysis. Future research studies could comprehensively examine the impacts of human resource accounting on the decisions of financial market participants across countries. Additionally, future research studies can be devoted to explore the possible problems in accounting treatment of human capital.

REFERENCES

Abeysekera, I. (2007). Intellectual capital reporting between a developing and developed nation. *Journal of Intellectual Capital*, *8*(2), 329–345. doi:10.1108/14691930710742871

Abeysekera, I., & Guthrie, J. (2004). Human capital reporting in a developing nation. *The British Accounting Review*, *36*(3), 251–268. doi:10.1016/j.bar.2004.03.004

Ahmed, A. D., Cheng, E., & Messinis, G. (2011). The role of exports, FDI and imports indevelopment: Evidence from Sub-Saharan African countries. *Applied Economics*, *43*(26), 3719–3731. doi:10.1080/00036841003705303

Amabile, T. M. (1988). A model of creativity and innovation in organizations. *Research in Organizational Behavior*, *10*(1), 123–167.

Andrikopoulos, A. (2005). Using intellectual capital statements to determine value drivers and priorities for organizational change: A portfolio selection approach. *Knowledge Management Research and Practice*, *3*(3), 166–172. doi:10.1057/palgrave.kmrp.8500065

Asimakou, T. (2009). *Innovation, knowledge and power in organizations*. London: Routledge.

Bartel, A. (1991). *Formal Employee Training Programs and their Impact on Labour Productivity: Evidence From A Human Resources Survey*. Working Paper Draft, 1-51.

Beattie, V. (2005). Moving the financial accounting research front forward: The UK contribution. *The British Accounting Review*, *37*(1), 85–114. doi:10.1016/j.bar.2004.09.004

Becker, G. (1975). *Human Capital*. Chicago: Chicago University Press.

Bontis, N. (1999). Managing organizational knowledge by diagnosing intellectual capital: Framing and advancing the state of the field. *International Journal of Technology Management, 18*(5), 433–462. doi:10.1504/IJTM.1999.002780

Bontis, N. (2003). Intellectual capital disclosure in Canadian corporations. *Journal of Human Resource Costing & Accounting*, *7*(1), 9–20. doi:10.1108/eb029076

Bozzolan, S., Favotto, F., & Ricceri, F. (2003). Italian annual intellectual capital disclosure: An empirical analysis. *Journal of Intellectual Capital*, *4*(4), 543–558. doi:10.1108/14691930310504554

Brennan, N. (2001). Reporting intellectual capital in annual reports: Evidence from Ireland. *Accounting, Auditing & Accountability Journal*, *14*(4), 423–436. doi:10.1108/09513570110403443

Bullen, M. L., & Eyler, K. A. (2010). Human resource accounting and international developments: Implications for measurement of human capital. *Journal of International Business and Cultural Studies*, *3*, 1–16.

Carel, B. (2010). The Knowledge Society: Refounding the Socius. In Organizational, Business, and Technological Aspects of the Knowledge Society: Third World Summit on the Knowledge Society (pp. 266-277). Springer.

Carlucci, D., Marr, B., & Schiuma, G. (2004). The knowledge value chain: How intellectual capital impacts on business performance. *International Journal of Technology Management*, *27*(6-7), 575–590. doi:10.1504/IJTM.2004.004903

Chen, M. C., Cheng, S. J., & Hwang, Y. (2005). An empirical investigation of the relationship between intellectual capital and firms' market value and financial performance. *Journal of Intellectual Capital*, *6*(2), 159–176. doi:10.1108/14691930510592771

D'amore, R., Iorio, R., & Lubrano Lavadera, G. (2017). Exploring the Relationship between Human Capital and Innovation at the Firm Level: A study on a Sample of European Firms (No. 144). CELPE-Centre of Labour Economics and Economic Policy, University of Salerno, Italy.

Dakhli, M., & De Clercq, D. (2004). Human capital, social capital, and innovation: A multi-country study. *Entrepreneurship and Regional Development*, *16*(2), 107–128. doi:10.1080/08985620410001677835

Deegan, C. (2000). *Financial Accounting Theory*. Sydney, Australia: McGraw-Hill Publishing.

Dyer, J. H., & Singh, H. (1998). The relational view: Cooperative strategy and sources of interorganizational competitive advantage. *Academy of Management Review, 23*(4), 660–679. doi:10.5465/amr.1998.1255632

Edvinsson, L., & Malone, M. S. (1997). *Intellectual capital—realizing your company's true value by finding its hidden roots*. New York, NY: Harper Business.

Flamholtz, E. (1976). The impact of human resource valuation on management decisions: A laboratory experiment. *Accounting, Organizations and Society, 1*(2-3), 153–165. doi:10.1016/0361-3682(76)90019-2

Flamholtz, E. G., Bullen, M. L., & Hua, W. (2002). Human resource accounting: A historical perspective and future implications. *Management Decision, 40*(10), 947–954. doi:10.1108/00251740210452818

Flamholtz, E. G., & Randle, Y. (2012). Corporate culture, business models, competitive advantage, strategic assets and the bottom line: Theoretical and measurement issues. *Journal of Human Resource Costing & Accounting, 16*(2), 76–94. doi:10.1108/14013381211284227

García-Meca, E., Parra, I., Larrán, M., & Martínez, I. (2005). The explanatory factors of human capital disclosure to financial analysts. *European Accounting Review, 14*(1), 63–94. doi:10.1080/0963818042000279713

Gelübcke, J. P. (2013). The performance of foreign affiliates in German manufacturing: Evidence from a new database. *Review of World Economics, 149*(1), 151–182. doi:10.100710290-012-0142-1

Gray, R., Kouhy, R., & Lavers, S. (1995). Corporate social and environmental reporting: A review of the literature and a longitudinal study of UK disclosure. *Accounting, Auditing & Accountability Journal, 8*(2), 47–77. doi:10.1108/09513579510146996

Grossman, G., & Helpman, E. (1991). *Innovation and Growth in the Global Economy*. London: MIT Press.

Guthrie, J., & Parker, L. D. (1990). Corporate social disclosure practice: A comparative international analysis. *Advances in Public Interest Accounting, 3*(1), 159–175.

Guthrie, J., Petty, R., Yongvanich, K., & Ricceri, F. (2004). Using content analysis as a research method to inquire into intellectual capital reporting. *Journal of Intellectual Capital, 5*(2), 282–293. doi:10.1108/14691930410533704

Hansson, B. (2004). Human capital and stock returns: Is the value premium an approximation for return on human capital? *Journal of Business Finance & Accounting, 31*(3-4), 333–358. doi:10.1111/j.0306-686X.2004.00542.x

Jasrotia, P. (2004). *The Need for Human Resource Accounting*. Retrieved from http://www.itpeopleindia.com/20021216/cover.shtml

Lev, B., & Schwartz, A. (1971). On the use of the economic concept of human capital in financial statements. *The Accounting Review*, *46*(1), 103–112.

Malhotra, Y. (1998). Knowledge management for the new world of business. *Asian Strategy Leadership Institute Review, 6*.

Mankiw, N. G., Romer, D., & Weil, D. N. (1992). A contribution to the empirics of economic growth. *The Quarterly Journal of Economics*, *107*(2), 407–437. doi:10.2307/2118477

Miller, R. (1996). *Measuring What People Know. Human Capital Accounting for the Knowledge Economy*. Washington, DC: OECD Publications and Information Center.

Minai, M. H. (2016). Leading for innovation. In Human Capital and Innovation: Examining the Role of Globalization (pp. 39-72). Palgrave Macmillan.

Möller, K., Gamerschlag, R., & Guenther, F. (2011). Determinants and effects of human capital reporting and controlling. *Journal of Management Control*, *22*(3), 311–333. doi:10.100700187-011-0138-3

Nazari, J. A., & Herremans, I. M. (2007). Extended VAIC model: Measuring intellectual capital components. *Journal of Intellectual Capital*, *8*(4), 595–609. doi:10.1108/14691930710830774

Oyewo, B. M. (2013). Comparative analyses of human resources accounting disclosure practices in Nigerian financial service and manufacturing companies. *IOSR Journal of Humanities and Social Science*, *16*(1), 20–26. doi:10.9790/0837-1612026

Rahman, M. R. C. A., & Ahmed, R. M. (2016). Disclosure of Human Capital Information in Annual Reports: A Case of Malaysian Banking and Financial Institution Sector. *International Journal of Business*, *1*(1), 83–104.

Romer, P. (1986). Increasing returns and long-run growth. *Journal of Political Economy*, *94*(5), 1002–1037. doi:10.1086/261420

Schultz, T. W. (1961). Investment in Human Capital. *The American Economic Review*, *51*(1), 1–17.

Scott, S. G., & Bruce, R. A. (1994). Determinants of innovative behavior: A path model of individual innovation in the workplace. *Academy of Management Journal*, *37*(3), 580–607.

Slaughter, M. J. (2002). *Does Inward Foreign Direct Investment Contribute to Skill Upgrading in Developing Countries?* SCEPA Working Paper No. 2002-08. New York, NY: Schwartz Center for Economic Policy Analysis, New School University.

Solow, R. M. (1956). A contribution to the theory of economic growth. *The Quarterly Journal of Economics*, *70*(1), 65–94. doi:10.2307/1884513

Stewart, T. A. (1999). *Intellectual capital—the new wealth of organizations.* New York, NY: Crown Business.

Tapp, L. (1997). Emerging triumphant. *Business Quarterly*, *61*(3).

Teixeira, A. A., & Shu, L. (2012). The level of human capital in innovative firms located in China. Is foreign capital relevant? *Journal of the Asia Pacific Economy*, *17*(2), 343–360. doi:10.1080/13547860.2012.668095

Teixeira, A. A., & Tavares-Lehmann, A. T. (2014). Human capital intensity in technology-based firms located in Portugal: Does foreign ownership matter? *Research Policy*, *43*(4), 737–748. doi:10.1016/j.respol.2014.01.001

Van Uden, A., Knoben, J., & Vermeulen, P. (2014). *Human capital and innovation in developing countries: A firm level study.* Radboud University.

Vomberg, A., Homburg, C., & Bornemann, T. (2015). Talented people and strong brands: The contribution of human capital and brand equity to firm value. *Strategic Management Journal*, *36*(13), 2122–2131. doi:10.1002mj.2328

Chapter 6
How Are Innovation, Growth, and HCIF Affected by Natural Resources?

Seyed Mohammad Amir Mousavi
National Iranian Oil Refining and Distribution Company, Iran & Université Côte d'Azur, France

ABSTRACT

This chapter demystifies in detail the transmission mechanisms of how the natural resource industry (NRI) harms the growth and innovation in human capital-intensive firms (HCIF). Two important phenomena were studied qualitatively: rent seeking (RS) and Dutch disease (DD) which result from the abundance of natural resources (NR). RS pushes down the return of production and DD results in uncompetitive production. The empirical results for a cross-section of 81 countries show a significant evidence that with recent data, oil rent hinders human capital as a proxy for innovation. Meanwhile, the indicators of resource governance show a significant and positive impact on human capital accumulation. A growing amount of literature focuses on growth and human capital, while this chapter emphasizes HCIF and innovation, elaborating the transmission mechanisms of underperforming economic growth through the hindrance of innovation in the firms and awkwardness of HC.

DOI: 10.4018/978-1-5225-7426-2.ch006

INTRODUCTION

Although a growing body of literature studies the HCIF boundary and governance, few try to focus on these firms when the abundance of NRs is involved in the economy. This chapter tries to highlight this gap, elaborating on the relationships between the two perspectives. Natural resources are said to be detrimental to development if there are no benefits from well-established institutions and good governance (Blanco, 2012; Kaufmann, Kraay, & Mastruzzi, 2009; Kim, 2017). This well-known phenomenon is called the *resource curse* and has been the focus of a growing number of researchers since the early 20th century. This theory states that countries with an abundance of NRs or a dependence on them show little economic growth compared to their counterparts with scarce natural resources. On the contrary, a few researchers criticize the destructive effects of resources on human capital accumulation. (Shao & Yang, 2014; Weber, 2014; Stijns, 2006; Davis, 1995; Kim & Lin, 2017). Moreover, the main body of literature in this field explores the link between NRA and economic growth, whereas a few studies show the effect of NRA on growth through human capital (HC) and innovation (Mousavi, Ben Youssef, & Nouri, 2017).

Economic growth is dependent on several factors including capital stock. Capital is divided into physical and human capital and the latter is considered of the utmost importance by Schultz (as cited in Ross, 2001). As a labor force is likely to work more efficiently with better physical capital— more efficient machinery, better tools, and raw material—it is analogously plausible to do a better job if the labor force is also healthy and has superior knowledge and skills—assuming the same production input consumption.

The firms, however, do not provide all the requirements regarding innovation and HC intangible assets within their boundaries. Accordingly, one requirement for a better engagement in production is the education provided by the government (Papyrakis & Gerlagh, 2007; Rosser 2006). Even learning by doing might have positive results if the laborers or employees already have the prerequisite knowledge and skills. States usually invest in human capital accumulation. Accordingly, the countries—in terms of economic growth and evidently, human development— are ranked differently regarding their level of HC development in public and private sectors.

According to the literature, HC reinforces innovation (Badinger & Tondl, 2003; D'Este, Rentocchini, & Vega-Jurado, 2014; Dakhli & Clercq, 2004; Marvel & Lumpkin, 2007). Furthermore, if one looks more precisely at HC and divides it into a macro public-level and micro firm-level, innovation could be considered mostly related to the latter. Although the public provision of HC—like education is essential, however, the innovation dynamics in HCIF plays a more important role in completing the chain of creating innovation.

This chapter sheds some light on the transmission mechanism of NR's impact on HC, innovation, and growth. This chapter will mostly focus on the Rent Seeking (RS) and Dutch Disease (DD) concepts and investigate how the lack of innovation in HCIF could influence economic growth. DD and RS refer to the undesirable impact of the NRA on the economy of one country; so the research question in this chapter is: under which circumstances do natural resources impact growth in a country and the human capital in the firms. Moreover, the effect of good governance on the human capital will be explored.

The rest of the chapter is organized as follows. First, broad definitions of the topic and the literature review will be discussed. Then the dynamics of RS and DD will be explained relating to the dynamics of innovation. In the empirical section, the methodology adopted to achieve the objectives of the chapter will be presented with explanations about results from the model estimation and the econometric interpretation. Finally, the policy implications of the results are discussed, followed by the conclusion.

BACKGROUND

While many scholars try to define HC, its notion remains vague or even ambiguous. The concept of HC refers to a complicated living being called a human. The author believes that it is debatable to cover all aspects of its being and its surroundings by the current proxy in the literature. Citing a poem by a Persian poet and philosopher Jalal al-Din Muhammad Balkhi (1258), HC resembles an elephant located in a dark room and the researcher touches only one part and tries to explain the whole concept. Therefore, sufficient margins of error should be kept when quantifying and interpreting it. Winter argues that *knowledge itself is nearly as ambiguous an idea as value or importance, and it has many guises* (as cited in Starbuck, 1992) In this regard, one may say that even the top-ranked developed countries or even firms in terms of HC are cutting edge only in a relative comparison with others, i.e. there may be more potential to discover.

In spite of this difficulty, investigating the literature allows scholars such as Ehrenberg to characterize HC as the skills and the knowledge of workers, often derived from education and training, which contribute to productivity (as cited in Ross, 2001). Moreover, Burton-Jones and Spender (2011) define HC as, *the skills, knowledge, and capabilities of the workforce of a firm, or of the population of a country, as well as the organizational arrangement and networks of relationship those people have formed that enables them to be more innovative and productive.* According to this definition, HC and innovation are closely related. In this regard, the definition of the HCIF is clear as the firms that their productivity is mostly based on the human capital.

In passing, according to the literature, it is crystal clear how much the stock of HC is vital for development. HC is the fourth factor of production (Burton-Jones & Spender, 2011) and strengthens the path towards economic and social development. Moreover, HC is the main part of people's income in developing countries more so than the influence of physical and natural capital (Auty, 2001). Put differently, the principle origin of sustainable economic growth is claimed to be technological development based on human capital and innovation—which is mainly inspired by education (Abramovitz, 1989; Becker, 1994; Easterlin, 1981; Lucas, 1988; Nelson & Phelps, 1966; Schultz, 1961). The rationale for this is obvious: the more people are healthy and skillful, the more they are likely to contribute to better and innovative production. The notion of HC is of great importance, insofar as in the resource curse theory, the endowment of NR per se is not considered as the main obstacle for economic growth except when it is accompanied by a low level of HC (Ross, 2001). Moreover, in certain cases, the HC may offset the adverse effect of NR on economic growth (Bravo-Ortega & De Gregorio, 2005).

Furthermore, it is very important to know the environment in which the firms are running. NR, as another factor of production, may point toward this circumstance. In the early stage of development, mainstream economists such as Viner (1952), Lewis (1955) and neoliberal economists, highlighted NRs as the lead engine of economic growth and development (Krueger, 1980; Balassa, 1980). These supportive points of view, however, stayed in the lead into the 1990s, when pioneering studies showed that the abundance of NRs could prone the sustainable development of a country compared with the economies with NR deficiency (Birdsall, Pinckney, & Sabot, 2000; Gylfason, 2001; Sachs &Warner, 1995). In other words, the economic growth of countries with an abundance of NRs has been lower in comparison with that of countries with a shortage in terms of NR (Daniele, 2011). This may affect the performance of the firms as well, in such an economy. As the example in figure 1 shows —the bar graph of the GDP per capita for different regions such as North America, European Union, Latin America, and the Middle East & North Africa (MENA) —there is a remarkable income drop when moving from left to write, i.e. the regions comprising the natural-resource-dependent economies (NRDEs) have a lower GDP per capita than the regions with economies less dependent on NR. Interestingly, economic historians such as de Ferranti, Perry, Lederman, and Maloney argue that US development *stemmed in large part from the country's playing to its strength-resource abundance in a large range of minerals-while heavily investing in knowledge accumulation in and around the resource sector* (as cited in Stijns, 2005). This shows that the resource curse could be considered a condition of the bedrock of human capital and knowledge.

Figure 1. GDP per capita, data for 2016 (constant 2010 in trillions US$)
Source: Author elaboration / Data: World Development Indicators

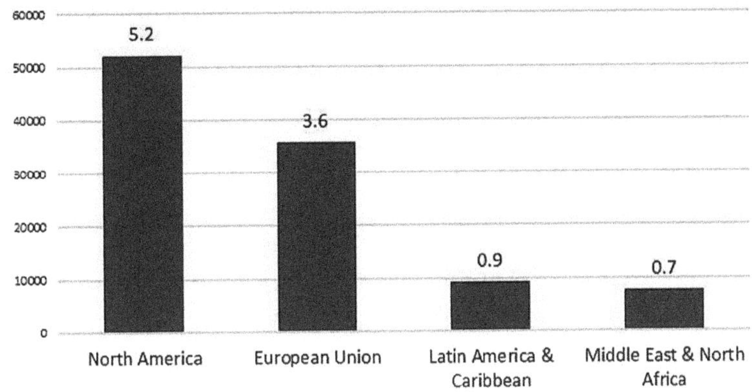

Accordingly, one should not put all the countries in the same basket. According to the institutional ambiance of an economy, one country may get affected by the abundance of NRs while the other economies may not only escape the malediction of resources but also use it optimally in favor of the firms for higher development and growth. Regarding governance, the literature on the resource curse has increasingly highlighted the key role of good governance in defining how resource abundance affects economic growth and human capital. There are two main contributions in the literature on this subject according to Blanco (2012). The first strand of literature argues the negative impact of NRs on institutions (Bulte, Damania, & Deacon, 2005; Isham, Woolcock, Pritchett, & Busby, 2005). Furthermore, as Philippot (2010) argues the impact would be more detrimental if the resources are centralized rather than diffused. On the other hand, the impact of natural resources on development and human capital is considered to be dependent on the type of institutions. Mehlum, Moene and Torvik (2006) who define *grabber-friendly* institutions versus *producer-friendly*, argue that for the latter, the production and rent-seeking are competing activities. However, for the former, they are complementary activities.

As Murphy, Shleifer and Vishny (1993) argue, the innovation in the firms flourishes in an economy that is removed from RS. Put differently, the more rigorous and uncontaminated the institution of an economy is, the more incentive there will be to create innovation within the firms. Accordingly, the HCIF will grow more when an economy has a better indicator of accountability, political stability and absence of violence, government effectiveness, regulatory quality, rule of law, and control of corruption (the Worldwide Governance Indicator (WGI) from World Bank). Alternatively, there are a few researchers who argue that the notion of good governance theory is mostly in favor of investors' investment and not for the law or corruption, per se. For example, Naderi (2011) argues that this theory —good governance— was proposed when the World Bank policies underperformed. He asserts that the concept of capitalism is behind the good governance theory and the critiques applied to capitalism apply to this theory as well.

MAIN FOCUS OF THE CHAPTER

In this section, the author explores two important phenomena which are both induced by NRA: the so-called Dutch Disease and Rent Seeking. The author considers the consequences of NRA on growth and innovation in HCIF.

Dutch Disease (DD)

Dutch disease (DD) is the term for a phenomenon that affects countries that are dependent on their NRA—especially on oil, natural gas (NG) and minerals. It was first observed in the Netherlands after that country discovered natural gas in the 1960s, with some paradoxical consequences like loose of the comparative advantage of manufacturing export. DD starts because oil, gas or minerals tend to bring windfall revenue into the country which gives rise to a strengthened currency, the so-called appreciation of the real exchange rate (RER). A huge field of gas or oil accounts for magnifying the export of the relevant products. This probably leads to the surplus of exports over imports — a trade surplus. Therefore, it causes an increase in demand for domestic currency since foreign purchasers need the domestic currency to pay for the oil and gas, which exerts a rising pressure on the exchange rate. This is illustrated in Figure 2.

For most exporters of petroleum products, such as OPEC, oil is traded in US dollars. In this case, the mechanism is different, but the result is the same; i.e. the huge amount of foreign currency enters the economy and, in the absence or malfunctioning of a sovereign wealth fund, the demand for foreign currency decreases. This finally results in the appreciation of RER.

From a consumer point of view, RER appreciation is beneficial because people can now afford more imported commodities more cheaply. Their money is more valuable — so-called hard currency — although, the currency is still the same inside the country, therefore, the problem arises when the firms find it more expensive to export goods and services. Concurrently, since they find it cheaper to import goods and services from abroad than to manufacture it domestically, there would be less incentive for production, leading those kinds of firms— that in normal condition could contribute to production— to shrivel up and the country becomes more and more dependent on one resource: the oil, gas or mineral.

Figure 2. Appreciation of domestic currency due to Dutch Disease
D represents the demand curve, S represents the supply curve, and EP act for the equilibrium point

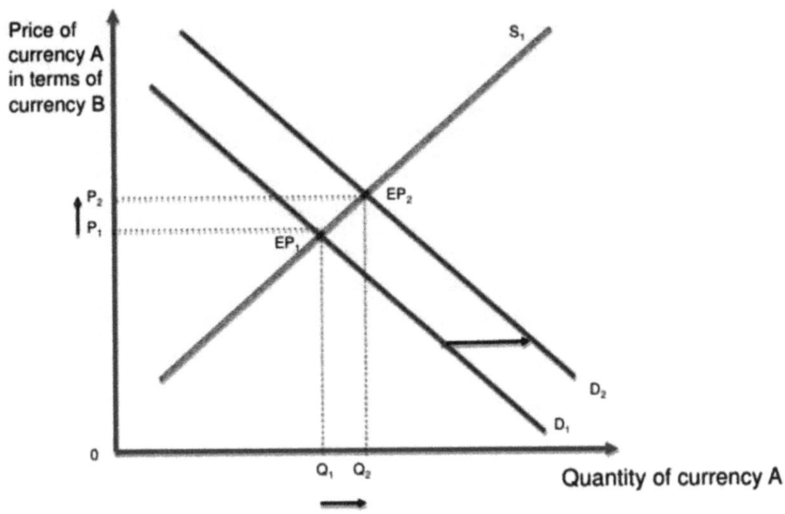

Figure 3. Patent applications, residents—the order of the regions in each year is the same order indicated above
Source: Author elaboration / Data: World Development Indicators

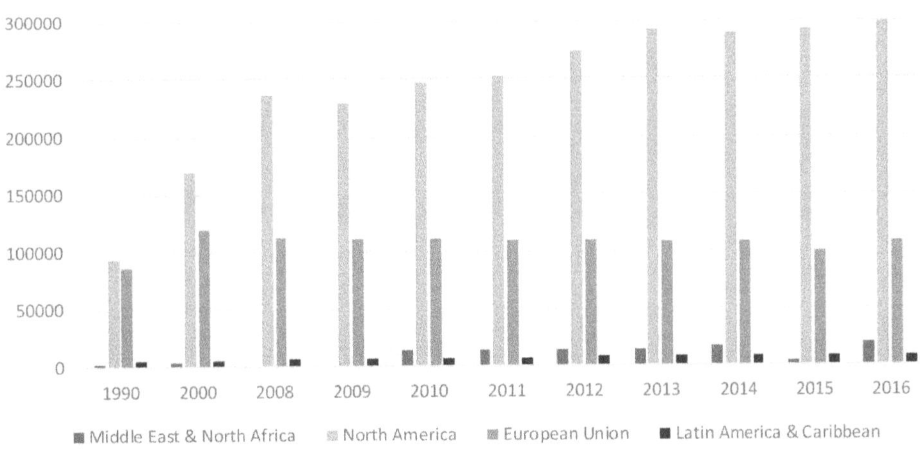

In this regard, the appreciation of RER which is caused by the massive NR-revenue contribution to the economy provides fewer opportunities for the production industries which are generally innovative-promoting ones compared with the NRIs that are usually extractive-based industries.[1] As a result, as the non-booming sector fails to be prosperous[2], the firms' goods and services are no longer competitive in the domestic and world market. Consequently, no incentive will remain for HCIF management and employees to create innovation within their boundaries. Figure 3 shows, for example, the patent applications for the same regions as in Figure 1. It is clear that there is a big difference in patent applications — as a proxy of innovation (Dakhli & De Clercq, 2004) — between the regions that are highly dependent on NR, demonstrating that the firms are remarkably underperforming in the creation of innovation, skills, and knowledge in the former types of economies.

Figure 4 comprehensively shows the mechanism of how DD impacts growth through innovation awkwardness and retardation of HC accumulation. Consequently, manufacturing would not be dynamic and competitive anymore. Moreover, considering the uncompetitive production sector, NRs per se, don't create many jobs to replace those that are lost (Stiglitz, 2004). Therefore, fewer people have jobs in manufacturing and more and more people try to find a way to get jobs in the NR sector even though corrupt or illegal means.

Figure 4. Dutch disease dynamics
Source: Author elaboration
** Direct deindustrialization: the transfer of labor from the lagging sector to the NRI*
*** Indirect deindustrialization: the shift from the lagging sector to the non-tradable sector*
 # The lagging sector: non-booming tradable sector e.g. manufacturing or agriculture

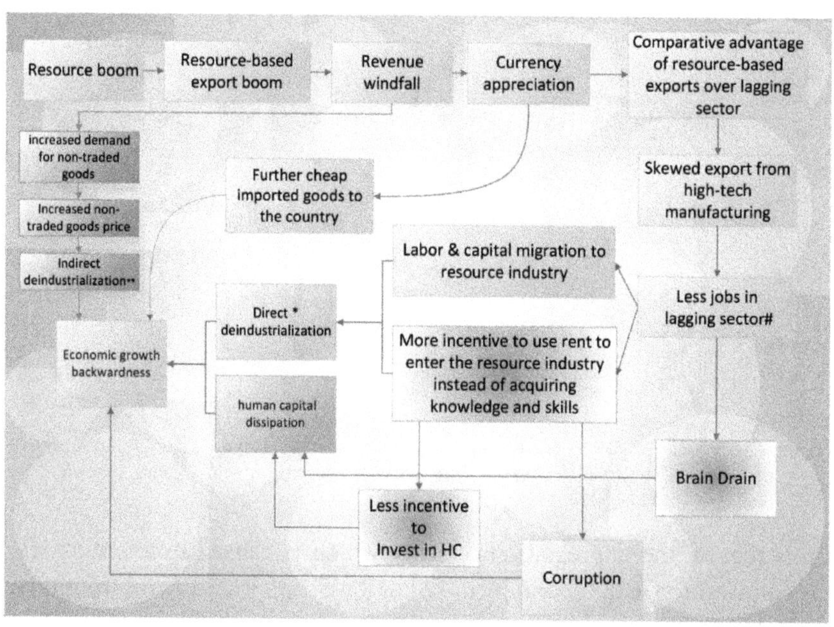

Rent Seeking (RS)

In economics, rent is any possible income or earning paid to a factor of production in excess of what is required to keep it in its ongoing service. In this regard, rent-seeking refers to any kind of earning that does not create any wealth. This may happen through exclusive privilege, authorizations, loan subsidies supported by the state and tariff production. In other words, rent-seeking activities imply earning without any contribution to production. Any policymaking for resource allocation that results in the disturbance of input production price, commodity price, and any interference on the competitive-free market will account for the rent-seeking activities.

According to the public choice school of economic thought, the existence of rent is a reason for the failure of government intervention in the economy and asserts that rent creation is caused by state exclusive privileges. (Abrishami & Hadian, 2005) Moreover, rent-seeking results in the underperformance of economic growth through the following transition mechanisms — ambiguous resource allocation, vanished government income, the social class gap in terms of income generation, likely national failure, and reduced wealth-creation. For instance, Iqbal and Daly (2014), in an empirical study, find that rent-seeking activities impede economic growth. They also find that the reduction in corruption is helpful for growth when it is accompanied by good governance. Rent seeking, like corruption, is a non-productive activity which takes from the productive side of the economy. Rent seeking doesn't have to be illegal, however.

According to Baland and Francois (2000), when entrepreneurship activities are initially low in an economy, a resource boom is plausible to intensify rent-seeking activities. However, they assert that if a large portion of the population is already engaged in entrepreneurship activities, the resource abundance fortifies it. To shed some light on how rent-seeking steals from the productive sector, the author explains the model propounded by Murphy et al. (1993). The basic idea is that rent-seeking can harm productive activities in passing from a good equilibrium to a bad one. (Tabarrok & Cowen, 2018) According to this model, one can think of the economy as having three activities; first, producing a *cash crop* for sale to turn a profit. The second possibility is subsistence production as one can produce for his own use but has negligible market value. The third is going towards capital bargaining, where one can tax, steal and create cartels which enable to rent seek from the producers of the cash crop.

Moreover, Murphy et al. (1993) study the rent-seeking model in three different situations regarding the protection of property rights. In the first and simplest case, property rights are well protected. Regardless of the number of rent seekers in the society, the return to the production sector is always higher than the rent-seeker returns and there is a high cost to diverting capital from the productive sector of the economy. In this case, there would be no incentive to be a rent seeker because, thanks to good governance and protected property rights, there is only good equilibrium and it costs more to be a capital stealer than to be a cash crop producer.

The second circumstance regards the economies with poorly-protected-property rights. In this case, the rent-seeking return curve exceeds the production return curve in that people find rent-seeking activities more profitable. Moreover, as the number of the rent seekers increases, the two decreasing curves tend to converge at the bad equilibrium point —where the returns from all three sectors become alike. Put differently, the rent seekers drive the economy to such a low level that everyone is getting a bad return. However, a third case may be the more common case: Multiple Equilibria could be considered as a mixed composition of the two first cases. (Figure 5)

As Figure 5 shows, if there are few rent seekers, the return to production is above that of rent seeking. However, if the number of rent seekers for any reason (such as bad institutions, social or political conflict or war) increases, they change their role, i.e. after the tipping point, the return to rent seeking becomes superior than that of production in that the higher the number of rent seekers, the more the economy tends to go towards bad equilibrium. It is denominated bad equilibrium, as it is very difficult for a country to return to the level before the tipping point where the return from rent seeking is less than that of production.

Figure 5. The rent-seeking model in the multiple equilibria
(Source: author elaboration inspired from Tabarrok & Cowen, 2018—MRUniversity)

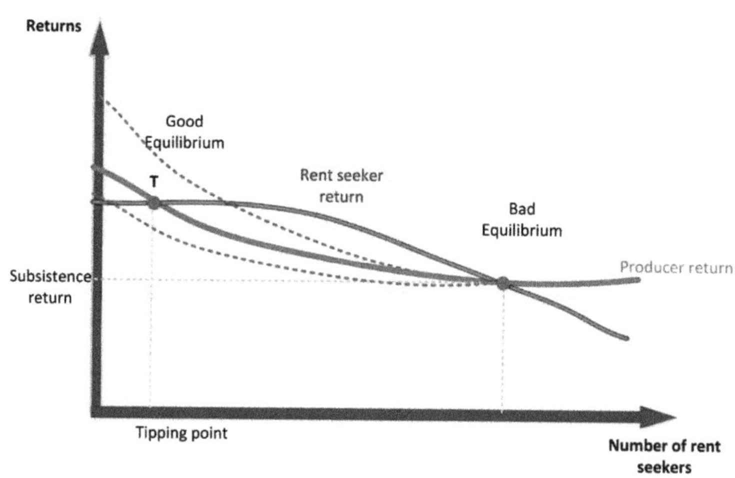

Natural Resources and Rent Seeking

NRA is very likely to transform an economy into a rent-seeking one. As figure 6 shows, NR windfall opens up a big opportunity to rent seekers to steal huge amounts of capital stock from the nation. Rent seekers are usually in power or have their agents in the government to leverage or do some rent-seeking activities like tariff protection, special loans and authorization for elites. Moreover, rent-seeking activity in a natural resource abundant economy (NRAE) has more a tendency towards illegal rent-seeking rather than legal. Regarding the fact that the political system in NRA countries is not in favor of property rights protection, the rent seeking (RS) economy is prone to the second model of Murphy et al. (1993). Moreover, in an RS environment, the elites — already engaged in the production market — use their leverage in the government to place tariffs on importation to preserve their monopoly. Bardhan argues that the literature confirms that import protection programs and corruption both result in economic underperformance (as cited in Gylfason, 2001).

Rent Seeking and Innovation in HCIF

To address the vulnerability of innovation to RS, Murphy et al. (1993) distinguish between private RS and public. They argue that private RS impedes production while public RS depreciates innovation. Inspired by this model, the author tries to

Figure 6. Rent Seeking vs. Growth and Innovation in HCIF
Source: author elaboration

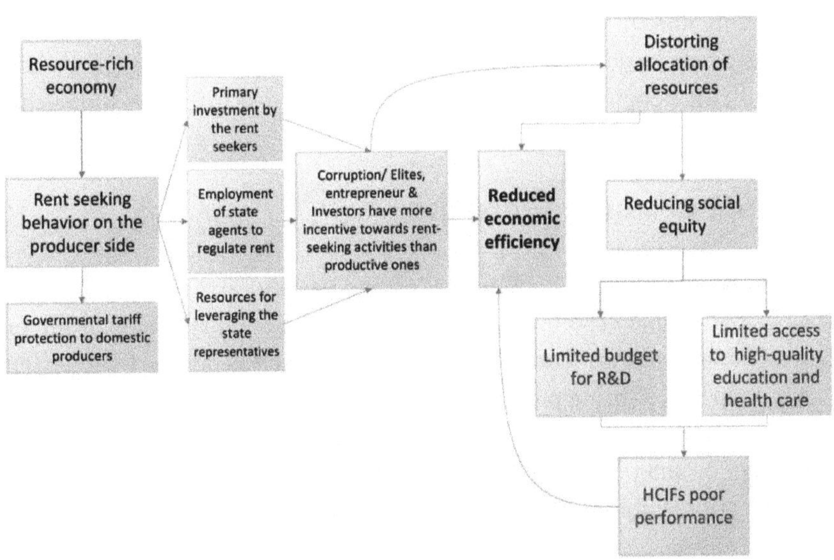

explain how the RS mechanism exerts influence on HCIF and innovation. As can be seen in Figure 7, contrary to well-established incumbents, HCIFs are considered the outsiders when it comes to getting involved in the power structure. Mutually opposing interests could make the situation more complicated. Moreover, in an RS economy, bribery plays an important role in facilitating certification, administration and even during project execution. In this regard, however, the firms that are often new startups are not able to pay for bribes and collaterals as they are credit-constrained and their projects are capital-intensive. This situation creates a further obstacle to the HCIF to play an innovative role in the market.

Another negative impact of public RS on HCIFs is the expropriation of patents and discoveries. Usually, innovative entrepreneurship projects are long term which increases the possibility of expropriation by rent seekers. Finally, innovative projects are risky by nature casting doubt about the future success of the project. In this regard, if the project succeeds, the probability of expropriation will increase as well. Otherwise, the firms are the one who must carry the burdens. Accordingly, when there is a possibility of expropriation, the HCIFs that are highly dependent on human capital have less incentive to contribute to innovation.

However, in RS circumstances, the de-motivation of innovators, scholars and even students is a big obstacle to innovative entrepreneurship. When the innovators do not achieve the desired outcomes from their spontaneous endeavors and additionally, their efforts have the likelihood of being expropriated, they become disappointed. If the same result occurs in other parts of the economy, despair dominates society which is surely very detrimental to the creation of any new ideas and innovation. This negatively affects growth, as well. In this case, the talented individuals, instead of contributing to HCIFs, use their aptitude to take a share from rents by entering in NRI or investing in non-tradable goods. Like the DD situation, a booming natural resources sector can be described as an overcrowded lifeboat with people swimming towards it with the people already in it trying to stay in control. This shows that the country's economy would be in real trouble.

Issues, Controversies, Problems

The problem is not only the abundance or dependence of an economy on the NRI, but lack of governance. The institutional quality of a country plays an important role. Once a country suffers from lack of institutions such as property rights, the NR —which is supposed to bring prosperity — will, on the contrary, drive the economy towards bad equilibrium in that rent seekers dominate the economy and the DD makes production uncompetitive. Consequently, it will diminish the incentive to invest in education and innovative entrepreneurship that are vital for HCIF.

Figure 7. Innovation in a Rent-Seeking economy
Source: author elaboration
**in weak protected property right condition*

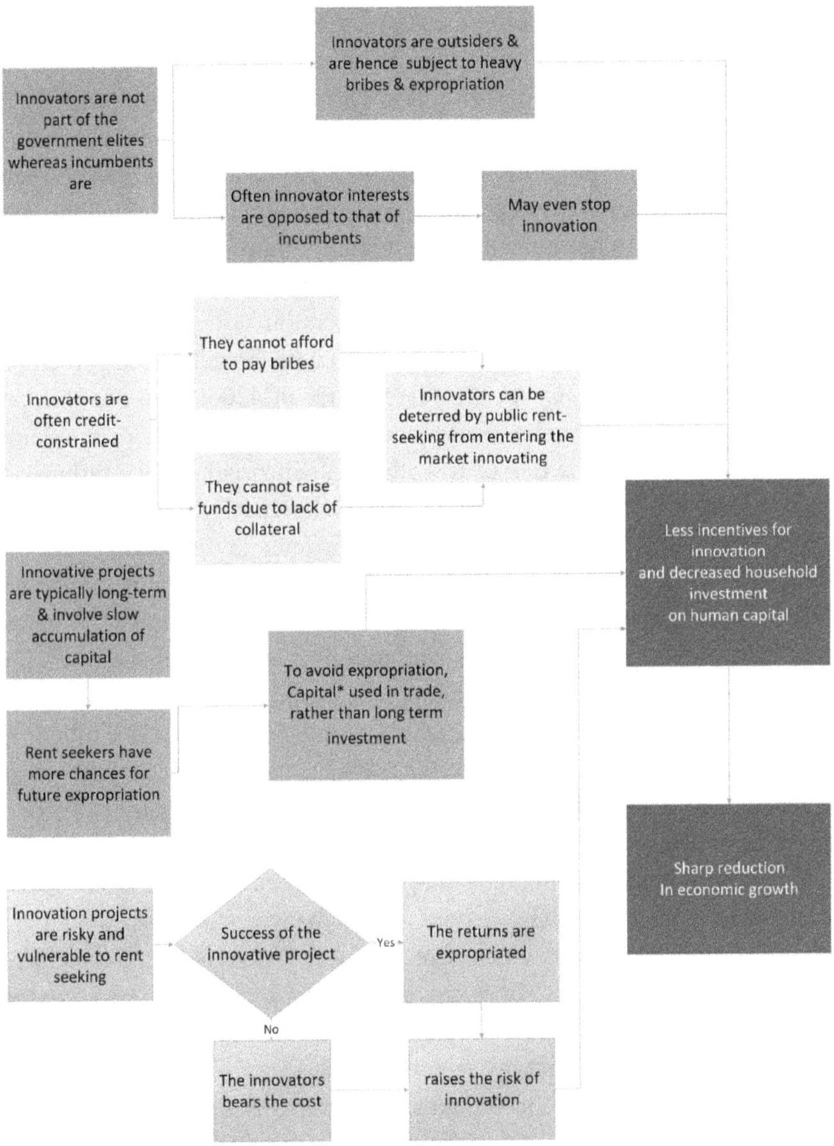

Tullock presents three reasons why RS has a negative impact on economic growth; the initial investment of rent seekers, government recruitment in favor of the agents that facilitate rent regulation and, the allocation of resources by rent seekers in order to leverage government representatives. He argues that the consequences are a waste of resources and lower growth (as cited in Abrishami & Hadian, 2005). For example, the Iranian economy struggles with a rent-seeking structure because of a widespread intervention of the government in resource allocation. Despite the launch of a privatization program to reduce the dominance of the government on economic activities, the results were not remarkable (Azad, 2010). The opportunity for RS in Iran is mostly because of the dichotomy between prices, especially the foreign exchange rate. Setting the foreign exchange rate much lower than that of the market value and discrimination in resource allocation is the origin of RS in Iran. Recently, the Iranian government, having predicted the breach of the agreement by the U.S. government about JCPA[3], set a fixed price of 42000 Rial per U.S. dollar. Despite the political decision, the consequences will not be good for the domestic economy as it could raise the risk of RS activities. Surprisingly, the failure of this plan exposed during after nearly one month. In this short period, the foreign exchange rate soared, and it was hard to find the foreign currency in the country.

Moreover, one important concern about NRA countries and why they are often underdeveloped is related to the hegemony of developed countries. Colonization has an adverse and negative impact on a country as it is accompanied by civil wars and it forecloses the political independence of the local government in order to follow the colonizer's policies (Chamarbagwala & Morán, 2011; Collier, 1999; Murdoch & Sandler, 2002). Moreover, the NRAEs, especially oil abundant ones, were/are considered a seductive target for colonizers. In this regard, the economic infrastructure of the country would be more beneficial for the colonizers. In this case, the people in power are not only supported by their domestic agents, but also by the foreigner governments. Hla Myint argues that the nature of colonization is to suppress education and that which is related to the awareness and insight of the people, thus ensuring *the supply of cheap unskilled labor for mines and plantations run by white settlers,* which causes development failure (as cited in Douangngeune, Hayami, & Godo, 2005). This is why according to the Natural Resource Governance Index (NRGI)[4] report, 75% out of 81 countries are ranked as weak, poor, and failing in terms of how good they are at governing their natural resources rents. Most of these countries had colonization experience.

SOLUTIONS AND RECOMMENDATIONS

Empirical Analysis

Empirically, this chapter studies the relationship between oil rent and the indicator of education. The hypothesis of this research is that the oil rent is detrimental to the HC. Moreover, this chapter hypothesizes that the institutional quality of an economy reinforces HC. This chapter applies a system of multiple linear regression models—ordinary least squares (OLS) — for a cross-section of 81 RGI ranked countries, to test the hypothesis.

Data

This chapter analyzes the empirical analysis using data from the World Bank and the NRGI. The Natural Resource Governance Index (NRGI) indicators assess strategies that authorities implement to rule their countries' oil, gas and mining industries. See figure 8 for all index and sub-index of NRGI—of which one subcomponent (enabling Environment) is the same as WGI with a different name. The explanatory variable of interest is the oil rent percentage of GDP, as oil is more likely to impose on an economy rent-seeking or Dutch Disease phenomena. Moreover, point resources, specifically petroleum ones, are more insidious when it comes to bringing about the curse on the growth and development of a country. (Philippot, 2010) Regarding the outcome variables and given the lack of data on innovation for most of NRGI sample countries, the author applies educational variables as a proxy for innovation, all sourced from the World Bank and UNESCO. Scholars commonly use secondary schooling indicators as a proxy of education (Mankiw, Romer, & Weil, 1992). In this way, the dependent (educational) variables are gross enrollment data. See table 1 for the definitions of all variables. All of the outcome variables are a simple average from 2010-2014.

In addition, the author applies the Global Human Capital Index (GHCI) as a recent outcome variable which ranks countries on how well they are developing their human capital (data for 2017). The choice of the RGI list of countries is based on the fact that from the set of 81 countries in the RGI report, nearly 70% are mainly petroleum abundant. According to the World Bank, oil rents are the difference between the value of crude oil production at world prices and the total costs of production.

To control the dependent variables of the economic development level, the author applies GDP per capita (constant 2010 US$). According to Wagner's law, when national income increases, the people solicit more from the government and hence, they are more involved in the economy. Consequently, there may be more demand for public goods, including human capital. In other words, the more people

Table 1. Description of GER (gross enrollment ratio): Simple average from 2010-2014

Gross enrolment ratio, lower secondary, both sexes (%)	Total enrollment in lower secondary education, regardless of age, expressed as a percentage of the total population of official lower secondary education age. GER can exceed 100% due to the inclusion of over-aged and under-aged students because of early or late school entrance and grade repetition.
Gross enrolment ratio, lower secondary, female (%)	Total female enrollment in lower secondary education, regardless of age, expressed as a percentage of the total female population of official lower secondary education age.
Gross enrolment ratio, secondary, gender parity index (GPI)	Ratio of female gross enrolment ratio for secondary to male gross enrolment ratio for secondary. It is calculated by dividing the female value for the indicator by the male value for the indicator.

Source: World Bank

Figure 8. Natural resource governance sub-indexes
Source: Natural Resource Governance Institute 2017

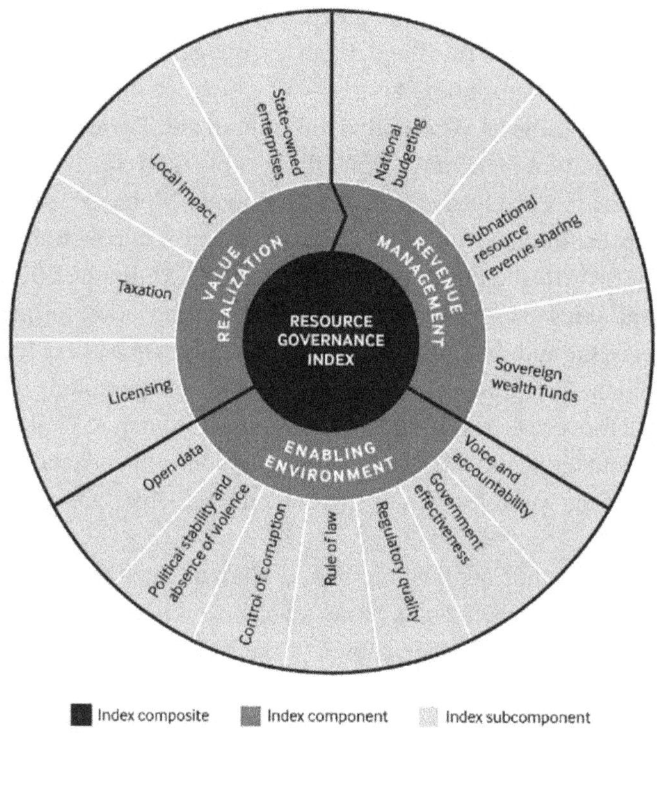

earn, the more they are likely to pay for their education. As a result, there is human capital accumulation, and the possibility to innovate will increase. Hence, the author expects to detect a positive link between GDP per capita and the stock of human capital. (Farzanegan & Thum, 2017; Philippot, 2010; Shao & Yang, 2014)

Moreover, population growth may affect the establishment of human capital as a public good. On one hand, a population boom may increase enrollment. On the other hand, it might reduce the per capita national budget dedicated to education programs. Therefore, population growth (annual %) is the second control variable. In addition, to have investment and an attractive market, the authorities should develop a proper infrastructure for human capital, which is why the trade should be controlled as well (Farzanegan & Thum, 2017; Philippot, 2010). Furthermore, another important factor to control is the institutional quality of a country. If the economy of study is high ranked in terms of governance, the provision for education by the government increases and the household demand for education does likewise. This more educated society then does a better job in terms of innovative entrepreneurship which leads HC based firms to flourish.

Oil rent, as the dependent variable, and all the control variables (except the NRGI and its subcomponent variables) are a simple average from 2005-2009. Regarding the simple average of dependent variables from 2010-2014, this method prevents the risk of reverse feedback. As Farzanegan and Thum (2017) argue, it *acknowledges* the needed time for explanatory variables to influence the dependent variable. It is important to point out that all the variables are represented in natural logarithms except the Oil Rent and Governance Indicators.

The econometric model is defined as multiple linear regression models using OLS estimation, which is widely used in econometric empirical analysis. It is very often applied by scholars to analyze the impact of natural resources on human capital and economic growth (Behbudi et al., 2010; Manning, 2004; Philippot, 2010; Stijns, 2006):

$$HC_i = C + \beta_1 Oil\_R_i + \beta_2 Gov_i + \beta_5 X_i + U_i \tag{1}$$

where HC is the indicator of human capital, Oil_R is the oil rent, and X is the set of control variables. Gov, is a set of variables measuring governance and the institutions for each country. Equation (1) implies that human capital depends on the stock of NRA and the set of control variables which include per capita income, governance, trade, and population growth.

Table 2. Descriptive statistics of the variables

	Variables	Span	Obs	Mean	Std. Dev.	Min	Max	Abbreviated Var Names
Human capital Variables	Gross enrolment ratio, lower secondary, both sexes (%)	Simple Average 2010-2014	76	78.37	27.18	17.08	130.82	GER_LwrSec_both
	Gross enrolment ratio, lower secondary, female (%)		76	76.65	29.29	12.15	130.54	GER_LwrSec_Fml
	Gross enrolment ratio, secondary, gender parity index (GPI)		69	0.92	0.16	0.44	1.21	GER_Sec_GPI
	The Global Human Capital Report 2017	2017	62	58.69	8.53	35.48	77.12	GHCI
Governance Index	Revenue Management	2017	81	43.01	18.12	0.00	85.48	Rev_Mang_Score
	Enabling Environment (WGI)		81	49.05	23.64	5.49	97.05	En_Enviornmt
Control Variabl	Population growth (annual %)	Average 2005-2009	81	2.35	2.19	-0.60	14.80	Pop_Growth
	GDP		81	7.99	1.51	5.61	11.41	LnGDP
*	Oil rents (% of GDP) * Explanatory Variable		70	12.79	16.62	0.00	57.84	Oil_rent

Descriptive Statistics

Table 2 shows the descriptive statistics of all variables in the model. There are 81 observations, but this number fluctuates according to the availability of the data. Quite a large variance can be seen for the two first gross enrollment ratios (GER). The highest variance is related to the female gross enrollment ratios, indicating that this variable is very diverse across countries; this diversity is near zero for the gender parity index of the GER.

Furthermore, figure 9 shows the scatter plot of the GHCI versus oil rents. As can be seen, the general trend is negative, indicating that the abundance of oil revenues, will decrease the rate of GHCI.

It is surprising that the above-mentioned scatter plot changes its behavior by disaggregating the countries regarding their NR governance performance. The same oil rent appears to be less harmful to economies with a higher GHCI (see figure 10, diagrams 1 - 3). In general, the NRGI has 5 different levels of governance, ranking from 1 (highest) to 5 (lowest). Note that only for this special variable (GHCI), the fifth group is omitted due to lack of data.

Results

The regression model is as follows:

$$HC_i = C + \beta_1 Oil\_R_i + \beta_2 X_i + \beta_4 Gov_i + U_i \quad (2)$$

Figure 9. The scatterplot of the global human capital index (GHCI) versus oil rents

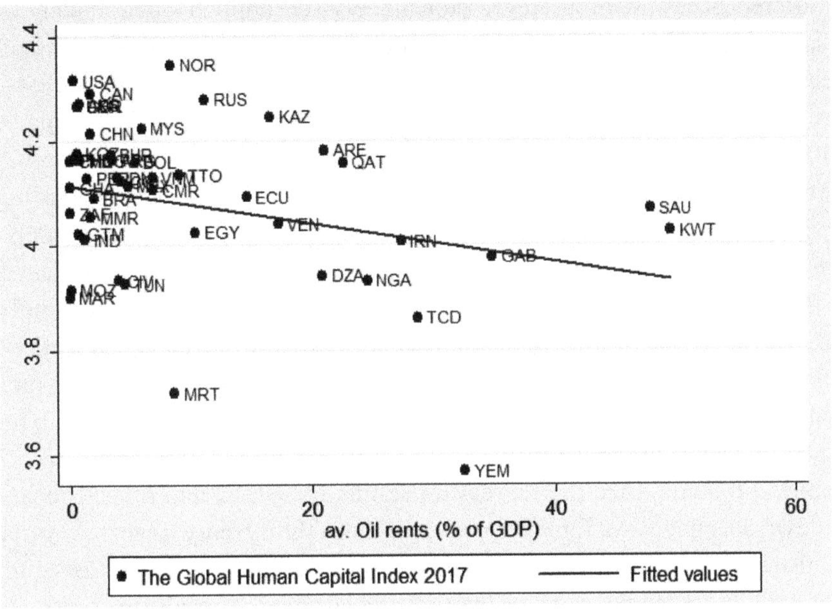

Figure 10. Global Human Capital Index (GHCI) for different NR governance levels

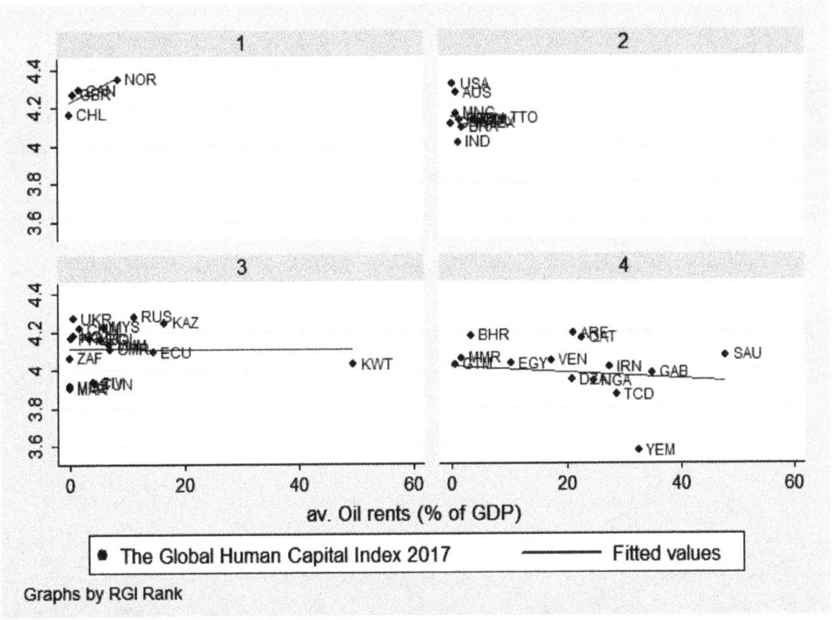

Four dependent variables regressed on the oil rent. For each dependent variable, eight different backward robust regression models were applied—denominated set of regressions in this chapter. The first four models are distinguished from the remaining models by Revenue Management and Enabling Environment, respectively— two governance indictors. See table 7 in appendix 1 for configuration of the explanatory variables.

The results for all sets are significant at a 1% level of confidence regarding the general regression F-statistic test, i.e. for all 32 models (8 different models × 4 dependent variables). The p-value for all regression sets is near zero, thus the outcomes show the significant and negative effect of oil rents on human capital accumulation for all sets of regressions. If innovation is considered a proxy for education, the author can deduct from the results that, in the countries highly dependent on their natural wealth, the HCIF may not perform efficiently, since these firms are highly dependent on HC and innovation.

Tables 3-6 summarize the regression results for GHCI and other educational variables, respectively. As Table 3 shows, all eight of the oil rent explanatory variables are statistically significant and negative at a 1% level of confidence. For example, the one-unit increase in oil rent for the first and last models results in an impedance of GHCI by 0.0051% and 0.00315%, respectively. The model 6 (Table 3) is the best-fitted model, in which the maximum obtained R-Squared value is 0.634. This means that nearly 63% of the GHCI variable, as the dependent variable, is explained by

Table 3. Regression sets for Global Human Capital Index 2017

	(1) GHCI	(2) GHCI	(3) GHCI	(4) GHCI	(5) GHCI	(6) GHCI	(7) GHCI	(8) GHCI
Oil_rent	-0.00509*** (-3.84)	-0.00485*** (-3.70)	-0.00491*** (-3.68)	-0.00486*** (-3.32)	-0.00595*** (-4.64)	-0.00302*** (-3.27)	-0.00312*** (-3.26)	-0.00315*** (-3.37)
LnGDP	0.0694*** (8.13)	0.0681*** (8.03)	0.0648*** (7.53)	0.0682*** (7.20)	0.0742*** (8.05)	0.0494*** (4.87)	0.0420*** (3.70)	0.0501*** (4.92)
Rev_Mang~e	0.0702* (2.00)	0.0754** (2.19)	0.0747** (2.12)	0.0753** (2.18)				
En_Envio~e						0.103** (2.12)	0.128** (2.38)	0.107** (2.12)
Pop_Growth						-0.0296* (-1.73)		-0.0303* (-1.75)
Trade							-0.0218* (-1.72)	
_cons	3.277*** (20.56)	3.259*** (20.89)	3.293*** (20.55)	3.259*** (20.76)	3.509*** (42.98)	3.291*** (21.23)	3.335*** (24.98)	3.271*** (19.87)
N	53	51	50	50	53	51	50	50
R-sq	0.599	0.625	0.612	0.609	0.561	0.634	0.625	0.622

Notes: All data are sourced from WDI
Robust standards errors are in the parentheses. ***, ** and * denote significance at 1%,5%,and 10%, respectively.

the explanatory variable — the oil rent. The least fitted model, however, belongs to GER, secondary, gender parity index, with an R-squared value of 0.414 which shows that the model is less successful in explaining this HC variable. Nevertheless, the quite high amount of R-squared values in the results, considering the cross-section analysis, show that the models are well fitted in general (Gujarati, 2009).

The resource-human capital equation discloses that oil rent is inversely related to human capital accumulation for the cross of 81 countries. This implies that the higher the share of oil rent in the national income, the more likelihood there is for the government to concentrate on its natural resource windfall, therefore neglecting other capitals like education which is the vital essence of HCIF.

Analogously, the same negative trend between oil rent and HC (educational) indicators holds for all other regression sets through Table 4, Table 5 and Table 6. However, a fewer number of the oil-rent coefficients are statistically significant than the GHCI. It can be argued that the educational variables do not capture all aspects of human capital, whereas the GHCI can measure human capital in a more comprehensive way as it applies across four thematic dimensions and five distinct age groups to capture the full human capital potential profile of a country (The Global Human Capital Report, 2017). Despite the fewer numbers of significant coefficients, all the significant ones are negative, reconfirming a negative trend between the gross enrollment variables and the oil rent. The results are in line with the author's initial expectations —the hypothesis that the oil rent is detrimental for HC.

Table 4. Regression sets for GER, secondary -both sexes

	(1) GER_Lwr~h	(2) GER_Lwr~h	(3) GER_Lwr~h	(4) GER_Lwr~h	(5) GER_Lwr~h	(6) GER_Lwr~h	(7) GER_Lwr~h	(8) GER_Lwr~h
Oil_rent	-0.0117***	-0.00810**	-0.00841**		-0.00658**			
	(-3.15)	(-2.14)	(-2.20)		(-2.31)			
LnGDP	0.181***	0.174***	0.171***	0.138***	0.106***	0.0815**	0.0753**	0.102***
	(6.48)	(6.33)	(5.87)	(6.37)	(2.86)	(2.54)	(2.18)	(3.34)
Pop_Growth		-0.149***	-0.166***	-0.207***		-0.162***	-0.158***	-0.173***
		(-3.01)	(-3.00)	(-4.11)		(-3.31)	(-3.16)	(-3.72)
Trade			0.0485**					
			(2.66)					
En_Envio~e					0.243***	0.279***	0.287***	0.147**
					(2.77)	(3.09)	(3.14)	(2.43)
_cons	2.997***	3.097***	2.933***	3.384***	2.644***	2.719***	2.741***	3.100***
	(13.38)	(14.44)	(13.77)	(18.81)	(10.47)	(10.27)	(10.25)	(17.62)
N	65	63	61	59	66	64	62	60
R-sq	0.474	0.526	0.524	0.513	0.544	0.583	0.577	0.557

Notes: All data are sourced from WDI
Robust standards errors are in the parentheses. ***, ** and * denote significance at 1%,5%,and 10%, respectively.

Table 5. Regression sets for GER, secondary-female

	(1) GER_Lwr~1	(2) GER_Lwr~1	(3) GER_Lwr~1	(4) GER_Lwr~1	(5) GER_Lwr~1	(6) GER_Lwr~1	(7) GER_Lwr~1	(8) GER_Lwr~1
Oil_rent	-0.0142***	-0.0102**	-0.0104**		-0.00778**			
	(-3.21)	(-2.28)	(-2.33)		(-2.29)			
LnGDP	0.214***	0.206***	0.204***	0.159***	0.120***	0.0902**	0.0840**	0.112***
	(6.37)	(6.18)	(5.74)	(6.73)	(2.77)	(2.52)	(2.16)	(3.52)
Pop_Growth		-0.167***	-0.183***	-0.233***		-0.184***	-0.179***	-0.191***
		(-3.01)	(-2.92)	(-4.19)		(-3.24)	(-3.08)	(-3.81)
Trade			0.0443*					
			(1.97)					
En_Envio~e					0.304***	0.351***	0.359***	0.191***
					(3.03)	(3.37)	(3.39)	(3.16)
_cons	2.713***	2.826***	2.671***	3.198***	2.272***	2.351***	2.373***	2.831***
	(10.22)	(11.02)	(10.25)	(16.39)	(7.91)	(7.70)	(7.67)	(16.04)
N	65	63	61	59	66	64	62	60
R-sq	0.491	0.538	0.534	0.544	0.571	0.605	0.599	0.605

Notes: All data are sourced from WDI
Robust standards errors are in the parentheses. ***, ** and * denote significance at 1%,5%,and 10%, respectively.

Furthermore, the results show a statistically significant and positive nexus between two resource governance variables, i.e. Revenue Management and Enabling Environment as control variables and human capital accumulation. The Enabling Environment is the World Governance Indicator which, according to the results, seems to control better the HC than that of Revenue Management. According to Table 3, all seven significant coefficients of the governance indicators—in line with the results of Murphy et al. (1993)— are positive, demonstrating the fact that the higher the level of a country's governance, the more the accumulation of human capital in that country, which plausibly makes the situation more convenient for HCIF activities. The related coefficients of the governance explanatory variables are all significant for GHCI, except one model, however, for the GER variables, significance evidence is available only for the Enabling Environment variable, in contrary with that Revenue Management. It may be because of the fact that Revenue Management captures only financial aspects of the governance which is less related to the educational variables, while Enabling Environment is a more comprehensive one as it is the same as WGI. Table 8 in appendix 2, summarizes all regression sets (each of the Tables 3-6)

The model with three of the dependent variables identified as having heteroscedasticity, however, shows no sign of auto-correlation and auto collinearity. The regression model is robust and has been controlled for autocorrelation. In that the Durbin-Watson coefficient is also not far from 2 for all the models, the null hypothesis of autocorrelation is rejected, and the models show no evidence of serial autocorrelation. Therefore, the estimators are linear, unbiased, consistent, and efficient (minimum variance).

Table 6. Regression sets for GER, secondary, gender parity index (GPI)

	(1) GER_Sec~I	(2) GER_Sec~I	(3) GER_Sec~I	(4) GER_Sec~I	(5) GER_Sec~I	(6) GER_Sec~I	(7) GER_Sec~I	(8) GER_Sec~I
Oil_rent	-0.00627***	-0.00627***	-0.00585***		-0.00406**	-0.00404**		
	(-3.55)	(-3.53)	(-3.25)		(-2.23)	(-2.20)		
LnGDP	0.0763***	0.0764***	0.0778***	0.0504***	0.0398*	0.0396*		
	(4.10)	(4.08)	(3.83)	(3.18)	(1.80)	(1.76)		
Trade			-0.0279**				-0.0544***	
			(-2.28)				(-4.27)	
Pop_Growth				-0.0741*				
				(-1.81)				
En_Envio~e					0.112**	0.112**	0.199***	0.141***
					(2.15)	(2.13)	(5.19)	(3.51)
_cons	-0.637***	-0.637***	-0.538***	-0.422***	-0.779***	-0.779***	-0.595***	-0.584***
	(-4.13)	(-4.11)	(-3.64)	(-3.07)	(-4.64)	(-4.63)	(-4.34)	(-3.57)
N	58	56	54	52	59	57	55	53
R-sq	0.416	0.414	0.424	0.316	0.471	0.470	0.463	0.312

Notes: All data are sourced from WDI
Robust standards errors are in the parentheses. ***, ** and * denote significance at 1%,5%,and 10%, respectively.

Moreover, to check for multicollinearity, the Variance Inflation Factor (VIF) has been applied which quantifies the severity of multicollinearity in an OLS regression analysis.[5] In the model, this index is far less than 10 and ensures that there is no strong evidence of multicollinearity between the explained variables.

Lastly, to check for heteroscedasticity, two tests were applied. For the first one, i.e. Breusch-Pagan / Cook-Weisberg test, three models are detected to have heteroscedasticity. Because the P-value is smaller than 5%, the null hypothesis is rejected and there is significant evidence of heteroscedasticity. Secondly, by applying the white test, only one model was identified as having heteroscedasticity because the P-value is less than 5%. Accordingly, the models related to the other variables, i.e. GHCI, appear to be better at explaining the impact on human capital.

Regarding the limitation of the model, one may say that the education variables are preliminary good, but they could bias the results as they do not measure well the innovation. Another limitation is regarding the human capital variables that do not capture all aspects of human capital. Besides, one inadequacy is lack of data in terms of innovation for developing and underdevelopment countries.

Discussion

The negative impact of NRs on growth is broadly studied in the literature, however, the innovation and HC as a main driver of HCIF were not in the focus of researchers. In this chapter, the transmission channels that could impact growth explained profoundly through the channel of HC and innovation. The RS and DD are two main sources of this inefficiency. Moreover, cross-country regression in this chapter shows that oil rent is negatively related to human capital accumulation for the cross of 81 countries. The applied model in this chapter predicted that this negative effect takes place because the production industries lose the comparative advantage and because the NR sector deters the proper allocation of the resource. Bravo (2005) find NRs as a hindrance for growth through the low level of HC because NR sector *draws resources from other economic sectors that could generate further economic growth.* Moreover, the results of this chapter confirm that of Birdsall (2000); he argues that DD tends to decrease the return to HC investment as NRs prone proper development strategy, social equality, and incentives for investment in education. In the same line, Polterovich, Popov and Tonis (2010) argue that in resource abundant countries, RER is generally higher, accumulation of HC is lower, and the condition of the good governance is worse. Moreover, the empirical results from this chapter are supportive of a major stream of the literature in resource curse theory such as Blanco (2012), Cockx and Francken (2014), Douangngeune et al. (2005), Papyrakis and Gerlagh (2007), and Zhan, Duan and Zeng (2015). The results, however, are in contrary with a minor stream of the literature that find a positive or neutral relationship between two variables of interest (Shao & Yang, 2014; Weber, 2014; Stijns, 2006; Davis, 1995; Kim & Lin, 2017). Put differently, regarding the qualitative analysis of rent-seeking and Dutch disease theories, the findings of this chapter are that the HCIF are likely to underperform in the NRAEs, through different channels, such as uncompetitive production sector or deindustrialization, brain drain, corruption, demotivation, and most importantly the retardation of human capital.

DD economy impacts growth negatively through innovation awkwardness and retardation of HC accumulation. Consequently, manufacturing would not be dynamic and competitive anymore. The consequence would be more unemployment in the productive lagging sector. (Gylfason, 2001; Davis, 1995). Because of this, the laborers and elites will try to enter the NRI, the so-called direct deindustrialization. It may occur through bribery, corruption or any rent-seeking activity (Davis, 1995), or by leaving the country which is the so-called brain drain that accounts for a big loss of HC. Both cases trigger the dissipation of HC accumulation within the boundaries of the firm or the economy of the country as well, which is consequently detrimental to economic growth (Nelson & Phelps, 1966; Schultz, 1961; Abramovitz, 1989; Becker, 1993). In other words, the DD-affected economy tends to crowd out the incentive for the HCIF management to support human capital. In this case, the investment in HC and funding innovation and R&D is cut. Whereas, in Natural-Resource-Poor economy (NRPE), the HCIF are more likely to flourish since they have no alternative other than being competitive in the global market (recall figure 4).

In passing, indirect deindustrialization refers to the shift of laborers from the lagging sector to the non-tradable market because of the DD economy. This makes brokerage more profitable and leaves less incentive for knowledge-based development. In this regard, the elites and even the graduate students use their talents, not in the creation of innovation and entrepreneurship in the firms, but in non-tradable market and brokerage. Furthermore, there may be a loss of motivation among young students because of the non-applicability of what they are investing in at colleges and universities. The HCIF cannot be formed easily in these circumstances, let alone evolve and prosper. In any case, either directly or indirectly, the result will be the same: deindustrialization diverts the economy away from the productive-based knowledge-demanding sector toward resources-based industries which finally results in retardation of HC accumulation and economic development (Corden, 1984; Corden & Neary, 1982).

Moreover, focusing on the HCIF performance in NRDEs, the RS behavior breeds corruption in both the government and the business environments that not only impedes growth but also results in the skewed allocation of the resources (Gylfson, 2001). This triggers a reduction in social equity. In this regard, the access of the poor to proper education and health care services would be limited, research and development expenditure shrinks up and eventually negatively impacts the HCIF. Concerning two types of HC (Cézanne & Saglietto, 2014), NR could impede general HC (labor market) as well as specific HC (within the firm) which both cases impede the economic development.

Recommendation

In this chapter, the author studied in detail the transmission mechanisms that harm a country's growth, innovation, and HCIF. Logically, the next step would be to determine how to avoid the adverse impacts of NRs on the economy and on HC. For example, there are some ways to reduce the negative effects of the DD phenomenon, such as limiting the appreciation of the RER: by increasing the savings in the economy, saving some of the revenues abroad, and by establishing a sovereign wealth fund to save part of the revenue for future generations. This can also be achieved by boosting the competitiveness of lagging sectors (productive industries) of which the most secure approach is to drive the governance of NRs in a pathway that creates more incentives for the firms to invest in education, R&D, and innovative entrepreneurship. However, a state protectionism plan to protect domestic manufacturing could be considered as a short run solution, yet it could have some side effects on the economy. Moreover, it is important to note that rising the institutions of a country up plays an important role to prevent the negative effects of NR on development of that country.

Regarding RS, an appropriate public policy seems to be very important in overcoming this phenomenon; that is, keeping the economy in a state of well-protected property rights which makes the return to production high enough and at the same time, reducing the return to RS activities. Recalling Figure 5, in the lower curve, the tipping point is immediately accessible. However, smarter policymakers try to mold the economy in such a way that the production-return dashed line remains at the highest possible position so that for a larger span of rent seekers, a return to production stays superior to that of RS, i.e. the higher dashed curve.

In spite of the effort made in this chapter to link NR to HCIFs, the problems should be approached macroeconomically. Even if firms were HC promoting, they would not be able to remove the negative effects of NRs from the economy, per se. By imagining society as a pyramid, policies and implementation start from the upper parts of the pyramid and the results flow towards all other parts of the economy, including HCIF. The main point, however, is related to the investment in human capital, taking an even higher priority than institutional quality. It is important to note that good governance and even democracy will not work well unless the people have a certain level of perception and understanding that can be achieved through the accumulation of HC. Consequently, the result would be fruitful for the HCIF in that they could straightforwardly progress and makes innovative startups for the evolving modern market.

FUTURE RESEARCH DIRECTIONS

While this chapter tried to link between general and specific HC— by observing the mechanisms through which NRs could affect this link— this subject is an area of research that still needs more attention. This comes through understanding how the mechanisms of public education and health provisions affect HC at the micro level empirically, i.e. the skills and knowledge of the laborers on the HCIF level. However, one can apply better proxies for innovation to find the direct impact of NRI on innovation.

Recalling the expropriation concern in RS economies, the author believes that one of the missing indicators in the analysis of NRA impact on growth and HCIF could be considered the people's confidence in their governance system. In some ways, this indicator may be more important in that innovation and entrepreneurship may not be beneficial to growth, lacking confidence in the government even if they have been provided with a high-quality education.

Moreover, it may be interesting to simulate the Multiple Equilibria model of Murphy et al. (1993) for oil-rich countries to find the bad equilibrium level which could be communicated to the government in order to implement prevention policies.

In this respect, the return to production, subsistence and RS should be calculated and graphed in a diagram with the number of rent seekers on the x-axis. While doing the same procedure with resource-poor countries, one would be able to compare between the two, recalling the two-dashed lines in Figure 5.

CONCLUSION

While the impact of NRs on HCIF is not underexplored by the existing literature, this chapter tried to highlight the linkage between the two-dominant impacts of NR, i.e. RS and DD, on the growth and firms that are highly dependent on the stock of HC and innovation. This chapter tried, as well, to connect the HC and growth influenced by NRA, through a macroeconomic and microeconomic perspective. The author concludes that NRs may easily lower economic growth by deterring HCIF. This may happen through the production sector having a less competitive advantage, corruption, demotivation, expropriation, and poorly-protected-property right institution. In other words, NR sector has the potential to harm growth directly and indirectly through the HCIF channel.

Moreover, as the empirical analysis of this chapter show, oil rent does hinder the stock of HC as a proxy for innovation. In this regard, the outcome of the HCIFs will be impeded. In other words, failure in a public-level HC does hinder the HC in HCIF, which finally roughs the development path. The results comply with the resource curse theory in that as long as RS activities and DD overshadow the economy, the investment on HC, which is the basis of the innovation, will fall. Furthermore, the results for the control variables confirm author's hypothesis concerning good governance theory in that as long as the country's policies are in favor of good institutional quality, the curse on NRs does not harm HC.

REFERENCES

Abramovitz, M. (1989). *Thinking about growth: And other essays on economic growth and welfare*. Cambridge University Press. doi:10.1017/CBO9780511664656

Abrishami, H & Hadian, M (2005). Rent seeking and Economic Growth (Empirical Evidence from Iran). *Journal of Economic Studies, 67,* 1-28. (in Persian)

Arthur, L. (1955). *The theory of economic growth.* Routledge.

Auty, R. M. (2001). *Resource abundance and economic development.* Oxford University Press.

Azad, S. (2010). The politics of privatization in Iran. *Middle East Review of International Affairs, 14*(4), 60.

Badeeb, R. A., Lean, H. H., & Clark, J. (2017). The evolution of the natural resource curse thesis: A critical literature survey. *Resources Policy, 51*, 123-134.

Badinger, H., & Tondl, G. (2003). Trade, human capital and innovation: the engines of European regional growth in the 1990s. In *European regional growth* (pp. 215–239). Berlin: Springer. doi:10.1007/978-3-662-07136-6_8

Baland, J. M., & Francois, P. (2000). Rent-seeking and resource booms. *Journal of Development Economics, 61*(2), 527–542. doi:10.1016/S0304-3878(00)00067-5

Balassa, B. (1980). *The process of industrial development and alternative development strategies*. The World Bank.

Becker, G. S. (1994). Human capital revisited. In Human Capital: A Theoretical and Empirical Analysis with Special Reference to Education (3rd ed.; pp. 15-28). The University of Chicago Press.

Birdsall, N., Pinckney, T. C., & Sabot, R. H. (2000). Natural resources, human capital, and growth. *Global Policy Program.*

Blanco, L., & Grier, R. (2012). Natural resource dependence and the accumulation of physical and human capital in Latin America. *Resources Policy, 37*(3), 281–295. doi:10.1016/j.resourpol.2012.01.005

Bravo-Ortega, C., & De Gregorio, J. (2005). *The relative richness of the poor? Natural resources, human capital, and economic growth*. The World Bank. doi:10.1596/1813-9450-3484

Bulte, E., Damania, R., & Deacon, R. (2005). Resource intensity, institutions and development. *World Development, 33*(7), 1029–1044. doi:10.1016/j.worlddev.2005.04.004

Burton-Jones, A., & Spender, J. C. (Eds.). (2011). *The Oxford handbook of human capital*. Oxford University Press. doi:10.1093/oxfordhb/9780199532162.001.0001

Cézanne, C., & Saglietto, L. (2014). Human capital-Intensive firms and symbolic value creation. *Timisoara. Journal of Economics and Business, 7*(1), 70–88.

Chamarbagwala, R., & Morán, H. E. (2011). The human capital consequences of civil war: Evidence from Guatemala. *Journal of Development Economics, 94*(1), 41–61. doi:10.1016/j.jdeveco.2010.01.005

Cockx, L., & Francken, N. (2014). Extending the concept of the resource curse: Natural resources and public spending on health. *Ecological Economics, 108*, 136–149. doi:10.1016/j.ecolecon.2014.10.013

Collier, P. (1999). On the economic consequences of civil war. *Oxford Economic Papers, 51*(1), 168–183. doi:10.1093/oep/51.1.168

Corden, W. M. (1984). Boom Sector and Dutch Disease Economics: Survey and Consolidation. *Oxford Economic Papers, 36*(3), 362. doi:10.1093/oxfordjournals.oep.a041643

Corden, W. M., & Neary, J. P. (1982). Booming sector and de-industrialisation in a small open economy. *Economic Journal (London), 92*(368), 825–848. doi:10.2307/2232670

D'Este, P., Rentocchini, F., & Vega-Jurado, J. (2014). The role of human capital in lowering the barriers to engaging in innovation: Evidence from the Spanish innovation survey. *Industry and Innovation, 21*(1), 1–19. doi:10.1080/13662716.2014.879252

Dakhli, M., & De Clercq, D. (2004). Human capital, social capital, and innovation: A multi-country study. *Entrepreneurship and Regional Development, 16*(2), 107–128. doi:10.1080/08985620410001677835

Daniele, V. (2011). Natural resources and economic growth: a curse or a blessing? *Rivista Italiana degli Economisti, 16*(3), 507-0.

Davis, G. A. (1995). Learning to Love the Dutch Disease: Evidence from the Mineral Economies. *World Development, 23*(10), 1765–1779. doi:10.1016/0305-750X(95)00071-J

Dolan, E. G. (2014). *The Curse of Riches: Resource Wealth and Social Progress*. Retrieved from http://dolanecon.blogspot.fr

Douangngeune, B., Hayami, Y., & Godo, Y. (2005). Education and natural resources in economic development: Thailand compared with Japan and Korea. *Journal of Asian Economics, 16*(2), 179–204. doi:10.1016/j.asieco.2004.12.004

Easterlin, R. A. (1981). Why isn't the whole world developed? *The Journal of Economic History, 41*(1), 1–17. doi:10.1017/S0022050700042674

Farzanegan, M. R., & Thum, M. (2017). *More oil, less quality of education? New empirical evidence* (No. 09/17). CEPIE Working Paper.

Gujarati, D. N. (2009). *Basic econometrics*. Tata McGraw-Hill Education.

Gylfason, T. (2001). Natural resources, education, and economic development. *European Economic Review*, *45*(4), 847–859. doi:10.1016/S0014-2921(01)00127-1

Iqbal, N., & Daly, V. (2014). Rent seeking opportunities and economic growth in transitional economies. *Economic Modelling*, *37*, 16–22. doi:10.1016/j.econmod.2013.10.025

Isham, J., Woolcock, M., Pritchett, L., & Busby, G. (2005). The varieties of resource experience: Natural resource export structures and the political economy of economic growth. *The World Bank Economic Review*, *19*(2), 141–174. doi:10.1093/wber/lhi010

Jalal al-Din Muhammad Balkhi. (1258). *Masnavi*.

Kaufmann, D., Kraay, A., & Mastruzzi, M. (2009). Governance matters VIII: Aggregate and individual governance indicators, 1996-2008. *World Bank Policy Research Working Paper*, 4978.

Kim, D. H., & Lin, S. C. (2017). Human capital and natural resource dependence. *Structural Change and Economic Dynamics*, *40*, 92–102. doi:10.1016/j.strueco.2017.01.002

Krueger, A.O. (1980). *Trade policy as an input to development*. Academic Press.

Lucas, R. E. Jr. (1988). On the mechanics of economic development. *Journal of Monetary Economics*, *22*(1), 3–42. doi:10.1016/0304-3932(88)90168-7

Mankiw, N. G., Romer, D., & Weil, D. N. (1992). A contribution to the empirics of economic growth. *The Quarterly Journal of Economics*, *107*(2), 407–437. doi:10.2307/2118477

Marvel, M. R., & Lumpkin, G. T. (2007). Technology entrepreneurs' human capital and its effects on innovation radicalness. *Entrepreneurship Theory and Practice*, *31*(6), 807–828. doi:10.1111/j.1540-6520.2007.00209.x

Mehlum, H., Moene, K., & Torvik, R. (2006). Institutions and the resource curse. *Economic Journal (London)*, *116*(508), 1–20. doi:10.1111/j.1468-0297.2006.01045.x

Mousavi, S. M. A., Nouri, M., & BenYousef, A. (2017b, October). *Natural resource abundance and Human Capital nexus, concerning the governance*. Paper presented at 29th European Association for Evolutionary Political Economy, Budapest, Hungry.

Murdoch, J. C., & Sandler, T. (2002). Economic growth, civil wars, and spatial spillovers. *The Journal of Conflict Resolution*, *46*(1), 91–110. doi:10.1177/0022002702046001006

Murphy, K. M., Shleifer, A., & Vishny, R. W. (1993). Why is rent-seeking so costly to growth? *The American Economic Review*, *83*(2), 409–414.

Naderi, M. M. (2011). Good Governance; Introduction and criticism. Islām va Pazhūheshhāye Modirīyatī, 1(1). (in Persian)

Nelson, R. R., & Phelps, E. S. (1966). Investment in humans, technological diffusion, and economic growth. *The American Economic Review*, *56*(1/2), 69–75.

Palangkaraya, A., Spurling, T., & Webster, E. (2016). *What drives firm innovation? A review of the economics literature*. Academic Press.

Papyrakis, E., & Gerlagh, R. (2007). Resource abundance and economic growth in the United States. *European Economic Review*, *51*(4), 1011–1039. doi:10.1016/j.euroecorev.2006.04.001

Philippot, L. M. (2010). *Are Natural Resources a Curse for Human Capital Accumulation*. Centre d'Etudes et de Recherches sur le Développement International (CERDi-CNRS).

Polterovich, V., Popov, V., & Tonis, A. (2010). *Resource abundance: A curse or blessing?* Academic Press.

2017 . Resource Governance Index. (2017). Retrieved from https://resourcegovernance.org/ analysis-tools/publications/2017-resource-governance-index

Ross, M. L. (2001). Does oil hinder democracy? *World Politics*, *53*(3), 325–361. doi:10.1353/wp.2001.0011

Rosser, A. (2006). *The political economy of the resource curse: A literature survey*. Academic Press.

Sachs, J. D., & Warner, A. M. (1995). *Natural resource abundance and economic growth (No. w5398)*. National Bureau of Economic Research. doi:10.3386/w5398

Schultz, T. W. (1961). Investment in human capital. *The American Economic Review*, *51*(1), 1–17.

Shahbaz, M., Naeem, M., Ahad, M., & Tahir, I. (2017). Is natural resource abundance a stimulus for financial development in the USA? *Resources Policy*.

Shao, S., & Yang, L. (2014). Natural resource dependence, human capital accumulation, and economic growth: A combined explanation for the resource curse and the resource blessing. *Energy Policy*, *74*, 632–642. doi:10.1016/j.enpol.2014.07.007

Starbuck, W. H. (1992). Learning by knowledge-intensive firms. *Journal of Management Studies, 29*(6), 713–740. doi:10.1111/j.1467-6486.1992.tb00686.x

Stiglitz, J. (2004). *We can now cure Dutch disease.* Retrieved from https://www.theguardian.com/business /2004/ aug/18/comment.oilandpetrol

Stijns, J. P. (2006). Natural resource abundance and human capital accumulation. *World Development, 34*(6), 1060–1083. doi:10.1016/j.worlddev.2005.11.005

Stijns, J. P. C. (2005). Natural resource abundance and economic growth revisited. *Resources Policy, 30*(2), 107–130. doi:10.1016/j.resourpol.2005.05.001

Tabarrok, A., & Cowen, T. (2018). *MRUniversity.* Available at http://mruniversity.com/

The Global Human Capital Report 2017, Preparing people for the future of work. (2017). Retrieved from http://www3.weforum.org/docs/WEF_Global_Human_Capital_Report_2017.pdf

Viner, J. (1952). America's aims and the progress of underdeveloped countries. *The Progress of Underdeveloped Areas,* 175-202.

Wade, M. P., & Dabla-Norris, M. E. (2001). Rent Seeking and Endogenous Income Inequality (No. 1-15). International Monetary Fund.

Weber, J. G. (2014). A decade of natural gas development: The makings of a resource curse? *Resource and Energy Economics, 37,* 168–183. doi:10.1016/j.reseneeco.2013.11.013

Zhan, J. V., Duan, H., & Zeng, M. (2015). Resource dependence and human capital investment in China. *The China Quarterly, 221,* 49–72. doi:10.1017/S0305741014001556

ENDNOTES

1. One exception is the oil and gas industry which requires advanced technical knowledge. However, those advanced services are usually provided by giant international companies that import high-skilled employees and recruit only casual domestic employees.
2. the so-called "resource movement effect" or "pulling effect" (Badeeb et al. 2017).

3 The Joint Comprehensive Plan of Action, commonly known as the Iran nuclear deal or the Iran deal, is an agreement on the nuclear program of Iran reached in Vienna on July 14th, 2015 between Iran and the P5+1. However, on May 8, 2018, the United States officially withdrew from the agreement after Donald Trump signed a Presidential Memorandum ordering the reinstatement of harsher sanctions.

4 Natural Resource Governance Index (NRGI) is a report ranking the countries according to their success in terms of governance and institution. (See the references for more information).

5 It provides an index that measures how much the variance (the square of the estimate's standard deviation) of an estimated regression coefficient is increased because of collinearity.

APPENDIX 1

Table 7. Explanatory variable configuration in the models

Models	Oil Rent	GDP	Revenue Management	Enabling Environment	Population growth	Trade
1	■	■	■			
2	■	■	■		■	
3	■	■	■		■	■
4	■	■	■		■	■
5	■	■		■		
6	■	■		■	■	
7	■	■		■	■	■
8	■	■		■	■	■

APPENDIX 2

Table 8. Summary of regression sets (each of the Tables 3 – 6 is abstracted in each row)

Variables	Nubmer of significant oil rent coefficient in set of regression (best&worst level of confidence)	Nubmer of significant resource governance coefficients [En_Enviornmt & Value_R_Score] in set of regression (max level of confidence for each var. respectivly)	R-squared obtained (max-min)	Abbriviated Var Names
The Global Human Capital I	8 (1% & 1%)- all NEGATIVE	[4 & 3]- (5% & 10%)- all POSITIVE	(0.634 -0.561)	GHCI
Gross enrolment ratio, lower secondary, both sexes (%)	4 (5% & 1%)- all NEGATIVE	[4 & 0]- (5% & n.a)- all POSITIVE	(0.583 - 0.474)	GER_LwrSec_both
Gross enrolment ratio, lower secondary, female (%)	4 (5% & 1%)- all NEGATIVE	[4 & 0]- (1% & n.a)- all POSITIVE	(0.605-0.491)	GER_LwrSec_Fml
Gross enrolment ratio, secondary, gender parity index (GPI)	5 (5% & 1%)- all NEGATIVE	[4 & 0]- (5% & n.a)- all POSITIVE	(0.471 -0.414)	GER_Sec_GPI

Section 3

Capabilities, Innovation, and Performance

Chapter 7
Knowledge Inflows and Knowledge Creation Capabilities Among MNC Subsidiaries in Malaysia:
Human Capital in Host Country as a Moderator

Vijayalakchimi Subramaniam
University Science Malaysia, Malaysia

Shankar Chelliah
University Science Malaysia, Malaysia

ABSTRACT

In a volatile business environment and a global landscape, knowledge creation capability plays an important role in ensuring that MNC subsidiaries stay competitive. In this respect, knowledge inflows from different parts of the MNC knowledge network are vital to a subsidiary's capability to create new knowledge. Briefly, knowledge creation capability refers to the successful implementation of creative ideas within an organization. However, innovation-based competitiveness always starts with creativity that is rooted in individual workers in an organization. The human capital of the organization, therefore, is considered to be one of the main sources of knowledge-based competitive advantage. Therefore, besides knowledge inflows from the MNC network, subsidiaries also need human capital to allow for knowledge flows to be utilized creatively in order to remain competitive.

DOI: 10.4018/978-1-5225-7426-2.ch007

INTRODUCTION

"How can subsidiaries of multinational corporation (MNC) gain sustainable competitive advantage in the host countries that they operate in?" This issue has been a matter of interest among the industry key stakeholders, government bodies, as well as academics. According to the existing literature, the ways in which a firm potentially sustains its competitive advantage can be explained in three (3) different ways. From an industry market-based view (MBV), a firm should concentrate on its competitive analysis. A resource-based view (RBV), on the other hand, focuses on the usage of firm resources. The third perspective is through the knowledge-based view (KBV) that emphasizes knowledge to be the main driver of superior performance in organizations (Wang, 2014).

In the current fast-paced changes in technological advancement and the growth of economies, the knowledge we learn today may not necessarily solve the problems of tomorrow. To compete effectively in this day and age, an organization needs to be alert of the changes and developments of its business environment. It means that as the industrial sector grows in complexity, organizations come under increasing pressure to reconstruct themselves. Knowledge turns into a major asset with regards to competitive advantage from the knowledge-based market perspective. As discussed and acknowledge in previous literatures, knowledge has become a critical driver of the world's economy today. Drucker (2009), for example, argues that "knowledge has become the key economic resource and the dominant – and perhaps even the only – source of comparative advantage".

Knowledge refers to information combined with experience, context, interpretation, and reflection. Basically, knowledge is a high value form of information that is ready to apply to decisions and actions (Jarrar, Zairi, & Schiuma, 2010). Knowledge is a pivotal part for todays' knowledge-based companies. The performance of an organization depends on the knowledge the organization can acquire and utilize (Andreeva & Kianto, 2012). Organizations must have the technological and organizational capability to adapt to the current knowledge to ensure greater opportunity to react against and overcoming the growing complexity of the current market requirements. Globalization has caused rapid knowledge changes, which forces firms to constantly develop and innovate their technological capabilities, while also ensuring minimization of costs in order to maximise profits. In short, knowledge is key in an organization's pursuit for competitive advantage. An organization increases its opportunity to produce better value-added products and services and enhance business growth through a rapid and effective process of generating knowledge (Subramaniam & Youndt, 2005). Business success depends on how quickly and effectively knowledge is exchanged.

On the other hand, KBV of a company recognizes the capability of leveraging and managing knowledge in the organization. Subsidiaries of a MNC are usually dispersed geographically. As such, in order for the MNC to remain competitive as a global group, each subsidiary must also be competitive in each locality. As knowledge quickly becomes outdated due to rapid progress in science and technology, the subsidiary cannot rely solely on the knowledge residing within its organizational boundary because this may not be adequate to maintain and upkeep knowledge within the organization. Subsidiaries need to gather knowledge externally and combine it with in-house knowledge to generate more and value-added knowledge (Perri & Andersson, 2014). Organizational embedded knowledge and inflow of external knowledge (i.e. internal and external network) present vital opportunities for the competitive advantage of a subsidiary (Andersson, Björkman & Forsgren, 2005). Through the knowledge inflow and existing knowledge, an organization can create new knowledge and achieve innovative performance as well as develop a sustainable competitive advantage (Liao, Chen, Hu, Chung, & Yang, 2016).

Knowledge inflow can increase the competitiveness of the subsidiary, but some literature claims that the gain of valuable fresh knowledge does not, in itself, improve a subsidiary's performance. A subsidiary must regularly generate fresh knowledge to build a sustainable competitive advantage (Ahlstrom,Su, Li, & Cheng, 2013). The way that a subsidiary is able to reshape current competencies and generate fresh knowledge by sourcing new knowledge and linking it to the current knowledge stock is a strategically important capability to stay competitive. The argument here is there should not be a vacuum in knowledge search in a time continuum. Subsidiaries need to respond to the opposing demands of global integration and local calls of responsiveness to learn from both the internal and the external environments for competitive advantage (Ghoshal et al., 1988).

BACKGROUND

Subsidiary's Knowledge Inflow

A subsidiary operates within two well-defined systems—the internal MNC network, made up of the HQ and subsidiaries of the same organization; and the external network partners (Demeter, Szász, & Rácz, 2016). Therefore, the strategies adopted by a subsidiary can be designed from an internal and external perspective. Through the externally-oriented network, a subsidiary seeks to pick out the requirements of the new customers, establish fresh suppliers and build fresh alliance connection. With regards to the internal network, on the other hand, a subsidiary seeks to ensure that current relationship within the subsidiary functions effectively (Birkinshaw, 1998). The creation of fresh knowledge is conducted via the connection with external network actors (customers, suppliers, competitors etc.) and internal network actors (headquarters and sister units) (Holm & Sharma, 2006).

Meyer, Mudambi, & Narula (2011) has termed the integration of internal and external knowledge inflow by subsidiary as "dual embeddedness". Dual embeddedness is focused on the way in which knowledge from the present market can be derived from the host knowledge and transmitted throughout the subsidiary. If a subsidiary gains new knowledge from a source in terms of product development and better production planning, the knowledge gained needs to be distributed amongst other parties in the network to ensure that it is incorporated into the day-to-day operations (Mahnke, Pedersen, & Venzin, 2005), after the knowledge is validated to be operationally sound.

The breadth and depth of knowledge that exists within a subsidiary is enhanced through the different knowledge inflows from outside the boundary of the organization, thereby increasing opportunities for combining different types of knowledge increases the competitiveness of the subsidiary (Cohen & Levinthal, 1990). Knowledge inflow has been a vital element in comprehending the way subsidiaries are able to deepen their knowledge to make themselves more efficient, flexible and globally integrated (Gupta & Govindarajan, 1991).

Subsidiary's ability to facilitate and manage various sources of knowledge influence the competitive advantage of subsidiaries (Gupta & Govindarajan, 2000). In view of these trends, and recognizing that knowledge has great potential value. Thus, internal and external knowledge inflow are vital to the success of the firm. Organizational knowledge inflow associated with higher levels of subsidiary performance and the proper balance between internal and external knowledge maximize its overall competitiveness (Bierly & Chakrabarti, 1996).

Subsidiary's Knowledge Creation Capability (KCC)

In this rapidly changing and globalized world, innovation is key to any business company. It therefore underscores the importance of the KCC for competitive advantage. The ability to self-generate knowledge can be explained as an organization's KCC (Smith, Collins, & Clark, 2005). In this present time, the capabilities such as acquisition, integration and implementation of knowledge to create fresh competencies is more important. According to Smith et al., (2005), organizations with greater KCC are able to generate more knowledge in order to be competitive. As a result of the presence of KCC, companies are able to design product and services towards innovation and gain competitive advantage (Mudambi, 2002).

The continuous increase in business competitiveness globally, the KCC of subsidiaries becomes a vital competitive asset. Teece, Pisano, & Shuen, (1997) have stressed that subsidiaries must develop 'capabilities' so that they can adapt and help determine the ever changing and challenging business environment. Teece et al. 1997 explains that 'capabilities' as '*firms' ability to integrate, build and reconfigure internal and external competencies to address rapidly changing environments*'. Subsidiary needs to understand the nature of knowledge to transform the knowledge into new knowledge to match with the existing knowledge and create a value-added knowledge base. Subsidiary must have the ability to understand and utilize knowledge to create improved value add in order to gain competitive advantage, especially in high-velocity business environments (Bueno, Anton, & Salmador, 2008).

Knowledge inflow from different networks influences the level and standard of subsidiary capability to create knowledge. Subsidiary needs to have KCC to integrate between home and host network knowledge by leveraging knowledge (product and process related) from their networks and convey into subsidiary level operational performance (Demeter et al., 2016). Subsidiaries' capabilities to create knowledge by assimilating new external knowledge will increase their performance (Lane et al., 2001). Therefore, competitiveness of a subsidiary depends on its ability to transform these knowledge inflows into value-added activities. Liao, Wu, Hu, & Tsui, (2010) claims that KCC enables subsidiaries to survive and achieve a high level of competitiveness both in the national and international marketplace. Subsidiary while lacking resources, vulnerable and unsure in a volatile business environment as well as facing demands of suppliers and customers, should be able to gain competitive advantage by utilizing KCC. In a situation where the life cycle of a product is limited and knowledge quickly becomes outdated, KCC has become essential is order to survive (Roy & Therin, 2008).

On account of KCC, organizations are better equipped to face changes in the environment and can respond in a more efficient and effective manner. It contributes to opportunities and then improves firm performance (Ahlstrom et al., 2013). A subsidiary existence in an environment which is highly technological needs to absorb new technology quickly. Knowledge needs to be gained from outside sources, however, the significant amount of knowledge transfer to improve the competitive advantage of subsidiary depends on organizational capability (Liao et al., 2016). Since, competitive advantage consists of knowledge and capabilities of a firm (Cardy & Selvarajan, 2006), the approach taken to apply knowledge both efficiently and effectively will greatly enhance the competitive capability of the organizations. KCC could help businesses to establish routines in their organization and transform knowledge into planned actions (Teece et al., 1997). KCC would enable firms to respond to the external environment in a timely efficient manner, which helps with their overall performance. Those subsidiaries with higher KCC can derive more use of their knowledge, in turn become more innovative. Conversely, subsidiaries that lacks KCC would fail to benefit from their knowledge, and consequently adversely affect the performance of the organization (Ferraris, Santoro, & Dezi, 2017).

As a result, knowledge inflow and KCC are seen with more appreciation with regards to improve subsidiary's competitive advantage (Najim Abdullah, Hashim, & Ali, 2015). In a study by Teece et al. (1997), it has shown that companies which do not possess the capabilities are unable to be competitive even though the company accumulates a large amount of knowledge. Choi & Lee (2002) added that firms which are capable of coordinating and redeploying both in-house and external knowledge, as well as respond timely with quick and flexible innovative solutions are the winners in the global market. Therefore, it is vital for companies to set themselves apart through KCC without which the performance of an organization will be doomed. KCC is emphasized as the determining factor of success or failure of firms globally.

Basically a subsidiary needs to have KCC which are fundamental for competitive advantage and must be consistent over time (Eisenhardt & Martin, 2000). Such capabilities comprise certain strategic and organizational obligation towards distinct procedure and processes which allow a subsidiary to configure new knowledge. Similarly, Ahlstrom, Su, Li, & Cheng (2013) stated that since knowledge becomes obsolete with frequent advancements in science and technology, organizations need to generate new knowledge on regular basis through the leverage of KCC to build and sustain competitive advantage. Therefore, a subsidiary's KCC can provide a competitive advantage for a subsidiary to compete in the global market place. A subsidiary needs to continuously construct knowledge from its capability to innovate and abandon old and outdated ones to achieve sustainable competitive advantage (Mudalige, Ismail, & Malek, 2016).

MAIN FOCUS OF THE CHAPTER: COMPETITIVE ADVANTAGE OF SUBSIDIARY

Generally, the main property of any organization in today's economy is knowledge and it is the key driver of the organization's competitive advantage (Teece et al.,1997). In the current environment, the competitiveness of a company depends on knowledge creation and successful subsidiary refers to those with capabilities of creating knowledge and converting it into applicable practices that will boost performance. The faster a company generates knowledge, the greater opportunity it has to produce growth with added value (Subramaniam & Youndt, 2005). A subsidiary would be considered having high competitive advantage when the knowledge of the subsidiary is novel and hindered from being re-produced by others in addition to being relevant on a global scale. Whereas, duplicative knowledge would not be relevant to the business and a subsidiary's competitive advantage would remain low (Gupta & Govindarajan, 2000). Therefore, for the business of a subsidiary to flourish in the current business environment, it must have the capability to be innovative and creative. A subsidiary's KCC would provide that competitive advantage defining the subsidiary's success.

As widely accepted among international management scholars that subsidiaries act as agents of competency creation, since they are simultaneously embedded in two different knowledge contexts: (1) the internal multinational firm network, composed of the headquarters and other sister units; (2) the external set of host country firm, composed of customers, suppliers, competitors and government institution (Almeida & Phene, 2004). Subsidiaries are significant sources of knowledge, ideas and knowledge creation for new and improved products, processes, systems, and structures that can be utilized locally, regionally and globally (Colakoglu & Jiang, 2013).

In essence, subsidiaries have an integrative character that could bridge local competencies and environments to the entire group, thus enabling competence creation, and it facilitates the use of knowledge throughout the organization (Mudambi, Pedersen, & Andersson, 2014). Linkages to host country knowledge provide the best inputs for innovation (Phene & Almeida, 2008). Taking into account, all the aspect of knowledge-based organization, subsidiaries in the manufacturing sector are considered knowledge reliant, as knowledge in its intangible form has a major impact on the competitive advantage of an organization. It is imperative for subsidiaries to learn on handling the demands of its environment as it has a critical effect on the competitive advantage of the organisation (Shih et al., 2010).

Malaysia: Lack of Knowledge Creation Capability

The subsidiary needs to focus on constantly improving KCC as a platform to make organization more effective. However, despite the focus on KCC, many companies in Malaysia have not reached the required capability with regards to generating knowledge (Wai Yi & Jayasingam, 2012). Malaysia remains far behind advanced economies, such as South Korea and Taiwan, as far as KCC are concerned. According to Choy Chong, (2006), while most organization acknowledges the merits of KCC, in practice, the benefits of KCC is not fully implemented or utilized to the same degree.

While the Malaysian government is committed towards developing the nation into a knowledge-intensive society, KCC level in Malaysia remains low. Practically, Malaysia should be able to demonstrate high level of innovation capabilities since the economy is reliant on Foreign Direct Investment (FDI). In FDI-led economies, attention should be centred on the development of human capital (HC) in host country (Ritchie, 2002), especially when the level of HC development is a critical determinant of FDI inflows. However, according to the National Economic Advisory Council (2010) report, Malaysia lacks in skilled HC for the necessary development of technology. According to a comparative study between Malaysia, Korea, Singapore and Taiwan, the supply of skilled HC in Malaysia is one of the lowest (Lai & Yap,

2004). Moreover, the World Bank (2005) reported that the issue of HC is prevalent in Malaysia. Inadequate skilled HC stifles the country's growth towards achieving a knowledge-based economy status. Nambiar (2011) claims that Malaysia's growth objectives were threatened due to the discrepancy between the requirements of the economy and the supply of HC.

This shortcoming alerted the government to concentrate on establishing ways to create knowledge and activities which generate value. Developing HC is of an increasing importance in supporting subsidiaries of MNC. Having skilled workforce is essential for subsidiaries, particularly in filling the requirements of organizations that desires high technology competencies. The way in which HC is valued depends on its ability to contribute to the main business of the firm and its competitive advantage (Nambiar, 2011). According to the theory of HC, an individual must bring economic value to organization with their respective competencies and knowledge (Seleim & Khalil, 2011). It stresses the importance of HC in acquiring and transforming knowledge. Consequently, the strength of a knowledge-based organization rests in their knowledge inflow and HC of the organization. Competent HC is as essential as any of the other resources in an organization.

Unleash the Human Capital in Subsidiary

Literature has shown just how essential HC is in the firm, as proven by Amabile (1988), KCC always starts with creativity that is rooted in individual workers in an organization, with regards to the successful implementation of creative ideas within an organization. Therefore, the KCC of the organization relies on an individual or a group of individuals who introduce beneficial concepts which can be integrated and developed further. Basically an organization's creative and innovative concepts stem from HC (Ahmad, Mohamad, & Ibrahim, 2013). In the context of a subsidiary, although knowledge from the parent MNC combined with the host country is essential to a subsidiary's KCC, HC is the most important factor affecting organizational performance (Seleim & Khalil, 2011). As the workforce is the greatest asset of an organization, it has the potential of conceiving knowledge. Therefore, a subsidiary's growth depends on the human factor since it is the most important element in determining an organization's KCC.

Seleim & Khalil (2011) stated as well that HC is the most fundamental element of organization's knowledge stock which has a major impact in the performance of an organization. The HC theory explains that HC brings value to the investment of an organization. HC engages a range of different knowledge which in turn allows for various perspectives and opinions for the same challenge (Chiang, 2007). In order to perform well across the board, HC needs to perform effectively (Morris

& Snell, 2011). In an organization, HC is the source of knowledge creation and strategic reconstruct. HC creates awareness of the organization's technological limitations so as to improve its ability to absorb and apply the knowledge spheres (Huang & Wu, 2010).

As a whole, countries with a large supply of HC will be at the forefront of the world economy. This is due to the fact that HC is essential for adopting technology and its respective improvement activities. In the context of MNC subsidiaries, the HC facilitates the inflow of knowledge from one department or unit to another that enables the generation of knowledge (Minbaeva et al., 2003). It was proven in Minbaeva et al., (2003), with a sample size of 169 subsidiaries based in the USA, Russia, and Finland, that HC is required to help with the knowledge inflow between subsidiary and other parts of the MNC to generate new knowledge. Gupta and Govindarajan (2000) also noted that the knowledge input in a subsidiary has a positive correlation with the desire and ability to gain and absorb knowledge and its transference to absorb incoming knowledge. HC is a critical source of intangible value of an organization (Huang & Wu, 2010) and these factors are critical for a subsidiary seeking to gain competitive advantage in the current challenging economy (Mehralian, Nazari, Akhavan, & Rasekh, 2014).

SOLUTIONS AND RECOMMENDATIONS

Literature has proven that knowledge inflow, KCC and HC in the subsidiary will create new knowledge and bring value add to stay competitive in this globalized world of economy. Previous literature provides sufficient evidence indicating the role and importance of workforce development in organizational strategy. The effectiveness of knowledge development strategy further becomes the reason for organizational performance. The strategic management in acquiring knowledge, the capability of the organization and workforce enable firms to deal appropriately with changes in circumstances and enhance the competitive advantage and capability within the organization.

Basically the relationship between knowledge inflow and knowledge creation capacity depends on being more grounded when a subsidiary has workers who have the necessary knowledge, skills, abilities and experience which will help them exploit the acquired knowledge (Gupta & Govindarajan, 2000; Minbaeva et al., 2003). Consequently, a high level of HC will positively affect the flow of KCC in a company due to the skilled and ambition employees at hand of the company (in-house and local knowledge).

HC is essential in order to create value, it provides the opportunity for new knowledge outside of the organization and combined with existing knowledge which is necessary for KCC (Dishon & Yabs, 2017). Subsidiaries learn new elements of knowledge externally beyond the organization's boundary through the knowledge network (in-house and local knowledge). Thus, knowledge is defined as being tacit, as it remains with the individual. In order for this knowledge to be transmitted effectively, needs to be turned onto explicit knowledge through knowledge creation. Explicit knowledge can then be successfully integrated into the subsidiary and combine new knowledge will enable the employee to transform it into their personal tacit knowledge. The organization further enhances its knowledge stock to establish a wealth of prior knowledge which improves its KCC and develops competitive advantage. Consequently, the cycle continues (Liao et al., 2016).

The Integration of Human Capital and Knowledge Creation Capability of Subsidiary

HC comprises of all aspects relating to the employees of a company. Their experience, talent and their innovativeness and creative aptitudes, enable the organization to be innovative and sustainable. The effective use of knowledge depends on human skills. Different knowledge requires different skills. HC plays a major role in an organization's competitiveness in the industry and at a national level. Innovation will become stagnant without the necessary HC. HC and knowledge creation are related to each other (Bontis, 2004). Innovation of product development and the establishment of novel service or program depends on individuals or groups of people who are capable of generating unique approaches and having the foresight to think beyond the implementation stage (Ahmad et al., 2013).

It is necessary for HC to have the right expertise in each department such as operations, marketing and so forth since HC is important to understand knowledge inflow in the organization (Lane et al., 2001). Organization's HC focuses on specific knowledge areas that enable a firm to function better than other firms. A high standard of HC is required to carry out challenging activities. HC affects the quality of a product and the speed for it to be manufactured. This can be explained by the fact that employees with a high level of expertise are able to acquire new knowledge and apply it well in the task at hand. Highly talented and skilled employees favourably influence KCC of an organization (Hsu & Sabherwal, 2012). A firm with a higher ability to absorb new knowledge will have the competitive advantage over other firms compared with lower absorbing abilities. However, an organization needs to have a capable HC to be able to absorb and use new knowledge. Without existing knowledgeable employees, an organization may never be able to absorb new knowledge and may be locked out from acquiring subsequent knowledge and technological development (Miles, 2013). New knowledge and knowledge creation are related to the existing fields of expertise of the worker (Lane et al., 2001).

Therefore, KCC of an organization highly depends on its HC. HC is viewed as an essential element for developing its competitive advantage, hence companies aim at recruiting the best individuals to achieve this (Rahimli, 2012). In order to achieve success, a company needs to have a good working team of knowledgeable creative individuals as this will have a big difference on the KCC of the entire firm. The employees will support the KCC of the organization through knowledge sharing. In short, the KCC is extremely HC sensitive (Urbancova, 2013). The more specialized an individual is, the greater the value he/she brings to the firm, which in return has a big impact on the organization's competitive advantage (Chahal, H., & Bakshi, 2015).

Due to the requirement of technological experts in planning and penetrating new markets, HC is more important than ever before. A subsidiary need not only recognize the existence and value of the new knowledge to understand its knowledge inflow i.e. home and host network knowledge (Cohen and Levinthal, 1990). In addition, a subsidiary needs such skilled workforce and enough HC in order to comply with the requirement of local organizations looking for high technology expertise. The HC of a subsidiary helps expertise to move freely from one department to another in MNC to establish a knowledge stock (Minbaeva et al., 2003).

Human Capital as Enabler

As subsidiaries are exposed to a range of expertise and operate at different levels of the market and MNCs (Chiang, 2007), subsidiaries' HC have a critical effect on its competitiveness (Huang & Wu, 2010). Technical expertise and insights along with HC can equip an organization with the ability to pick vital knowledge and distinguish possible knowledge channel (Phene & Almeida, 2008). Furthermore, according to Phene & Almeida (2008), HC helps to identify and digest external knowledge, thus improving the sourcing capability of the subsidiary. Depending on the employees' capability, they will be able to acquire more knowledge with great diversity enabling them to develop a variety of solutions to potential issues. Having the right knowledge at hand, will heighten the productivity and efficiency of the employees when they are faced with the inflow of new knowledge. Employees' ability allows them access to more knowledge, or diverse knowledge, with the potential for multiple views on similar problems. The more relevant knowledge is made available to employees, the more efficient and productive they will be in dealing with knowledge inflows (Chiang, 2007).

Since HC is the source of innovation and competitiveness, the accessibility of capable, talented, and motivated employees in a subsidiary's workforce will increase the capabilities of the organization in gaining competitive advantage (Chiang, 2007). High knowledge background will allow employees to take on board and comprehend new knowledge (Cohen and Levinthal, 1990). The firms that have HC with greater expertise or knowledge are commonly in a better position to create fresh knowledge because they have a strong knowledge platform in which they can build. This supports the theory of HC which advocates that expertise and capability of the employees along with collective knowledge constitute a form of capital that will provide value as a result of the time and effort invested in them (Subramaniam & Youndt, 2005).

HC generates value to the organization by bringing a wide source of knowledge (Chiang, 2007). Employees and hence the subsidiary will be more competitive when the right knowledge is made available to them. The workforce in a subsidiary needs to operate efficiently to reach an optimal level of performance due to the responsibility it has in a subsidiary's KCC (Morris & Snell, 2011). Making sure new knowledge is at hand will enhance a subsidiaries capability of remaining competitive, particularly through HC.

Essentially subsidiaries need in-house capacity to fully comprehend and transform knowledge inflow from internal and external knowledge source into functional expertise (Cohen & Levinthal, 1990). Employees who are able to set the firm apart from its competitors are vital to the organization especially as today's society has moved to a knowledge society. Such employees are deemed a necessity to ensure that knowledge creation abilities are achieved by the firm. It can also be said that innovation generated from knowledge itself and being able to adapt in the face of challenges in the environment leads to greater profitability and success. Consequently, it is imperative that subsidiaries focus on developing knowledgeable workers, training programs, flexibility, positive working culture and so forth. By doing this, the internal HC will be able to produce a competitive advantage which is unique to the organization. The more discrete this knowledge remains, the easier it will be to sustain especially with regards to the competitive advantage of the firm (Rahimli, 2012).

Therefore, taking into consideration that HC theory is an evolving concept, HC is a necessary requirement for the competitive advantage of a subsidiary. It means that the development of a skilled workforce in Malaysia is necessary to innovate, assimilate and diffuse new knowledge and to adapt to it, for subsidiaries in Malaysia to achieve competitive advantage. In other words, without the HC, subsidiaries would not be able to create new knowledge even though there are knowledge inflows (Cohen & Levinthal, 1990). The strength of HC can determine the extent of ability for a subsidiary to create KCC of the organization in order to stay competitive in the industry (Morris & Snell, 2011). This relationship of HC as a moderator in between knowledge inflow and KCC of subsidiary can be summarized in Figure 1.

FUTURE RESEARCH DIRECTIONS

KCC of subsidiary depends of how HC is recruited, groomed and utilized. HC plays a vital role in the dynamics of an organization to transform its product and services to position in the mind of the consumer for a long time. The KCC of subsidiary depends on the effective utilization of HC that enable the organization to grow to an industrial leader status. The local talents can guide subsidiaries to seek home-grown knowledge to become more innovative in its products or services offering in order to increase its sales and profit. The more the subsidiary is able to uncover and appreciate the tacit knowledge that is distinct from the home country, the motivation of the local talent increases. Then the local management would be able to devise better strategies, processes and methods to stay competitive.

Besides that, future research needs to establish other aspect of a subsidiary's intellectual capital which can enhance the KCC of a subsidiary. For example, the growing influence of social capital in the host country in determining the survival of the subsidiary. Most importantly, the collaboration of the subsidiaries with the local SME who could be the suppliers in the total supply value chain between HQ and the subsidiary. The existing knowledge exchanges between the subsidiaries and the local SMEs are equally important to create KCC. The knowledge exchanges could have taken place in a formal and informal ways which is worth to be understood.

CONCLUSION

In summary, organization which has the capacity to be creative and integrative with respect to knowledge and can quickly put it into practice in the market, in the era of knowledge, will gain the sharpest competitive edge. An organization is able to

Figure 1. Relationship between knowledge inflow, human capital and knowledge creation capabilities

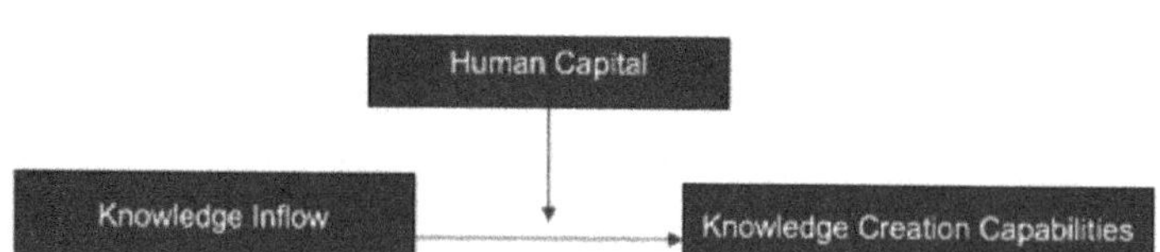

enhance its products and services by being innovative and transmitting its knowledge on a continuous basis. Hence the knowledge-based capability of a subsidiary is of greater significance compared to the entity-based capability as the only way for a firm's competitive advantage to be sustained is through its learning capabilities (Luo, 2000).

A firm's competitive advantage is generated from the firm's capabilities and a firm's KCC are strengthened by responding to environment changes. A firm develops its capacity to combine, organize and restructure in house and external knowledge to meet the challenges of the evolving environment (Teece et al., 1997). Subsidiaries with abundant HC will be able to boost their operational efficiency and also become a vital input with respect to the knowledge inflow activities (Seleim & Khalil, 2011). Greater expertise of HC leads to a better knowledge inflow. HC comprising tacit knowledge (such as experience, beliefs and attitudes) and explicit knowledge (such as understanding industry requirements and best practices) is necessary to establish and retain relevant knowledge in the subsidiary to gain competitive edge.

Committed, inspired and skilful HC forms the backbone of innovative procedures in the subsidiary. Such intellectual capital is a major starting point for establishing fresh ideas and knowledge (Martín-de Castro, Delgado-Verde, Navas-López, & Cruz-González, 2013). The benefits of HC are essential for eliminating a subsidiary's technological limits, augmenting its ability to take in and use completely different spheres of knowledge (Subramaniam & Youndt, 2005). Even though, very committed and skilled employees may suggest organizational structures into question, such HC is vital in propelling the subsidiary to its technological boundaries and it's the best encouragement for innovating and generating fresh knowledge (Nonaka, 1991). Subsidiaries which have the greatest pool of HC will be the most innovative, with HC being the well of ideas driving innovation (Martín-de Castro et al., 2013).

To conclude, KCC is a way for a subsidiary to ensure its survival in a volatile business environment. External and internal knowledge inflows help to improve an organization's performance. An improved HC increases the KCC of the subsidiary (Ahlstrom et al., 2013). The impact of KCC contributes to the overall competitiveness of the subsidiary in the market. KCC is able to direct knowledge beyond the boundary of organization and generate new knowledge with which it can combine. However, even though a subsidiary is able to generate new knowledge through leveraging its KCC, the subsidiary is incapable of knowledge generation alone by itself. HC helps the organization to gather and use external knowledge which can fill the gaps in knowledge left by KCC. Thus, HC helps to channel what is achieved from KCC into product innovation. Subsidiaries' KCC will be more beneficial in subsidiaries with a higher level of HC. In a subsidiary with higher KCC and stronger HC, will achieve a higher competitive advantage.

REFERENCES

Ahmad, F., Mohamad, O., & Ibrahim, H. I. (2013). Absorptive Capacity and Innovative Behavior among Engineers in Malaysia. *Elixir International Journal, 56*.

Almeida, P., & Phene, A. (2004). Subsidiaries and knowledge creation: The influence of the MNC and host country on innovation. *Strategic Management Journal, 25*(89), 847–864. doi:10.1002mj.388

Amabile, T. M. (1988). A Model of Creativity and Innovation in Organizations. *Research in Organizational Behavior, 10*, 123.

Andersson, U., Bjorkman, I., & Forsgren, M. (2005). Managing subsidiary knowledge creation: The effect of control mechanisms on subsidiary local embeddedness. *International Business Review, 14*(5), 521–538. doi:10.1016/j.ibusrev.2005.07.001

Andreeva, T., & Kianto, A. (2012). Does knowledge management really matter? Linking knowledge management practices, competitiveness and economic performance. *Journal of Knowledge Management, 16*(4), 617–636. doi:10.1108/13673271211246185

Bierly, P., & Chakrabarti, A. (1996). Generic knowledge strategies in the u.s. pharmaceutical industry. *Strategic Management Journal, 17*(S2), 123–135. doi:10.1002mj.4250171111

Birkinshaw, J. (1998). Corporate entrepreneurship in network organizations. *European Management Journal, 16*(3), 355–364. doi:10.1016/S0263-2373(98)00012-7

Bontis, N. (2004). National Intellectual Capital Index: A United Nations Initiative for the Arab Region. *Journal of Intellectual Capital, 5*(1), 13–39. doi:10.1108/14691930410512905

Bueno, E., Anton, J. M. R., & Salmador, M. P. (2008). Knowledge creation as a dynamic capability: Implications for innovation management and organisational design. *International Journal ofTechnology Management, 41*(1/2), 155. doi:10.1504/IJTM.2008.015989

Cardy, R. L., & Selvarajan, T. T. (2006). Competencies: Alternative frameworks for competitive advantage. *Business Horizons, 49*(3), 235–245. doi:10.1016/j.bushor.2005.09.004

Chahal, H., & Bakshi, P. (2015). Examining intellectual capital and competitive advantage relationship: role of innovation and organizational learning. *International Journal of Bank Marketing, 33*(3), 376-399.doi:10.1108/IJBM-07-2013-0069

Chiang, J. (2007). Subsidiary performance in MNCs: The influences of absorptive capacity and social capital on knowledge transfer. *International Business & Economics Research Journal*, *6*(10), 43–50.

Choi, B., & Lee, H. (2002). Knowledge management strategy and its link to knowledge creation process. *Expert Systems with Applications*, *23*(3), 173–187. doi:10.1016/S0957-4174(02)00038-6

Chong, S. C. (2006). KM critical success factors: A comparison of perceived importance versus implementation in Malaysian ICT companies. *The Learning Organization*, *13*(3), 230–256. doi:10.1108/09696470610661108

Cohen, W. M., & Levinthal, D. A. (1990). Absorptive Capacity : A New Perspective on Learning and Innovation. *Administrative Science Quarterly*, *35*(1), 128–152. doi:10.2307/2393553

Colakoglu, S., & Jiang, Y. (2013). Subsidiary-level outcomes of expatriate staffing: An empirical examination of MNC subsidiaries in the USA. *European Journal of International Management*, *7*(6), 696–718. doi:10.1504/EJIM.2013.057107

Collins, C. J., & Smith, K. G. (2006). Knowledge exchange and combination: The role of human resource practices in the performance of high-technology firms. *Academy of Management Journal*, *49*(3), 544–561. doi:10.5465/amj.2006.21794671

Demeter, K., Szász, L., & Rácz, B. (2016). The impact of subsidiaries ' internal and external integration on operational performance. *International Journal of Production Economics*, *182*, 73–85. doi:10.1016/j.ijpe.2016.08.014

Dishon, W. M., & Yabs, D. J. (2017). A Critical Literature Review On The Link Between Multinational Enterprises Presence, Absorptive Capacity And Competitive Advantage Of Firms. *Archives of Business Research*, *5*(3), 101–114. doi:10.14738/abr.53.2711

Drucker, P. F. (2009). A century of social transformation: Emergence of knowledge society. In *Managing in a time of great change*. Boston, MA: Harvard Business Press.

Eisenhardt, K. K. M., & Martin, J. J. A. (2000). Dynamic capabilities: What are they? *Strategic Management Journal*, *21*(10-11), 1105–1121. doi:10.1002/1097-0266(200010/11)21:10/11<1105::AID-SMJ133>3.0.CO;2-E

Ferraris, A., Santoro, G., & Dezi, L. (2017). How MNC's subsidiaries may improve their innovative performance? The role of external sources and knowledge management capabilities. *Journal of Knowledge Management*, *21*(17).

Ghoshal, S., Bartlett, C. A., & Wyplosz, C. (1988). Creation, Adoption and Diffusion of Innovations by Subsidiaries of Multinational Corporations. *Journal of International Business Studies*, *19*(3), 365–388. doi:10.1057/palgrave.jibs.8490388

Gupta, A. K., & Govindarajan, V. (1991). Knowledge Flows and the Structure of Control Within Multinational Corporations. *Academy of Management Review, 16*(4), 768–792. doi:10.5465/AMR.1991

Gupta, A. K., & Govindarajan, V. (2000). Knowledge flows within multinational corporations. *Strategic Management Journal, 496*, 473–496.

Holm, U., & Sharma, D. D. (2006). Subsidiary marketing knowledge and strategic development of the multinational corporation. *Journal of International Management*, *12*(1), 47–66. doi:10.1016/j.intman.2005.11.001

Hsu, I.-C., & Sabherwal, R. (2012). Relationship between Intellectual Capital and Knowledge Management: An Empirical Investigation. *Decision Sciences*, *43*(3), 489–524. doi:10.1111/j.1540-5915.2012.00357.x

Huang, Y.-C., & Wu, Y.-C. J. (2010). Intellectual capital and knowledge productivity: The Taiwan biotech industry. *Management Decision*, *48*(4), 580–599. doi:10.1108/00251741011041364

Jarrar, Y., Zairi, M., & Schiuma, G. (2010). Defining Organisational Knowledge: A Best Practice Perspective. *ECBPM, Copyright*(September), 1–10.

Lai, M.-C., & Yap, S.-F. (2004). Technology Development in Malaysia and the Newly Industrializing Economies: A Comparative Analysis. *Asia-Pacific Development Journal*, *11*(2), 53–80.

Lane, P. J., Salk, J. E., & Lyles, M. A. (2001). Absorptive capacity, learning, and performance in international joint ventures. *Strategic Management Journal*, *22*(12), 1139–1161. doi:10.1002mj.206

Liao, S.-H., Chen, C.-C., Hu, D.-C., Chung, Y., & Yang, M.-J. (2016). Developing a sustainable competitive advantage: Absorptive capacity, knowledge transfer and organizational learning. *The Journal of Technology Transfer*. doi:10.100710961-016-9532-1

Liao, S.-H., Wu, C.-C., Hu, D.-C., & Tsui, K.-A. (2010). Relationships between knowledge acquisition, absorptive capacity and innovation capability: An empirical study on Taiwan's financial and manufacturing industries. *Journal of Information Science*, *36*(1), 19–35. doi:10.1177/0165551509340362

Luo, Y. (2000). Dynamic Capabilities in International Expansion. *Journal of World Business*, *35*(4), 355–378. doi:10.1016/S1090-9516(00)00043-2

Mahnke, V., Pedersen, T., & Venzin, M. (2005). Why do MNC subsidiaries engage in knowledge sharing with other subsidiaries and what are the implications for performance. In *Dynamics of Industry and Innovation*. Organizations, Networks and Systems.

Marr, B., Gupta, O., Pike, S., & Roos, G. (2003). Intellectual capital and knowledge management effectiveness. *Management Decision*, *41*(8), 771–781. doi:10.1108/00251740310496288

Martín-de Castro, G., Delgado-Verde, M., Navas-López, J. E., & Cruz-González, J. (2013). The moderating role of innovation culture in the relationship between knowledge assets and product innovation. *Technological Forecasting and Social Change*, *80*(2), 351–363. doi:10.1016/j.techfore.2012.08.012

Mehralian, G., Nazari, J. A., Akhavan, P., & Rasekh, H. R. (2014). Exploring the relationship between the knowledge creation process and intellectual capital in the pharmaceutical industry. *The Learning Organization*, *21*(4), 258–273. doi:10.1108/TLO-07-2013-0032

Meyer, K. E., Mudambi, R., & Narula, R. (2011). Multinational Enterprises and Local Contexts: The Opportunities and Challenges of Multiple Embeddedness. *Journal of Management Studies*, *48*(2), 235–252. doi:10.1111/j.1467-6486.2010.00968.x

Miles, J. A. (2013). Absorptive Capacity Theory. In Management and Organization Theory. Academic Press.

Minbaeva, D., Pedersen, T., Björkman, I., Fey, C. F., Park, H. J., Bjorkman, I., ... Park, H. J. (2003). MNC knowledge transfer, subsidiary absorptive capacity and HRM. *Journal of International Business Studies*, *34*(6), 586–599. doi:10.1057/palgrave.jibs.8400056

Morris, S. S., & Snell, S. (2011). Intellectual capital configurations and organizational capability: An empirical examination of human resource subunits in the multinational enterprise. *Journal of International Business Studies*, *42*(6), 805–827. doi:10.1057/jibs.2011.14

Mudalige, D., Ismail, N. A., & Malek, M. M. (2016). Application of theory of dynamic capabilities to explicate internationalization of SMEes in Sri Lanka. *Ipbj*, *8*(2), 1–18.

Mudambi, R., Pedersen, T., & Andersson, U. (2014). How subsidiaries gain power in multinational corporations. *Journal of World Business*, *49*(1), 101–113. doi:10.1016/j.jwb.2013.02.001

Mudambi, R. (2002). Knowledge management in multinational firms. *Journal of International Management, 8*(1), 1–9. doi:10.1016/S1075-4253(02)00050-9

Najim Abdullah, M., Hashim, M. A., & Ali, A. (2015). Review of the Elements of Knowledge Management Capabilities. *Journal of Information Systems Research and Innovation*, *9*(2), 28–34.

Nambiar, S. (2011). Problems with human capital in Malaysia East Asia Forum. *East Asia Forum*, (Part 1), 2–4.

National Economic Advisory Council. (2010). *New economic model for Malaysia: Strategic policy direction*. Author.

Nonaka, I. (1991). The Knowledge Creating Company. *Harvard Business Review*, *69*, 96–104. doi:10.1016/0024-6301(96)81509-3

Perri, A., & Andersson, U. (2014). Knowledge outflows from foreign subsidiaries and the tension between knowledge creation and knowledge protection: Evidence from the semiconductor industry. *International Business Review*, *23*(1), 63–75. doi:10.1016/j.ibusrev.2013.08.007

Phene, A., & Almeida, P. (2008). Innovation in multinational subsidiaries: The role of knowledge assimilation and subsidiary capabilities. *Journal of International Business Studies*, *39*(5), 901–919. doi:10.1057/palgrave.jibs.8400383

Rahimli, A. (2012). Knowledge Management and Competitive Advantage. *Information and Knowledge Management, 2*(7), 37–43.

Ritchie, B. K. (2002). Foreign direct investment and intellectual capital. *OECD Working Paper, 194*. Retrieved from http://www.oecd.org/indonesia/1949901.pdf

Roy, M. J., & Therin, F. (2008). Knowledge acquisition and environmental commitment in SMEs. *Corporate Social Responsibility and Environmental Management*, *15*(5), 249–259. doi:10.1002/csr.145

Seleim, A. A. S., & Khalil, O. E. M. (2011). Understanding the knowledge management-intellectual capital relationship: a two-way analysis. *Journal of Intellectual Capital*, *12*. doi:10.1108/14691931111181742

Shih, K. H., Chang, C., & Lin, B. (2010). Assessing knowledge creation and intellectual capital in banking industry. *Journal of Intellectual Capital*, *11*(1), 74–89. doi:10.1108/14691931011013343

Smith, K. G., Collins, C. J., & Clark, K. D. (2005). Existing knowledge, knowledge creation capability, and the rate of new product introduction in high technology firms. *Academy of Management Journal*, *48*(2), 346–357. doi:10.5465/amj.2005.16928421

Su, Z., Ahlstrom, D., Li, J., & Cheng, D. (2013, November). Knowledge creation capability, absorptive capacity, and product innovativeness. *R&D Management*. doi:10.1111/radm.12033

Subramaniam, M., & Youndt, M. A. (2005a). The Influence of Intellectual Capital On The Types Of Innovation Capabilities. *Academy of Management Journal*, *48*(3), 450–463. doi:10.5465/amj.2005.17407911

Teece, D. J., Pisano, G., & Shuen, A. (1997). Dynamic Capabilities and Strategic Management. *Strategic Management Journal*, *18*(7), 509–533. doi:10.1002/(SICI)1097-0266(199708)18:7<509::AID-SMJ882>3.0.CO;2-Z

Urbancova, H. (2013). Competitive Advantage Achievement through Innovation and Knowledge. *Journal of Competitiveness*, *5*(1), 82–96. doi:10.7441/joc.2013.01.06

Wang, H. (2014). Theories for competitive advantage. In H. Hasan (Ed.), Being Practical with Theory: A Window into Business Research (pp. 33–43). Wollongong, Australia: Academic Press.

Yi, W. (2012). L., & Jayasingam, S. (2012). Factors Driving Knowledge Creation among Private Sector Organizations: Empirical Evidence from Malaysia. *Journal of Organizational Knowledge Management*, *12*. doi:10.5171/2012.199983

Chapter 8
Organizational Learning and Collective Human Capital Relationship With Firm Performance Among MNEs in the Northern Region of Malaysia

Phynthamilkumaran Siea Dass
Universiti Sains Malaysia, Malaysia

Shankar Chelliah
Universiti Sains Malaysia, Malaysia

ABSTRACT

The main objective in this chapter is to understand the organizational learning challenges of multinational enterprises and their performance in Malaysia. At the same time, it also explores how organizational learning and collective human capital with competitive advantage as a mediating factor affect MNEs' performance in Malaysia through employee movement. This research concluded knowledge acquisition, knowledge distribution, and organizational memory is positively significant towards competitive advantage. Only knowledge acquisition and organizational memory are positively significant when competitive advantage mediates organizational learning towards firm performance. Collective human capital is positively significant towards competitive advantage as well as towards firm performance when competitive advantage mediates. Through this research it was found that MNEs in Malaysia are weak in knowledge interpretation and knowledge distribution due to employee movement in the northern region of Malaysia.

DOI: 10.4018/978-1-5225-7426-2.ch008

INTRODUCTION

This chapter provides an introduction to the piece of research by drawing a comprehensive picture of this study as a whole and as such, laying the foundations for the following chapters. It starts with an overview of the research background. The importance of the study is then discussed in the problem statement and the broad gaps in current literature are addressed as well as the significance of the research towards theoretical perspectives and its estimated practical contributions. Through the problem statement the research is addressed by specific research questions and research objectives as well as by defining the scope. The chapter also defines the important terms used in the study.

MNEs have been taking the lead in terms of innovation and moving the market trend in order to meet ever changing customer demand. As well as meeting the changes they have to meet the challenges in the market presented by the customer, regardless of whether it is with product, service or quality. From meeting the customer demand, there is now the expectation to meet the customer differences which determine the performance of the MNEs in industry (Azmi, 2008).

It also needs to be acknowledged that MNEs have a wealth of experience in operating in crises in both the internal and external environment. Some of the firms who acknowledged this earlier have made the significant changes required to prepare to meet these crises and those firms who haven't, have eventually been phased out of the industry (Collins, 2001). Examples Kodak, Nokia and so forth.

Thus, this study has been carried out to further understand organizational learning and collective human capital significance in MNEs in Malaysia. This research explores the latest significance of the relationship of these variables with MNEs in Malaysia which have had significant growth and have contributed to the growth of SMEs as well as the GDP of the country over the years (Penang Investment, 2015). Thus, the aim of this research is to understand the reason for the retention of the MNEs in Malaysia.

RESEARCH BACKGROUND

This study explores the determinants of Multinational Enterprises (MNE) performance in Malaysia. Therefore, the influence of organizational learning and collective human capital on establishing competitive advantage that improves firm performance has also been investigated.

Referring to Sampe (2012), most firms practice the sustaining and fundamentals of the economy model of having cost leadership, market or product differentiation and niche orientation to attain firm performance. The above three segments are widely used in domestic environments when referring to competitive advantage being analyzed in terms of business continuity with rapid changes, development in technology and market demands and requirements. Operational cost and product cost is one of the main contributing factors in order for MNEs to remain in the industry. Despite having a huge or limited product variant, it has to ensure meeting the end user's demand. By having a huge variant of products MNEs have to ensure they meet their end user's affordability so that the products can remain in the industry. All this has to be done without lowering the quality and safety standards of the product. One of the drawing factors for MNEs to venture into external resources is due to the knowledge and skills as well as the abilities that the labour force has to acquire. Furthermore with the establishment of the learning mechanisms or structure establishment in the organization in terms of sustainability as well as managing the crises and developing the new work force to demonstrate the firm performance (Nkundabanyanga, 2016), only an experienced work force has the ability to develop a new work force and repeat the organizational learning to ensure the self-sustainability is retained (Sampe, 2012).

Thus, this study expects to analyze the significance of organizational learning establishment by MNEs as well as knowledge, skills and abilities developed by MNEs towards the employees. It is found that MNEs with the affordability in establishing right problem solving methodology, training development as well as standardization practices have indirectly helped long serving employees in the firm to gain such experience in order for them to increase and sustain firm performance (Chang & Lee, 2007). Malaysia has been one of the countries for MNEs to invest in heavily over the few decades. Therefore, the significance of organizational learning and collective human capital practices among MNEs in Malaysia have been studied. With this, organizational learning and human capital abilities and skills among Malaysians have been analyzed. This, would result in Malaysians having a higher competitive advantage in the market which continues to attract MNEs allowing them to increase their performance in Malaysia. Subsequent subchapters will provide the foreign and domestic investment trends by states as well as in the manufacturing sectors in Malaysia. This is expected to highlight Malaysian manufacturing economic progress and its relevance to this study.

PROBLEM STATEMENT

In recent years MNEs have made their decision to shut down their operations in Malaysia and some have even outsourced their operations locally. They are MNEs investing as well as expanding in Malaysia as explained in the figures above. This drastic decision made by MNEs impacts organizational learning and skill enhancement in Malaysia. There have been minimal studies which explore how organizational learning and skill enhancement impact competitive advantage as well as firm performance when MNEs in Malaysia exit, expand or invest. Thus, this study is designated to address organizational learning and collective human capital impact towards sustaining MNEs in Malaysia when other MNEs leave, expand or invest. By understanding the current organizational practices towards organizational learning and collective human capital deliverables respectively, the study measures the sustaining MNEs competitive advantage capabilities and their performance in Malaysia, which eventually indicates, whether these MNEs have the potential to leave or to expand.

One of the key observations acknowledged when MNEs leave, expand or invest is the employee movement within MNEs. It is very common for employees to job hop in such an environment to protect their income or seek better opportunities. In such an environment it creates a knowledge halt or vacuum in the organizational learning process in existing organizations or firms (Coyle, 2009), which increases the chances of existing MNEs losing their competitive advantage as well as performance in Malaysia. This eventually leads such MNEs to exit their operations from Malaysia. The more such situation are faced by sustaining MNEs in Malaysia, the chances of them exiting is higher which will reduce the manufacturing growth in the Malaysian economy in the coming years.

10, 000 hours or ten years of deliberate practice studies done by Ericsson, Krampe & Tesch-Romer (1997) and Ericsson, Preitula & Cokely (2007) were only being studied and evaluated amongst athletes and musicians as well as sports individual contributors, which require repeated practice and skill enhancement. It was proven from research that when athletes or musicians have adequate amount of hours or years of deliberate practice, they have the ability to outperform the rest in the field. Since this research is being evaluated in matured MNEs with more than ten years of operation experience would have established organizational learning systems in order to self-sustain the productivity and revenue growth. Thus, this study relates the significance of 10,000 hours or ten years of deliberate experience in organizational learning performance towards MNEs competitive advantage and firm performance.

Similarly for collective human capital, when the employees have gained the required knowledge, skills and abilities throughout their employability in MNEs it would directly relate to firm performance and the contribution towards the success and sustaining of the organization. Human capital was found to be an intangible asset in the organization and considered as one of the inimitable assets. Nevertheless, when employees decide to move around to another organization or firm, the organization or firm has to ensure the continuity of the knowledge, skills as well as abilities are retained within the organization (Sirmon, Hitt, Ireland & Glbert, 2012). The revolution of collective human capital should have developed and be enhanced as well as well-crafted in organizational practices. Thus, this study relates the significance of collective human capital knowledge, skills as well as the ability in the organization of MNE performance.

In summary, this is research addresses the current sustaining challenges of MNEs in practicing organizational learning as well as the importance of collective human capital in MNEs in Malaysia, which answers the implications towards competitive advantage and MNE performance respectively.

LITERATURE REVIEW

Resource-Based View Theory

Barney (1991) defines the resource-based view theory as a competitive advantage developed by acquiring, developing, combining as well as developing organizational resources and employees in such a way that it is difficult to imitate and it creates unique value compared to its competitors. For sources of competitive advantage, the resource-based view theory suggests that the firm explore the physical and intellectuality of their internal resources. Once the resources become rare, inimitable, valuable and non-substitutable, as mentioned by researchers Takeuchi, Wang & Takeuchi (2007) and Newbert (2008) and they classified it as central visions that would lead to competitive advantages. Resources which are set for exploiting opportunities as well as minimizing incoming threats are classified as value, whereas, resources that are advancing in the large organization and are a threat for future competitors are classified as rare. The difficulty faced by competitors reproducing or copying the resources for their own use is classified as inimitability. When the resources cannot be replicated by competitors for their own benefit it is classified as non-substitutable. With all these views in the above being achieved, it would allow respective firms to pass on the resources which have potential to lead and sustain competitive advantage in the long run (Allen & Wright, 2007). Figure 1 illustrates the Barney (1991) VRIO model.

Due to the influence of highly skilled and highly motivated human capital a firm is able to achieve sustainable competitive advantage. Inspite of skill and motivation, productive behavior has a significant correlation with competitive advantage (Seidu, 2011). Firm performance was determined by creating competitive advantage with the resource-based view theory. It requires internal resources as employee skills as well as knowledge, motivation and behavior. The current piece of research, tests the relationship of the resource-based view theory between collective human capital and competitive advantage as mediating with firm performance.

Figure 1. Resource-based view theory developed and named as VRIO model

Organizational Learning Theory

Leavitt (2011) highlights the significance of human capital in today's organization as intangible assets in the organization, employees tend to create the capacity to think, act and collaborate. Employees tend to work together by encouraging each other's thought process through beliefs and assumptions. With the rising complexity in the market it requires organizational learning as well as intelligent, capable and knowledgeable people to face the challenges. Organizational learning has been divided into three main theories by Leavitt (2011). As well as being summarized in Figure 2.

The learning process and systems were established through the organization to enhance and retain knowledge acquisition, to store and disseminate. Organizational learning is valued as a medium to create competitive advantage in today's competitive market environment. It serves as a mechanism to rejuvenate and reinvent for individuals as well as the organization. Nevertheless retaining and developing organizational learning are the challenges focused on by firms today to improve their financial as well as operational performance.

Organizational Learning

Despite having its roots in individual learning, organizational learning tends to emerge from the learning process towards organizational perspective. Previous studies

Figure 2. Integrated organization learning model between organization, group/team and Individual respectively.

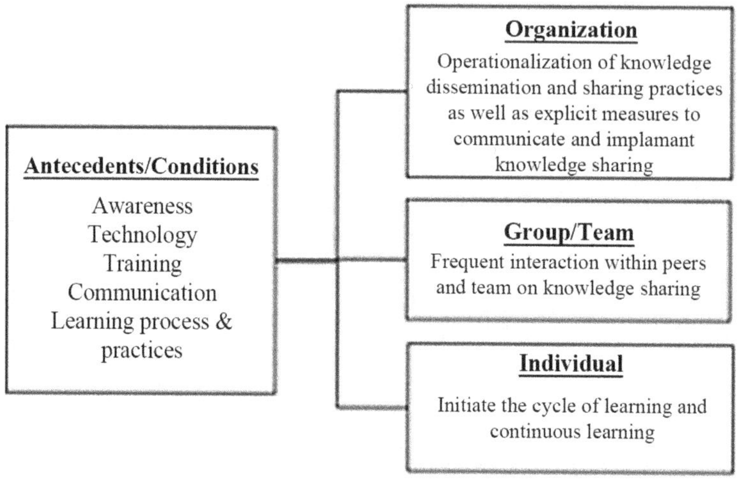

have related organizational learning towards internal organization and management practices which allowed it to be one-dimensional in the past study. However the use of organizational learning in terms of understanding knowledge acquisition, distribution and interpretation or utilization in the organization itself, was more suitable to be multidimensional (Jimenez-Jimenez & Sans-Valle, 2011). This was explained by analyzing knowledge acquisition, distribution and interpretation in organizational learning in this research, it has adapted the theory of assimilation in organizational learning theory as explained in Figure 2.

In a study by Seidu (2011) it was mentioned that the organization would only attain its sustainability of peak performance when the human capital blended into the organization. In terms of the knowledge acquired by respective individuals and having the collaboration to comprehend each other in delivering towards firm performance, this study in referring to Ericsson et al., (1993) adopted the experienced human capital who have been developing their knowledge in the assigned job for almost 10,000 hours or ten years. During these progress years it allows them to blend adequately in order to fit and progress in the organization and firm resulting in firm performance. It requires continuous improvement for the organization to grow and to gather respective human capital aligned and to deliver to the organizational goal and objectives. By having the right knowledge it would strengthen the organization and firm as years pass by with continuous improvement. Thus, this could be related to the study by Ericsson et al., (1993) that it requires ten years to have an international growth in terms knowledge. By adopting these findings in this research it would help it focus on the actual knowledge acquired by the employees who would have contributed significantly towards the firm's growth or performance respectively.

Collective Human Capital

In the business and economic forum, human capital is addressed as employees with knowledge, skills and abilities (KSA). The value of the wages would go higher depending on the KSA acquired by the human capital which increases the demand and it is also unable to be imitated when human capital is in collective environment. Since human capital is not able to be imitated, is rare and non-substitutable it is related to resource-based view theory. The multidimensional study is more relevant to be studied when human capital is measured from an individual perspective. In the collective environment it is recommended that a one-dimensional study be done as it is gathering the different levels of human capital which varies in terms of KSA. It then aligns them to the organization as well as firm goals and direction respectively. It is expected that with the collective human capital environment it would allow the work force to be more directive and objective as well as improvising productivity and performance overall (Takeuchi et al., 2007).

Collective human capital was adopted for this research to understand the significance of sustaining MNE performance in Malaysia with competitive advantage as a mediating factor. Seidu (2011) has researched this model specifically in the banking industry and has compared the performance of two banks in this model. Thus, it requires knowledge, skills, abilities, creativity and the independency of the employees as sub elements in collective human capital to be measured in order to determine the relativity towards firm performance with a competitive advantage as a mediating factor. The above mentioned sub elements were evaluated by Subramaniam and Yount (2005) and by Seidu (2011) in their respective studies. However, it would take several years of experience for the organization to regain the competitive advantage which they have lost through employee movement. It requires heavy investment in training and development as well as system establishments to develop the KSA of the existing employee so as to have higher skill sets to compete. This is the current predicament that MNEs in Malaysia are experiencing due to employee movement. With this, the above sub elements have been adopted in this research to relate the collective human capital towards MNE performance in Malaysia with a competitive advantage as a mediating factor.

Competitive Advantage

According to Luu (2014) a product has to go through eight basic quality dimensions such as esthetics, conformance, durability, serviceability, reliability, perceived quality, performance and features before it is marketed or sent for customer consumption. Thus, severe criteria are being placed by ensuring adequate quality standards are being followed to sustain and upscale to meet the customers' requirements and standards. Despite the sustaining of MNEs, SMEs are improving quality standards and raising their standards to be on a par with MNEs performance in terms of quality with higher competitive advantage regardless the cost or personalization.

For this research, innovation, quality, service and market differentiation respectively as well as low cost leadership are adopted to measure the performance of MNEs in Malaysia as a mediator. This research explores an interplay with both organization learning and collective human capital relations together and its effect on competitive advantage of MNEs in Malaysia which is not conclusive in the literature. With employee movement practices in Malaysia, it makes this piece of research different from past studies which would be assessing the effectiveness of organizational learning practices as well as collective human capital towards competitive advantage.

Firm Performance

Dubey et al. (2014) articulated, they are several approaches to relate firm performance to utilization. It also depends on the industry and the nature of the business to define the right approach as some rely on service based industry and others on a manufacturing base. There was considerable debate on the appropriateness of various approaches to the concept utilization and measurement of organizational performance. Unlike small firms, most of the bigger firms have listed themselves in share markets for investors to invest in them. Thus, quarterly and yearly financial performance and strategy have to be revealed for investors to value the firms. Usually their financial records are accurate as they have been audited by a third party audit firm before revealing the data compared to a small firm which truly depends to its internal audit and CEO approval. Since CEOs of MNEs are answerable to a board of directors and investors, their evaluation and progress is being valued in a very meticulous manner (Abebe & Alvarado, 2013).

Overall a firm's performance was measured based on its financial gains. Those financial gains would reflect its profitability in terms of sales, investments and assets of returns and total profits respectively. For growth, it governs profit and sales growth respectively. Nevertheless, the below highlighted financial gains not only reflects firm's performance, but also highlights Chief Executive Officer (CEO)'s satisfaction of firm performance (Beal, 2000).

Later studies, Return on Assets (ROA) and Return on Total Global Sales (ROS) become key factors in determining firm performance in financial terms. Both of these variables determines the time of investments to generate growth as well as depreciation of the assets as they are utilized. Thus, as illustrated by Azadegan & Dooley (2010) cost, quality, new product, delivery and flexibility performance would determine a firm's performance. These determinants have been adopted as high relevance in determining firm performance for this study on MNEs in Malaysia.

Gaps in the Literature

Based on the literature review, a few research gaps can be derived. Firstly, the application of organizational learning among MNEs is still ambiguous in Malaysia. The research gaps found in organizational learning in terms of knowledge acquisition, knowledge storing and disseminating is alarming with the people movement in the industry in Malaysia. This is clear when Seidu (2011) emphasizes collective human capital and firm performance with competitive advantage as a mediating variable, but is unable to point out the importance of organizational learning which the current study would like to compliment. Similarly, studies by Cheng et al. (2010) and Sim (2012) in Malaysia at that point of time did not foresee the importance of organizational learning and its implications towards the competitive advantage of MNEs.

Secondly, Wang & Yang (2011) have stated that organizational learning can be improved when an individual creates the ability to spare additional time for development and improvement. This can be attained by experience gained collectively in the organization as organizational learning. In the theoretical framework explained by Wang & Yang (2011) it clearly defined the capability of an employee as having a high correlation with the success of organizational learning. Thus, the present study will comprehend years of experience as part of the organizational learning which determines the firm's performance in MNEs which supports Ericsson el at. (2007) on deliberate practice. By adding deliberate practices it enhances the organizational memory element in organizational memory as well as governing data base effectiveness in the organization.

In summary, the present study will govern the antecedents of competitive advantage and its relevance towards firm performance amongst MNEs in Northern Malaysia as well as the relationships between organizational learning, and collective human capital respectively. For this research purpose, organizational learning, and collective human capital are defined as independent variables. Competitive advantage is the mediating variable and firm performance is the dependent variable. The conceptual framework for this research is discussed in the next section.

Theoretical Framework

The main sets of variables have been categorized into independent, dependent and mediating variable. The conceptual framework is based on the model established by Lopez et al. (2005) as illustrated in Figure 2.3 for organizational learning interactions with firm performance and the model established by Seidu (2011) as illustrated in Figure 2.8 for collective human capital interactions with firm performance. The competitive advantages behave as a mediating factor in both models. Also this framework comprehends the combination of assimilation theory and the resourced-based view theory. With this, the variables are engaged to summarize the firm performance as the dependent variable in this study. The independent variables of this study are organizational learning, and collective human capital. Competitive advantage has been integrated as a mediating variable in this study. Based on the above illustration the conceptual model is shown in Figure 3.

Organizational Learning and Competitive Advantage

In a study done by Goh and Ryan (2008) it was found, for a firm to have long term financial gain in the market as well as becoming a market leader, financial performance of the firm determines the success. The only competitive advantage can be achieved through a series of developments in organizational learning and should have strong bonding between both of the factors. When a similar study was done in Dutch and Belgian owned firms, similar results were obtained where knowledge sharing and organizational learning were found to be in an incremental mode. This resulted in a higher return on profits, product range expansion and the sustainability of higher skilled and experienced as well as knowledgeable employees.

Figure 3. The conceptual framework: organizational learning and collective human capital relationship with firm performance.

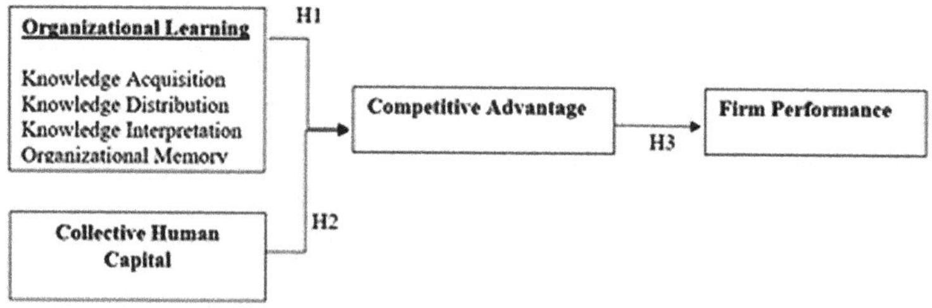

Alegre & Chiva (2008) found a willingness on risk taking, high external environment interaction, and a decision making approach in organizing, highly correlates the competitive advantage when it was measured against the relativity of innovation of a product in Spain respectively. In Greece found to sustain the firm's performance it requires continues development in acquiring, disseminating and storing the knowledge in the organization. The research further articulates that organizational learning consists of reducing machinery errors as well as poor decision making errors, advanced technology introduction and enhancement of old or outdated technology and enhancing employee capability by challenging the current state.

In this thesis research, organizational learning is posited as having a relationship with competitive advantage and the following hypotheses were tested.

H.1: Knowledge acquisition has a positive significant relationship with the competitive advantage of MNEs.
H.2: Knowledge distribution has a positive significant relationship with the competitive advantage of MNEs.
H.3: Knowledge interpretation has a positive significant relationship with the competitive advantage of MNEs.
H.4: Organizational memory has a positive significant relationship with the competitive advantage of MNEs.

Collective Human Capital and Competitive Advantage

In today's emerging market SMEs have been competing globally as well as being able to deliver a similar quality performance as MNEs. With new innovative development, marketing differentiation, quality differentiation, service differentiation and low cost leadership as well as re-using old technology for new products and adequate distribution systems (Clarke et al., 2011) the performance of SMEs has been made sustainable. To achieve such a sustainable performance it requires the right talent in terms of valuable knowledge, the right skill sets as well as the ability to reproduce the performance and quality of the performance in a repeated manner. Nevertheless the similar significance in MNEs has to be sustained to retain the competitiveness. MNEs were the pioneer in guiding domestic SMEs on how to improve the performance through supply chain management (Tseng & Liao, 2015). This shows that MNEs are having local manufacturers as competitors, as they are able to challenge them in competitive advantage leadership. MNEs have difficulties being competitive as well as being unable to be market leaders, despite having high knowledge, skills as well as capable human capital.

Thus, human capital has significantly determined the competitive advantage of the firm or MNEs (Tiep, 2007). It is equally important and valuable for an employee in the organization to have creativity as well as to be independent in performing day to day tasks and making the human capital in the organization as well as the firm even more capable and inimitable. Despite MNE and SME growth, truly collective human capital has a strong correlation with competitive advantage (Clarke et al., 2011). Thus, the present study examines the positive relationship between collective human capital and competitive advantage as shown in the hypothesis below.

H.5: Collective human capital has a positive significant relationship with the competitive advantage of MNEs.

The Mediating Role of Competitive Advantage

Firms which are able to sustain their competitive advantage have the ability and capability to increase firm performance (Luu, 2014). Achieving this requires adequate and well established organizational learning as it governs intellectual capital as one of the core competences of firm performance. Knowledge management captured in organizational learning would create years of competitive advantage experience internationally. As it requires the experiences to face the challenges and counter the issues to ensure there is no impact on firm performance at any point of time (Santos et al., 2011). Jimenez-Jimenez & Sanz-Valle (2011) have strongly quoted that it requires structured organizational learning to sustain competitive advantage to achieve high performance by the firm. Knowledge acquisition, knowledge distribution, knowledge, interpretation and organizational memory determines the challenges faced to overcome competitive advantage through innovation, marketing, quality and service differentiation as well as low cost leadership which determines the firm's performance. For such practices to be in place only MNEs are able to deliver due to their vast experience in knowledge management as well as abilities to invest in high technology and database for that data to be stored and processed in a timely manner to minimize the decision making and to have an accurate decision (Luu, 2014).

The firm's performance has a high correlation with collective human capital through competitive advantage by Seidu (2011). To have effective human capital it requires employees with sufficient knowledge, skills as well as abilities and capabilities, creativity as well as the competency of working independently. Only with this criteria, it would result and gain the abilities and overcome the competitive advantage which determines the performance of the firm. Not only does it determine the performance of the firm but it also determines the sustainability of the firm for long servicing years. It also requires years of deliberate practice and experiences to have the ability to overcome crisis and manage the difficult situation with human capital. To achieve a healthy or self-sustaining, willingness to develop ideas and creativity and willingness to be proactive would lead for betterment in human capital (Wang et al., 2014).

H.6: Competitive advantage of MNEs mediates significantly the relationship between knowledge acquisition and firm performance.
H.7: Competitive advantage of MNEs mediates significantly the relationship between knowledge distribution and firm performance.
H.8: Competitive advantage of MNEs mediates significantly the relationship between knowledge interpretation and firm performance.
H.9: Competitive advantage of MNEs mediates significantly the relationship between organizational memory and firm performance.
H.10: Competitive advantage of MNEs mediates significantly the relationship between collective human capital and firm performance.

DISCUSSION

Organizational Learning and Competitive Advantage

In organizational learning, there were four dimensions illustrated being knowledge acquisition, knowledge distribution, knowledge interpretation and organizational memory. The outcome from direct hypothesis testing between organizational learning and competitive advantage revealed that only knowledge interpretation was not supported and that the rest, knowledge acquisition, knowledge distribution and organizational memory were supported.

The employees did not see the presence of knowledge interpretation in the organization, due to the following practices being implanted in the organization. They comprise voluntary separation package (VSP) announcements, contingent worker practice, contracted worker practice, foreign worker practice for operator and technician positions, headcount reduction to optimize operation model and cost and lastly younger generation workforce (Ahmad & Oranye, 2010).

In recent years some of the MNEs in Malaysia experience people movement whom are mostly seniors or long serving employees due to business needs (Penang investment, 2015). Coyle (2009) claimed that usually the first group to leave are the tier one group whom are experienced employees from all levels of management and expertise. Once the tier one group employees leave, tier two employees take over the task done by them. Tier two employees are good employees but not as good as tier one employees. Thus, this would result in tier two employees having greater burden in their daily job and facing difficulties meeting their job expectations. Soon or later the tier two employees would leave due to being unable to strike an effective work life balance and being unable to cope with the challenges and expectations of business needs. When the tier two employees leave they would also leave unfinished work with no proper documentation or job procedures. The tier three employees whom are new employees or middle performing employees take over the task left by tier two employees, making the daily task even more difficult and challenging to complete due to their lack of capability and competency. Thus, many work procedures, systems, checklists and methods have to be established in order to guide and train the third tier of employees to meet the business challenges.

Figure 4 illustrates the landscape of knowledge interpretation faced by MNEs in Malaysia where employees leaving the organizations leave a permanent connectivity breakdown in terms of teamwork and expertise resulting in MNEs losing their competitive advantage over time. It requires a tremendous effort from the management of MNEs to redevelop the capability of the balance pool of employees in order to meet the desired results which usually come with hefty investments. Each circle explains the level of knowledge gain being stored in the organization.

In conclusion, even though there was knowledge acquisition, knowledge distribution and organizational memory with sophisticated databases and trainers with ten or more years' experience in the organizations'; it still requires knowledge interpretation to take place in order to make the organizational learning complete in an organization. In the context of MNEs in Malaysia, organizational learning does not function completely as it lacks knowledge interpretation. Here the organization would lose its high level of knowledge in relation to competitive advantage. The reasoning

Figure 4. Knowledge halting from tier 1 to tier 3 employees.

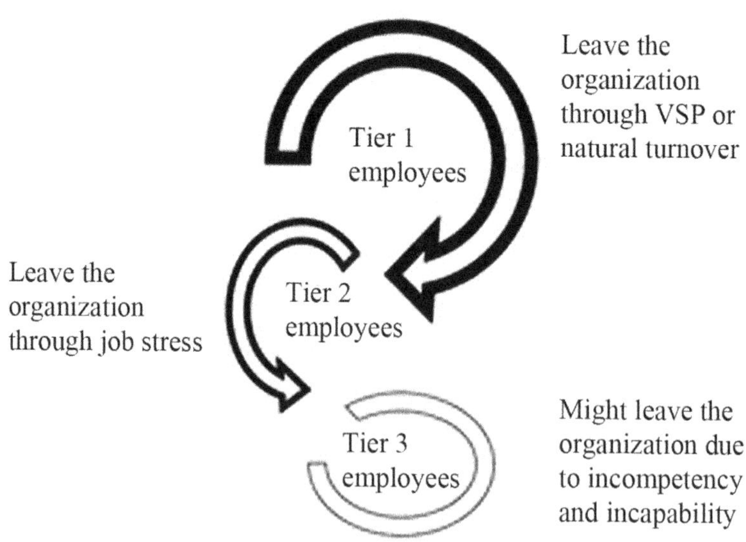

for MNEs being unable to sustain or build knowledge interpretation is illustrated in figure 4 respectively as the phenomenon of the expert or experienced leaving the organization, as explained by Coyle (2009). Thus, in order to be competitive in terms organizational learning MNEs in Malaysia have to foster the culture of teamwork as well as establishing experts and a forum to share and discuss amongst employees to enhance as well as to cultivate knowledge.

Collective Human Capital and Competitive Advantage

It creates a vast number of years of experience and practice to have the right balance in the organization through a pool of human capital which is not able to be imitated. With collective human capital the firm has the tendency to overcome the crisis and be competitive, which ensures productivity capabilities through human resources in the firm. MNEs strongly believe in human capital as their primary investment which results in them returning long-lasting sustainability (Subramaniam & Youndt, 2005).

MNEs utilize their developed collective human capital, who are highly skilled, widely knowledgeable, highly creative and experts in their respective task as well as have the ability to work independently to reduce cost, exploit opportunities, minimize or neutralize threats to have a competitive advantage. Only in a collective manner is an individual who is skilled, knowledgeable, an expert and independent, able to integrate with other skilled, knowledgeable, experts to continuously enhance the status quo. Collective human capital creates an avenue for these employees to interact and build competitive advantage by following the practices which are rare and inimitable. By having the right human capital with superior knowledge and skills, results in the potentiality and productivity of the firm by reducing the cost, maximizing environmental opportunities as well as minimizing threats. With effective collective human capital practice there is greater competitive advantage (Seidu, 2011). This is being experienced by employees in MNEs here, thus showing the significance and direct relationship with competitive advantage.

The collective human capital construct proves MNEs in Malaysia have highly skilled, creative and bright experts who are widely knowledgeable and independent in their respective tasks. In the perspective of the organization or MNE they all have the desired and required knowledge, skills and abilities which can be used in MNEs in Malaysia to have competitive advantage. This is very important as only through employees with a high KSA can, a MNE overcome a crisis as well as help SMEs grow through supply chain management. In conclusion, it also highlights that Malaysia has employees with the right knowledge, skill and ability who are able to ensure that MNEs in Malaysia are able to be competitive in the market which in turn ensures a long lasting sustainability in Malaysia.

The Mediating Role of Competitive Advantage

The above findings highlight that there was a limited sharing of knowledge and discussion as well as teamwork with regards to competitive advantage differentiation towards firm performance in MNEs in Malaysia. From the differentiation list in competitive advantage it stated that each differential would be operating as an individual organization. As an organization they would have gained a good knowledge which would be shared among their peers respectively. However the results as a firm showed that there was low cross functional collaboration, knowledge sharing and teamwork. With poor cross functional collaboration, knowledge sharing and teamwork the organization is not able to provide the right support of expertise when needed at the right time (Nkundabanyanga, 2016). Hence knowledge distribution and interpretation was not supported in this research.

Out of four dimensions in organizational learning only two relations knowledge acquisition and organizational memory were supported. Therefore, with strong knowledge acquisition in subject matter by employees, organizational memory with sophisticated databases and experienced employees the firm performance will be stimulated through competitive advantage. Nevertheless, MNEs in Malaysia have to focus on knowledge distribution and interpretation in order to make it complete and achieve greater performance results. This finding also highlights, knowledge interpretations could influence knowledge distribution in organizational learning when competitive advantage mediates as far as knowledge sharing is concerned.

For collective human capital indirect relations showed it to be well supported towards firm performance with competitive advantage as a mediator. It proves, highly knowledgeable, skilled and able employees contribute towards the firm and make the firm even more competitive and unable to be imitated by employees in Malaysia.

Therefore, it is no longer possible to treat employees only as a labour cost without taking into consideration their intangible advantage such as their creativity, talent and expertise that a particular employee brings to an organization (Wang et al., 2014). Consequently an optimal structure for the management of collective human capital has become necessary as it is an important criterion to ensure a sustainable growth for a firm.

Where an individual carries certain expertise, skill, talent and knowledge, it becomes a vital asset of a firm because such intangible property cannot be removed from an individual. Therefore, it becomes important for management to be able to manage the knowledge residing within its employees to ensure that potential valuable knowledge is not lost through the individual. An individual's knowledge becomes an asset that can only be retained for the future benefit of an organization if it can be managed well (Clarke et al., 2011). This needs to be taken into consideration by the management of MNEs in Malaysia. This phenomenon can be illustrated in figure 5.2, where competitive advantage mediates organizational learning and firm performance. Knowledge interpretation and knowledge distribution were not supported despite, these two elements being positioned in the high quadrant for competitive advantage, which illustrates that when these elements were not supported, MNEs in Malaysia eventually lose their competitive advantage in the long run resulting in poor firm performance. Through knowledge acquisition and restoring organizational memory, MNEs will not be able to sustain the performance in Malaysia. This answers the initial problem statement of this research of why MNEs tend to leave Malaysia. It is because they lose their competitive advantage through knowledge interpretation and distribution.

CONCLUSION

Only an experienced work force has the ability to develop a new work force and repeat the organizational learning to ensure that self-sustainability is retained (Sampe, 2012). It was found that MNEs with the affordability in establishing the right problem solving methodology, training development as well as standardization practices have directly helped long serving employees in the firm to gain such experiences, in order for them to increase and sustain firm performance (Chang & Lee, 2007). This, would result in Malaysians having higher competitive advantage in the market and continuing to attract MNEs and allowing them to increase their performance in Malaysia.

The reviews were done to understand the expansion, sustaining as well as how to overcome the barriers of MNEs. Only a few studies were done on how these variables would contribute to the significance of MNEs to retain the firm performances overseas. Despite having multiple knowledge management application, it was found that acquiring, disseminating and sharing are the key principles which link to the assimilation theory. In the context of MNEs in Malaysia knowledge acquisition and organizational memory were well established. Knowledge distribution and interpretation has to enhance MNEs here through teamwork and relationships between employees. This is also true for collective human capital, where employees have gained the required knowledge, skills and abilities throughout their employability in MNEs with development structures in place. This study has confirmed that employees in MNEs in Malaysia have a high KSA which allows MNEs to sustain themselves in Malaysia.

When MNEs in Malaysia have the rightfully skilled experts, they could revamp and overcome crises even during catastrophic events as well support other factories in other countries (Sim, 2012). MNEs do establish a strong supply chain management and business sustainability with local SMEs. MNEs start to generate or improve the socioeconomic condition, by providing systems to improve the operation and also by auditing their process and seeking their process improvement while guiding to reduce their cost by sustaining the product quality (Saru, 2007). By having highly skilled employees in MNEs it would add value to SMEs in Malaysia by establishing international standards and practices to improve and grow.

This research intends to be a guide and reference for MNEs in Malaysia to pursue and retain their operation by expending their knowledge acquisition and organizational memory practices while retaining their performance. It is also anticipated that MNE owners and local senior level management will take note of knowledge interpretation and knowledge distribution which were not significantly related towards firm performance when competitive advantage takes place caused by employee movement in the manufacturing industry in the northern region of Malaysia. Wang & Yang (2011) explained that with the right strategic planning in organizational learning strategic firm performance would ensue. Through teamwork, and building employee relationships knowledge interpretation and knowledge distribution would be enhanced respectively.

As a conclusion, this research adds value to the Malaysian government as it can influence MNEs to retain themselves and improve the domestic economy as well as SMEs. Finally, this research is expected to lead future research in organizational learning and collective human capital in Malaysian MNEs subsequently retaining them in Malaysia.

REFERENCES

Abebe, M., & Alvarado, D. A. (2013). Founder-CEO status and firm performance: An exploratory study of alternative perspectives. *Journal of Strategy and Management*, *6*(4), 343–357. doi:10.1108/JSMA-03-2013-0014

Ahmad, N., & Oranye, O. (2010). Empowerment, Job Satisfaction and Organizational Commitment: A Comparative Analysis of Nurses Working in Malaysia and England. *Journal of Nursing Management*, *18*(5), 582–591. doi:10.1111/j.1365-2834.2010.01093.x PMID:20636507

Allen, M. R., & Wright, P. (2007). Strategic Management and HRM. In The Oxford Handbook of Human Resource Management. New York: Oxford University Press.

Anders Ericsson, K. (1993). The Role of Deliberate Practice in the Acquisition of Expert Performance. *Psychological Review*, *100*(3), 363–406. doi:10.1037/0033-295X.100.3.363

Azadegan, A., & Dooley, K. J. (2010). Supplier innovativeness, organizational learning styles and manufacturer performance: An empirical assessment. *Journal of Operations Management*, *28*(6), 488–505. doi:10.1016/j.jom.2010.02.001

Azmi, F. T. (2008). Organizational learning: Crafting a strategic framework. ICFAI. *The Journal of Business Strategy*, *5*(2), 58–70.

Barney, J. (1991). Firm resources and sustained competitive advantage. *Journal of Management*, *17*(1), 99–120. doi:10.1177/014920639101700108

Chang, S.-C., & Lee, M.-S. (2007). A study on relationship among leadership, organizational culture, the operation of learning organization and employee's job satisfaction. *The Learning Organization*, *14*(2), 155–185. doi:10.1108/09696470710727014

Chiva, R., & Alegre, J. (2009). Organizational learning capability and job satisfaction: An empirical assessment in the ceramic tile industry. *British Journal of Management*, *20*(3), 323–340. doi:10.1111/j.1467-8551.2008.00586.x

Clarke, M., Seng, D., & Whiting, R. H. (2011). Intellectual capital and firm performance in Australia. *Journal of Intellectual Capital*, *12*(4), 505–530. doi:10.1108/14691931111181706

Cohen, J. (1998). *Statistical Power Analysis for the Behavioral Sciences*. Hillside, NJ: L. Erlbaum Associates.

Collins, J. (2001). Good to Great. Harper Collins Publisher Inc.

Coyle. (2009). *The talent code*. Bantam.

Darroch, J. (2005). Knowledge management, innovation and firm performance. *Journal of Knowledge Management*, *9*(3), 101–115. doi:10.1108/13673270510602809

Ding, L., Velicer, W.F., & Harlow, L.L. (1995). Effects of estimation methods, number of indicators per factor, and improper solutions on structural equation modelling fit indices. *Structural Equation Modelling: A Multidisciplinary Journal*, *2*(2), 119-143.

Dubey, Singh, & Ali, Venkatesh, & Gupta. (2014). Exploring dimensions of firm competencies and their impact on performance: Some exploratory empirical results, Benchmarking. *International Journal (Toronto, Ont.)*, *21*(6).

Ericsson, K. A., Preitula, M. J., & Cokely, E. T. (2007). *The Making of an Expert*. Harvard Business Review.

Goh, S. C., & Ryan, P. J. (2008). The organizational performance of learning companies - a longitudinal and competitor analysis using market and accounting financial data. *The Learning Organization*, *15*(3), 225–239. doi:10.1108/09696470810868855

Hair, J. F., Anderson, R. E., Tatham, R. L., & Black, W. C. (2006). *Multivariate Data Analysis* (6th ed.). Prentice-Hall.

Jiménez-Jiménez, D., & Sanz-Valle, R. (2011). Innovation, organizational learning, and performance. *Journal of Business Research*, *64*(4), 408–417. doi:10.1016/j.jbusres.2010.09.010

Leavitt,, C.C. (2011). A Comparative Analysis of Three Unique Theories of Organizational Learning. *Journal of Knowledge Management*.

Ling, T. C., & Nasurdin, A. M. (2010). Human Resource Management Practices and Organizational Innovation: An Empirical Study In Malaysia. *Journal of Applied Business Research*, *26*(4), 105–115. doi:10.19030/jabr.v26i4.311

Luu, T. (2014). Knowledge sharing and competitive intelligence. *Marketing Intelligence & Planning*, *32*(3), 269–292. doi:10.1108/MIP-05-2013-0077

Newbert, S. L. (2008). Value, Rareness, Competitive Advantage, and Performance: A Conceptual-Level Empirical Investigation of the Resource-Based View of the Firm. *Strategic Management Journal*, *29*(3), 745–768. doi:10.1002mj.686

Penang Investment. (2015). Retrieved from www.investpenang.gov.my/

Beal & Yasai-Ardekani. (2000). Performance Implications of aligning CEO functional experiences with competitive strategies. *Journal of Management*, *25*(4), 733–762.

Sampe, F. (2012). *The influence of organizational learning on performance in Indonesian SMEs* (DBA thesis). Southern Cross University.

Santos-Vijande, M. L., López-Sánchez, J. Á., & Trespalacios, J. A. (2012). How organizational learning affects a firm's flexibility, competitive strategy, and performance. *Journal of Business Research*, *65*(8), 1079–1089. doi:10.1016/j.jbusres.2011.09.002

Saru, E. (2007). Organisational learning and HRD: How appropriate are they for small firms? *Journal of European Industrial Training*, *31*(1), 36–51. doi:10.1108/03090590710721727

Seidu, Y. (2011). *Human Resource Management and Organizational Performance: Evidence from the Retail Banking Sector* (DBA thesis). Southern Cross University.

Sim, A. (2012). A comparative case study of the internationalization strategies of Malaysian, Singaporean and Taiwanese firms. *Journal of Asian Business, 24*(3), 85–108.

Sirmon, D. G., Hitt, M. A., Ireland, R. D., & Gilbert, B. A. (2011). Resource Orchestration to Create Competitive Advantage. *Journal of Management*, 37.

Smit, A. J. (2010). The competitive advantage of nations: Is Porter's Diamond Framework a new theory that explains the international competitiveness of countries. *Southern African Business Review*.

Takeuchi, H. (1998). *Beyond knowledge management: lessons from Japan*. Available at: www.sveiby.com/articles/lessons

Takeuchi, R., Lepak, D., Wang, H., & Takeuchi, K. (2007). An Empirical Examination of the Mechanisms Mediating Between High-Performance Work Systems and the Performance of Japanese Organizations. *The Journal of Applied Psychology, 92*(4), 1060–1083. doi:10.1037/0021-9010.92.4.1069 PMID:17638466

Tiep, N. D. (2007). The Honda motorcycle business in the Vietnamese emerging market. *International Journal of Emerging Markets, 2*(3), 298–309. doi:10.1108/17468800710758413

Tseng, P.-H., & Liao, C.-H. (2015). Supply chain integration, information technology, market orientation and firm performance in container shipping firms. *International Journal of Logistics Management, 26*(1), 82–106. doi:10.1108/IJLM-09-2012-0088

Wang, D., Su, Z., & Yang, D. (2011). Organisational culture and knowledge creation capability. *Journal of Knowledge Management, 15*(3), 363–373. doi:10.1108/13673271111137385

Wang, Y.-L., Wang, Y.-D., & Horng, R.-Y. (2010). Learning and innovation in small and medium enterprises. *Industrial Management & Data Systems, 110*(2), 175–192. doi:10.1108/02635571011020296

Chapter 9
A Supply Chain Management View of Human Capital-Intensive Firms

Laurence Saglietto
Université Côte d'Azur, France

Dominique Bonet Fernandez
IPAG Business School, France

Alban Quillaud
Independent Researcher, France

Gilles Paché
Aix-Marseille University, France

ABSTRACT

Logistics and supply chain management (SCM) is benefiting from today's disruptive information technologies. Disruptive technologies based on massive data capabilities offer new opportunities for growth in international trade, through supply networks and real-time management. The authors aim to shed light on the impact of digitization and digitalization and disruptive technologies on human-capital-intensive firms (HCIFs), particularly in the logistics sector. Three case studies of control towers, business spheres, and supply chain cockpits seem to indicate that a new generation of high value-added human capital is entering the logistics sector in the context of massive data.

DOI: 10.4018/978-1-5225-7426-2.ch009

INTRODUCTION

At the heart of global competition and technological change is the growing conviction among organizations that human capital is a key driver of competitive advantage, and especially for high human capital intensive firms (HCIFs) (Hatch and Dyer 2004; Coff and Kryscynski 2011; Campbell *et al.*, 2012a,b; Carnahan *et al.*, 2012; Nyberg *et al.*, 2014; Della Torre *et al.*, 2018). In many HCIFs, the increased importance of specific human capital is coinciding with similarly increased exploitation of massive data, and the control over results and forecasting which they allow. While much research attention has focused on HCIFs (Campbell *et al.*, 2012b; Carnahan *et al.*, 2012) and massive data (Wang *et al.*, 2016), few studies have examined the management of massive data within HCIFs to understand the changes they induce. The management of massive data has transformed data management methods quite radically, making it possible to adapt data technologies and strategies by providing information critical for targeted and optimized actions. Data management is providing opportunities to access new business opportunities and better control the inherent risks. The quality and governance of Big Data are major concerns for HCIFs. Development tools are being implemented to increase the uptake of these new technologies but the importance of human-capital-intensive employees (such as highly skilled developers) should not be overlooked.

Our approach to HCIFs focuses on the logistics sector. This sector is an example of the transformation of the traditional "old economy" such as manufacturing (and automotives in particular) to an economy in which innovation capacity linked to the immaterial is an important part of value creation. In the logistics sector in particular, disruptive technologies linked to Big Data management along global supply chains are being implemented. Productive activity no longer involves traditional factors such as fixed capital and labor; it requires specialized skills, organizational structures and procedures, a corporate culture, and a myriad other resources described as "*intangible assets*" (Brynjolfsson *et al.*, 2002). This is making it difficult to keep human assets subordinate to physical assets. The growing intensity of globalized competition, and the technological progress and the increased financing possibilities in financial markets are reinforcing the substantial nature of innovation. Innovation necessarily requires employees with specific and specialized human capital. The race to innovate is driven essentially by human capital, and especially those working in R&D but increasingly also, employment in all other phases of the production process. In this dynamic perspective, tangible assets are losing their importance in favor of the individuals employed in the productive activities of firms.

This chapter aims to shed pragmatic light on the management of the disruptive technologies underlying Big Data within HCIFs in the field of logistics and supply chain management (SCM). How do HCIFs mobilize and value disruptive technologies based on massive data? The chapter is structured in five sections. The first section discusses how HCIFs mobilize and value disruptive technologies, based on massive data, in the context of the existing literature. In the second section, we identify the dimensions of digitization and digitalization by studying three emblematic HCIF cases that rely on these disruptive technologies–namely the control towers of logistics service providers (LSPs), and the business spheres and supply chain cockpits of shippers. These three cases make it possible to identify what is at stake for the HCIF, and the limits imposed by massive data management. In the third section, we propose some solutions and recommendations to mitigate the limitations identified. We suggest that a new generation of functional and informational integration tools is emerging based on the *human capital and SCM in the context of massive data*. The final two sections discuss some future perspectives, and outline our conclusions.

BACKGROUND

HCIFs are defined as companies whose productive activity depends mainly on intangible assets such as specific human assets and skills, corporate culture, etc. (Cézanne and Saglietto, 2014; Clarke and Gholamshahi, 2018). These intangible assets include a wide variety of organizations ranging from knowledge-intensive business services or KIBS (Freel, 2016; Miles *et al.*, 2018), to high-tech manufacturing industry jobs such as analyst, programmer, financial scientist, and lawyer (Qian, 2003). Human capital investments are more important for technology-intensive firms (Boxall, 2011), and the involvement of human capital-intensive employees varies according to the technological intensity of the company's activities (Della Torre *et al.*, 2018). Finally, companies and human capital-intensive employees are essential although not sufficient for the efficiency of the firm's production (Li, 2015), have strong power (Qian, 2003), and remain a source of business growth (Amoroso and Link, 2018).

However, it is not just in industries in which competition is based on technology that companies rely on the skills and knowledge of employees to maximize their investments in advanced technologies. Human capital theory suggests that the productivity of any enterprise relies on the knowledge and skills embodied by employees (individually and collectively) and the capabilities of employees (Becker, 1994; Myers, 1999; Ployart *et al.*, 22014; Della Torre *et al.*, 2018). A well-trained workforce will increase productivity which is the key to economic growth (Faggian *et al.*, 2017). For example, training and work experience can determine the organization's human capital level by enabling employees to acquire skills and competencies (Smith *et al.*, 2005). Finally, the importance of human capital for organizational performance depends on the context in which it operates (Boxall and Purcell, 2008; Della Torre *et al.*, 2018).

In the areas in which HCIFs (services, high technology, manufacturing processes) operate, the level of complexity required for many current operations such as management of massive data is continuously increasing. Thus, it is of concern to all industries and HCIFs that rely on management of massive data to control flows (physical and informational). Big Data analytics can be operational (short-term) for responsive, tactical (medium-term) decision-making, proactive decision-making and continuous improvement, or strategic (long-term) for structural transformations. Also, massive data, both endogenous and exogenous, are heterogeneous which implies the need for prior knowledge to understand and treat them. They are characterized by the concepts of volumetry, velocity, variety and value, and their management embodies the evolution of various organizational models and requires new knowledge and skills. Human capital plays a vital role in improving and making visible decision-making that is depends heavily on quality related on the one hand to the technical treatment of Big Data, and on the other to how it is interpreted to achieve and maintain competitive advantage. Any technological advance such as Big Data management, reduces the pool of these talents and increases their external attractiveness (Eisfeldt and Papanikolaou, 2013). Since job creation has become a major challenge for the economy, the focus should be on labor-intensive sectors. This applies especially to some HCIFs in the logistics sector; logistics traditionally has been a human capital-intensive sector.

The influence of digitalization of the economy on this sector has highlighted its intensive nature in relation to high value-added skills and trades. Among HCIFs, logistics professionals for many years have been promoting new value creation through a complete rethinking of how to handle the massive data generated by new global production networks and international SCM (Waller and Fawcett, 2013; Wang *et al.*, 2016; Kache and Seuring, 2017; Tiwari *et al.*, 2018). The differentiation proposed by Ackoff (1989) and Sambamurthy and Zmud (2000) between data, information, knowledge, understanding and wisdom is particularly useful to capture the issues at stake for these HCIFs. Massive data as a new information resource, open up almost infinite exploitation horizons in terms of the realization of multiple future scenarios to anticipate behaviors, advance efficient decisions, and improve the performance of firms internal logistics operations (or outsource them to LSPs). However, in this context, the organization of human assets and their decisions and choices are crucial for success. Thus, digitization and digitalization are emerging as realities which are shaking up companies, questioning working methods, and suggesting the need for deep changes to organizational models and ways of thinking.

Digitization refers to the digitalization of data on certain tasks which allow their processing and exchange through objects (connected and/or able to calculate), software (processes) and the Internet infrastructure (omni-connectivity to a fast and reliable network). It relies on the dematerialization of data to facilitate their transfer, and encompasses the concepts of volumetry, velocity, variety and value among the many singular characteristics of massive data. Digitalization (or massive "*datification*") embodies the evolution of organizational models requiring new knowledge and new decision-making methodologies. Digitization and digitalization are contributing to the emergence of a new form of control of physical flows analogous to the 360 degree management model. In that model, both top management who define strategy and middle management responsible for day-to-day implementation perform within a more overall and more consensual approach allowed by access to massive data. Fagerjord and Storsul (2007) proposed that digitalization follows digitization, and in this understanding their conjunction creates a technological break: a *disruption*.

Disruptive technology radically disrupts the production, logistics, data processing, organizational model, value proposition and human resources management practices of the HCIF. Disruptive change is necessary for firms–and especially HCIFs–because they generate productivity gains related to traditional products and services (Danneels, 2004). Disruptive technologies based on massive data and their exploitation, also can create synergies with other technologies to create an environment conducive to the development of HCIFs. In the age of digitalization, companies are making decisions on the basis not only of their private information but also the rational inferences of information from partners, the market and customers. This makes the aggregation of information vital because it allows all the firm's stakeholders to have precise knowledge about the value of their assets (Li, 2017). Therefore, understanding the management of Big Data within a HCIF poses a major challenge to existing firm theories, and is in line with work on the "search for new foundations" for a theory of the modern corporation (Zingales, 2000; Acharya *et al.*, 2011; Rajan, 2012).

HCIFs seek to exploit the scarcity, the inimitability of their human capital (Barney, 1991; Castanias and Helfat, 1992; Wright *et al.*, 1994). According to Starbuck (1992:715), in a HCIF, "the workforce is of the greatest importance... because it implies that knowledge is more important than other inputs". As a result, HCIFs have a particular need for carefully configuration and reconfiguration of their most important assets for greater value creation (Meyer-Doyle *et al.*, 2017). Yet, unlike physical assets or tradable knowledge assets such as patents, human assets have features that can affect their configuration and deployment to achieve strategic goals (Coff, 1997; Meyer-Doyle *et al.*, 2017). We provide three case studies of disruptive technologies focused on Big Data: the control tower, the business sphere, and the supply chain cockpit. Although the literature emphasizes some limitations in their knowledge, we advance three propositions related to our research question:

Proposition 1: The effective management of Big Data depends on the HCIF' specific stock of human capital: "the value creation capacity of firms is much more dependent on the human capital they employ than on the physical capital they possess, especially for innovative firms" (Fulghieri and Sevilir, 2009:1291). Also, "firms are dynamic repositories of different sets of knowledge that are critically dependent upon the individual and collective human capital of the organization. Unique sets of knowledge, and the distinctive ways in which knowledge is integrated and organized by the firm, can generate capabilities" that either create or support disruptive technologies (Ranft and Lord, 2000:297).

Proposition 2: Efficient Big Data management depends on the expertise of the HCIF's stock of human capital. According to Starbuck (1992:716), "knowledge is a stock of expertise, not a flow of information", and the firm can be described as knowledge-intensive only if exceptional and valuable expertise dominates common place knowledge. The human capital intensity and related expertise can interact to hinder some transactions while promoting others (Coff, 1997). "Consequently, in HCIFs, those human assets with the greatest levels of firm-specific human capital are often among the most valuable resources controlled by the firm–yet, it is exactly those human assets that are likely to be in short supply" (Chatain and Meyer-Doyle, 2017:236).

Proposition 3: The effective management of disruptive data-centric technologies depends on the HCIF's technological opportunities when solving complex problems i.e. *the talent and experts it has recruited*. Development tools are needed to increase uptake of these new technologies and to reduce the need for developers to employ more interpretation experts.[1] "The quality of human capital is crucial for high-tech companies to maintain competitive advantages in knowledge economy era. However, high-technology companies suffering from high turnover rates often find it hard to recruit the right talents" (Chien and Chen, 2008:280). So, "critical technologies demand to firms to retain the services of the best-skilled knowledge workers, including hard to find engineers and programmers" (Ranft and Lord, 2000:296).

MAIN FOCUS: PRACTICAL APPROACH BASED ON THREE CASE STUDIES

The goal of this chapter is to provide an exploratory analysis of emergent disruptive technologies which radically alter the way that businesses and industries operate, and are widespread in the logistics sector. The three cases identified are based on public information–available on websites, in the theoretical literature and in the trade press–related to control towers, business spheres and supply chain cockpits.

Case Study 1: Control Towers

Control towers are a specialty of LSPs, created in the late 1990s and based on the airport control tower principle. Control towers are platforms designed to manage all of a customer's supply chain operations. They are driven by talented groups of people, and offer centralized and partially automated management, transport activities, and storage on behalf of the client. The control towers manage all of the client's relations with its LSP instead of its customers. By organizing the management of physical and information flows (storage, packaging, routing, distribution, etc.), and by offering process optimization and automation expertise in a single location they function as the prime contractor. The expected features of a control tower are: (1) collection of necessary data, whether proprietary or from external sources (Heaney, 2014); (2) detection of contingencies and risks (Cap Gemini 2012; Bentz and Kammerer, 2014) based on fixed and predetermined parameters and criteria, and the generation of relevant alerts (Pearson, 2014); (3) implementation of corrective actions (reactive or proactive) following these alerts, and proposals for new ideas, for example to reflect new capabilities (Bentz and Kammerer, 2014); and (4) communication to stakeholders via different communication channels of hazards and corrective actions (Pearson, 2014). These multiple needs mean that control towers are reliant on particular processes which can be summarized as:

- Cross-system connectivity, via EDI and/or web interfaces and also humans, for data entry or loading of scanned documents.
- Management of various types of master data on tariffs and transport times related to suppliers, factories, customers and LSPs.
- Order management (purchases, sales, restocking) processed using previously calibrated master data to integrate the information into the transport management system.
- Management of the above-mentioned transport system with a view to optimizing it, i.e. to minimize costs and reduce periods of overcapacity.
- Verification of LSP invoices related to relevant tariff agreements and to the firm's transport order history.
- Visibility and reporting to render data, information and knowledge transferable to all members of a global production network.

These aspects may use different information systems, or be grouped within a series of systems in the form of interfaced modules. More broadly, control towers often rely on an ecosystem of intra- and inter-organizational information systems which help to digitize some of the data inherent in supply chains while creating value. For reasons of competitiveness, and although each solution is tailored to the needs of each customer, the LSP tries to build its offers on a common base and on an organization which if necessary, can be shared by different customers, at least in its "repetitive" and not very cognitive dimensions. Other services such as continuous improvement in data collection and interpretation, or commercial and contractual management will be completely dedicated (Cap Gemini, 2012; Trzuskawska-Grzesinska, 2017).

Case Study 2: Business Spheres

Procter & Gamble (P&G) introduced the notion of business sphere in the early 2010s, and today, the company has more than 50 business spheres around the world. On a technological level, a business sphere is a circular room equipped with giant screens displaying management information in the form of graphs to allow processing and other decisions: "Around the world, P&G managers are conferring in such rooms, with embedded analysts from P&G's Information and Decision Solutions group aiding their deliberations with Spotfire-enabled visuals. Some of the displays are quite cool… but their purpose is not, of course, to dazzle managers with coolness and creativity. The real goal is to help them understand quickly what's going on in the business, and to decide what to do about it" (Davenport, 2013). P&G developed its business sphere idea in partnership with BOI, Cisco, HP, SAP, Nielsen and TIBCO Spotfire. They are interconnected and interactive meeting spaces located around the world to allow easy visualization of massive data and collective decisions. The idea behind the business sphere is that the cross-fertilization of these data should allow the extraction of new information and knowledge which ultimately, could be the source of shareholder value, and new partnerships for the firm. Its functioning requires effective digitization programs and significant investment in advanced analytical systems to assist decision-making (Bughin, 2016). It provides a way to instantly reveal new ideas, trends and opportunities.

The business sphere model relies on very sophisticated forecasting tools related to market share (and its evolution) and other important firm market performance parameters. Based on forecasts, the firm can adjust prices instantly, and adapt advertising investment, industrial and logistical capacity, etc., which allows it to respond quickly to market changes using complex data presented visually via the business sphere. Eliminating the time needed to manually collect and aggregate massive data allows productivity improvements, enables collaboration, simplifies work processes, and reduces decision-making time by allowing the firm to focus on innovation.[2] Thus, integrating the technology, visualization and information allows the management team to interpret massive amounts of data and obtain real-time solutions to the problems encountered (Xu, 2014). Preliminary results from P&G are encouraging: according to the company's Annual Report 2016, it achieved 25% reduction in inventories, and savings of tens of millions of dollars. Top management can focus on the solutions being implemented without having to (Sarangi, 2016) collect and process all the data. According to Kalakota (2012), creative solutions underlie P&G's success over 20 years in various markets. For many years, companies have mobilized different models of digitization in key areas of their organization to automate business processes and workflows. Digitized data are more easily integrated in a business sphere which is a truly immersive information-centric environment that provides data and knowledge essential for efficient value creation, and adaptations to the firm's value proposition.

Case Study 3: Supply Chain Cockpits

To face the growing need for new multidimensional measures, and to evaluate their commercial performance and satisfy customer demand, Intel has adapted and implemented a software called supply chain cockpit, in collaboration with SAP which exist in various industries. By mapping the movement of materials and products, the supply chain cockpit helps to align performance measurement systems to strategies and targets to achieve competitive advantage through sustainable performance within the global production network. The supply chain cockpit software is a visual tool for measuring performance and up to date reporting to allow better general management. The cockpit control software is a new generation decision support system (DSS). Each component of the software has been developed as a web-accessible application to provide structured information on logistics flows. The information is centralized and presented as a consolidated, aggregated or detailed view in the form of planned inventories, production capacities and production (Frayret *et al.*, 2007). The approach provides users with visualization capabilities (global and local) for supply chain planning and control (Rnolmayer *et al.*, 2002). It provides access to massive data related to individual components via the cockpit which centralizes access to information, and access rights to its management. Finally, the cockpit makes it possible to generate indicators to monitor the performance of the global production network. This solution reflects Intel's ability to provide the information needed to perform mass daily operations and avoid–or detect–emerging issues.

Companies' expectations in terms of improved flow management require real-time information on global production network performance from various sources (mobile, ERP, internal information, etc.), an alert capability potential, advanced analytical capacity and environmental scanning capability to support long-term business planning. The supply chain cockpit offers these functionalities, thanks to an intuitive graphical interface acting as a superior business planning layer which covers all logistics domains (manufacturing, demand, physical distribution, transport) (Setia *et al.*, 2008). The supply chain cockpit also allows individual work areas to be created to facilitate multiple planners working simultaneously on different segments of the global production network, and allows a fine-grained vision which minimizes the complexity of the relationships among its components. In conclusion, the benefits of a supply chain cockpit include an overview of alerts displayed by *applications* and *priorities* (Dickersbach, 2009).

SYNTHESIS OF THE THREE CASE STUDIES

The three emblematic case studies of disruptive technologies can be considered as technological paradigm shifts. These paradigm shifts are allowing new functionalities in proposed new products, their commercialization and their application in new solutions for a better customer satisfaction. Three findings emerge from the case studies:

Finding 1: Effective management of disruptive data-centric technologies depends on the specific human capital stock of the HCIF.

Finding 2: The effective management of disruptive technologies centered on Big Data depends on the expertise of the specific human capital of the HCIF.

Finding 3: The effective management of disruptive data-centric technologies depends on the HCIF's technological opportunities in the performance of complex tasks, that is, the talent and expertise of its employees.

The three case studies highlight essential points. These points are the following: (1) the collection of massive multidisciplinary, intra- and inter-organizational data is accomplished in near real time. Thus, it depends on the HCIF's stock of human capital; (2) access to the data and generation of new information (i.e., aggregated data) which are dependent on the expertise of HCIF staff in their interpretation. The opportunity for human operators to make reactive and proactive (i.e., predictive) decisions can lead to the development of new knowledge; (3) the efficiency of disruptive technologies centered on Big Data depends on relatively new and complex technologies which require better documentation to facilitate their use, tools to support the development and implementation of small projects (e.g., MapReduce, Hadoop, Pig, Hive, etc.), and mobilization of specific employees.

Disruptive technologies based on massive data represent significant opportunities but also significant difficulties. These latter are related in part to these technologies being relatively new and complex as described above. Appropriate data-processing solutions, talents and expertise are required .Disruptive technologies generally require considerable effort for their incorporation into a governance framework to manage projects and data at the HCIF scale. We identified various challenges faced by HCIFs. From a managerial perspective, greater customer satisfaction in terms of both cost and service quality are essential in parallel with massive data management. This involves combining huge amounts of internal and external data to allow real-time monitoring of materials and product flows. Complete mastery of these issues remains to be achieved by HCIFs. One of the biggest barriers to Big Data management within HCIFs is intra- and inter-organizational fragmentation, and the difficulties involved in sharing and maintaining central master data for the proper functioning of organizations. Information systems use algorithms that need to be calibrated to business parameters according to top management plans. However, master data change frequently which can render information systems useless or counterproductive. These changes are due to variations in pricing and customers' and suppliers' information, product references, and sales.

Digital media such as hardware, Internet networks, connectivity, mobility, and especially, prices, accelerate the creation of organizational models which are failing because of the dematerialization and automation of repetitive data processing and data processing information tasks. Downes and Nunes (2013) believe that the impact of disruptive technologies on control towers, business spheres and supply chain cockpits is more important for intensive technology and/or information industries and their management of global production networks. There tends to be a gap before organizations using "old technology" are affected in terms of turnover and net profit, by the arrival of new technologies associated to digitization and digitalization. This engenders complacency and lack of urgency to implement the new technologies. Also, the organizational models underlying these three disruptive technologies are at different levels of maturity. These innovations will be useful to only a limited number of users, and business spheres and supply chain cockpits are solutions developed by and on behalf of companies. The data they collect and process to create new information and knowledge and generate value, remain within the purview of these companies. However, the organizational model of control towers is based on a central hub with technology and processes to capture and use data to allow greater shared visibility.

SOLUTIONS AND RECOMMENDATIONS

The disruptive technologies are enabling new services, creating new uses and transforming the organization of HCIFs. They are attractive because they constitute a break with the established model. They also offer higher profits at lower cost. In the three emblematic cases examined, creating value from human capital requires co-specialization using specific resources which underlines the need to protect talented individuals and experts. Companies are seeking to set up appropriate incentive mechanisms to retain their highly skilled employees while enabling them to capture a share of the economic rents generated by the human capital they represent. Digitization and digitalization are reflected in many changes to the management of global production networks. The deployment of technologies is immediate, both in their diffusion through the almost universal accessibility allowed by Internet networks, and in their use as they become more ergonomic and easier to master and use. In the context of logistics management, the speed of dissemination of information systems is dependent on the strategic decisions of companies and thorough analysis of intra- and inter-organizational links.

Managerial (internal) and commercial (external) efforts are needed to convince the firm and its business partners, and to bypass the resistance to adopting Big Data technologies (Caesarius and Hohenthal, 2018). However, new entrants can disrupt the market through their more developed exploitation of massive data, better performance, lower prices and higher levels of customization. These conditions offer strong potential for productivity gains through the adoption of new technologies that reduce the weight of the labor factor in the composition of the usual factors of production. Standardizing and automating could allow better logistics management and ensure repetitiveness of non-physical operational tasks which also often respond well to the concept of pattern (Rinehart and Ragatz, 1996).

For a long period, in the field of information systems the technology did not allow extensive automation of non-physical processes. However, current software allows for a logical sequence of logistical tasks from engineering, to a chronological physical execution of tasks, to tactical and strategic activities including order management systems (OMS), transport management systems (TMS), warehousing management systems (WMS), inventory management systems (IMS), enterprise resource planning (ERP), logistics procurement platforms (LPP), process design systems (PDS), network design systems (NDS), and cloud-like solutions that act at the frontier and collect massive data which offers the relevant actors total visibility. New players tend to rely on the latest technologies for connectivity, database management and artificial intelligence. A critical mass of actors is required to obtain value that is superior to an intra-firm model. Connectivity technologies are changing and advancing rapidly, with the result that a critical mass should be achievable in the near future which will allow the related synergies to be realized. In this value creation, the attitude of human capital-intensive employees will be paramount.

We have several recommendations in this direction. First, expert employees are essential for interpreting the results but must retain an open mind to avoid becoming trapped into routine reactions based on past experience. Second, employees involved in decision making have different choice behaviors, and ways of grasping the real world and handling information; they must be able to adapt to different decision-making processes. Third, the difficulties related to decision making lie in the importance and the strength of the simplifying representations that emerge from the processing of massive data. They can be simultaneously an aid to understanding reality and an obstacle to it because they reduce the range of possibilities and create precedents. To monitor production workshops requires that meaning is given to a large volume of information from the machinery related to different production systems. Managers must focus on not being overwhelmed by massive data. The solution requires contextualization of the information which requires in turn simulations of potential scenarios involving the global supply chain.

On the other hand, the introduction of disruptive technologies in the management of global production networks is reflected in many immediate changes since their deployment is rapid in terms of their spread and the almost universal accessibility allowed by Internet networks. These advances have led to HCIFs being a vital part of Industry 4.0 which is the new industrial management paradigm (Hofmann and Rüsch, 2017; Moeuf *et al.*, 2017). Industry 4.0 will rely on the hyper-connection of firms, technology, processes and information systems. Although the changes will be rapid in strategic fields such as human resource management, production, marketing and logistics, they will depend on humans' specific and rare digital skills as well as the technology.

The human challenge includes significant human resources management tasks to make jobs attractive. The image of Industry 4.0 is tarnished by the possibility of it resulting in higher unemployment. There are issues related to commitment and change: decision-makers should acknowledge that Big Data, algorithms and robotics will not automatically replace human workers. Many employees are concerned about the possible disappearance of workstations, obsolescence caused by technology or deep transformations. Human resources managers will have to oversee the disappearance of some businesses and the emergence of new ones, and provide appropriate training, mentoring of young workers by older employees, introduction of new ways of working and collaborative approaches that will accelerate innovation.

The technological challenge posed by the rise of artificial intelligence, machine learning, cloud computing, the Internet of Things (IoT) or blockchain, is perceived as a threat to employment. HCIFs must reinvent their ways of innovating and working. Hyper-connected HCIFs that will mobilize the management of massive data, must be able to continue improving the efficiency and flexibility of their services or their supply chains by using real-time data exchange which is more reliable and faster. Compartmentalization will decline in favor of a hyper-connection. All machines will be directly or indirectly connected to networks, and this technological revolution will induce changes to how organizations integrate cyber-security. Automation engineers and computer engineers will have to work together since Industry 4.0 is based on the interconnection of the two worlds which induces greater vulnerability. The risks will multiply, and the threats will be of a different nature. Ongoing network monitoring and prevention will be needed to reduce the risk of cyber-attacks from a variety of origins.

FUTURE RESEARCH DIRECTIONS

A first research direction would be to explore connectivity: how far will these disruptive technologies increase connectivity (interconnectivity) and compensate for the fragmentation of supply chains? In practice, departments within firms (or interconnected firms), factory machinery (or interconnected factories), suppliers, warehouses, stores, etc., exchange information. The continuous and instantaneous communication among the various tools and workstations integrated in supply chains will make it possible to optimize industrial processes. It will allow improved flexibility to adapt to real-time demand and better meet the needs of individual customers. From this point of view, data and the number of actors are critical. Data are an essential link in this convergence, and for some professionals, human capital is key to moving from Big Data to Smart Data that is, being able to capture the right data, to contextualize it, and enable it to optimize production processes, reduce inventories, increase quality, satisfy the customer, etc.

The second research direction is related to the disruptive technologies which are enabling a new generation of functional and informational integration tools, and leading inevitably to use of multiple operational equipment in a "Atawad" ("Anytime, anywhere, any device") perspective. Atawad was coined by the French consultant Xavier Dalloz in 2002 and refers to the trend for consumers, especially the new generations Y and Z, desiring increasingly systematically to access content, information or market offers at whatever time and place and by whatever mode (TV, computer, mobile phone, tablet, etc.) is most convenient. More research on this will be fundamental to manage new tools and related consumer behaviors, and identify the efficiency gains from widespread interconnection, and its real contribution to the performance of HCIFs.

The third research direction concerns a unifying concept in information systems, representative of these disruptive technologies, i.e. transactional centers responsible for global management of all flows. The strategic alignment between disruptive practices, connectivity and supply chain monitoring must be considered in the context of different ways of creating intra and inter-organizational networking.

This idea reminds the debate introduced by Fulconis and Paché (2005) on the role played by a previous SCM approach in the implementation of strategic partnerships. A strategic partnership can succeed only if logistical conditions are met initially to catalyze the link between supply chain members around a common project. In the same way the firm's intra-organizational networking divisions and departments (vertical integration) and inter-organizational networking among firms (horizontal integration) constitute basic conditions for the success of Industry 4.0. We would suggest the need to measure the sustainability contribution of disruptive technologies and HCIFs, linked to a set of domains such as proposed by the 2016 Federal Big Data R&D Strategic Plan.[3]

The fourth research direction is related to measuring productivity gains and energy optimization related to the explosion of Big Data and the effect on societal issues. While the three case studies discussed in this paper should improve competitiveness greatly, by adapting supply and demand almost instantaneously in the context of product and services customization, the HCIFs envisage that this evolution will have a positive impact also on their energy consumption. Management of Big Data will involve huge series of computers which will have high energy and maintenance costs. It will be vital for firms to be able to assess the expected costs and benefits when deciding on the most appropriate trajectory.

CONCLUSION

The logistics sector is influenced heavily by the digitalization of the economy which is calling for high value-adding skills and trades. Our goal in this chapter was to shed light on the impact of digitization and digitalization and disruptive technologies on HCIFs, particularly in the logistics sector. Logistics is a human capital-intensive sector and requires high value-adding management skills. The three case studies of control towers, business spheres and supply chain cockpits suggest that a new generation of high value-added human capital will be required to manage the massive data in logistics. Human capital is one of the main drivers of competitive advantage and especially for high human capital intensive firms. The increase in the importance of specific human capital is coinciding in many HCIFs with growing exploitation of Big Data.

To conclude this chapter, we would suggest that the human factor i.e. the skills and knowledge of employees, is essential for efficient implementation of disruptive technologies in HCIFs along the supply chain. Although the focus in this chapter was on logistics HCIFs and disruptive technologies, the potential for future research is huge and includes multidisciplinary work in a context of perpetual and global technological innovation. Our future research agenda will be centered on studying and monitoring the implementation of innovations using performance indicators related to technological deployments in the various firms in this initial study. We plan to adopt a longitudinal approach based on our sample firms' annual reports. More precisely, the research agenda will have four axes: (1) connectivity of supply chains; (2) integration tools; (3) intermediation; and (4) the contribution of sustainability to organizational models.

REFERENCES

Acharya, V., Myers, S., & Rajan, R. (2011). The internal governance of firms. *The Journal of Finance*, *66*(3), 689–720. doi:10.1111/j.1540-6261.2011.01649.x

Ackoff, R. (1989). From data to wisdom. *Journal of Applied Systems Analysis*, *16*(1), 3–9.

Amoroso, S., & Link, A. (2018). Under the AEGIS of knowledge intensive entrepreneurship: Employment growth and gender of founders among European firms. *Small Business Economics*, *50*(4), 899–915. doi:10.100711187-017-9920-4

Barney, J. (1991). Firm resources and sustained competitive advantage. *Journal of Management*, *17*(1), 90–120. doi:10.1177/014920639101700108

Becker, G. (1994). *Human capital: a theoretical and empirical analysis with special reference to education* (3rd ed.). Chicago, IL: University of Chicago Press.

Bentz, B., & Kammerer, B. (2014). 3PL management: Building the dream house. *Logistics Management*, *53*(9), 30–32.

Boxall, P. (2011). Human capital, HR strategy, and organizational effectiveness. In A. Burton-Jones & J. Spencer (Eds.), *The Oxford handbook of human capital* (pp. 289–308). Oxford, UK: Oxford University Press; doi:10.1093/oxfordhb/9780199532162.003.0012

Boxall, P., & Purcell, J. (2008). *Strategy and human resource management* (2nd ed.). London: Palgrave-Macmillan.

Brynjolfsson, E., Hitt, L., & Yang, S. (2002). Intangible assets: Computers and organizational capital. *Brookings Papers on Economic Activity*, *1*(1), 137–198. doi:10.1353/eca.2002.0003

Bughin, J. (2016). Ten big lessons learned from Big Data analytics. *Applied Marketing Analytics*, *2*(4), 286–295.

Caesarius, L., & Hohenthal, J. (2018). Searching for Big Data: How incumbents explore a possible adoption of Big Data technologies. *Scandinavian Journal of Management*, *34*(2), 129–140. doi:10.1016/j.scaman.2017.12.002

Campbell, B., Coff, R., & Kryscynski, D. (2012a). Rethinking competitive advantage from human capital. *Academy of Management Review*, *37*(3), 376–395. doi:10.5465/amr.2010.0276

Campbell, B., Ganco, M., Franco, A., & Agarwal, R. (2012b). Who leaves, where to, and why worry? Employee mobility, entrepreneurship and effects on source firm performance. *Strategic Management Journal*, *33*(1), 65–87. doi:10.1002mj.943

Cap Gemini. (2012). Insights on supply chain agility. Fluctuating demand and market uncertainty: how to meet the challenge? Paris: Cap Gemini.

Carnahan, R., Agarwal, R., & Campbell, B. (2012). Heterogeneity in turnover: The effect of relative compensation dispersion of firms on the mobility and entrepreneurship of extreme performers. *Strategic Management Journal*, *33*(12), 1411–1430. doi:10.1002mj.1991

Castanias, R., & Helfat, C. (1992). Managerial and windfall rents in the market of corporate control. *Journal of Economic Behavior & Organization*, *18*(2), 153–184. doi:10.1016/0167-2681(92)90025-7

Cézanne, C., & Saglietto, L. (2014). Human capital-intensive firms and the creation of symbolic value. *Timisoara Journal of Economics & Business*, *7*(1), 70–88. doi:10.2478/tjeb-2014-0004

Chatain, O., & Meyer-Doyle, P. (2017). Alleviating managerial dilemmas in human-capital-intensive firms through incentives: Evidence from M&A legal advisors. *Strategic Management Journal*, *38*(2), 232–254. doi:10.1002mj.2473

Chien, C.-F., & Chen, L.-F. (2008). Data mining to improve personnel selection and enhance human capital: A case study in high-technology industry. *Expert Systems with Applications*, *34*(1), 280–290. doi:10.1016/j.eswa.2006.09.003

Clarke, T., & Gholamshahi, S. (2018). Developing human capital for knowledge based economies. In T. Clarke & K. Lee (Eds.), *Innovation in the Asia Pacific: from manufacturing to knowledge economy* (pp. 247–270). Singapore: Springer. doi:10.1007/978-981-10-5895-0_12

Coff, R. (1997). Human assets and management dilemmas: Coping with hazards on the road to resource-based theory. *Academy of Management Review*, *22*(2), 374–402. doi:10.5465/amr.1997.9707154063

Coff, R., & Kryscynski, D. (2011). Drilling for micro-foundations of human capital based competitive advantages. *Journal of Management*, *37*(5), 1429–1443. doi:10.1177/0149206310397772

Danneels, E. (2004). Disruptive technology reconsidered: A critique and research agenda. *Journal of Product Innovation Management*, *21*(4), 246–258. doi:10.1111/j.0737-6782.2004.00076.x

Davenport, T. (2013). How P&G presents data to decision-makers. *Harvard Business Review Blog Network*. Available on http://blogs.hbr.org/2013/04/how-p-and-g-presents-data/

Della Torre, E., Zatzick, C., Sikora, D., & Solari, L. (2018). Workforce churning, human capital disruption, and organizational performance in different technological contexts. *Human Resource Management Journal*, *28*(1), 112–127. doi:10.1111/1748-8583.12167

Dickersbach, T. (2009). *Supply chain management with SAP APO: structures, modeling approaches and implementation of SAP SCM 2008* (3rd ed.). Heidelberg, Germany: Springer. doi:10.1007/978-3-540-92942-0

Downes, L., & Nunes, P. (2013). Big bang disruption. *Harvard Business Review*, *91*(3), 44–56.

Eisfeldt, A., & Papanikolaou, D. (2013). Organization capital and the cross-section of expected returns. *The Journal of Finance*, *68*(4), 1365–1406. doi:10.1111/jofi.12034

Fagerjord, A., & Storsul, T. (2007). Questioning convergence. In T. Storsul & D. Stuedahl (Eds.), *Ambivalence towards convergence: digitalization and media change* (pp. 19–31). Göteborg: Nordicom.

Faggian, A., Partridge, M., & Malecki, E. (2017). Creating an environment for economic growth: Creativity, entrepreneurship or human capital? *International Journal of Urban and Regional Research*, *41*(6), 997–1009. doi:10.1111/1468-2427.12555

Frayret, J.-M., D'Amours, S., Rousseau, A., Harvey, S., & Gaudreault, J. (2007). Agent-based supply chain planning in the forest products industry. *International Journal of Flexible Manufacturing Systems*, *19*(4), 358–391. doi:10.100710696-008-9034-z

Freel, M. (2016). Inside KIBS' black box: exploring the existence and function of knowledge angels. In D. Doloreux, M. Freel, & R. Shearmur (Eds.), *Knowledge-intensive business services: geography and innovation* (pp. 229–250). London: Routledge. doi:10.4324/9781315591216

Fulconis, F., & Paché, G. (2005). Exploiting SCM as source of competitive advantage: The importance of cooperative goals revisited. *Competitiveness Review*, *15*(2), 92–100. doi:10.1108/10595420510818740

Fulghieri, P., & Sevilir, M. (2009). Organization and financing of innovation, and the choice between corporate and independent venture capital. *Journal of Financial and Quantitative Analysis*, *44*(6), 1291–1321. doi:10.1017/S0022109009990391

Hatch, N., & Dyer, J. (2004). Human capital and learning as a source of sustainable competitive advantage. *Strategic Management Journal*, *25*(12), 1155–1178. doi:10.1002mj.421

Heaney, B. (2014). *Supply chain visibility and segmentation: control tower approach.* Boston: Aberdeen Group.

Hofmann, E., & Rüsch, M. (2017). Industry 4.0 and the current status as well as future prospects on logistics. *Computers in Industry*, *89*, 23–34. doi:10.1016/j.compind.2017.04.002

Kache, F., & Seuring, S. (2017). Challenges and opportunities of digital information at the intersection of Big Data analytics and supply chain management. *International Journal of Operations & Production Management*, *37*(1), 10–36. doi:10.1108/IJOPM-02-2015-0078

Kalakota, R. (2012). Procter & Gamble: business sphere and decision cockpits. *Practical Analytics*. Available on https://practicalanalytics.co/2012/

Li, J. (2017). *Why do partnerships prevail in human capital-intensive industries? An information coordination perspective* (Unpublished Working Paper). Fairfax, VA: George Mason University.

Li, N. (2015). *Labor market peer firms*. Working Paper Series No. 2015-02. Chicago: Searle Center on Law, Regulation & Economic Growth.

Meyer-Doyle, P., Mawdsley, J., & Chatain, O. (2017). *Resource reconfiguration in human-capital-intensive firms*. Research Paper No. SPE-2017-1216. Jouy-en-Josas: HEC Paris.

Miles, I., Belousova, V., & Chichkanov, N. (2018). Knowledge intensive business services: Ambiguities and continuities. *Foresight*, *20*(1), 1–26. doi:10.1108/FS-10-2017-0058

Moeuf, A., Pellerin, R., Lamouri, S., Tamayo-Giraldo, S., & Barbaray, R. (2017). The industrial management of SMEs in the era of Industry 4.0. *International Journal of Production Research*, *56*(3), 1118–1136. doi:10.1080/00207543.2017.1372647

Myers, S. (1999). Financial architecture. *European Financial Management*, *5*(2), 133–141. doi:10.1111/1468-036X.00086

Nyberg, A., Moniterno, T., Hale, D., & Lepak, D. (2014). Resource-based perspective on unit-level human capital: A review and integration. *Journal of Management*, *40*(1), 316–346. doi:10.1177/0149206312458703

Pearson, M. (2014). Supply chain control towers are taking off. *Logistics Management*, *53*(8), 26–27.

Ployart, R., Nyberg, A., Reilly, G., & Maltarich, M. (2014). Human capital is dead; long live human capital resources! *Journal of Management*, *40*(2), 371–398. doi:10.1177/0149206313512152

Qian, Y. (2003). *Human capital-Intensive firms: incentives and capital structure* (Unpublished Working Paper). New York: Stern School of Management.

Rajan, R. (2012). Presidential address: The corporation in finance. *The Journal of Finance*, *67*(4), 1173–1217. doi:10.1111/j.1540-6261.2012.01745.x

Ranft, A., & Lord, M. (2000). Acquiring new knowledge: The role of retaining human capital in acquisitions of high-tech firms. *The Journal of High Technology Management Research*, *11*(2), 295–319. doi:10.1016/S1047-8310(00)00034-1

Rinehart, L., & Ragatz, G. (1996). Management of facility and human resources in materials and logistics management. *Journal of Business Logistics*, *17*(2), 1–18.

Rnolmayer, G., Merten, P., & Zeier, A. (2002). *Supply chain management based on SAP systems*. Heidelberg, Germany: Springer; doi:10.1007/978-3-540-24816-3

Sambamurthy, V., & Zmud, R. (2000). Research commentary: The organizing logic for an enterprise's IT activities in the digital era–A prognosis of practice and a call for research. *Information Systems Research*, *11*(2), 105–114. doi:10.1287/isre.11.2.105.11780

Sarangi, S. (2016). Business intelligence systems: A necessity for agile supply chains. *KIIT Journal of Management*, *12*(2), 52–65.

Setia, P., Sambamurthy, V., & Closs, D. (2008). Realizing business value of agile IT applications: Antecedents in the supply chain networks. *Information Technology Management*, *9*(1), 5–19. doi:10.100710799-007-0028-4

Smith, K., Collins, C., & Clark, K. (2005). Existing knowledge, knowledge creation capability, and the rate of new product introduction in high-technology firms. *Academy of Management Journal*, *48*(2), 346–357. doi:10.5465/amj.2005.16928421

Starbuck, W. (1992). Learning by knowledge-intensive firms. *Journal of Management Studies*, *29*(6), 713–740. doi:10.1111/j.1467-6486.1992.tb00686.x

Tiwari, S., Wee, H.-M., & Daryanto, Y. (2018). Big Data analytics in supply chain management between 2010 and 2016: Insights to industries. *Computers & Industrial Engineering*, *115*, 319–330. doi:10.1016/j.cie.2017.11.017

Trzuskawska-Grzesinska, A. (2017). Control towers in supply chain management–Past and future. *Journal of Economics & Management*, *27*, 114–133. doi:10.22367/jem.2017.27.07

Waller, M., & Fawcett, S. (2013). Data science, predictive analytics, and Big Data: A revolution that will transform supply chain design and management. *Journal of Business Logistics*, *34*(2), 77–84. doi:10.1111/jbl.12010

Wang, G., Gunasekaran, A., Ngai, E., & Papadopoulos, T. (2016). Big Data analytics in logistics and supply chain management: certain investigations for research and applications. *International Journal of Production Economics, 176*, 98-110. doi:10.1016/j.ijpe.2016.03.014

Watson, B. (2012). Data wrangling: how Procter & Gamble maximizes business analytics. *CIO Insight*. Available on http://www.cioinsight.com/

Wright, P., McMahan, G., & McWilliams, A. (1994). Human resources as a source of sustained competitive advantage. *International Journal of Human Resource Management*, *5*(2), 301–326. doi:10.1080/09585199400000020

Xu, J. (2014). *Managing digital enterprise: ten essential topics*. Amsterdam: Atlantis Press. doi:10.2991/978-94-6239-094-2

Zingales, L. (2000). In search of new foundations. *The Journal of Finance*, *55*(4), 1623–1653. doi:10.1111/0022-1082.00262

ENDNOTES

1 The majority of developers and architects who "understand" Big Data work for Big Data technology creators including among others Facebook, Google, Yahoo and Twitter, or for the many startups in the field such as Hortonworks, Cloudera and MapR. Since the technology is difficult to control, the rate of availability of resources for Big Data is low. Added to this, in this emerging market support tools for the development and implementation of projects are scarce.

2 According to Watson (2012), the business sphere offers executives the opportunity to leverage more than 500 million data points per month. These include retailers' point-of-sale and ERP data, shipping and internal inventories. The business sphere provides a quick and accurate way to identify opportunities and areas where inventions are needed. It is an innovative solution which satisfies the objective of end-to-end digitization of the company.

3 The international Group on Earth Observations (GEO) is a voluntary partnership of 96 governments and 87 participating organizations working to develop the Global Earth Observation System of Systems (GEOSS). 39 GEOSS links international earth observation resources in the areas of agriculture, biodiversity, climate, disasters, ecosystems, energy, health, water and weather. The goal is to provide the right Earth observation information in an appropriate, to the relevant people at the right time to allow the best decision. This requires Big Data analytics, infrastructure and principles around open data exchange. E.g., early agreement on a set of data sharing and data management principles has allowed the development of open-source software to collect worldwide data on health epidemics, assess the state of global water resources, produce fire-potential maps from weather data, and calculate and communicate earthquake risk (https://www.nitrd.gov/PUBS/).

Compilation of References

2017 . Resource Governance Index. (2017). Retrieved from https://resourcegovernance.org/analysis-tools/publications/2017-resource-governance-index

Abebe, M., & Alvarado, D. A. (2013). Founder-CEO status and firm performance: An exploratory study of alternative perspectives. *Journal of Strategy and Management*, *6*(4), 343–357. doi:10.1108/JSMA-03-2013-0014

Abeysekera, I. (2007). Intellectual capital reporting between a developing and developed nation. *Journal of Intellectual Capital*, *8*(2), 329–345. doi:10.1108/14691930710742871

Abeysekera, I., & Guthrie, J. (2004). Human capital reporting in a developing nation. *The British Accounting Review*, *36*(3), 251–268. doi:10.1016/j.bar.2004.03.004

Abramo, G., D'angelo, A. C., & Viel, F. (2013). Assessing the accuracy of the h- and g-indexes for measuring researchers' productivity. *Journal of the American Society for Information Science and Technology*, *64*(6), 1224–1234. doi:10.1002/asi.22828

Abramovitz, M. (1989). *Thinking about growth: And other essays on economic growth and welfare*. Cambridge University Press. doi:10.1017/CBO9780511664656

Abrishami, H & Hadian, M (2005). Rent seeking and Economic Growth (Empirical Evidence from Iran). *Journal of Economic Studies, 67,* 1-28. (in Persian)

Acharya, V., Myers, S., & Rajan, R. (2011). The internal governance of firms. *The Journal of Finance*, *66*(3), 689–720. doi:10.1111/j.1540-6261.2011.01649.x

Ackoff, R. (1989). From data to wisdom. *Journal of Applied Systems Analysis*, *16*(1), 3–9.

Aglietta, M., & Rebérioux, A. (2012). 23 Financialization and the firm. *Handbook on the Economics and Theory of the Firm*, 308.

Ahamed, Z., Inohara, T., & Kamoshida, A. (2013). The servitization of manufacturing: An empirical case study of IBM Corporation. *International Journal of Business Administration*, *4*(2), 18. doi:10.5430/ijba.v4n2p18

Ahmad, F., Mohamad, O., & Ibrahim, H. I. (2013). Absorptive Capacity and Innovative Behavior among Engineers in Malaysia. *Elixir International Journal, 56*.

Ahmad, N., & Oranye, O. (2010). Empowerment, Job Satisfaction and Organizational Commitment: A Comparative Analysis of Nurses Working in Malaysia and England. *Journal of Nursing Management, 18*(5), 582–591. doi:10.1111/j.1365-2834.2010.01093.x PMID:20636507

Ahmed, A. D., Cheng, E., & Messinis, G. (2011). The role of exports, FDI and imports indevelopment: Evidence from Sub-Saharan African countries. *Applied Economics, 43*(26), 3719–3731. doi:10.1080/00036841003705303

Al Ariss, A., Cascio, W. F., & Paauwe, J. (2014). Talent management: Current theories and future research directions. *Journal of World Business, 49*(2), 173–179. doi:10.1016/j.jwb.2013.11.001

Alchian, A. A., & Demsetz, H. (1972). Production, information xcosts, and economic organization. *The American Economic Review, 62*(5), 777–795.

Alchian, A., & Demsetz, H. (1972). Production, Information Costs, and Economic Organization. *The American Economic Review, 62*(5), 777–795.

Al-Laham, A., Tzabbar, D., & Amburgey, T. L. (2011). The dynamics of knowledge stocks and knowledge flows: Innovation consequences of recruitment and collaboration in Biotech. *Industrial and Corporate Change, 20*(2), 555–583. doi:10.1093/icc/dtr001

Allen, M. R., & Wright, P. (2007). Strategic Management and HRM. In The Oxford Handbook of Human Resource Management. New York: Oxford University Press.

Almeida, P., & Phene, A. (2004). Subsidiaries and knowledge creation: The influence of the MNC and host country on innovation. *Strategic Management Journal, 25*(89), 847–864. doi:10.1002mj.388

Amabile, T. (1988). A Model of Creativity and Innovation in Organizations. In B. Staw & L. Cummings (Eds.), *Research in Organizational Behavior* (pp. 123–167). Greenwich, CT: J.A.I. Press.

Amabile, T. (1993). Motivational Synergy: Toward New Conceptualizations of Intrinsic and Extrinsic Motivation in the Workplace. *Human Resource Management Review, 3*(3), 185–201. doi:10.1016/1053-4822(93)90012-S

Amabile, T. M. (1988). A model of creativity and innovation in organizations. *Research in Organizational Behavior, 10*(1), 123–167.

Amabile, T. M. (1988). A Model of Creativity and Innovation in Organizations. *Research in Organizational Behavior, 10*, 123.

Amit, R., & Schoemaker, P. J. H. (1993). Strategic assets and organizational rent. *Strategic Management Journal, 14*(1), 33–46. doi:10.1002mj.4250140105

Amoroso, S., & Link, A. (2018). Under the AEGIS of knowledge intensive entrepreneurship: Employment growth and gender of founders among European firms. *Small Business Economics, 50*(4), 899–915. doi:10.100711187-017-9920-4

Anders Ericsson, K. (1993). The Role of Deliberate Practice in the Acquisition of Expert Performance. *Psychological Review, 100*(3), 363–406. doi:10.1037/0033-295X.100.3.363

Anderson, C. (2012). *Makers: The New Industrial Revolution*. Crown Business.

Andersson, U., Bjorkman, I., & Forsgren, M. (2005). Managing subsidiary knowledge creation: The effect of control mechanisms on subsidiary local embeddedness. *International Business Review, 14*(5), 521–538. doi:10.1016/j.ibusrev.2005.07.001

Andreeva, T., & Kianto, A. (2012). Does knowledge management really matter? Linking knowledge management practices, competitiveness and economic performance. *Journal of Knowledge Management, 16*(4), 617–636. doi:10.1108/13673271211246185

Andrikopoulos, A. (2005). Using intellectual capital statements to determine value drivers and priorities for organizational change: A portfolio selection approach. *Knowledge Management Research and Practice, 3*(3), 166–172. doi:10.1057/palgrave.kmrp.8500065

Antonelli, G., Antonietti, R., & Guidetti, G. (2010). Organizational change, skill formation, human capital measurement: Evidence from Italian manufacturing firms. *Journal of Economic Surveys, 24*(2), 206–247. doi:10.1111/j.1467-6419.2009.00615.x

Aoki, M. (1988). *Information, Incentives and Bargaining in the Japanese Economy*. Cambridge, UK: Cambridge University Press. doi:10.1017/CBO9780511571701

Aoki, M. (1990). Towards an economic model of the Japanese firm. *Journal of Economic Literature, 28*(1), 1–27.

Appelbaum, E., Bailey, T., Berg, P. B., Kalleberg, A. L., & Bailey, T. A. (2000). *Manufacturing advantage: Why high-performance work systems pay off.* Cornell University Press.

Appelbaum, E., & Berg, P. (2000). High-Performance Work Systems: Giving Workers a Stake. In M. Blair & T. Kochan (Eds.), *The New Relationship: Human Capital in the American Corporation* (pp. 102–138). Washington, DC: Brookings Institution Press.

Appold, S. J. (2000). The control of high-skill labor and entrepreneurship in the early US semiconductor industry. *Environment & Planning A, 32*(12), 2133–2160. doi:10.1068/a3372

Armstrong, M., & Taylor, S. (2014). *Armstrong's handbook of human resource management practice*. Kogan Page Publishers.

Arthur, L. (1955). *The theory of economic growth*. Routledge.

Arundel, A., Lorenz, E., Lundvall, B. Å., & Valeyre, A. (2007). How Europe's economies learn: A comparison of work organization and innovation mode for the EU-15. *Industrial and Corporate Change, 16*(6), 1175–1210. doi:10.1093/icc/dtm035

Asimakou, T. (2009). *Innovation, knowledge and power in organizations*. London: Routledge.

Audretsch, D. B., Lehmann, E. E., & Plummer, L. A. (2009). Agency and governance in strategic entrepreneurship. *Entrepreneurship Theory and Practice*, *33*(1), 149–166. doi:10.1111/j.1540-6520.2008.00284.x

Augier, M., March, J. G., & Sullivan, B. N. (2005). Notes on the evolution of a research community: Organization studies in Anglophone North America, 1945–2000. *Organization Science*, *16*(1), 85–95. doi:10.1287/orsc.1040.0108

Auty, R. M. (2001). *Resource abundance and economic development*. Oxford University Press.

Azadegan, A., & Dooley, K. J. (2010). Supplier innovativeness, organizational learning styles and manufacturer performance: An empirical assessment. *Journal of Operations Management*, *28*(6), 488–505. doi:10.1016/j.jom.2010.02.001

Azad, S. (2010). The politics of privatization in Iran. *Middle East Review of International Affairs*, *14*(4), 60.

Azmi, F. T. (2008). Organizational learning: Crafting a strategic framework. ICFAI. *The Journal of Business Strategy*, *5*(2), 58–70.

Baard, P., Deci, E., & Ryan, R. (2004). Intrinsic Need Satisfaction: A Motivational Basis of Performance and Well-Being in Two Work Settings. *Journal of Applied Social Psychology*, *34*(10), 2045–2068. doi:10.1111/j.1559-1816.2004.tb02690.x

Badeeb, R. A., Lean, H. H., & Clark, J. (2017). The evolution of the natural resource curse thesis: A critical literature survey. *Resources Policy, 51*, 123-134.

Badinger, H., & Tondl, G. (2003). Trade, human capital and innovation: the engines of European regional growth in the 1990s. In *European regional growth* (pp. 215–239). Berlin: Springer. doi:10.1007/978-3-662-07136-6_8

Baker, G., Gibbons, R., & Murphy, K. (2002). Relational Contracts and the Theory of the Firm. *The Quarterly Journal of Economics*, *117*(1), 39–84. doi:10.1162/003355302753399445

Baker, G., Jensen, M., & Murphy, K. (1988). Compensation and Incentives: Practice vs. Theory. *The Journal of Finance*, *43*(3), 593–616. doi:10.1111/j.1540-6261.1988.tb04593.x

Baland, J. M., & Francois, P. (2000). Rent-seeking and resource booms. *Journal of Development Economics*, *61*(2), 527–542. doi:10.1016/S0304-3878(00)00067-5

Balassa, B. (1980). *The process of industrial development and alternative development strategies*. The World Bank.

Balconi, M., & Fontana, R. (2011). Entry and innovation: An analysis of the fabless semiconductor business. *Small Business Economics*, *37*(1), 87–106. doi:10.100711187-009-9231-5

Baldwin, C., & Clark, K. (2000). *Design Rules: The Power of Modularity* (Vol. 1). Cambridge, MA: The MIT Press.

Ballot, G., Fakhfakh, F., & Taymaz, E. (2001). Firms' human capital, R&D and performance: A study on French and Swedish firms. *Labour Economics*, *8*(4), 443–462. doi:10.1016/S0927-5371(01)00038-0

Barnard, C. (1938). *The Functions of the Executive*. Cambridge, MA: Harvard University Press.

Barney, J. B., & Wright, P. M. (1998). On becoming a strategic partner: The role of human resources in gaining competitive advantage. *Human Resource Management (1986-1998)*, *37*(1), 31.

Barney, J. B. (1991). Firm resources and sustained competitive advantage. *Journal of Management*, *17*(1), 99–120. doi:10.1177/014920639101700108

Barney, J., & Felin, T. (2013). What are microfoundations? *The Academy of Management Perspectives*, *27*(2), 138–155. doi:10.5465/amp.2012.0107

Baron, A. (2007). *Human capital management: Achieving added value through people*. Kogan Page Publishers.

Baron, J., & Kreps, D. (1999). *Strategic Human Resources: Frameworks for General Managers*. New York: Wiley and Sons.

Bartel, A. (1991). *Formal Employee Training Programs and their Impact on Labour Productivity: Evidence From A Human Resources Survey*. Working Paper Draft, 1-51.

Beal & Yasai-Ardekani. (2000). Performance Implications of aligning CEO functional experiences with competitive strategies. *Journal of Management*, *25*(4), 733–762.

Beattie, V. (2005). Moving the financial accounting research front forward: The UK contribution. *The British Accounting Review*, *37*(1), 85–114. doi:10.1016/j.bar.2004.09.004

Becker, G. S. (1964). Human Capital: A Theoretical and Empirical Analysis, with Special Reference to Education (3rd ed.). University of Chicago Press.

Becker, G. S. (1994). Human capital revisited. In Human Capital: A Theoretical and Empirical Analysis with Special Reference to Education (3rd ed.; pp. 15-28). The University of Chicago Press.

Becker, B. E., Huselid, M. A., Pickus, P. S., & Spratt, M. F. (1997). HR as a source of shareholder value: Research and recommendations. *Human Resource Management*, *36*(1), 39–47. doi:10.1002/(SICI)1099-050X(199721)36:1<39::AID-HRM8>3.0.CO;2-X

Becker, G. (1975). *Human Capital*. Chicago: Chicago University Press.

Becker, G. (1994). *Human capital: a theoretical and empirical analysis with special reference to education* (3rd ed.). Chicago, IL: University of Chicago Press.

Becker, G. S. (1964). *Human capital: A theoretical and empirical analysis, with special reference to education*. New York: University of Chicago Press and NBER.

Bénabou, R., & Tirole, J. (2003). Intrinsic and Extrinsic Motivation. *The Review of Economic Studies*, *70*(3), 489–520. doi:10.1111/1467-937X.00253

Bénabou, R., & Tirole, J. (2006). Incentives and Prosocial Behavior. *The American Economic Review, 96*(5), 1652–1678. doi:10.1257/aer.96.5.1652

Bentz, B., & Kammerer, B. (2014). 3PL management: Building the dream house. *Logistics Management, 53*(9), 30–32.

Berg, P. (1999). The Effects of High Performance Work Pratices on Job Satisfaction in the United States Steel Industry. *Relations Industrielles. Industrial Relations, 54*(1), 111–134. doi:10.7202/051222ar

Berle, A., & Means, G. (1932). *The Modern Corporation and Private Property*. New York: Harcourt, Brace and World.

Bierly, P., & Chakrabarti, A. (1996). Generic knowledge strategies in the u.s. pharmaceutical industry. *Strategic Management Journal, 17*(S2), 123–135. doi:10.1002mj.4250171111

Biondi, Y., & Rebérioux, A. (2012, December). The governance of intangibles: Rethinking financial reporting and the board of directors. *Accounting Forum, 36*(4), 279–293. doi:10.1016/j.accfor.2012.03.003

Birdsall, N., Pinckney, T. C., & Sabot, R. H. (2000). Natural resources, human capital, and growth. *Global Policy Program.*

Birkinshaw, J. (1998). Corporate entrepreneurship in network organizations. *European Management Journal, 16*(3), 355–364. doi:10.1016/S0263-2373(98)00012-7

Blair, M. M. (2011). An economic perspective on the notion of 'human capital. In The Oxford Handbook of Human Capital, Part 1: The nature of human capital. Oxford.

Blair, M. M. (2012). In the best interest of the corporation: Directors' duties in the wake of the global crisis. In The SAGE Handbook of Corporate Governance (pp. 62-80). Sage. doi:10.4135/9781446200995.n3

Blair, M. (1999). Firm-Specific Human Capital and Theories of the Firm. In M. Blair & M. Roe (Eds.), *Employees and Corporate Governance* (pp. 58–90). Washington, DC: Brookings Institution Press.

Blair, M. M. (1995). *Ownership and Control: Rethinking Corporate Governance for the Twenty-First Century*. Washington, DC: Brookings Institution Press.

Blair, M. M. (2010). *Wealth creation and wealth sharing: A colloquium on corporate governance and investments in human capital*. Brookings Institution Press.

Blair, M. M., & Roe, M. J. (Eds.). (2010). *Employees and corporate governance*. Brookings Institution Press.

Blanco, L., & Grier, R. (2012). Natural resource dependence and the accumulation of physical and human capital in Latin America. *Resources Policy, 37*(3), 281–295. doi:10.1016/j.resourpol.2012.01.005

Bögenhold, D., & Klinglmair, A. (2016). Independent work, modern organizations and entrepreneurial labor: Diversity and hybridity of freelancers and self-employment. *Journal of Management & Organization*, *22*(6), 843–858. doi:10.1017/jmo.2016.29

Bontis, N. (1999). Managing organizational knowledge by diagnosing intellectual capital: Framing and advancing the state of the field. *International Journal of Technology Management*, *18*(5), 433–462. doi:10.1504/IJTM.1999.002780

Bontis, N. (2003). Intellectual capital disclosure in Canadian corporations. *Journal of Human Resource Costing & Accounting*, *7*(1), 9–20. doi:10.1108/eb029076

Bontis, N. (2004). National Intellectual Capital Index: A United Nations Initiative for the Arab Region. *Journal of Intellectual Capital*, *5*(1), 13–39. doi:10.1108/14691930410512905

Bontis, N., Dragonetti, N. C., Jacobsen, K., & Roos, G. (1999). The knowledge toolbox: A review of the tools available to measure and manage intangible resources. *European Management Journal*, *17*(4), 391–402. doi:10.1016/S0263-2373(99)00019-5

Boon, C., Eckardt, R., Lepak, D. P., & Boselie, P. (2018). Integrating strategic human capital and strategic human resource management. *International Journal of Human Resource Management*, *29*(1), 34–67. doi:10.1080/09585192.2017.1380063

Bornay-Barrachina, M., De la Rosa-Navarro, D., López-Cabrales, A., & Valle-Cabrera, R. (2012). Employment relationships and firm innovation: The double role of human capital. *British Journal of Management*, *23*(2), 223–240. doi:10.1111/j.1467-8551.2010.00735.x

Bosma, N., van Praag, M., Thurik, R., & de Wit, G. (2004). The value of human and social capital investments for the business performance of start-ups. *Small Business Economics*, *23*(3), 227–236. doi:10.1023/B:SBEJ.0000032032.21192.72

Boxall, P. (1998). Achieving competitive advantage through human resource strategy: Towards a theory of industry dynamics. *Human Resource Management Review*, *8*(3), 265–288. doi:10.1016/S1053-4822(98)90005-5

Boxall, P. (2011). Human capital, HR strategy, and organizational effectiveness. In A. Burton-Jones & J. Spencer (Eds.), *The Oxford handbook of human capital* (pp. 289–308). Oxford, UK: Oxford University Press; doi:10.1093/oxfordhb/9780199532162.003.0012

Boxall, P., & Macky, K. (2009). Research and theory on high-performance work systems: Progressing the high-involvement stream. *Human Resource Management Journal*, *19*(1), 3–23. doi:10.1111/j.1748-8583.2008.00082.x

Boxall, P., & Purcell, J. (2000). Strategic human resource management: Where have we come from and where should we be going? *International Journal of Management Reviews*, *2*(2), 183–203. doi:10.1111/1468-2370.00037

Boxall, P., & Purcell, J. (2008). *Strategy and human resource management* (2nd ed.). London: Palgrave-Macmillan.

Boyatsis, R. E. (1982). *The competent manager: A model for effective performance*. New York: Wiley.

Bozzolan, S., Favotto, F., & Ricceri, F. (2003). Italian annual intellectual capital disclosure: An empirical analysis. *Journal of Intellectual Capital*, *4*(4), 543–558. doi:10.1108/14691930310504554

Bravo-Ortega, C., & De Gregorio, J. (2005). *The relative richness of the poor? Natural resources, human capital, and economic growth*. The World Bank. doi:10.1596/1813-9450-3484

Brennan, N. (2001). Reporting intellectual capital in annual reports: Evidence from Ireland. *Accounting, Auditing & Accountability Journal*, *14*(4), 423–436. doi:10.1108/09513570110403443

Brown, S. L., & Eisenhardt, K. M. (1997). The art of continuous change: Linking complexity theory and time-paced evolution in relentlessly shifting organizations. *Administrative Science Quarterly*, *42*(1), 1–34. doi:10.2307/2393807

Brummans, B., Cooren, F., Robichaud, D., & Taylor, J. R. (2014). Approaches in research on the communicative constitution of organizations. In L. L. Putnam & D. Mumby (Eds.), *The SAGE Handbook of Organizational Communication* (3rd ed.; pp. 173–194). London, UK: Sage.

Brynjolfsson, E., Hitt, L. M., & Yang, S. (2002). Intangible Assets: Computers and Organizational Capital. *Brookings Papers on Economic Activity*, *1*(1), 137–198. doi:10.1353/eca.2002.0003

Bueno, E., Anton, J. M. R., & Salmador, M. P. (2008). Knowledge creation as a dynamic capability: Implications for innovation management and organisational design. *International Journal of Technology Management*, *41*(1/2), 155. doi:10.1504/IJTM.2008.015989

Bughin, J. (2016). Ten big lessons learned from Big Data analytics. *Applied Marketing Analytics*, *2*(4), 286–295.

Bullen, M. L., & Eyler, K. A. (2010). Human resource accounting and international developments: Implications for measurement of human capital. *Journal of International Business and Cultural Studies*, *3*, 1–16.

Bulte, E., Damania, R., & Deacon, R. (2005). Resource intensity, institutions and development. *World Development*, *33*(7), 1029–1044. doi:10.1016/j.worlddev.2005.04.004

Burke, A. (Ed.). (2015). *The Handbook of Research on Freelancing and Self-Employment*. Dublin, Ireland: Senate Hall Academic Publishing.

Burns, T., & Stalker, G. M. (1961). *The Management of Innovation*. London, UK: Tavistock.

Burton-Jones, A., & Spender, J. (2011). *The Oxford handbook of human capital*. Oxford, UK: Oxford University Press. doi:10.1093/oxfordhb/9780199532162.001.0001

Caesarius, L., & Hohenthal, J. (2018). Searching for Big Data: How incumbents explore a possible adoption of Big Data technologies. *Scandinavian Journal of Management*, *34*(2), 129–140. doi:10.1016/j.scaman.2017.12.002

Calder, B., & Staw, B. (1975). Self-Perceptions of Intrinsic and Extrinsic Motivation. *Journal of Personality and Social Psychology*, *31*(4), 599–605. doi:10.1037/h0077100 PMID:1159610

Campbell, B., Coff, R., & Kryscynski, D. (2012a). Rethinking competitive advantage from human capital. *Academy of Management Review*, *37*(3), 376–395. doi:10.5465/amr.2010.0276

Campbell, B., Ganco, M., Franco, A., & Agarwal, R. (2012b). Who leaves, where to, and why worry? Employee mobility, entrepreneurship and effects on source firm performance. *Strategic Management Journal*, *33*(1), 65–87. doi:10.1002mj.943

Cap Gemini. (2012). Insights on supply chain agility. Fluctuating demand and market uncertainty: how to meet the challenge? Paris: Cap Gemini.

Capaldo, G., Iandoli, L., & Zollo, G. (2006). A situationalist perspective to competency management. *Human Resource Management*, *45*(3), 429–448. doi:10.1002/hrm.20121

Cappelli, P., & Keller, J. R. (2013). Classifying work in the new economy. *Academy of Management Review*, *38*(4), 575–596. doi:10.5465/amr.2011.0302

Cardy, R. L., & Selvarajan, T. T. (2006). Competencies: Alternative frameworks for competitive advantage. *Business Horizons*, *49*(3), 235–245. doi:10.1016/j.bushor.2005.09.004

Carel, B. (2010). The Knowledge Society: Refounding the Socius. In Organizational, Business, and Technological Aspects of the Knowledge Society: Third World Summit on the Knowledge Society (pp. 266-277). Springer.

Carlucci, D., Marr, B., & Schiuma, G. (2004). The knowledge value chain: How intellectual capital impacts on business performance. *International Journal of Technology Management*, *27*(6-7), 575–590. doi:10.1504/IJTM.2004.004903

Carnahan, R., Agarwal, R., & Campbell, B. (2012). Heterogeneity in turnover: The effect of relative compensation dispersion of firms on the mobility and entrepreneurship of extreme performers. *Strategic Management Journal*, *33*(12), 1411–1430. doi:10.1002mj.1991

Castanias, R., & Helfat, C. (1992). Managerial and windfall rents in the market of corporate control. *Journal of Economic Behavior & Organization*, *18*(2), 153–184. doi:10.1016/0167-2681(92)90025-7

Cater, T. (2004). The relevance of the knowledge-based school of thought on the sources of a firm's competitive advantage. *Management*, *9*(1), 1–26.

Cézanne, C. (2008). Modern corporate changes: Reinstating the link between the nature, boundaries and governance of the Firm. *International Review of Applied Economics*, *22*(4), 447–461. doi:10.1080/02692170802137596

Cézanne, C., & Rubinstein, M. (2012). The role of CSR in the governance of the 'new firm': An empirical study of the French telecommunications industry. *The IUP Journal of Corporate Governance*, *11*(4), 17–38.

Cézanne, C., & Saglietto, L. (2014). Human capital-Intensive firms and symbolic value creation. *Timisoara. Journal of Economics and Business*, *7*(1), 70–88.

Cézanne, C., & Saglietto, L. (2014). Human Capital-Intensive Firms and symbolic value creation. *Timisoara. Journal of Economics and Business*, *7*(1), 70–88.

Cézanne, C., & Saglietto, L. (2014). Human capital-intensive firms and the creation of symbolic value. *Timisoara Journal of Economics & Business*, *7*(1), 70–88. doi:10.2478/tjeb-2014-0004

Cézanne, C., & Saglietto, L. (2016). Human Capital-Intensive Firms and 4PLs: A Specific Partnership. *Journal of Economics and Management*, *12*(1), 61–83.

Chabault, D., Hulin, A., & Soparnot, R. (2012). Talent management in clusters. *Organizational Dynamics*, *41*(4), 327–335. doi:10.1016/j.orgdyn.2012.08.008

Chahal, H., & Bakshi, P. (2015). Examining intellectual capital and competitive advantage relationship: role of innovation and organizational learning. *International Journal of Bank Marketing, 33*(3), 376-399.doi:10.1108/IJBM-07-2013-0069

Chamarbagwala, R., & Morán, H. E. (2011). The human capital consequences of civil war: Evidence from Guatemala. *Journal of Development Economics*, *94*(1), 41–61. doi:10.1016/j.jdeveco.2010.01.005

Chang, S.-C., & Lee, M.-S. (2007). A study on relationship among leadership, organizational culture, the operation of learning organization and employee's job satisfaction. *The Learning Organization*, *14*(2), 155–185. doi:10.1108/09696470710727014

Chassagnon, V. (2011). The law and economics of the modern firm: A new governance structure of power relationships. *Revue d'Economie Industrielle*, (2): 25–50. doi:10.4000/rei.4983

Chassagnon, V., & Hollandts, X. (2014). Who are the owners of the firm: Shareholders, employees or no one? *Journal of Institutional Economics*, *10*(1), 47–69. doi:10.1017/S1744137413000301

Chatain, O., & Meyer-Doyle, P. (2017). Alleviating managerial dilemmas in human-capital-intensive firms through incentives: Evidence from M&A legal advisors. *Strategic Management Journal*, *38*(2), 232–254. doi:10.1002mj.2473

Chen, M. C., Cheng, S. J., & Hwang, Y. (2005). An empirical investigation of the relationship between intellectual capital and firms' market value and financial performance. *Journal of Intellectual Capital*, *6*(2), 159–176. doi:10.1108/14691930510592771

Chiang, J. (2007). Subsidiary performance in MNCs: The influences of absorptive capacity and social capital on knowledge transfer. *International Business & Economics Research Journal*, *6*(10), 43–50.

Chia, R. (1995). From Modern to Postmodern Organizational Analysis. *Organization Studies*, *16*(4), 579–604. doi:10.1177/017084069501600406

Chia, R. (1997). Essai: Thirty years on: From organizational structures to the organization of thought. *Organization Studies, 18*(4), 684–707. doi:10.1177/017084069701800406

Chia, R. (1999). A "rhizomic" model of organizational change and transformation: Perspective from a metaphysics of change. *British Journal of Management, 10*(3), 209–227. doi:10.1111/1467-8551.00128

Chia, R. (2003). Organization theory as postmodern science. In H. Tsoukas & C. Knudsen (Eds.), *The Oxford Handbook of Organization Theory*. Oxford University Press.

Chien, C.-F., & Chen, L.-F. (2008). Data mining to improve personnel selection and enhance human capital: A case study in high-technology industry. *Expert Systems with Applications, 34*(1), 280–290. doi:10.1016/j.eswa.2006.09.003

Chiva, R., & Alegre, J. (2009). Organizational learning capability and job satisfaction: An empirical assessment in the ceramic tile industry. *British Journal of Management, 20*(3), 323–340. doi:10.1111/j.1467-8551.2008.00586.x

Choi, B., & Lee, H. (2002). Knowledge management strategy and its link to knowledge creation process. *Expert Systems with Applications, 23*(3), 173–187. doi:10.1016/S0957-4174(02)00038-6

Chong, S. C. (2006). KM critical success factors: A comparison of perceived importance versus implementation in Malaysian ICT companies. *The Learning Organization, 13*(3), 230–256. doi:10.1108/09696470610661108

Chou, E. S. (2007). The boundaries of firms as information barriers. *The Rand Journal of Economics, 38*(3), 733–746. doi:10.1111/j.0741-6261.2007.00109.x

Clarke, M., Seng, D., & Whiting, R. H. (2011). Intellectual capital and firm performance in Australia. *Journal of Intellectual Capital, 12*(4), 505–530. doi:10.1108/14691931111181706

Clarke, T. (2014). Dangerous frontiers in corporate governance. *Journal of Management & Organization, 20*(3), 268–286. doi:10.1017/jmo.2014.37

Clarke, T. (2015). Changing paradigms in corporate governance: New cycles and new responsibilities. *Society and Business Review, 10*(3), 306–326. doi:10.1108/SBR-07-2015-0027

Clarke, T., & Gholamshahi, S. (2018). Developing human capital for knowledge based economies. In T. Clarke & K. Lee (Eds.), *Innovation in the Asia Pacific: from manufacturing to knowledge economy* (pp. 247–270). Singapore: Springer. doi:10.1007/978-981-10-5895-0_12

Coase, R. H. (1937). The nature of the firm. *Economica, 4*(16), 386–405. doi:10.1111/j.1468-0335.1937.tb00002.x

Cockx, L., & Francken, N. (2014). Extending the concept of the resource curse: Natural resources and public spending on health. *Ecological Economics, 108*, 136–149. doi:10.1016/j.ecolecon.2014.10.013

Coff, R. W. (1997). Human assets and management dilemmas: Coping with hazards on the road to resource-based theory. *Academy of Management Review*, *22*(2), 374–402. doi:10.5465/amr.1997.9707154063

Coff, R. W. (1999). When competitive advantage doesn't lead to performance: The resource-based view and stakeholder bargaining power. *Organization Science*, *10*(2), 119–133. doi:10.1287/orsc.10.2.119

Coff, R. W. (2002). Human capital, shared expertise, and the likelihood of impasse in corporate acquisitions. *Journal of Management*, *28*(1), 107–128. doi:10.1177/014920630202800107

Coff, R. W. (2011). Maximizing value from human capital. In *The Oxford Handbook of Human Capital* (pp. 359–381). Oxford, UK: Oxford University Press.

Coff, R., & Kryscynski, D. (2011). Drilling for micro-foundations of human capital-based competitive advantages. *Journal of Management*, *37*(5), 1429–1443. doi:10.1177/0149206310397772

Cohen, J. (1998). *Statistical Power Analysis for the Behavioral Sciences*. Hillside, NJ: L. Erlbaum Associates.

Cohen, W. M., & Levinthal, D. A. (1990). Absorptive Capacity : A New Perspective on Learning and Innovation. *Administrative Science Quarterly*, *35*(1), 128–152. doi:10.2307/2393553

Colakoglu, S., & Jiang, Y. (2013). Subsidiary-level outcomes of expatriate staffing: An empirical examination of MNC subsidiaries in the USA. *European Journal of International Management*, *7*(6), 696–718. doi:10.1504/EJIM.2013.057107

Collier, P. (1999). On the economic consequences of civil war. *Oxford Economic Papers*, *51*(1), 168–183. doi:10.1093/oep/51.1.168

Collings, D. G., & Mellahi, K. (2009). Strategic talent management: A review and research agenda. *Human Resource Management Review*, *19*(4), 304–313. doi:10.1016/j.hrmr.2009.04.001

Collins, J. (2001). Good to Great. Harper Collins Publisher Inc.

Collins, C. J., & Smith, K. G. (2006). Knowledge exchange and combination: The role of human resource practices in the performance of high-technology firms. *Academy of Management Journal*, *49*(3), 544–561. doi:10.5465/amj.2006.21794671

Colombo, M. G., Delmastro, M., & Grilli, L. (2004). Entrepreneurs' human capital and the start-up size of new technology-based firms. *International Journal of Industrial Organization*, *22*(8–9), 1183–1211. doi:10.1016/j.ijindorg.2004.06.006

Cooren, F., Kuhn, T. R., Cornelissen, J. P., & Clark, T. (2011). Communication, organizing and organization: An overview and introduction to the special issue. *Organization Studies*, *32*(9), 1149–1170. doi:10.1177/0170840611410836

Corden, W. M. (1984). Boom Sector and Dutch Disease Economics: Survey and Consolidation. *Oxford Economic Papers*, *36*(3), 362. doi:10.1093/oxfordjournals.oep.a041643

Corden, W. M., & Neary, J. P. (1982). Booming sector and de-industrialisation in a small open economy. *Economic Journal (London)*, *92*(368), 825–848. doi:10.2307/2232670

Cordonnier, L., & Van de Velde, F. (2014). The demands of finance and the glass ceiling of profit without investment. *Cambridge Journal of Economics*, *39*(3), 871–885. doi:10.1093/cje/beu064

Cornell, B., & Shapiro, A. (1987). Corporate Shareholders and Corporate Finance. *Financial Management*, *16*(1), 5–14. doi:10.2307/3665543

Corporaal, G. F., & Lehdonvirta, V. (2017). *Platform Sourcing: How Fortune 500 Firms Are Adopting Online Freelancing Platforms*. Oxford, UK: Oxford Internet Institute - University of Oxford.

Coyle. (2009). *The talent code*. Bantam.

Cyert, R. M., & March, J. G. (1963). *A Behavioral Theory of the Firm*. Englewood Cliffs, NJ: Prentice-Hall.

D'amore, R., Iorio, R., & Lubrano Lavadera, G. (2017). Exploring the Relationship between Human Capital and Innovation at the Firm Level: A study on a Sample of European Firms (No. 144). CELPE-Centre of Labour Economics and Economic Policy, University of Salerno, Italy.

D'Este, P., Rentocchini, F., & Vega-Jurado, J. (2014). The role of human capital in lowering the barriers to engaging in innovation: Evidence from the Spanish innovation survey. *Industry and Innovation*, *21*(1), 1–19. doi:10.1080/13662716.2014.879252

Dakhli, M., & De Clercq, D. (2004). Human capital, social capital, and innovation: A multi-country study. *Entrepreneurship and Regional Development*, *16*(2), 107–128. doi:10.1080/089 85620410001677835

Daniele, V. (2011). Natural resources and economic growth: a curse or a blessing? *Rivista Italiana degli Economisti*, *16*(3), 507-0.

Danneels, E. (2004). Disruptive technology reconsidered: A critique and research agenda. *Journal of Product Innovation Management*, *21*(4), 246–258. doi:10.1111/j.0737-6782.2004.00076.x

Darroch, J. (2005). Knowledge management, innovation and firm performance. *Journal of Knowledge Management*, *9*(3), 101–115. doi:10.1108/13673270510602809

Davenport, T. (2013). How P&G presents data to decision-makers. *Harvard Business Review Blog Network*. Available on http://blogs.hbr.org/2013/04/how-p-and-g-presents-data/

David, R. J., & Han, S.-K. (2004). A systematic assessment of the empirical support for transaction cost economics. *Strategic Management Journal*, *25*(1), 39–58. doi:10.1002mj.359

Davis, G. A. (1995). Learning to Love the Dutch Disease: Evidence from the Mineral Economies. *World Development*, *23*(10), 1765–1779. doi:10.1016/0305-750X(95)00071-J

Deakin, S., Hobbs, R., Konzelmann, S., & Wilkinson, F. (2002). Partnership, ownership and control: The impact of corporate governance on employment relations. *Employee Relations*, *24*(3), 335–352. doi:10.1108/01425450210428480

Deakin, S., Hobbs, R., Konzelmann, S., & Wilkinson, F. (2006). Anglo-American Corporate Governance and the Employment Relationship: A Case to Answer? *Socio-economic Review*, *4*(1), 155–174. doi:10.1093/SER/mwj037

Deakin, S., & Rebérioux, A. (2009). Corporate Governance, Labour Relations and Human Resource Management in Britain and France: Convergence or Divergence? In J.-P. Touffut (Ed.), *Does Company Ownership Matter?* Cheltenham, UK: Edward Elgar. doi:10.4337/9781781953297.00014

Deci, E. L., & Ryan, R. M. (Eds.). (2002). *Handbook of self-determination research.* University Rochester Press.

Deci, E., & Ryan, R. (1985). *Intrinsic Motivation and Self-Determination in Human Behavior.* New York: Plenum Press. doi:10.1007/978-1-4899-2271-7

Deci, E., & Ryan, R. (2000). Self-Determination Theory and the Facilitation of Intrinsic Motivation, Social Development, and Well-Being. *The American Psychologist*, *55*(1), 68–78. doi:10.1037/0003-066X.55.1.68 PMID:11392867

Deegan, C. (2000). *Financial Accounting Theory.* Sydney, Australia: McGraw-Hill Publishing.

Defélix, C., Klarsfeld, A., & Oiry, E. (2006). *Introduction de l'ouvrage – Nouveaux regards sur la gestion des compétences* (pp. 1–9). Paris: Vuibert.

Dejoux, C., & Thévenet, M. (2012). *Talent management.* Paris: Dunod.

Delaney, J. T., & Huselid, M. A. (1996). The impact of human resource management practices on perceptions of organizational performance. *Academy of Management Journal*, *39*(4), 949–969.

Delery, J. E., & Roumpi, D. (2017). Strategic human resource management, human capital and competitive advantage: Is the field going in circles? *Human Resource Management Journal*, *27*(1), 1–21. doi:10.1111/1748-8583.12137

Della Torre, E., Zatzick, C., Sikora, D., & Solari, L. (2018). Workforce churning, human capital disruption, and organizational performance in different technological contexts. *Human Resource Management Journal*, *28*(1), 112–127. doi:10.1111/1748-8583.12167

Demeter, K., Szász, L., & Rácz, B. (2016). The impact of subsidiaries ' internal and external integration on operational performance. *International Journal of Production Economics*, *182*, 73–85. doi:10.1016/j.ijpe.2016.08.014

De, S. (2009). Intangible determinants of market value in the new economy: A dynamic panel data analysis of the Indian software industry. *The Singapore Economic Review*, *54*(3), 379–398. doi:10.1142/S0217590809003392

De, S., & Dutta, D. (2007). Impact of intangible capital on productivity and growth: Lessons from the Indian information technology software industry. *The Economic Record*, *83*(s1), S73–S86. doi:10.1111/j.1475-4932.2007.00406.x

Desmarchelier, B., Djellal, F., & Gallouj, F. (2013). Knowledge intensive business services and long term growth. *Structural Change and Economic Dynamics*, *25*(0), 188–205. doi:10.1016/j.strueco.2012.07.003

Dickersbach, T. (2009). *Supply chain management with SAP APO: structures, modeling approaches and implementation of SAP SCM 2008* (3rd ed.). Heidelberg, Germany: Springer. doi:10.1007/978-3-540-92942-0

Ding, L., Velicer, W.F., & Harlow, L.L. (1995). Effects of estimation methods, number of indicators per factor, and improper solutions on structural equation modelling fit indices. *Structural Equation Modelling: A Multidisciplinary Journal*, *2*(2), 119-143.

Dishon, W. M., & Yabs, D. J. (2017). A Critical Literature Review On The Link Between Multinational Enterprises Presence, Absorptive Capacity And Competitive Advantage Of Firms. *Archives of Business Research*, *5*(3), 101–114. doi:10.14738/abr.53.2711

Dobusch, L., & Schoeneborn, D. (2015). Fluidity, identity, and organizationality: The communicative constitution of Anonymous. *Journal of Management Studies*, *52*(8), 1005–1035. doi:10.1111/joms.12139

Dolan, E. G. (2014). *The Curse of Riches: Resource Wealth and Social Progress*. Retrieved from http://dolanecon.blogspot.fr

Domenech, J., Escamilla, R., & Roig-Tierno, N. (2016). Explaining knowledge-intensive activities from a regional perspective. *Journal of Business Research*, *69*(4), 1301–1306. doi:10.1016/j.jbusres.2015.10.096

Dore, R. (2008). Financialization of the global economy. *Industrial and Corporate Change*, *17*(6), 1097–1112. doi:10.1093/icc/dtn041

Douangngeune, B., Hayami, Y., & Godo, Y. (2005). Education and natural resources in economic development: Thailand compared with Japan and Korea. *Journal of Asian Economics*, *16*(2), 179–204. doi:10.1016/j.asieco.2004.12.004

Dougherty, D. (2012). The maker movement. *Innovations*, *7*(3), 11–14. doi:10.1162/INOV_a_00135

Dougherty, D., & Conrad, A. (2016). *Free to Make: How the Maker Movement is Changing our Schools, our Jobs, and our Minds*. Berkeley, CA: North Atlantic Books.

Downes, L., & Nunes, P. (2013). Big bang disruption. *Harvard Business Review*, *91*(3), 44–56.

Drucker, P. F. (2009). A century of social transformation: Emergence of knowledge society. In *Managing in a time of great change*. Boston, MA: Harvard Business Press.

Dubey, Singh, & Ali, Venkatesh, & Gupta. (2014). Exploring dimensions of firm competencies and their impact on performance: Some exploratory empirical results, Benchmarking. *International Journal (Toronto, Ont.)*, *21*(6).

Dyer, J. H., & Singh, H. (1998). The relational view: Cooperative strategy and sources of interorganizational competitive advantage. *Academy of Management Review*, *23*(4), 660–679. doi:10.5465/amr.1998.1255632

Easterlin, R. A. (1981). Why isn't the whole world developed? *The Journal of Economic History*, *41*(1), 1–17. doi:10.1017/S0022050700042674

Edvinsson, L., & Malone, M. S. (1997). *Intellectual capital—realizing your company's true value by finding its hidden roots*. New York, NY: Harper Business.

Eisenberg, N. (1982). *The Development of Prosocial Behavior*. London: Academic Press.

Eisenhardt, K. K. M., & Martin, J. J. A. (2000). Dynamic capabilities: What are they? *Strategic Management Journal*, *21*(10-11), 1105–1121. doi:10.1002/1097-0266(200010/11)21:10/11<1105::AID-SMJ133>3.0.CO;2-E

Eisenhardt, K. M. (1989). Building theories from case study research. *Academy of Management Review*, *14*(4), 532–550. doi:10.5465/amr.1989.4308385

Eisenhardt, K. M., & Graebner, M. E. (2007). Theory building from cases: Opportunities and challenges. *Academy of Management Journal*, *50*(1), 25–32. doi:10.5465/amj.2007.24160888

Eisfeldt, A., & Papanikolaou, D. (2013). Organization capital and the cross-section of expected returns. *The Journal of Finance*, *68*(4), 1365–1406. doi:10.1111/jofi.12034

Elias, J., & Scarbrough, H. (2004). Evaluating human capital: An exploratory study of management practice. *Human Resource Management Journal*, *14*(4), 21–40. doi:10.1111/j.1748-8583.2004.tb00131.x

Ellingsen, T., & Johannesson, M. (2008). Pride and Prejudice: The Human Side of Incentive Theory. *The American Economic Review*, *98*(3), 990–1008. doi:10.1257/aer.98.3.990

Engelen, P.-J., & Vanderberghe, A.-S. (2005). Boundary Defense in Human Capital Intensive Firms: Coping With the Problem of Collective Departure of Employees. *22nd Annual Conference of the European Association for Law and Economics*, 15-17.

Ericsson, K. A., Preitula, M. J., & Cokely, E. T. (2007). *The Making of an Expert*. Harvard Business Review.

Fagerjord, A., & Storsul, T. (2007). Questioning convergence. In T. Storsul & D. Stuedahl (Eds.), *Ambivalence towards convergence: digitalization and media change* (pp. 19–31). Göteborg: Nordicom.

Faggian, A., Partridge, M., & Malecki, E. (2017). Creating an environment for economic growth: Creativity, entrepreneurship or human capital? *International Journal of Urban and Regional Research, 41*(6), 997–1009. doi:10.1111/1468-2427.12555

Farndale, E., Scullion, H., & Sparrow, P. (2010). The role of the corporate HR function in global talent management. *Journal of World Business, 45*(2), 161–168. doi:10.1016/j.jwb.2009.09.012

Farzanegan, M. R., & Thum, M. (2017). *More oil, less quality of education? New empirical evidence* (No. 09/17). CEPIE Working Paper.

Ferraris, A., Santoro, G., & Dezi, L. (2017). How MNC's subsidiaries may improve their innovative performance? The role of external sources and knowledge management capabilities. *Journal of Knowledge Management, 21*(17).

Ferris, G. R., Hall, A. T., Royle, M. T., & Martocchio, J. J. (2004). Theoretical development in the field of human resources management: Issues and challenges for the future. *Organizational Analysis, 12*(3), 231–254.

Flamholtz, E. (1976). The impact of human resource valuation on management decisions: A laboratory experiment. *Accounting, Organizations and Society, 1*(2-3), 153–165. doi:10.1016/0361-3682(76)90019-2

Flamholtz, E. G., Bullen, M. L., & Hua, W. (2002). Human resource accounting: A historical perspective and future implications. *Management Decision, 40*(10), 947–954. doi:10.1108/00251740210452818

Flamholtz, E. G., & Randle, Y. (2012). Corporate culture, business models, competitive advantage, strategic assets and the bottom line: Theoretical and measurement issues. *Journal of Human Resource Costing & Accounting, 16*(2), 76–94. doi:10.1108/14013381211284227

Foss, K., Foss, N., & Vazquez, X. (2006). 'Tying the Manager's Hands': Constraining Opportunistic Managerial Intervention. *Cambridge Journal of Economics, 30*(5), 797–818. doi:10.1093/cje/bei107

Foss, N. (2000). The Dangers and Attractions of Theoretical Eclectism. *Journal of Macromarketing, 20*(1), 65–67. doi:10.1177/0276146700201007

Frayret, J.-M., D'Amours, S., Rousseau, A., Harvey, S., & Gaudreault, J. (2007). Agent-based supply chain planning in the forest products industry. *International Journal of Flexible Manufacturing Systems, 19*(4), 358–391. doi:10.100710696-008-9034-z

Freel, M. (2016). Inside KIBS' black box: exploring the existence and function of knowledge angels. In D. Doloreux, M. Freel, & R. Shearmur (Eds.), *Knowledge-intensive business services: geography and innovation* (pp. 229–250). London: Routledge. doi:10.4324/9781315591216

French, J., & Rosenstein, J. (1984). Employee Ownership Work Attitudes and Power Relationships. *Academy of Management Journal, 27*(4), 861–869.

Frey, B. (1997). *Not Just for the Money - An Economic Theory of Personal Motivation*. Cheltenham, UK: Edward Elgar.

Frey, B., & Jegen, R. (2001). Motivation Crowding Theory. *Journal of Economic Surveys*, *15*(5), 589–611. doi:10.1111/1467-6419.00150

Fukuda, S., & Owen, R. F. (2008). Human capital and economic growth: Dynamic implications of insider-outsider problem for macroeconomics. *Public Policy Review*, *4*(1), 133–158.

Fulconis, F., & Paché, G. (2005). Exploiting SCM as source of competitive advantage: The importance of cooperative goals revisited. *Competitiveness Review*, *15*(2), 92–100. doi:10.1108/10595420510818740

Fulghieri, P., & Sevilir, M. (2009). *Size and scope of human capital intensive firms*. Working paper, CEPR and ECGI University of North Carolina.

Fulghieri, P., & Sevilir, M. (2009). Organization and financing of innovation, and the choice between corporate and independent venture capital. *Journal of Financial and Quantitative Analysis*, *44*(6), 1291–1321. doi:10.1017/S0022109009990391

Fulmer, I. S., & Ployhart, R. E. (2014). "Our most important asset": A multidisciplinary/multilevel review of human capital valuation for research and practice. *Journal of Management*, *40*(1), 161–192. doi:10.1177/0149206313511271

Gagné, M. (Ed.). (2014). *The Oxford handbook of work engagement, motivation, and self-determination theory*. Oxford Library of Psychology. doi:10.1093/oxfordhb/9780199794911.001.0001

Gagné, M., & Deci, E. (2005). Self-Determination Theory and Work Motivation. *Journal of Organizational Behavior*, *26*(4), 331–362. doi:10.1002/job.322

Gallardo-Gallardo, E., Dries, N., & González-Cruz, T. F. (2013). What is the meaning of 'talent' in the world of work? *Human Resource Management Review*, *23*(4), 290–300. doi:10.1016/j.hrmr.2013.05.002

Gambardella, A., Panico, C., & Valentini, G. (2015). Strategic incentives to human capital. *Strategic Management Journal*, *36*(1), 37–52. doi:10.1002mj.2200

Gandini, A. (2015). The rise of coworking spaces: A literature review. *Ephemera*, *15*(1), 193–215.

García-Meca, E., Parra, I., Larrán, M., & Martínez, I. (2005). The explanatory factors of human capital disclosure to financial analysts. *European Accounting Review*, *14*(1), 63–94. doi:10.1080/0963818042000279713

Garicano, L., & Hubbard, T. N. (2005). Hierarchical sorting and learning costs: Theory and evidence from the law. *Journal of Economic Behavior & Organization*, *58*(2), 349–369. doi:10.1016/j.jebo.2004.03.021

Garicano, L., & Hubbard, T. N. (2007). Managerial leverage is limited by the extent of the market: Hierarchies, specialization, and the utilization of lawyers' human capital. *The Journal of Law & Economics*, *50*(1), 1–43. doi:10.1086/508313

Geel, R., Mure, J., & Backes-Gellner, U. (2011). Specificity of occupational training and occupational mobility: An empirical study based on Lazear's skill-weights approach. *Education Economics*, *19*(5), 519–535. doi:10.1080/09645291003726483

Gelübcke, J. P. (2013). The performance of foreign affiliates in German manufacturing: Evidence from a new database. *Review of World Economics*, *149*(1), 151–182. doi:10.100710290-012-0142-1

Gersbach, H., & Schmutzler, A. (2003). Endogenous technological spillovers: Causes and consequences. *Journal of Economics & Management Strategy*, *12*(2), 179–205. doi:10.1162/105864003766754198

Gherardi, S. (2000). Practice-based theorizing on learning and knowing in organizations. *Organization*, *7*(2), 211–223. doi:10.1177/135050840072001

Ghoshal, S., Bartlett, C. A., & Wyplosz, C. (1988). Creation, Adoption and Diffusion of Innovations by Subsidiaries of Multinational Corporations. *Journal of International Business Studies*, *19*(3), 365–388. doi:10.1057/palgrave.jibs.8490388

Gibbons, R. (2005). Four formal(izable) theories of the firm? *Journal of Economic Behavior & Organization*, *58*(2), 200–245. doi:10.1016/j.jebo.2004.09.010

Glenn, A., McGarrity, J. P., & Weller, J. (2001). Firm-specific human capital, job matching, and turnover: Evidence from major league baseball, 1900–1992. *Economic Inquiry*, *39*(1), 86–93. doi:10.1093/ei/39.1.86

Goh, S. C., & Ryan, P. J. (2008). The organizational performance of learning companies - a longitudinal and competitor analysis using market and accounting financial data. *The Learning Organization*, *15*(3), 225–239. doi:10.1108/09696470810868855

Gómez, J., & Vargas, P. (2012). Intangible resources and technology adoption in manufacturing firms. *Research Policy*, *41*(9), 1607–1618. doi:10.1016/j.respol.2012.04.016

Gottschalg, O., & Zollo, M. (2007). Interest Alignment and Competitive Advantage. *Academy of Management Review*, *32*(2), 418–437. doi:10.5465/amr.2007.24351356

Grandori, A. (2013). Human capital and property rights. Handbook of Economic Organization: Integrating Economic and Organization Theory, 273.

Grandori, A., & Soda, G. (2004). Governing with Multiple Principals: An Empirically-Based Analysis of Capital Providers' Preferences and Superior Governance Structures. In A. Grandori (Ed.), *Corporate Governance and Firm Organization: Microfoundations and Structural Forms* (pp. 67–88). New York: Oxford University Press. doi:10.1093/acprof:oso/9780199269761.003.0004

Grant, A. M., & Berry, J. W. (2011). The necessity of others is the mother of invention: Intrinsic and prosocial motivations, perspective taking, and creativity. *Academy of Management Journal*, *54*(1), 73–96. doi:10.5465/amj.2011.59215085

Gray, R., Kouhy, R., & Lavers, S. (1995). Corporate social and environmental reporting: A review of the literature and a longitudinal study of UK disclosure. *Accounting, Auditing & Accountability Journal*, *8*(2), 47–77. doi:10.1108/09513579510146996

Green, F. (2004). Whay Has Work Effort Become More Intense? *Relations Industrielles. Industrial Relations*, *43*(4), 709–741. doi:10.1111/j.0019-8676.2004.00359.x

Griffith, D. A., Yalcinkaya, G., & Calantone, R. J. (2010). Do marketing capabilities consistently mediate effects of firm intangible capital on performance across institutional environments? *Journal of World Business*, *45*(3), 217–227. doi:10.1016/j.jwb.2009.09.008

Grossman, G., & Helpman, E. (1991). *Innovation and Growth in the Global Economy*. London: MIT Press.

Grossman, S. J., & Hart, O. D. (1986). The costs and benefits of ownership: A theory of vertical and lateral integration. *Journal of Political Economy*, *94*(4), 691–719. doi:10.1086/261404

Guilhon, B. (2004). Markets for Knowledge: Problems, Scope and Economic Implications. *Economics of Innovation and New Technology*, *13*(2), 165–181. doi:10.1080/1043859041000 1628134

Gujarati, D. N. (2009). *Basic econometrics*. Tata McGraw-Hill Education.

Gupta, A. K., & Govindarajan, V. (1991). Knowledge Flows and the Structure of Control Within Multinational Corporations. *Academy of Management Review*, *16*(4), 768–792. doi:10.5465/ AMR.1991

Gupta, A. K., & Govindarajan, V. (2000). Knowledge flows within multinational corporations. *Strategic Management Journal*, *496*, 473–496.

Guthrie, J., & Parker, L. D. (1990). Corporate social disclosure practice: A comparative international analysis. *Advances in Public Interest Accounting*, *3*(1), 159–175.

Guthrie, J., Petty, R., Yongvanich, K., & Ricceri, F. (2004). Using content analysis as a research method to inquire into intellectual capital reporting. *Journal of Intellectual Capital*, *5*(2), 282–293. doi:10.1108/14691930410533704

Gylfason, T. (2001). Natural resources, education, and economic development. *European Economic Review*, *45*(4), 847–859. doi:10.1016/S0014-2921(01)00127-1

Hair, J. F., Anderson, R. E., Tatham, R. L., & Black, W. C. (2006). *Multivariate Data Analysis* (6th ed.). Prentice-Hall.

Håland, E., & Tjora, A. (2006). Between asset and process: Developing competence by implementing a learning management system. *Human Relations*, *59*(7), 993–1016. doi:10.1177/0018726706067599

Hall, P., & Soskice, D. (2001). Introduction. In P. Hall & D. Soskice (Eds.), *Varieties of Capitalism* (pp. 1–68). Oxford, UK: Oxford University Press. doi:10.1093/0199247757.003.0001

Hansson, B. (2004). Human capital and stock returns: Is the value premium an approximation for return on human capital? *Journal of Business Finance & Accounting*, *31*(3-4), 333–358. doi:10.1111/j.0306-686X.2004.00542.x

Hart, O. (1995). Corporate Governance: Some Theory and Implications. *Economic Journal (London)*, *105*(430), 678–689. doi:10.2307/2235027

Hart, O. D. (1995). *Firms, Contracts, and Financial Structure*. Oxford, UK: Oxford University Press – Clarendon Press. doi:10.1093/0198288816.001.0001

Hart, O. D., & Moore, J. (1990). Property rights and the nature of the firm. *Journal of Political Economy*, *98*(6), 1119–1158. doi:10.1086/261729

Hart, O., & Moore, J. (1994). A theory of debt based on the inalienability of human capital. *The Quarterly Journal of Economics*, *109*(4), 841–879. doi:10.2307/2118350

Hatch, M. (2013). *The Maker Movement Manifesto: Rules for Innovation in the New World of Crafters, Hackers, and Tinkerers*. McGraw-Hill Professional.

Hatch, N. W., & Dyer, J. H. (2004). Human capital and learning as a source of sustainable competitive advantage. *Strategic Management Journal*, *25*(12), 1155–1178. doi:10.1002mj.421

Hayton, J. C. (2005). Competing in the new economy: The effect of intellectual capital on corporate entrepreneurship in high-technology new ventures. *R & D Management*, *35*(2), 137–155. doi:10.1111/j.1467-9310.2005.00379.x

Heaney, B. (2014). *Supply chain visibility and segmentation: control tower approach*. Boston: Aberdeen Group.

Helin, J., Hernes, T., Hjorth, D., & Holt, R. (Eds.). (2014). *Process Philosophy and Organization Studies*. Oxford, UK: Oxford Press University. doi:10.1093/oxfordhb/9780199669356.001.0001

Hernes, T. (2014). *A Process Theory of Organization*. Oxford, UK: Oxford University Press. doi:10.1093/acprof:oso/9780199695072.001.0001

Hirsch, J. E. (2005). An index to quantify an individual's scientific research output. *Proceedings of the National Academy of Sciences of the United States of America*, *102*(46), 16569–16572. doi:10.1073/pnas.0507655102 PMID:16275915

Hofmann, E., & Rüsch, M. (2017). Industry 4.0 and the current status as well as future prospects on logistics. *Computers in Industry*, *89*, 23–34. doi:10.1016/j.compind.2017.04.002

Holm, U., & Sharma, D. D. (2006). Subsidiary marketing knowledge and strategic development of the multinational corporation. *Journal of International Management, 12*(1), 47–66. doi:10.1016/j.intman.2005.11.001

Hsu, I.-C., & Sabherwal, R. (2012). Relationship between Intellectual Capital and Knowledge Management: An Empirical Investigation. *Decision Sciences, 43*(3), 489–524. doi:10.1111/j.1540-5915.2012.00357.x

Huang, H.-C., Lai, M.-C., & Lin, T.-H. (2011). Aligning intangible assets to innovation in biopharmaceutical industry. *Expert Systems with Applications, 38*(4), 3827–3834. doi:10.1016/j.eswa.2010.09.043

Huang, H.-C., Lai, M.-C., & Lo, K.-W. (2012). Do founders' own resources matter? The influence of business networks on start-up innovation and performance. *Technovation, 32*(5), 316–327. doi:10.1016/j.technovation.2011.12.004

Huang, L.-H. (2001). Industry-specific human capital and wage determination in Taiwan. *Asian Economic Journal, 15*(1), 19–37. doi:10.1111/1467-8381.00121

Huang, L.-H. (2003). Industry-specific human capital, occupation and firm size: Evidence from Taiwan. *Small Business Economics, 20*(3), 205–218. doi:10.1023/A:1022845929500

Huang, Y.-C., & Wu, Y.-C. J. (2010). Intellectual capital and knowledge productivity: The Taiwan biotech industry. *Management Decision, 48*(4), 580–599. doi:10.1108/00251741011041364

Hunter, L., Beaumont, P., & Lee, M. (2002). Knowledge management practice in Scottish law firms. *Human Resource Management Journal, 12*(2), 4–21. doi:10.1111/j.1748-8583.2002.tb00061.x

Hussenot, A., De Vaujany, F. X., & Chanlat, J. F. (2016). Changements socio-économiques et théories des organisations. In *Théories des organisations: nouveaux tournants* (pp. 11–24). Paris, France: Economica.

Hussenot, A., & Missonier, S. (2016). Encompassing stability and novelty in organization studies: An events-based approach. *Organization Studies, 37*(4), 523–546.

Iqbal, N., & Daly, V. (2014). Rent seeking opportunities and economic growth in transitional economies. *Economic Modelling, 37*, 16–22. doi:10.1016/j.econmod.2013.10.025

Isham, J., Woolcock, M., Pritchett, L., & Busby, G. (2005). The varieties of resource experience: Natural resource export structures and the political economy of economic growth. *The World Bank Economic Review, 19*(2), 141–174. doi:10.1093/wber/lhi010

Jalal al-Din Muhammad Balkhi. (1258). *Masnavi.*

Jamali, D., Safieddine, A. M., & Rabbath, M. (2008). Corporate governance and corporate social responsibility synergies and interrelationships. *Corporate Governance, 16*(5), 443–459. doi:10.1111/j.1467-8683.2008.00702.x

Jarrar, Y., Zairi, M., & Schiuma, G. (2010). Defining Organisational Knowledge: A Best Practice Perspective. *ECBPM, Copyright*(September), 1–10.

Jasrotia, P. (2004). *The Need for Human Resource Accounting*. Retrieved from http://www.itpeopleindia.com/20021216/cover.shtml

Jensen, A., Thuesen, C., & Geraldi, J. (2016). The projectification of everything: Projects as a human condition. *Project Management Journal, 47*(3), 21–34.

Jensen, M. C., & Meckling, W. H. (1976). Theory of the firm: Managerial behavior, agency costs and ownership structure. *Journal of Financial Economics, 3*(4), 305–360. doi:10.1016/0304-405X(76)90026-X

Jiménez-Jiménez, D., & Sanz-Valle, R. (2011). Innovation, organizational learning, and performance. *Journal of Business Research, 64*(4), 408–417. doi:10.1016/j.jbusres.2010.09.010

Johnson, L. D., Neave, E. H., & Pazderka, B. (2002). Knowledge, innovation and share value. *International Journal of Management Reviews, 4*(2), 101–134. doi:10.1111/1468-2370.00080

Kache, F., & Seuring, S. (2017). Challenges and opportunities of digital information at the intersection of Big Data analytics and supply chain management. *International Journal of Operations & Production Management, 37*(1), 10–36. doi:10.1108/IJOPM-02-2015-0078

Kalakota, R. (2012). Procter & Gamble: business sphere and decision cockpits. *Practical Analytics*. Available on https://practicalanalytics.co/2012/

Kaufmann, D., Kraay, A., & Mastruzzi, M. (2009). Governance matters VIII: Aggregate and individual governance indicators, 1996-2008. *World Bank Policy Research Working Paper*, 4978.

Kaya, F. B., Sahin, G. G., & Gurson, P. (2010). Intellectual capital in organizations. *Problems and Perspectives in Management, 8*(1), 153–160.

Keenan, J., & Aggestam, M. (2001). Corporate Governance and Intellectual Capital: Some Conceptualizations. *Empirical Research-Based and Theory-Building Papers, 9*(4), 259–275.

Kessler, A. S., & Lulfesmann, C. (2006). The theory of human capital revisited: On the interaction of general and specific investments. *Economic Journal (London), 116*(514), 903–923. doi:10.1111/j.1468-0297.2006.01116.x

Ketchen, D. J. Jr, Crook, T. R., Todd, S. Y., Combs, J. G., & Woehr, D. J. (2017). *Managing human capital*. The Oxford Handbook of Strategy Implementation.

Kianto, A., Sáenz, J., & Aramburu, N. (2017). Knowledge-based human resource management practices, intellectual capital and innovation. *Journal of Business Research, 81*, 11–20. doi:10.1016/j.jbusres.2017.07.018

Kim, D. H., & Lin, S. C. (2017). Human capital and natural resource dependence. *Structural Change and Economic Dynamics, 40*, 92–102. doi:10.1016/j.strueco.2017.01.002

Klein, B., Crawford, R., & Alchian, A. (1978). Vertical integration, appropriable rents, and the competitive contracting process. *The Journal of Law & Economics, 21*(2), 297–326. doi:10.1086/466922

Kleinknecht, R. H. (2015). Employee participation in corporate governance: Implications for company resilience. *European Journal of Industrial Relations, 21*(1), 57–72. doi:10.1177/0959680114523820

Klein, P. G., Mahoney, J. T., McGahan, A. M., & Pitelis, C. N. (2012). Who is in charge? A property rights perspective on stakeholder governance. *Strategic Organization, 10*(3), 304–315. doi:10.1177/1476127012453108

Kochan, T., & Rubinstein, S. (2000). Toward a Stakeholder Theory of the Firm: The Saturn Partnership. *Organization Science, 11*(4), 367–386. doi:10.1287/orsc.11.4.367.14601

Kor, Y. Y., & Leblebici, H. (2005). How do interdependencies among human-capital deployment, development, and diversification strategies affect firms' financial performance? *Strategic Management Journal, 26*(10), 967–985. doi:10.1002mj.485

Kraaijenbrink, J. (2011). Human capital in the Resource-Based View. In A. Burton-Jones & J.-C. Spender (Eds.), *The Oxford Handbook of Human Capital, Part 2: The nature of human capital and the firm* (pp. 218–237). Oxford.

Kramer, J.-P., Revilla Diez, J., Marinelli, E., & Iammarino, S. (2010). Intangible assets and MNEs' locational strategies for innovation-or: Why the regional matters: Empirical insights from Germany and the UK. *Review of Regional Research, 30*(2), 129–157. doi:10.100710037-010-0046-2

Kreps, D. (1997). Intrinsic Motivation and Extrinsic Incentives. *The American Economic Review, 87*(2), 359–364.

Krueger, A.O. (1980). *Trade policy as an input to development.* Academic Press.

Lai, M.-C., & Yap, S.-F. (2004). Technology Development in Malaysia and the Newly Industrializing Economies: A Comparative Analysis. *Asia-Pacific Development Journal, 11*(2), 53–80.

Lajili, K., & Zéghal, D. (2006). Market performance impacts of human capital disclosures. *Journal of Accounting and Public Policy, 25*(2), 171–194. doi:10.1016/j.jaccpubpol.2006.01.006

Lallement, M. (2015). *L'âge du faire. Hacking, travail, anarchie.* Paris, France: Seuil.

Lane, P. J., Salk, J. E., & Lyles, M. A. (2001). Absorptive capacity, learning, and performance in international joint ventures. *Strategic Management Journal, 22*(12), 1139–1161. doi:10.1002mj.206

Langley, A., Smallman, C., Tsoukas, H., & Van de Ven, A. H. (2013). Process studies of change in organization and management: Unveiling temporality, activity, and flow. *Academy of Management Journal, 56*(1), 1–13. doi:10.5465/amj.2013.4001

Langley, A., & Tsoukas, H. (2010). Introducing "Perspectives on process organization studies.". In T. Hernes & S. Maitlis (Eds.), *Process, Sensemaking and Organizing* (pp. 1–26). Oxford, UK: Oxford University Press. doi:10.1093/acprof:oso/9780199594566.003.0001

Langley, A., & Tsoukas, H. (2017). Introduction: Process thinking, process theorizing and process researching. In A. Langley & H. Tsoukas (Eds.), *The SAGE Handbook of Process Organization Studies* (pp. 1–26). London, UK: Sage. doi:10.7765/MG/9781526125491.01

Lawrence, P. R., & Lorsch, J. W. (1967). Differentiation and integration in complex organizations. *Administrative Science Quarterly*, *12*(1), 1–47. doi:10.2307/2391211

Lazear, E. (2000). The Power of Incentives. *The American Economic Review*, *90*(2), 410–414. doi:10.1257/aer.90.2.410

Lazonick, W. (2011). From innovation to financialization: how shareholder value ideology is destroying the US Economy. The handbook of the political economy of financial crises, 491-511.

Lazonick, W. (2010). Innovative business models and varieties of capitalism: Financialization of the US corporation. *Business History Review*, *84*(4), 675–702. doi:10.1017/S0007680500001987

Lazonick, W., & O'Sullivan, M. (2000). Maximizing Shareholder Value: A New Ideology for Corporate Governance. *Economy and Society*, *29*(1), 13–35. doi:10.1080/030851400360541

Le Deist, F. D., & Winterton, J. (2005). What is competence? *Human Resource Development International*, *8*(1), 27–46. doi:10.1080/1367886042000338227

Leavitt,, C.C. (2011). A Comparative Analysis of Three Unique Theories of Organizational Learning. *Journal of Knowledge Management.*

Lee, J. Y., Swink, M., & Pandejpong, T. (2011). The roles of worker expertise, information sharing quality, and psychological safety in manufacturing process innovation: An intellectual capital perspective. *Production and Operations Management*, *20*(4), 556–570. doi:10.1111/j.1937-5956.2010.01172.x

Leibniz, G. W. (2011). *«La monadologie». Les classiques des sciences sociales.* Retrieved from http://classiques.uqac.ca/classiques/Leibniz/La_Monadologie/La_Monadologie.html

Leighton, P. (2016). Professional self-employment, new power and the sharing economy: Some cautionary tales from Uber. *Journal of Management & Organization*, *22*(6), 859–874. doi:10.1017/jmo.2016.30

Leiponen, A. (2005). Skills and innovation. *International Journal of Industrial Organization*, *23*(5–6), 303–323. doi:10.1016/j.ijindorg.2005.03.005

Lengnick-Hall, M. L., Lengnick-Hall, C. A., Andrade, L. S., & Drake, B. (2009). Strategic human resource management: The evolution of the field. *Human Resource Management Review*, *19*(2), 64–85. doi:10.1016/j.hrmr.2009.01.002

Leonard-Barton, D. (1992). Core Capabilities and Core Rigidities: A Paradox in Managing New Product Development. *Strategic Management Journal, 13*(special issue), 111–125. doi:10.1002mj.4250131009

Lepak, D. P., & Snell, S. A. (1999). The human resource architecture: Toward a theory of human capital allocation and development. *Academy of Management Review, 24*(1), 31–48. doi:10.5465/amr.1999.1580439

Lepak, D. P., & Snell, S. A. (2002). Examining the human resource architecture: The relationships among human capital, employment, and human resource configurations. *Journal of Management, 28*(4), 517–543. doi:10.1177/014920630202800403

Lev, B., & Schwartz, A. (1971). On the use of the economic concept of human capital in financial statements. *The Accounting Review, 46*(1), 103–112.

Lew, Y. K., & Sinkovics, R. R. (2013). Crossing borders and industry sectors: Behavioral governance in strategic alliances and product innovation for competitive advantage. *Long Range Planning, 46*(1-2), 13–38. doi:10.1016/j.lrp.2012.09.006

Li, J. (2017). *Why do partnerships prevail in human capital-intensive industries? An information coordination perspective* (Unpublished Working Paper). Fairfax, VA: George Mason University.

Li, N. (2015). *Labor market peer firms.* Working Paper Series No. 2015-02. Chicago: Searle Center on Law, Regulation & Economic Growth.

Liao, S.-H., Chen, C.-C., Hu, D.-C., Chung, Y., & Yang, M.-J. (2016). Developing a sustainable competitive advantage: Absorptive capacity, knowledge transfer and organizational learning. *The Journal of Technology Transfer.* doi:10.100710961-016-9532-1

Liao, S.-H., Wu, C.-C., Hu, D.-C., & Tsui, K.-A. (2010). Relationships between knowledge acquisition, absorptive capacity and innovation capability: An empirical study on Taiwan's financial and manufacturing industries. *Journal of Information Science, 36*(1), 19–35. doi:10.1177/0165551509340362

Lindberg, O., & Rantatalo, O. (2015). Competence in professional practice: A practice theory analysis of police and doctors. *Human Relations, 68*(4), 561–582. doi:10.1177/0018726714532666

Ling, T. C., & Nasurdin, A. M. (2010). Human Resource Management Practices and Organizational Innovation: An Empirical Study In Malaysia. *Journal of Applied Business Research, 26*(4), 105–115. doi:10.19030/jabr.v26i4.311

Linnehan, F., & De Carolis, D. (2005). Strategic frameworks for understanding employer participation in school-to-work programs. *Strategic Management Journal, 26*(6), 523–539. doi:10.1002mj.467

Lippert, I., Huzzard, T., Jürgens, U., & Lazonick, W. (2014). *Corporate governance, employee voice, and work organization: sustaining high-road jobs in the automotive supply industry.* Oxford University Press. doi:10.1093/acprof:oso/9780199681075.001.0001

Lööf, H., & Heshmati, A. (2002). Knowledge capital and performance heterogeneity: A firm-level innovation study. *International Journal of Production Economics*, *76*(1), 61–85. doi:10.1016/S0925-5273(01)00147-5

Lucas, R. E. Jr. (1988). On the mechanics of economic development. *Journal of Monetary Economics*, *22*(1), 3–42. doi:10.1016/0304-3932(88)90168-7

Luo, X., Koput, K., & Powell, W. (2009). Intellectual capital or signal? The effects of scientists on alliance formation in knowledge-intensive industries. *Research Policy*, *38*(8), 1313–1325. doi:10.1016/j.respol.2009.06.001

Luo, Y. (2000). Dynamic Capabilities in International Expansion. *Journal of World Business*, *35*(4), 355–378. doi:10.1016/S1090-9516(00)00043-2

Luu, T. (2014). Knowledge sharing and competitive intelligence. *Marketing Intelligence & Planning*, *32*(3), 269–292. doi:10.1108/MIP-05-2013-0077

Lynskey, M. (2004). Knowledge, finance and human capital: The role of social institutional variables on entrepreneurship in Japan. *Industry and Innovation*, *11*(4), 373–405. doi:10.1080/1366271042000289379

Macky, K., & Boxall, P. (2007). The relationship between 'high-performance work practices' and employee attitudes: An investigation of additive and interaction effects. *International Journal of Human Resource Management*, *18*(4), 537–567. doi:10.1080/09585190601178745

Macpherson, A., & Holt, R. (2007). Knowledge, learning and small firm growth: A systematic review of the evidence. *Research Policy*, *36*(2), 172–192. doi:10.1016/j.respol.2006.10.001

Mahnke, V., Pedersen, T., & Venzin, M. (2005). Why do MNC subsidiaries engage in knowledge sharing with other subsidiaries and what are the implications for performance. In *Dynamics of Industry and Innovation*. Organizations, Networks and Systems.

Mahoney, J., & Pandian, J. (1992). The resource-based view within the conversation of strategic management. *Strategic Management Journal*, *15*(5), 363–380. doi:10.1002mj.4250130505

Makani, J., & Marche, S. (2010). Towards a typology of knowledge-intensive organizations: Determinant factors. *Knowledge Management Research and Practice*, *8*(3), 265–277. doi:10.1057/kmrp.2010.13

Makimoto, T., & Manners, D. (1997). *Digital Nomad*. Chichester, UK: Wiley.

Makri, M., & Scandura, T. A. (2010). Exploring the effects of creative CEO leadership on innovation in high-technology firms. *The Leadership Quarterly*, *21*(1), 75–88. doi:10.1016/j.leaqua.2009.10.006

Malhotra, Y. (1998). Knowledge management for the new world of business. *Asian Strategy Leadership Institute Review, 6*.

Mankiw, N. G., Romer, D., & Weil, D. N. (1992). A contribution to the empirics of economic growth. *The Quarterly Journal of Economics*, *107*(2), 407–437. doi:10.2307/2118477

Marchand, O. (1998). Salariat et non-salariat dans une perspective historique. *Economie & Statistique*, *319-320*(1), 3–11. doi:10.3406/estat.1998.2666

Marchington, M., Wilkinson, A., Donnelly, R., & Kynighou, A. (2016). *Human resource management at work*. Kogan Page Publishers.

March, J. G. (1991). Exploration and exploitation in organizational learning. *Organization Science*, *2*(1), 71–87. doi:10.1287/orsc.2.1.71

March, J. G. (2007). The study of organizations and organizing since 1945. *Organization Studies*, *28*(1), 9–19. doi:10.1177/0170840607075277

March, J. G., & Simon, H. A. (1958). *Organizations*. New York, NY: Wiley.

Marr, B., Gupta, O., Pike, S., & Roos, G. (2003). Intellectual capital and knowledge management effectiveness. *Management Decision*, *41*(8), 771–781. doi:10.1108/00251740310496288

Martín-de Castro, G., Delgado-Verde, M., Navas-López, J. E., & Cruz-González, J. (2013). The moderating role of innovation culture in the relationship between knowledge assets and product innovation. *Technological Forecasting and Social Change*, *80*(2), 351–363. doi:10.1016/j.techfore.2012.08.012

Marvel, M. R., & Lumpkin, G. T. (2007). Technology entrepreneurs' human capital and its effects on innovation radicalness. *Entrepreneurship Theory and Practice*, *31*(6), 807–828. doi:10.1111/j.1540-6520.2007.00209.x

Marx, K. (1867). *Le Capital*. Presses Universitaires de France, Coll. Quadridge.

McClelland, D. C. (1973). Testing for competence rather than for "intelligence". *The American Psychologist*, *28*(1), 1–14. doi:10.1037/h0034092 PMID:4684069

McGregor, D. (1960). *The Human Side of Enterprise*. New York: McGraw-Hill.

Mehlum, H., Moene, K., & Torvik, R. (2006). Institutions and the resource curse. *Economic Journal (London)*, *116*(508), 1–20. doi:10.1111/j.1468-0297.2006.01045.x

Mehralian, G., Nazari, J. A., Akhavan, P., & Rasekh, H. R. (2014). Exploring the relationship between the knowledge creation process and intellectual capital in the pharmaceutical industry. *The Learning Organization*, *21*(4), 258–273. doi:10.1108/TLO-07-2013-0032

Merton, R. K. (1968). *Social Theory and Social Structure*. New York, NY: The Free Press.

Meyer-Doyle, P., Mawdsley, J., & Chatain, O. (2017). *Resource reconfiguration in human-capital-intensive firms*. Research Paper No. SPE-2017-1216. Jouy-en-Josas: HEC Paris.

Meyer, K. E., Mudambi, R., & Narula, R. (2011). Multinational Enterprises and Local Contexts: The Opportunities and Challenges of Multiple Embeddedness. *Journal of Management Studies*, *48*(2), 235–252. doi:10.1111/j.1467-6486.2010.00968.x

Meyers, M. C., Van Woerkom, M., & Dries, N. (2013). Talent – Innate or acquired? Theoretical considerations and their implications for. *Human Resource Management Review*, *23*(4), 305–321. doi:10.1016/j.hrmr.2013.05.003

Midler, C. (1995). Projectification of the firm: The Renault case. *Scandinavian Journal of Management*, *11*(4), 363–375. doi:10.1016/0956-5221(95)00035-T

Miles, J. A. (2013). Absorptive Capacity Theory. In Management and Organization Theory. Academic Press.

Miles, I., Belousova, V., & Chichkanov, N. (2018). Knowledge intensive business services: Ambiguities and continuities. *Foresight*, *20*(1), 1–26. doi:10.1108/FS-10-2017-0058

Miles, M. B., & Huberman, A. M. (1994). *Qualitative data analysis: An expanded sourcebook*. Sage Publications, Incorporated.

Milgrom, P., & Roberts, D. (1995). Complementarities and Fit: Strategy, Sructure, and Organizational Change in Manufacturing. *Journal of Accounting and Economics*, *19*(2-3), 179–208. doi:10.1016/0165-4101(94)00382-F

Miller, R. (1996). *Measuring What People Know. Human Capital Accounting for the Knowledge Economy*. Washington, DC: OECD Publications and Information Center.

Minai, M. H. (2016). Leading for innovation. In Human Capital and Innovation: Examining the Role of Globalization (pp. 39-72). Palgrave Macmillan.

Minbaeva, D., Pedersen, T., Björkman, I., Fey, C. F., Park, H. J., Bjorkman, I., ... Park, H. J. (2003). MNC knowledge transfer, subsidiary absorptive capacity and HRM. *Journal of International Business Studies*, *34*(6), 586–599. doi:10.1057/palgrave.jibs.8400056

Mincer, J. (1958). Investment in human capital and personal income distribution. *Journal of Political Economy*, *66*(4), 281–302. doi:10.1086/258055

Mincer, J. (1970). The distribution of labor incomes: A survey with special reference to the human capital approach. *Journal of Economic Literature*, *8*(1), 1–26.

Moavenzadeh, J., Bernard, M., Giffi, C. A., & Powers, D. (2012). *Manufacturing for growth strategies for driving growth and employment*. A World Economic Forum Report, April.

Moen, J. (2005). Is mobility of technical personnel a source of R&D spillovers? *Journal of Labor Economics*, *23*(1), 81–114. doi:10.1086/425434

Moeuf, A., Pellerin, R., Lamouri, S., Tamayo-Giraldo, S., & Barbaray, R. (2017). The industrial management of SMEs in the era of Industry 4.0. *International Journal of Production Research*, *56*(3), 1118–1136. doi:10.1080/00207543.2017.1372647

Möller, K., Gamerschlag, R., & Guenther, F. (2011). Determinants and effects of human capital reporting and controlling. *Journal of Management Control*, *22*(3), 311–333. doi:10.100700187-011-0138-3

Molloy, J. C., Ployhart, R. E., & Wright, P. M. (2011). The myth of "the" micro-macro divide: Bridging system-level and disciplinary divides. *Journal of Management*, *37*(2), 581–609. doi:10.1177/0149206310365000

Morris, S. S., & Snell, S. (2011). Intellectual capital configurations and organizational capability: An empirical examination of human resource subunits in the multinational enterprise. *Journal of International Business Studies*, *42*(6), 805–827. doi:10.1057/jibs.2011.14

Mousavi, S. M. A., Nouri, M., & BenYousef, A. (2017b, October). *Natural resource abundance and Human Capital nexus, concerning the governance*. Paper presented at 29th European Association for Evolutionary Political Economy, Budapest, Hungry.

Mudalige, D., Ismail, N. A., & Malek, M. M. (2016). Application of theory of dynamic capabilities to explicate internationalization of SMEes in Sri Lanka. *Ipbj*, *8*(2), 1–18.

Mudambi, R. (2002). Knowledge management in multinational firms. *Journal of International Management*, *8*(1), 1–9. doi:10.1016/S1075-4253(02)00050-9

Mudambi, R., Pedersen, T., & Andersson, U. (2014). How subsidiaries gain power in multinational corporations. *Journal of World Business*, *49*(1), 101–113. doi:10.1016/j.jwb.2013.02.001

Murdoch, J. C., & Sandler, T. (2002). Economic growth, civil wars, and spatial spillovers. *The Journal of Conflict Resolution*, *46*(1), 91–110. doi:10.1177/0022002702046001006

Murphy, K. M., Shleifer, A., & Vishny, R. W. (1993). Why is rent-seeking so costly to growth? *The American Economic Review*, *83*(2), 409–414.

Myers, M. B., Griffith, D. A., Daugherty, P. J., & Lusch, R. F. (2004). Maximizing the human capital equation in logistics: Education, experience and skills. *Journal of Business Logistics*, *25*(1), 211–232. doi:10.1002/j.2158-1592.2004.tb00175.x

Myers, S. C. (1999). Financial architecture. *European Financial Management*, *5*(2), 133–141. doi:10.1111/1468-036X.00086

Naderi, M. M. (2011). Good Governance; Introduction and criticism. Islām va Pazhūheshhāye Modirīyatī, 1(1). (in Persian)

Nagin, D., Rebitzer, J., Sanders, S., & Taylor, L. (2002). Monitoring, Motivation and Management: The Determinants of Opportunistic Behavior in a Field Experiment. *The American Economic Review*, *92*(4), 850–873. doi:10.1257/00028280260344498

Najim Abdullah, M., Hashim, M. A., & Ali, A. (2015). Review of the Elements of Knowledge Management Capabilities. *Journal of Information Systems Research and Innovation*, *9*(2), 28–34.

Nambiar, S. (2011). Problems with human capital in Malaysia East Asia Forum. *East Asia Forum*, (Part 1), 2–4.

Nash, C., Jarrahi, M. H., Sutherland, W., & Phillips, G. (2018). Digital nomads beyond the buzzword: Defining digital nomadic work and use of digital technologies. In G. Chowdhury, J. McLeod, V. Gillet, & P. Willett (Eds.), Lecture Notes in Computer Science: Vol. 10766. *Transforming Digital Worlds. iConference 2018*. Cham, Switzerland: Springer. doi:10.1007/978-3-319-78105-1_25

National Economic Advisory Council. (2010). *New economic model for Malaysia: Strategic policy direction*. Author.

Nazari, J. A., & Herremans, I. M. (2007). Extended VAIC model: Measuring intellectual capital components. *Journal of Intellectual Capital*, *8*(4), 595–609. doi:10.1108/14691930710830774

Negassi, S. (2004). R&D co-operation and innovation a microeconometric study on French firms. *Research Policy*, *33*(3), 365–384. doi:10.1016/j.respol.2003.09.010

Nelson, R. R., & Phelps, E. S. (1966). Investment in humans, technological diffusion, and economic growth. *The American Economic Review*, *56*(1/2), 69–75.

Newbert, S. L. (2007). Empirical research on the resource-based view of the firm: An assessment and suggestions for future research. *Strategic Management Journal*, *28*(2), 121–146. doi:10.1002mj.573

Newbert, S. L. (2008). Value, Rareness, Competitive Advantage, and Performance: A Conceptual-Level Empirical Investigation of the Resource-Based View of the Firm. *Strategic Management Journal*, *29*(3), 745–768. doi:10.1002mj.686

Ngo, H. Y., Lau, C. M., & Foley, S. (2008). Strategic human resource management, firm performance, and employee relations climate in China. *Human Resource Management*, *47*(1), 73–90. doi:10.1002/hrm.20198

Nonaka, I. (1991). The Knowledge Creating Company. *Harvard Business Review*, *69*, 96–104. doi:10.1016/0024-6301(96)81509-3

Nyberg, A., Moniterno, T., Hale, D., & Lepak, D. (2014). Resource-based perspective on unit-level human capital: A review and integration. *Journal of Management*, *40*(1), 316–346. doi:10.1177/0149206312458703

Osnowitz, D. (2010). *Freelancing Expertise: Contract Professionals in the New Economy*. Cornell University Press.

Osterloh, M., & Frey, B. (2000). Motivation, Knowledge Transfer, and Organizational Forms. *Organization Science*, *11*(5), 538–550. doi:10.1287/orsc.11.5.538.15204

Osterloh, M., & Frey, B. (2004). Corporate Governance for Crooks? The Case for Corporate Virtue. In A. Grandori (Ed.), *Corporate Governance and Firm Organization: Microfoundations and Structural Forms* (pp. 191–211). New York: Oxford University Press. doi:10.1093/acprof:oso/9780199269761.003.0009

Ouchi, W. (1980). Markets, Bureaucracies and Clans. *Administrative Science Quarterly*, *25*(1), 129–141. doi:10.2307/2392231

Oyewo, B. M. (2013). Comparative analyses of human resources accounting disclosure practices in Nigerian financial service and manufacturing companies. *IOSR Journal of Humanities and Social Science*, *16*(1), 20–26. doi:10.9790/0837-1612026

Padmasiri, H. M. N. (2011). The role of human capital in the development process of industrial clusters: Evidence from metalworking clusters in Sri Lanka. *Economic Papers*, *30*(1), 109–117. doi:10.1111/j.1759-3441.2010.00092.x

Palangkaraya, A., Spurling, T., & Webster, E. (2016). *What drives firm innovation? A review of the economics literature*. Academic Press.

Pantzalis, C., & Park, J. C. (2009). Equity market valuation of human capital and stock returns. *Journal of Banking & Finance*, *33*(9), 1610–1623. doi:10.1016/j.jbankfin.2009.03.008

Papyrakis, E., & Gerlagh, R. (2007). Resource abundance and economic growth in the United States. *European Economic Review*, *51*(4), 1011–1039. doi:10.1016/j.euroecorev.2006.04.001

Parker, M. (1992). Post-modern organizations or postmodern organization theories. *Organization Studies*, *13*(1), 1–17. doi:10.1177/017084069201300103

Patel, P. C., & Fiet, J. O. (2011). Knowledge combination and the potential advantages of family firms in searching for opportunities. *Entrepreneurship Theory and Practice*, *35*(6), 1179–1197. doi:10.1111/j.1540-6520.2011.00497.x

Pearson, M. (2014). Supply chain control towers are taking off. *Logistics Management*, *53*(8), 26–27.

Penang Investment. (2015). Retrieved from www.investpenang.gov.my/

Peneder, M. (2002). Intangible investment and human resources. *Journal of Evolutionary Economics*, *12*(1-2), 107–134. doi:10.100700191-002-0103-2

Penrose, E. T. (1959). The Theory of the Growth of the Firm. Oxford University Press.

Perdreau, F., Nadant, L., & Cliquet, G. (2015). Human capital intangibles and performance of franchise networks: A complementary view between agency and critical resource perspectives. *Managerial and Decision Economics*, *36*(2), 121–138. doi:10.1002/mde.2656

Peretto, P. F. (1999). Industrial development, technological change, and long-run growth. *Journal of Development Economics*, *59*(2), 389–417. doi:10.1016/S0304-3878(99)00018-8

Perraudin, C., Petit, H., & Rebérioux, A. (2008). The stock market and human resource management: Evidence from a survey of French establishments. *Recherches Economiques de Louvain*, *74*(4), 541–581. doi:10.3917/rel.744.0541

Perri, A., & Andersson, U. (2014). Knowledge outflows from foreign subsidiaries and the tension between knowledge creation and knowledge protection: Evidence from the semiconductor industry. *International Business Review*, *23*(1), 63–75. doi:10.1016/j.ibusrev.2013.08.007

Phene, A., & Almeida, P. (2008). Innovation in multinational subsidiaries: The role of knowledge assimilation and subsidiary capabilities. *Journal of International Business Studies*, *39*(5), 901–919. doi:10.1057/palgrave.jibs.8400383

Philippot, L. M. (2010). *Are Natural Resources a Curse for Human Capital Accumulation.* Centre d'Etudes et de Recherches sur le Développement International (CERDi-CNRS).

Pinder, C. C. (2014). *Work motivation in organizational behavior.* Psychology Press.

Ployhart, R. E., & Moliterno, T. P. (2011). Emergence of the human capital resource: A multilevel model. *Academy of Management Review*, *36*(1), 127–150. doi:10.5465/amr.2009.0318

Ployhart, R. E., Nyberg, A. J., Reilly, G., & Maltarich, M. A. (2014). Human capital is dead; Long live human capital resources! *Journal of Management*, *40*(2), 371–398. doi:10.1177/0149206313512152

Polterovich, V., Popov, V., & Tonis, A. (2010). *Resource abundance: A curse or blessing?* Academic Press.

Prahalad, C. K., & Hamel, G. (1990). The core competence of the corporation. *Harvard Business Review*, *68*(3), 79–91.

Purcell, J., & Hutchinson, S. (2007). Front-line managers as agents in the HRM-performance causal chain: Theory, analysis and evidence. *Human Resource Management Journal*, *17*(1), 3–20. doi:10.1111/j.1748-8583.2007.00022.x

Qian, Y. (2003). *Human capital-Intensive firms: incentives and capital structure* (Unpublished Working Paper). New York: Stern School of Management.

Qian, Y. (2003). *Human capital-Intensive firms: Incentives and capital structure.* Working Paper Series, University of Iowa – Department of Finance.

Rahimli, A. (2012). Knowledge Management and Competitive Advantage. *Information and Knowledge Management, 2*(7), 37–43.

Rahman, M. R. C. A., & Ahmed, R. M. (2016). Disclosure of Human Capital Information in Annual Reports: A Case of Malaysian Banking and Financial Institution Sector. *International Journal of Business*, *1*(1), 83–104.

Rajan, R. (2012). Presidential address: The corporation in finance. *The Journal of Finance*, *67*(4), 1173–1217. doi:10.1111/j.1540-6261.2012.01745.x

Rajan, R. G., & Zingales, L. G. (1998). Power in a theory of the firm. *The Quarterly Journal of Economics*, *113*(2), 387–432. doi:10.1162/003355398555630

Rajan, R. G., & Zingales, L. G. (2000). The Governance of the New Enterprise. In X. Vives (Ed.), *Corporate Governance: Theoretical and Empirical Perspectives* (pp. 201–227). Cambridge, UK: Cambridge University Press. doi:10.1017/CBO9781139175333.007

Rajan, R. G., & Zingales, L. G. (2001). The influence of the financial revolution on the nature of firms. *The American Economic Review*, *91*(2), 206–211. doi:10.1257/aer.91.2.206

Ramirez, P. G., & Hachiya, T. (2006). Measuring firm-specific organizational capital and its impact on value and productivity: Evidence from Japan. *Review of Pacific Basin Financial Markets and Policies*, *9*(4), 549–574. doi:10.1142/S0219091506000860

Ramsey, H., Scholarios, D., & Harley, B. (2000). Employees and High-Performance Work Systems: Testing Inside the Black Box. *British Journal of Industrial Relations*, *38*(4), 501–531. doi:10.1111/1467-8543.00178

Ranft, A. L., & Lord, M. D. (2000). Acquiring new knowledge: The role of retaining human capital in acquisitions of high-tech firms. *The Journal of High Technology Management Research*, *11*(2), 295–319. doi:10.1016/S1047-8310(00)00034-1

Ravix, J. L. (2008). Nature and governance of the firm: In search of an integrated perspective. *International Review of Applied Economics*, *22*(4), 463–478. doi:10.1080/02692170802137620

Rescher, N. (2012, Summer). Process philosophy. *The Stanford Encyclopedia of Philosophy*. Retrieved from https://plato.stanford.edu/archives/sum2012/entries/process-philosophy/

Rescher, N. (1996). *Process Metaphysics: An Introduction to Process Philosophy*. New York: State University of New York Press.

Rinehart, L., & Ragatz, G. (1996). Management of facility and human resources in materials and logistics management. *Journal of Business Logistics*, *17*(2), 1–18.

Ritchie, B. K. (2002). Foreign direct investment and intellectual capital. *OECD Working Paper, 194*. Retrieved from http://www.oecd.org/indonesia/1949901.pdf

Rnolmayer, G., Merten, P., & Zeier, A. (2002). *Supply chain management based on SAP systems*. Heidelberg, Germany: Springer; doi:10.1007/978-3-540-24816-3

Roberts, J., & Van den Steen, E. (2000). *Stakeholder interests, human capital investment and corporate governance*. Stanford GSB Working Paper Series, n°1631.

Romer, P. (1986). Increasing returns and long-run growth. *Journal of Political Economy*, *94*(5), 1002–1037. doi:10.1086/261420

Rosser, A. (2006). *The political economy of the resource curse: A literature survey*. Academic Press.

Ross, M. L. (2001). Does oil hinder democracy? *World Politics*, *53*(3), 325–361. doi:10.1353/wp.2001.0011

Roy, M. J., & Therin, F. (2008). Knowledge acquisition and environmental commitment in SMEs. *Corporate Social Responsibility and Environmental Management*, *15*(5), 249–259. doi:10.1002/csr.145

Sacconi, L., Blair, M., & Freeman, R. E. (2010). *Corporate social responsibility and corporate governance: The contribution of economic theory and related disciplines*. Springer.

Sachs, J. D., & Warner, A. M. (1995). *Natural resource abundance and economic growth (No. w5398)*. National Bureau of Economic Research. doi:10.3386/w5398

Sambamurthy, V., & Zmud, R. (2000). Research commentary: The organizing logic for an enterprise's IT activities in the digital era–A prognosis of practice and a call for research. *Information Systems Research*, *11*(2), 105–114. doi:10.1287/isre.11.2.105.11780

Sampe, F. (2012). *The influence of organizational learning on performance in Indonesian SMEs* (DBA thesis). Southern Cross University.

Sandberg, J. (2000). Understanding human competence at work: An interpretative approach. *Academy of Management Journal*, *43*(1), 9–25.

Sandberg, J., & Pinnington, A. H. (2009). Professional competence as ways of being: An existential ontological perspective. *Journal of Management Studies*, *46*(7), 1138–1170. doi:10.1111/j.1467-6486.2009.00845.x

Santos-Vijande, M. L., López-Sánchez, J. Á., & Trespalacios, J. A. (2012). How organizational learning affects a firm's flexibility, competitive strategy, and performance. *Journal of Business Research*, *65*(8), 1079–1089. doi:10.1016/j.jbusres.2011.09.002

Sarangi, S. (2016). Business intelligence systems: A necessity for agile supply chains. *KIIT Journal of Management*, *12*(2), 52–65.

Saru, E. (2007). Organisational learning and HRD: How appropriate are they for small firms? *Journal of European Industrial Training*, *31*(1), 36–51. doi:10.1108/03090590710721727

Schmidt, F. L., & Hunter, J. E. (1998). The validity and utility of selection methods in personnel psychology: Practical and theoretical implications of 85 years of research findings. *Psychological Bulletin*, *124*(2), 262–274. doi:10.1037/0033-2909.124.2.262

Schmitz, P. W. (2001). The Hold-Up Problem and Incomplete Contracts: A Survey of Recent Topics in Contract Theory. *Bulletin of Economic Research*, *53*(1), 1–17. doi:10.1111/1467-8586.00114

Schneider, L., Gunther, J., & Brandenburg, B. (2010). Innovation and skills from a sectoral perspective: A linked employer-employee analysis. *Economics of Innovation and New Technology*, *19*(1-2), 185–202. doi:10.1080/10438590902872887

Schuler, R. S., & Jackson, S. E. (2007). *Strategic human resource management* (2nd ed.). Oxford, UK: Blackwell.

Schultz, T. W. (1961). Investment in human capital. *The American Economic Review*, *51*(1), 1–17.

Schultz, T. W. (1961). Investment in Human Capital. *The American Economic Review*, *51*(1), 1–17.

Schultz, T. W. (1982). *Investing in people: The economics of population quality*. University of California Press.

Scott, S. W. (2000). Ivanhoe. London, UK: Wordsworth Classics. (Original work published 1820)

Scott, S. G., & Bruce, R. A. (1994). Determinants of innovative behavior: A path model of individual innovation in the workplace. *Academy of Management Journal*, *37*(3), 580–607.

Seidu, Y. (2011). *Human Resource Management and Organizational Performance: Evidence from the Retail Banking Sector* (DBA thesis). Southern Cross University.

Seleim, A. A. S., & Khalil, O. E. M. (2011). Understanding the knowledge management-intellectual capital relationship: a two-way analysis. *Journal of Intellectual Capital*, *12*. doi:10.1108/14691931111181742

Selznick, P. (1948). Foundations of the theory of organization. *American Sociological Review*, *13*(1), 25–35. doi:10.2307/2086752

Serneels, P. (2008). Human capital revisited: The role of experience and education when controlling for performance and cognitive skills. *Labour Economics*, *15*(6), 1143–1161. doi:10.1016/j.labeco.2007.10.003

Setia, P., Sambamurthy, V., & Closs, D. (2008). Realizing business value of agile IT applications: Antecedents in the supply chain networks. *Information Technology Management*, *9*(1), 5–19. doi:10.100710799-007-0028-4

Shahbaz, M., Naeem, M., Ahad, M., & Tahir, I. (2017). Is natural resource abundance a stimulus for financial development in the USA? *Resources Policy*.

Shao, S., & Yang, L. (2014). Natural resource dependence, human capital accumulation, and economic growth: A combined explanation for the resource curse and the resource blessing. *Energy Policy*, *74*, 632–642. doi:10.1016/j.enpol.2014.07.007

Shih, K. H., Chang, C., & Lin, B. (2010). Assessing knowledge creation and intellectual capital in banking industry. *Journal of Intellectual Capital*, *11*(1), 74–89. doi:10.1108/14691931011013343

Siggelkow, N. (2007). Persuasion with case studies. *Academy of Management Journal*, *50*(1), 20–24. doi:10.5465/amj.2007.24160882

Sim, A. (2012). A comparative case study of the internationalization strategies of Malaysian, Singaporean and Taiwanese firms. *Journal of Asian Business*, *24*(3), 85–108.

Simonen, J., & McCann, P. (2008). Firm innovation: The influence of R&D cooperation and the geography of human capital inputs. *Journal of Urban Economics*, *64*(1), 146–154. doi:10.1016/j.jue.2007.10.002

Simonen, J., & McCann, P. (2010). Knowledge transfers and innovation: The role of labour markets and R&D co-operation between agents and institutions. *Papers in Regional Science*, *89*(2), 295–309. doi:10.1111/j.1435-5957.2010.00299.x

Singleton, W. T. (1978). *Study of real skills: Vol. 1. The analysis of practical skills*. Academic Press.

Sirmon, D. G., Hitt, M. A., Ireland, R. D., & Gilbert, B. A. (2011). Resource Orchestration to Create Competitive Advantage. *Journal of Management*, 37.

Skaggs, B. C., & Youndt, M. (2004). Strategic positioning, human capital, and performance in service organizations: A customer interaction approach. *Strategic Management Journal*, *25*(1), 85–99. doi:10.1002mj.365

Slaughter, M. J. (2002). *Does Inward Foreign Direct Investment Contribute to Skill Upgrading in Developing Countries?* SCEPA Working Paper No. 2002-08. New York, NY: Schwartz Center for Economic Policy Analysis, New School University.

Smit, A. J. (2010). The competitive advantage of nations: Is Porter's Diamond Framework a new theory that explains the international competitiveness of countries. *Southern African Business Review*.

Smith, K. G., Collins, C. J., & Clark, K. D. (2005). Existing knowledge, knowledge creation capability, and the rate of new product introduction in high technology firms. *Academy of Management Journal*, *48*(2), 346–357. doi:10.5465/amj.2005.16928421

Solow, R. M. (1956). A contribution to the theory of economic growth. *The Quarterly Journal of Economics*, *70*(1), 65–94. doi:10.2307/1884513

Spencer, L. M., & Spencer, P. S. M. (2008). *Competence at Work models for superior performance*. John Wiley & Sons.

Spinuzzi, C. (2012). Working alone together: Coworking as emergent collaborative activity. *Journal of Business and Technical Communication*, *26*(4), 399–441. doi:10.1177/1050651912444070

Starbuck, W. (1992). Learning by knowledge-intensive firms. *Journal of Management Studies*, *29*(6), 713–740. doi:10.1111/j.1467-6486.1992.tb00686.x

Steinfield, C., Scupola, A., & López-Nicolás, C. (2010). Social capital, ICT use and company performance: Findings from the Medicon Valley Biotech Cluster. *Technological Forecasting and Social Change*, *77*(7), 1156–1166. doi:10.1016/j.techfore.2010.03.004

Stewart, T. A. (1999). *Intellectual capital—the new wealth of organizations*. New York, NY: Crown Business.

Stiglitz, J. (2004). *We can now cure Dutch disease*. Retrieved from https://www.theguardian.com/business /2004/ aug/18/comment.oilandpetrol

Stijns, J. P. (2006). Natural resource abundance and human capital accumulation. *World Development, 34*(6), 1060–1083. doi:10.1016/j.worlddev.2005.11.005

Stijns, J. P. C. (2005). Natural resource abundance and economic growth revisited. *Resources Policy, 30*(2), 107–130. doi:10.1016/j.resourpol.2005.05.001

Strauss, A., & Corbin, J. (1990). *Basics of qualitative research: Grounded theory procedures and techniques*. London: Sage Publications.

Su, Z., Ahlstrom, D., Li, J., & Cheng, D. (2013, November). Knowledge creation capability, absorptive capacity, and product innovativeness. *R&D Management*. doi:10.1111/radm.12033

Subramaniam, M., & Youndt, M. A. (2005a). The Influence of Intellectual Capital On The Types Of Innovation Capabilities. *Academy of Management Journal, 48*(3), 450–463. doi:10.5465/amj.2005.17407911

Subramanian, K. (2007). *Firm boundaries in the new economy: Theory and evidence*. 2007 Annual Meeting Allied Social Science Associations, AEA Conference, Chicago, IL.

Surinach, J., & Moreno, R. (2011). The role of intangible assets in the regional economic growth. *Investigaciones Regionales*, (20), 165-93.

Svendsen, G., & Sørensen, J. F. (2007). There's more to the picture than meets the eye: Measuring tangible and intangible capital in two marginal communities in rural Denmark. *Journal of Rural Studies, 23*(4), 453–471. doi:10.1016/j.jrurstud.2007.01.008

Swart, J., & Kinnie, N. (2003). Knowledge-intensive firms: The influence of the client on HR systems. *Human Resource Management Journal, 13*(3), 37–55. doi:10.1111/j.1748-8583.2003.tb00097.x

Tabarrok, A., & Cowen, T. (2018). *MRUniversity*. Available at http://mruniversity.com/

Taheri, M., & van Geenhuizen, M. (2011). How human capital and social networks may influence the patterns of international learning among academic spin-off firms. *Papers in Regional Science, 90*(2), 287–311. doi:10.1111/j.1435-5957.2011.00363.x

Takeuchi, H. (1998). *Beyond knowledge management: lessons from Japan*. Available at: www.sveiby.com/articles/lessons

Takeuchi, R., Lepak, D., Wang, H., & Takeuchi, K. (2007). An Empirical Examination of the Mechanisms Mediating Between High-Performance Work Systems and the Performance of Japanese Organizations. *The Journal of Applied Psychology, 92*(4), 1060–1083. doi:10.1037/0021-9010.92.4.1069 PMID:17638466

Tansley, C. (2011). What do we mean by the term "talent" in talent management? *Industrial and Commercial Training, 43*(5), 266–274. doi:10.1108/00197851111145853

Tapp, L. (1997). Emerging triumphant. *Business Quarterly*, *61*(3).

Teece, D. (2003). Expert Talent and the Design of (Professional Services) Firms. *Industrial and Corporate Change*, *12*(4), 895–916. doi:10.1093/icc/12.4.895

Teece, D. J., Pisano, G., & Shuen, A. (1997). Dynamic Capabilities and Strategic Management. *Strategic Management Journal*, *18*(7), 509–533. doi:10.1002/(SICI)1097-0266(199708)18:7<509::AID-SMJ882>3.0.CO;2-Z

Teixeira, A. A., & Shu, L. (2012). The level of human capital in innovative firms located in China. Is foreign capital relevant? *Journal of the Asia Pacific Economy*, *17*(2), 343–360. doi:10.1080/13547860.2012.668095

Teixeira, A. A., & Tavares-Lehmann, A. T. (2014). Human capital intensity in technology-based firms located in Portugal: Does foreign ownership matter? *Research Policy*, *43*(4), 737–748. doi:10.1016/j.respol.2014.01.001

The Global Human Capital Report 2017, Preparing people for the future of work. (2017). Retrieved from http://www3.weforum.org/docs/WEF_Global_Human_ Capital_Report_2017.pdf

Thomas, W. F., & Ong, P. (2002). Barriers to rehiring of displaced workers: A study of Aerospace engineers in California. *Economic Development Quarterly*, *16*(2), 167–178. doi:10.1177/0891242402016002006

Tiep, N. D. (2007). The Honda motorcycle business in the Vietnamese emerging market. *International Journal of Emerging Markets*, *2*(3), 298–309. doi:10.1108/17468800710758413

Tirole, J. (1988). *The theory of industrial organization*. MIT Press.

Tiwari, S., Wee, H.-M., & Daryanto, Y. (2018). Big Data analytics in supply chain management between 2010 and 2016: Insights to industries. *Computers & Industrial Engineering*, *115*, 319–330. doi:10.1016/j.cie.2017.11.017

Tregaskis, O., Daniels, K., Glover, L., Butler, P., & Meyer, M. (2013). High performance work practices and firm performance: A longitudinal case study. *British Journal of Management*, *24*(2), 225–244. doi:10.1111/j.1467-8551.2011.00800.x

Trzuskawska-Grzesinska, A. (2017). Control towers in supply chain management–Past and future. *Journal of Economics & Management*, *27*, 114–133. doi:10.22367/jem.2017.27.07

Tseng, P.-H., & Liao, C.-H. (2015). Supply chain integration, information technology, market orientation and firm performance in container shipping firms. *International Journal of Logistics Management*, *26*(1), 82–106. doi:10.1108/IJLM-09-2012-0088

Ulrich, D., & Smallwood, N. (2012). What is talent? *Leader to Leader*, *2012*(63), 55–61. doi:10.1002/ltl.20011

Urbancova, H. (2013). Competitive Advantage Achievement through Innovation and Knowledge. *Journal of Competitiveness*, *5*(1), 82–96. doi:10.7441/joc.2013.01.06

Van Uden, A., Knoben, J., & Vermeulen, P. (2014). *Human capital and innovation in developing countries: A firm level study*. Radboud University.

Viner, J. (1952). America's aims and the progress of underdeveloped countries. *The Progress of Underdeveloped Areas,* 175-202.

Vomberg, A., Homburg, C., & Bornemann, T. (2015). Talented people and strong brands: The contribution of human capital and brand equity to firm value. *Strategic Management Journal*, *36*(13), 2122–2131. doi:10.1002mj.2328

Wade, M. P., & Dabla-Norris, M. E. (2001). Rent Seeking and Endogenous Income Inequality (No. 1-15). International Monetary Fund.

Waller, M., & Fawcett, S. (2013). Data science, predictive analytics, and Big Data: A revolution that will transform supply chain design and management. *Journal of Business Logistics*, *34*(2), 77–84. doi:10.1111/jbl.12010

Wang, G., Gunasekaran, A., Ngai, E., & Papadopoulos, T. (2016). Big Data analytics in logistics and supply chain management: certain investigations for research and applications. *International Journal of Production Economics, 176*, 98-110. doi:10.1016/j.ijpe.2016.03.014

Wang, H. (2014). Theories for competitive advantage. In H. Hasan (Ed.), Being Practical with Theory: A Window into Business Research (pp. 33–43). Wollongong, Australia: Academic Press.

Wang, D., Su, Z., & Yang, D. (2011). Organisational culture and knowledge creation capability. *Journal of Knowledge Management*, *15*(3), 363–373. doi:10.1108/13673271111137385

Wang, H. C., He, J., & Mahoney, J. T. (2009). Firm-specific knowledge resources and competitive advantage: The roles of economic- and relationship-based employee governance mechanisms. *Strategic Management Journal*, *30*(12), 1265–1285. doi:10.1002mj.787

Wang, H., & Barney, J. (2006). Employee Incentives to Make Firm-Specific Investments: Implications for Resource-Based Theories of Corporate Diversification. *Academy of Management Review*, *31*(2), 466–476. doi:10.5465/amr.2006.20208691

Wang, H., & Lim, S. (2008). Real options and real value: The role of employee incentives to make specific knowledge investments. *Strategic Management Journal*, *29*(7), 701–721. doi:10.1002mj.681

Wang, Y.-L., Wang, Y.-D., & Horng, R.-Y. (2010). Learning and innovation in small and medium enterprises. *Industrial Management & Data Systems*, *110*(2), 175–192. doi:10.1108/02635571011020296

Watson, B. (2012). Data wrangling: how Procter & Gamble maximizes business analytics. *CIO Insight*. Available on http://www.cioinsight.com/

Weber, J. G. (2014). A decade of natural gas development: The makings of a resource curse? *Resource and Energy Economics*, *37*, 168–183. doi:10.1016/j.reseneeco.2013.11.013

Weber, M. (1922). *Economy and Society*. Routledge.

Wernerfelt, B. (1984). A resource-based view of the firm. *Strategic Management Journal*, *5*(2), 171–180. doi:10.1002mj.4250050207

Whitehead, A. N. (1978). *Process and Reality*. New York, NY: The Free Press. (Original work published 1929)

Williamson, O. E. (1975). *Markets and Hierarchy: Analysis and Antitrust Implications*. New York: Free Press.

Williamson, O. E. (1985). *The Economic Institutions of Capitalism: Firms, Markets, Relational Contracting*. New York: Free Press.

Williamson, O. E., Wachter, M. L., & Harris, J. E. (1975). Understanding the employment relation: The analysis of idiosyncratic exchange. *The Bell Journal of Economics*, *6*(1), 250–278. doi:10.2307/3003224

Wright, P. M., Gardner, T. M., Moynihan, L. M., & Allen, M. R. (2005). The relationship between HR practices and firm performance: Examining causal order. *Personnel Psychology*, *58*(2), 409–446. doi:10.1111/j.1744-6570.2005.00487.x

Wright, P. M., & McMahan, G. C. (2011). Exploring human capital: Putting "human" back into strategic human resource management. *Human Resource Management Journal*, *21*(2), 93–104. doi:10.1111/j.1748-8583.2010.00165.x

Wright, P. M., & Snell, S. A. (1991). Toward an integrative view of strategic human resource management. *Human Resource Management Review*, *1*(3), 203–225. doi:10.1016/1053-4822(91)90015-5

Wright, P., McMahan, G., & McWilliams, A. (1994). Human resources as a source of sustained competitive advantage. *International Journal of Human Resource Management*, *5*(2), 301–326. doi:10.1080/09585199400000020

Wynn, T., & Mueller, C. W. (1998). Product characteristics, human capital and labor market segments. *The Sociological Quarterly*, *39*(4), 597–622. doi:10.1111/j.1533-8525.1998.tb00520.x

Xu, J. (2014). *Managing digital enterprise: ten essential topics*. Amsterdam: Atlantis Press. doi:10.2991/978-94-6239-094-2

Yin, R. K. (2008). *Case study research: Design and methods* (4th ed.). London: Sage Publication.

Yi, W. (2012). L., & Jayasingam, S. (2012). Factors Driving Knowledge Creation among Private Sector Organizations: Empirical Evidence from Malaysia. *Journal of Organizational Knowledge Management, 12*. doi:10.5171/2012.199983

Zhan, J. V., Duan, H., & Zeng, M. (2015). Resource dependence and human capital investment in China. *The China Quarterly, 221*, 49–72. doi:10.1017/S0305741014001556

Zingales, L. (1998). Corporate Governance. In D. Newman (Ed.), *The New Palgrave Dictionary of Economics and the Law* (pp. 497–502). London: Stockton Press.

Zingales, L. (2000). In search of new foundations. *The Journal of Finance, 55*(4), 1623–1653. doi:10.1111/0022-1082.00262

About the Contributors

Cécile Cézanne is an Associate Professor accredited to supervise research in Economics at the University Côte d'Azur and a permanent researcher at the Research Group in Economics, Law and Management (GREDEG). She is specialized in Industrial Economics and more precisely her research is focused on the theory of the firm and corporate governance. These areas of expertise have led her to collaborate and compare viewpoints notably with researchers in Management on major subjects like intra- and inter-enterprises cooperation, the boundaries of organizations within networks and the role of fourth-party logistics providers in a context of growing importance of human capital in companies.

Laurence Saglietto is a Professor in Strategic Management at the University Côte d'Azur, France, and a Member of GREDEG 7321 UMR CNRS. Her research interests are in Intermediation and Human Capital in Network organization and Supply Chain Management. She manages the "International Network: on New Party Logistics".

* * *

Dominique Bonet Fernandez is a Researcher at the IPAG Business School Paris and associated to Aix-Marseille University Research Center for Logistics and Transport. She is head of the Global Supply Chain Management and Circular Economy programs and the Ipag European Chaire of Collaborative Economics. Member of the board of the French National Institute for circular economy, her work focuses on new business models of the circular and collaborative economy, and the role of logistics in an urban and international context. She co-authored the Circular Economics and Territories, published by the Presses Universitaires de Provence and Social Entrepreneurship in non-profit and profit sectors, published by Springer.

Shankar Chelliah is currently an Associate Professor with Universiti Sains Malaysia (USM), based in Penang, Malaysia. Prior becoming academician, he has fifteen years of corporate experiences by holding various positions in blue chip companies such as Motorola and Intel. Currently positioned in the section of International Business and teaching subjects such as international new venture, international trade law, and international business management. Apart from supervising students at postgraduate level, he is actively involved in consultancy services and social responsibility initiatives to key clients from the industry. His current research interests include: (a) internationalization – medical tourism, strategies in international trade, born global firms, SMEs etc, (b) green management as competitive capabilities in organizations and (c) strategic management in education – internationalization of education, holistic approach to education, and understanding the future challenges of education. Dr.Shankar Chelliah has published more than 100 publications in text books, chapter in books, high impact journals (SCOPUS/ISI), and both international and local conference proceedings. Has successfully received more than RM250,000 in total grant from the government in pursuing research in the above mentioned areas. Graduated more than 10 Phd and Master students. He also actively writes in the media mass on the areas relates to his research topics to outreach the community.

Sabrina Loufrani-Fedida, PhD, is Professor in human resource management and project management at the Graduate School of Management – IAE Nice at the Université Côte d'Azur in France. Her current research topics are competence and talent management, human resources communication, and development of project teams. Her work has appeared in international research journals such as Long Range Planning or International Journal of Project Management, and French famous review such as Revue de Gestion des Ressources Humaines.

Amir Mousav has more than 7 years of experience in the oil and gas industry. His last position was the supervisor of the Training Center in National Iranian Oil Refining and Distribution Company. Already having broad knowledge and experience in engineering and operations in the petroleum industry, he moved to the headquarters to find the gaps in the learning and training processes of the company. He accomplished several projects including the unification and integration of more than 2,500 training courses with the cooperation of the Iranian Ministry of Petroleum. Having been granted a company scholarship, he decided to pursue his Ph.D. in economics in the Université Côte d'Azur, France. His empirical research addresses the impact of natural resource abundance on human capital and growth.

Ahmet Özcan is an assistant professor in Faculty of Business at the Adana Science and Technology University where he has been a faculty member since 2015. Ahmet Özcan completed his PhD and his undergraduate studies at Marmara University.

Gilles Paché is Professor of Retailing and Supply Chain Management at the Aix-Marseille University, Aix-en-Provence (France). He is Deputy Director of the Centre de Recherche sur le Transport et la Logistique (CRET-LOG), and his major interests are network organizations, supply chain management, and retail operations management. Gilles has more than 380 publications in the forms of journal papers, books, edited books, edited proceedings, edited special issues, book chapters, conference papers, and reports.

Alban Quillaud is a logistics and supply chain management professional focusing on large outsourcing businesses. With 20 years of experience in that field, he is currently member of one division within a major logistics service provider company. He is regularly invited as guest speaker at business Schools and universities, as well as member of the GREDEG laboratory of Nice Côte d'Azur (France).

Viviane Sergi is Associate Professor in Management in the Department of management and technology at ESG UQAM in Montréal, Canada. Her research interests include process thinking, performativity, new work practices, leadership, and materiality. On top of her ongoing studies on collaborative workspaces and on freelancers, she is co-coordinator of the Montréal chapter of the Research group on Collaborative Spaces (RGCS), a network with chapters in various cities, like Paris, London and Barcelona. Her work has been published in journals such as Academy of Management Annals, Human Relations, Scandinavian Journal of Management, Long Range Planning, and in Qualitative Research in Organizations and Management.

Vijayalakchimi Subramaniam is a PhD student at School of Management in University Science Malaysia, Penang, Malaysia.

Index

A

accounting 99, 102-109, 111-112, 114-116
acquisition 3-4, 14, 106, 110, 159, 176, 181-182, 185, 188-190, 192-194
advantage 2-5, 12-15, 35, 44, 85, 101, 126, 144, 147, 156-167, 169, 176-181, 183-194, 199, 201, 206, 212
affordability 178, 193
analysis 1-3, 5-8, 10, 12, 17-18, 33-34, 38, 45-46, 99, 104-105, 111-112, 115-116, 135, 137, 141, 143-144, 146-147, 157, 203, 209

B

boundaries 2, 5, 12, 15-17, 56, 66, 76, 122, 128, 144, 169
business 6, 11, 33, 36, 39, 41-46, 58-59, 63, 65-66, 76, 99-102, 104, 106, 108-111, 115, 145, 156-157, 159-161, 163, 169, 178, 183-184, 189-190, 193, 198-200, 202-203, 205-206, 208-209, 212

C

capital-intensive 1-2, 30-31, 73, 75-76, 101, 121, 132, 198, 200-201, 209, 212
competencies 31-34, 36, 39-45, 158-160, 162-163, 200
competition 2, 5, 74, 101, 199-200
computer 6, 39, 41, 45, 76, 211
co-specialization 76, 80, 83-84, 89, 208
costs 3, 43, 74, 77, 84, 106, 109, 111-112, 115, 130, 135, 157, 212

D

digitization 198, 200-202, 205-206, 208-209, 212

E

education 3, 10, 13, 43, 64, 100, 104-106, 122-124, 132, 134-135, 137, 140-141, 143-146
empirical 1, 6, 8, 15, 18, 30, 37, 55, 73, 76, 104-105, 121, 123, 129, 135, 137, 144, 147
employees 2, 4-6, 12, 14-17, 30-32, 36-41, 43-46, 57-58, 64-66, 73-89, 100-102, 104-106, 111, 122, 128, 164-167, 169, 178-181, 183, 186, 188-194, 199-200, 207-210, 212
employment 4, 10, 12, 54, 57, 77, 79-80, 83-87, 113, 199, 210
environments 14, 31, 36, 145, 158, 160, 162, 178

F

firms 1-2, 4-6, 12-17, 30-31, 73, 75-76, 78-79, 88, 100-109, 111-112, 114-116, 121-128, 132, 137, 140, 145-147, 157, 160-161, 164-165, 167, 177, 179-181, 184, 186, 188, 198-202, 210-213

G

global 39, 81, 85, 89, 101, 103, 106, 135, 139, 141, 144, 156, 158, 161, 184, 199, 201, 207-211, 213

governance 15-17, 46, 55, 61-62, 64, 73-84, 86-89, 121-123, 125-126, 129-130, 132, 134-140, 142, 144-147, 199, 207
growth 14-16, 31, 81, 84, 88, 101, 103-104, 109, 121-126, 128-129, 131-132, 134-135, 137, 143-147, 157, 161, 163, 177, 179, 182-184, 188, 192, 198, 200

H

HCIF 1-2, 5-6, 8, 10-13, 15-18, 32, 45, 76, 84, 86, 88, 121-126, 128, 131-132, 140-147, 200, 202, 207
host 156-157, 159-160, 162-163, 166, 168

I

innovation 2-3, 6, 10, 12-16, 30-32, 37, 74-76, 82, 100-102, 104-105, 115, 121-126, 128, 131-133, 135, 140, 143-147, 159, 162, 165, 167, 169, 177, 184, 187-188, 199, 205, 210, 213
international 13, 31, 39, 41, 103, 107, 160, 162, 182, 194, 198, 201
inter-organizational 204, 207-209, 211-212
investment 3-4, 12-13, 32, 35, 99-101, 103-105, 109, 115, 125, 134, 137, 144, 146-147, 162-163, 177-178, 183, 189, 191, 205
investments 4, 14-15, 35, 76-78, 81, 83, 86, 89, 100, 105, 108-109, 184, 190, 200

K

knowledge-based 5, 100-101, 145, 156-157, 162-163, 169

L

legal 3, 13, 15, 17, 77-78, 88, 131
limitations 2, 18, 32, 46, 55, 108, 111, 164, 200, 202
literature 1-2, 5, 16, 30-36, 38, 45, 85, 87, 121-125, 131, 143-144, 147, 157-158, 163-164, 177, 180, 184-185, 200, 202-203
local 16, 134, 158, 162, 164-166, 168, 187, 193-194, 206
logistics 12, 198-203, 206, 209-210, 212

M

Malaysia 156, 162-163, 167, 176-180, 183-185, 189-194
management 6, 11-13, 16-17, 30-32, 35-37, 39, 41, 43-45, 58, 65-66, 74, 87-88, 100, 102, 104, 108, 111, 128, 140, 142, 144, 162, 164, 168, 182, 187-194, 198-202, 204-206, 208-212
managerial 2, 4-5, 14, 40-41, 45-46, 86, 207, 209
managers 3, 12, 38-41, 43-45, 56, 79, 205, 210
manufacturing 31, 44, 76, 105, 126, 128, 144-145, 162, 178-179, 184, 194, 199-201, 206
market 3, 13, 16, 39, 74, 77, 81, 99-104, 106, 111-112, 114-116, 128-129, 131-132, 134, 137, 144-146, 157, 159, 161, 166, 168-169, 177-178, 181, 184, 186-187, 191, 193, 202, 205, 209, 211
media 54, 56-58, 208
memory 176, 185, 188-190, 192-194
MNE 177, 180, 183, 188, 191, 194
modern 2, 6, 31, 87, 146, 202
multi-resource 73, 75, 78-89

N

NRA 122-123, 126, 131, 134, 137, 146-147

P

personal 38-41, 43, 45, 62, 65, 78, 165
perspective 3-4, 6, 12-13, 17, 33, 35-36, 46, 55, 61, 66, 79, 81, 83-85, 87-88, 147, 157-158, 181, 183, 191, 199, 207, 211
policy 11, 30, 32, 37, 40, 44, 88, 112, 123, 146
power 5, 12, 15-17, 73-81, 84, 86, 88-89, 108, 131-132, 134, 200

production 3-6, 11, 14, 31, 55, 74, 76-77, 80, 83, 85, 87, 100, 103-105, 121-122, 124-132, 135, 144, 146-147, 159, 199-202, 206-211

R

R and D 10, 14-16, 78, 144-145, 199, 212
relationships 3-4, 13, 15-16, 77-78, 80, 83, 86-89, 102, 122, 185, 193-194, 207
report 38, 100, 109, 114, 134-135, 141, 162, 205
reward 31, 35

S

scholars 54, 60, 66, 123, 132, 135, 137, 162
scope 1-2, 8, 11, 16, 18, 40, 61, 177
self-employed 54, 56
shareholder 73-75, 78-79, 205
SMEs 168, 177, 184, 187, 191, 193-194
Standards 103, 107, 112, 115, 178, 184, 194
study 2, 6, 8, 16-18, 30, 32, 36-39, 41, 45-46, 76, 115, 129, 137, 161-162, 177-180, 182-183, 185-186, 188, 193, 204-206, 213
subgroup 12-14, 16
subsidiaries 156-160, 162-169

T

talents 2, 5, 12, 14-16, 34, 40, 145, 168, 201, 207
technological 6, 14, 43, 76, 103-104, 106, 124, 157, 160, 164, 166, 169, 199-202, 205, 207, 210, 213
theme 10, 12-15
theoretical 1-2, 5, 15, 17-18, 35, 45-46, 60-61, 66, 73, 177, 185-186, 203
traditional 6, 12, 53, 55-56, 59-62, 65-66, 73, 75-76, 78-79, 88, 103, 108-109, 199, 202
trends 53, 62, 66, 74, 112, 159, 178, 205

Ensure Quality Research is Introduced to the Academic Community

Become an IGI Global Reviewer for Authored Book Projects

The overall success of an authored book project is dependent on quality and timely reviews.

In this competitive age of scholarly publishing, constructive and timely feedback significantly expedites the turnaround time of manuscripts from submission to acceptance, allowing the publication and discovery of forward-thinking research at a much more expeditious rate. Several IGI Global authored book projects are currently seeking highly qualified experts in the field to fill vacancies on their respective editorial review boards:

Applications may be sent to:
development@igi-global.com

Applicants must have a doctorate (or an equivalent degree) as well as publishing and reviewing experience. Reviewers are asked to write reviews in a timely, collegial, and constructive manner. All reviewers will begin their role on an ad-hoc basis for a period of one year, and upon successful completion of this term can be considered for full editorial review board status, with the potential for a subsequent promotion to Associate Editor.

If you have a colleague that may be interested in this opportunity, we encourage you to share this information with them.

www.ingramcontent.com/pod-product-compliance
Lightning Source LLC
LaVergne TN
LVHW081327300926
849161LV00008B/1901